The Light That Binds

The Light That Binds

*A Study in Thomas Aquinas's
Metaphysics of Natural Law*

STEPHEN L. BROCK

◆PICKWICK *Publications* · Eugene, Oregon

THE LIGHT THAT BINDS
A Study in Thomas Aquinas's Metaphysics of Natural Law

Copyright © 2020 Stephen L. Brock. All rights reserved. Except for brief quotations in critical publications or reviews, no part of this book may be reproduced in any manner without prior written permission from the publisher. Write: Permissions, Wipf and Stock Publishers, 199 W. 8th Ave., Suite 3, Eugene, OR 97401.

Pickwick Publications
An Imprint of Wipf and Stock Publishers
199 W. 8th Ave., Suite 3
Eugene, OR 97401

www.wipfandstock.com

PAPERBACK ISBN: 978-1-5326-4729-1
HARDCOVER ISBN: 978-1-5326-4730-7
EBOOK ISBN: 978-1-5326-4731-4

Cataloguing-in-Publication data:

Names: Brock, Stephen Louis, author.

Title: The light that binds : a study in Thomas Aquinas's metaphysics of natural law / Stephen L. Brock.

Description: Eugene, OR : Pickwick Publications, 2020 | Includes bibliographical references and index(es).

Identifiers: ISBN 978-1-5326-4729-1 (paperback) | ISBN 978-1-5326-4730-7 (hardcover) | ISBN 978-1-5326-4731-4 (ebook)

Subjects: LCSH: Thomas—Aquinas Saint—1225?–1274. | Natural law.

Classification: B765.T54 B76 2020 (print) | B765.T54 B76 (ebook)

Manufactured in the U.S.A.　　　　　　　　　　　　　　MARCH 26, 2020

To Charlie, Jim, Tom, and their families

Contents

Abbreviations and References | viii
Introduction | xi

1 The Question of the Legal Character of Natural Law | 1
2 The Relation between Natural Law and Eternal Law | 33
3 Natural Law, God's Will, and Positive Law | 61
4 Natural Inclinations in the Promulgation of Natural Law | 107
5 Nature and Human Nature in the Promulgation of Natural Law | 141
6 The Force of Natural Law | 180
7 The Naturalness of Natural Law | 215

Bibliography | 257
Index of Names | 263
Index of Subjects | 265

Abbreviations and References

De decem preceptis	*Collationes in decem preceptis* (Sermons on the Ten Commandments)
De malo	*Quaestiones disputatae De malo* (Disputed Questions on Evil)
De spir. creat.	*Quaestio disputata De spiritualibus creaturis* (Disputed Question on Spiritual Creatures)
De sub. sep.	*De substantiis separatis* (On Separate Substances)
De ver.	*Quaestiones disputatae De ueritate* (Disputed Questions on Truth)
De virt.	*Quaestiones disputatae De uirtutibus* (Disputed Questions on the Virtues)
In De an.	*Sentencia Libri De anima* (Commentary on Aristotle's *De anima*)
In De div. nom.	*Super Librum Dionysii De divinis nominibus* (Commentary on ps.-Dionysius's *On the Divine Names*)
In De Trin.	*Super Boetium De Trinitate* (Commentary on Boethius's *De Trinitate*)
In Eth.	*Sententia Libri Ethicorum* (Commentary on Aristotle's Nicomachean Ethics)
In Meta.	*Sententia super Metaphysicam* (Commentary on Aristotle's Metaphysics)
In Peryerm.	*Expositio Libri Peryermenias* (Commentary on Aristotle's *De interpretatione*)

Abbreviations and References

In Phys.	*Sententia super Physicam (Commentary on Aristotle's Physics)*
In Pol.	*Sententia Libri Politicorum (Commentary on Aristotle's Politics)*
In Post. an.	*Expositio Libri Posteriorum (Commentary on Aristotle's Posterior Analytics)*
In Rom.	*Super Epistolam Pauli Apostoli ad Romanos (Commentary on St Paul's Epistle to the Romans)*
In Sent.	*Scriptum super libros Sententiarum (Commentary on Peter Lombard's Sentences)*
QD De an.	*Quaestio disputata De anima (Disputed Question on the Soul)*
ScG	*Summa contra Gentiles*
ST	*Summa theologiae*

Passages of the *Summa theologiae* are cited as in these examples:

I.19.5	*Prima pars*, q. 19, a. 5
I.21.1*ad3*	*Prima pars*, q. 21, a. 1, ad 3
I.60.5*sc*	*Prima pars*, q. 60, a. 5, *Sed contra*
I–II.91.2*ad1/ad2*	*Prima secundae*, q. 91, a. 2, ad 1 and ad 2
I–II.94.3*obj1/ad1*	*Prima secundae*, q. 94, a. 3, obj. 1 and ad 1
II–II.57.2*c/ad3*	*Secunda secundae*, q. 57, a. 2, corpus and ad 3

The *Sentences* commentary and Disputed Questions are cited in similar ways. In *Sentences* commentary citations, *qc* stands for *quaestiuncula*.

Introduction

"The law of nature," declares Saint Thomas, "is nothing other than the light of the intellect instilled in us by God, through which we know what is to be done and what is to be avoided."[1] Of course it is not a physical light. "As it pertains to intellect, light is nothing other than a certain manifestation of truth."[2] In his more technical moments, Thomas will distinguish a little between the mind's light and natural law, the law being a set of truths, and the light being what manifests them and lets us understand them. But once lit up, the truths are also a light, showing us a path to follow. In some sense they even oblige us, bind us, to that path. Natural law is a light that binds.

The question running through the following pages is how exactly it is, for Aquinas, that the truths of natural law constitute a genuine law and carry real binding force. I shall motivate the question and survey various answers that it has received in chapter 1. There I shall also explain the plan of the rest. Here I would like to say something about my subtitle.

By far the bulk of Thomas's writing on natural law is found in his masterpiece, the *Summa theologiae*. So situated, it is obviously a theological teaching. I hope that I have kept its theological character sufficiently in view. Nevertheless, as with many of the topics presented in the *Summa*, its treatment of natural law involves very heavy use of philosophical sources and arguments. This is hardly surprising, if indeed natural law itself is a work of the human mind's natural light. For that is also philosophy's proper light. I see no need to apologize for wanting to concentrate on Thomas's philosophy of natural law.

---

1. *De decem preceptis*, 24, lines 7–8.
2. *ST* I.106.1.

Philosophy, though, has many parts. The truths of natural law, Thomas tells us, constitute the first principles of practical reason. The practical part of philosophy is moral philosophy or ethics. Metaphysics, by contrast, is speculative or theoretical, not practical. What has metaphysics got to do with natural law?

The truths of natural law are certainly not, for Thomas, the first principles of metaphysics itself. The field of metaphysics is all of reality, being itself, and its own principles are more far-reaching, and even more basic, than those that bear only on human conduct. Of course human conduct is a being too—it exists—and so its principles do somehow fall within the metaphysical purview. The metaphysician can speculate about anything. But the study of human conduct in light of the truths of natural law, both in its matter and in its purpose, is surely a practical undertaking. By that very fact, natural law pertains to moral philosophy.

It is one thing, however, to study a field in light of its principles. It is another thing to study the principles themselves. In Thomas's conception of philosophy, studying the principles of any field whatever is a metaphysical task. Every other part of philosophy takes the principles of its field for granted and seeks only to draw out the implications from them that make for full mastery of that field. Moral philosophy draws practical conclusions from the principles of natural law. But the fundamental treatment of all first principles, both those of metaphysics itself and those of the other parts of philosophy, whether speculative or practical, belongs to metaphysics. The mere fact that the principles are really principles and not conclusions—the fact that they do not need to be demonstrated, in light of other principles—does not preclude such treatment. For instance, the principles still need to be identified. The terms comprising them need to be clarified so as to achieve and to judge the precise formulations of them. And doubts or difficulties about them can arise and need to be resolved. These are metaphysical exercises.[3]

Moreover, if metaphysics has one primary task, it is to trace all the fields of philosophy and all of their principles back to the very first explanations or causes of all reality and all truth. This is metaphysics in its character as wisdom.[4] And among the various kinds of cause that Thomas recognizes, the dominant one—the one that explains the others—is the final cause, the end, that for the sake of which the others function as they do. Every final cause or end is some sort of good. Indeed the notion of the good is itself

---

3. I discuss various aspects of the relation between Thomas's metaphysics and his moral philosophy in Brock, *Philosophy of Saint Thomas*, chapter 6. On metaphysics and the self-evident truths of natural law, see 166–72.

4. See *ST* I–II.66.5ad4.

something metaphysical, "among the firsts."[5] And the absolutely ultimate end is the supreme good, which is God. Every other end and good is for the sake of His good. All of this gives metaphysics an obvious affinity with theology, and also a special bearing on natural law. For natural law rests entirely on the notion of the good, and the whole point of natural law is to provide us with our first guidance toward our own ultimate end.[6] Within philosophy, the final word on man's end belongs to metaphysics, not ethics. This is why Thomas can even say that metaphysics regulates all human activities, all of them being ordered to that end.[7] Practical thinking does not determine the end itself, but only assumes it and disposes the things that are for its sake.[8]

But perhaps most importantly, at least as far as this book is concerned, the very question of how Thomas thinks natural law constitutes a law is closely tied to the question of his view of its relation to God. In a sense, the whole book is an attempt to determine the meaning and drift of his famous description of natural law as "nothing other than a participation of the eternal law in the rational creature."[9] The eternal law is God's law. If only for this reason, the perspective cannot but be heavily metaphysical.

Let me stress, however, that this is only a study "in" Aquinas's metaphysics of natural law. I make no pretense of exhausting the matter. Much more could be said, for example, about his metaphysics of the good and the bad.

Some features of the book may make more sense to the reader if something is said about its rather protracted gestation. Three decades ago I defended a dissertation in Medieval Studies at the University of Toronto on "The Legal Character of Natural Law according to St Thomas Aquinas," under the direction of the late James P. Reilly. Wisely—he was a very practical man—Dr. Reilly advised me to follow the fairly common practice of Toronto medievalists and not to try at once to turn the dissertation into a book. Luckily I took the advice. Over the years the thing did spawn a few articles, and those, together with the degree, seemed to constitute a satisfactory yield. Lately, however, I have been encouraged to publish it after all. I dusted it off, and (for better or worse) I found myself still in substantial agreement with it. Having recently worked with Wipf and Stock and been

---

5. *In Eth.*, I.1, 5, lines 150–51.
6. See *ST* I–II.94.2; I–II.91.2ad2.
7. See *In Meta., proem.*
8. *ST* II–II.47.6.
9. *ST* I–II.91.2.

very happy with both the process and the result, I proposed it to them, and they kindly accepted.

Originally I thought that, beyond putting the material in book form, little more would be needed. The more I got back into it, however, the more I realized that my understanding of Aquinas's natural law teaching had actually evolved somewhat. An overhaul was called for. This showed the wisdom of Dr. Reilly's advice, and I regret that it is now too late to thank him.

The result has not been a complete transformation. The overall structure, the position that I take on the study's fundamental question, and most of the lines of argument, are the same. The changes are least in the first two chapters. Readers may notice that most of the scholarly literature surveyed in chapter 1 already existed when I wrote the dissertation. I think that the older literature is still interesting and that it does cover the main positions that can be taken on my question. At least, no significantly new position has come to my attention, and the chief purpose of the survey is simply to present the issues that I think need to be addressed. There are more references to subsequent publications in the later chapters. But this is not, after all, another dissertation, and it is quite long enough as it is.

Just in case anyone actually did see the dissertation, the main philosophical developments (if that is what they are) appear in what are now the third, sixth, and last chapters. Those in the third mostly regard the way in which the precepts of natural law can be seen as effects of the divine will and the divine command ordering all things toward the divine common good. This may be the book's philosophically most important moment, and I return to it in the last chapter. The last chapter also calls attention to what Thomas calls natural law "absolutely considered," which is a notion that had not previously struck me, and the chapter ends with a thought that came to me only recently about the relation between natural law and Thomas's definition of law in general. The chief development in the sixth chapter, vis-à-vis the dissertation, is a substantially different account of the general nature of obligation. As for the fourth and fifth chapters, they were originally one, of fewer pages; the division into two represents not so much a change in the views advanced as a desire to bolster the arguments, these being perhaps, in the current scholarly scene, the book's most contentious ones.

I hope it is clear that this is a historical study. I wish only to offer a tolerably accurate reading of Thomas on natural law. I am not proposing a natural law theory of my own, even a "Thomistic" one. There are several such theories out there that are quite worthy of study. Some of them I have engaged elsewhere. But here I try not to stray too far from Aquinas's texts. Perhaps this will account for at least some of the omissions, or near omissions, that some readers may otherwise find glaring.

As for Aquinas's texts themselves, for the most part I have not included the Latin originals. This is mainly in consideration of space and of their being so easily accessible nowadays, thanks especially to Enrique Alarcón's marvelous "Corpus Thomisticum" website. Unless otherwise indicated, translations in the book are mine.

My hearty thanks go to Professor Candace Vogler for her very key role in getting this project underway, and to Christine Jensen for her very generous help in bringing it to completion.

1

The Question of the Legal Character of Natural Law

The question is how the definition of law that Thomas Aquinas lays out in the *Summa theologiae* is meant to be applied to what he calls natural law.

Anyone moderately familiar with the section on law in the *Summa theologiae*, and not so familiar with the literature on natural law in Aquinas, may very well wonder why it is even a question. Can there be any doubt as to how his definition of law in general applies to natural law? Hardly any work of interpretation seems necessary.

In the very article in which he brings his definition of law to completion, Thomas says that "natural law has the nature of law to the highest degree (*maxime*)."[1] It is true that he makes this assertion in one of the article's objections, so that it cannot immediately be taken to express his own view. But the reply to the objection, far from denying the assertion or qualifying it in any way, only confirms it. It also seems to indicate rather clearly the precise manner in which natural law possesses the nature of law. The objection was against the proposition that promulgation belongs to the essence of law. Natural law, it said, is law to the highest degree, and yet needs no promulgation at all. The reply simply denies that natural law is without promulgation. If natural law stands in no need of promulgation, the reason

1. *ST* I–II.90.4*obj*1.

is that it has been promulgated already, "by the very fact that God has inserted it into the minds of men as something to be naturally known."² With this statement, how natural law fits under Thomas's definition of law in general seems quite easy to see. That definition, given in the same article, is "an ordination of reason, for the common good, promulgated by him who has care of the community."³ Natural law, then, would be an ordination of divine reason, for the common good of the universe, promulgated to man by God as governor of the universe, through the instilling of the natural light of the human intellect.⁴

Two articles later, Thomas offers a rigorous argument to show the existence of a natural law in us. It concludes with his description of natural law as "nothing other than a participation of the eternal law in the rational creature."⁵ Taken as a whole and as it exists in His own mind, the ordination by which God governs the universe is called the eternal law. This certainly fits the definition of law. And in the reply to the article's first objection, Thomas insists that natural law is not something diverse from the eternal law, but only a certain participation in it.

Still, unequivocal as these texts seem, Aquinas's subsequent treatment of natural law does raise one or two questions. The article that presents natural law as a participation of the eternal law in the rational creature belongs to a *quaestio* devoted to the "division of law." A little further on, Thomas devotes an entire *quaestio* to the subject of natural law.⁶ There he determines what sort of entity in man's mind it consists in, whether it has one or many precepts, and other characteristics of it. The curious thing is that, in this whole *quaestio*, the eternal law is not mentioned even once. Nor is its having God as its author—even though God's being Lord of the universe and author of a divine, supernaturally transmitted law is mentioned.⁷ Natural law is treated entirely on the human or natural level and is not referred to God at all.

This is one consideration that has led some interpreters to regard the description of natural law in terms of the eternal law as a mere function of

---

2. *ST* I–II.90.4*ad*1.

3. *ST* I–II.90.4.

4. This way of understanding natural law can be found, with some variations in the details, in a number of twentieth-century neo-Scholastic manuals. See, e.g., Merkelbach, *Summa*, 1:224–30; Prümmer, *Manuale*, 1:93–96; Boyer, *Cursus*, 2:429–35, 473–79; Gredt, *Elementa*, 2:385–92.

5. *ST* I–II.91.2.

6. *ST* I–II.94.

7. *ST* I–II.94.5*ad*2.

Aquinas's theological procedure, and not as his strict or sole definition of it. Nor is it the only such consideration. Alan Donagan offers others:

> From the fact that St Thomas, in a theological work, defines natural law theologically, it follows neither that it cannot be defined philosophically, nor that a philosophical definition would be incomplete, as, according to St Thomas, any account of the natural end of man that neglected divine revelation would be incomplete. Although this is not stated in terms by Aquinas, it is implied by his assertion that "all men know . . . the common principles of the natural law" [I–II.93.2]. It is also presupposed in his derivations of the various precepts of the natural law, in none of which does he make any appeal to revealed theology. Nor does he explicitly draw upon natural theology, except in deriving precepts having to do with divine worship.[8]

Donagan refers to Aquinas's derivations of the various precepts of natural law. Usually article 2 of *ST* I–II.94 is taken to lay the groundwork for these derivations. This article focuses entirely on things pertaining to human nature: the theoretical and practical truths naturally grasped by human reason and the natural inclinations of the human agent. The term *natural law*, as it is used there, appears to signify nothing other than the first principles of practical reason. Moreover, Thomas nowhere says that people need to have learned of God's legislative activity before they can grasp the truth of the first principles of practical reason. These principles are naturally *per se nota*, self-evident, to everyone.[9] By contrast, God's universal providence and legislation, on Thomas's view, are not naturally self-evident to us. This is the point that Donagan is making with his reference to Aquinas's assertion that all men know the common principles of the natural law.

The question that Donagan's claim raises is the following. Can an account of natural law that makes no mention of God, or of the eternal law, still present natural law as a law in the full sense, according to Thomas's definition of law? It seems easy to understand natural law in terms of that definition when reference is made to divine legislation. But without such reference, it is difficult to see how to apply almost any of the terms of the definition to natural law. Who is the one who oversees the community and promulgates it? Indeed, what is the community to which it applies? Is it mankind? Is mankind the sort of "complete community" that is regulated

---

8. Donagan, "Scholastic Theory," 328–29.

9. I follow the common practice of rendering *per se nota* as *self-evident*, although more literal would be something clumsier such as *known in virtue of themselves*.

by law?[10] Even the applicability of the first element of the definition, "an ordination of reason," seems doubtful. What Thomas means by this expression is a command issued by reason.[11] This leads back to the question of who promulgates natural law. There is no commanding without someone in command and someone commanded. Is natural law a command that every person's reason issues? Again, to what community? Moreover, Aquinas presents command as an act that presupposes a practical judgment and choice of the action commanded.[12] If natural law is a command issued by a man's own reason, then it depends upon man's own choice. This is problematic because natural law is supposed to consist precisely in first practical principles. These are prior to any choice.

Such considerations suggest that when Aquinas says that natural law has the nature of law to the highest degree, he must be thinking of natural law according to its "theological" definition, the one that refers to the eternal law. The "philosophical" definition would have to prescind from some of the elements of his definition of law and to employ a looser notion of law. One might then wonder, however, what the point would be of calling it a law in the first place.

And there are problems even for the theological definition. For if the text leaves no doubt that natural law is a law in the full sense, it also leaves no doubt that natural law is natural in a very strong sense. Natural law is promulgated "by the very fact that God has inserted it into the minds of men as something to be naturally known." How is this possible, if God's existence and legislative work are not naturally known? In the case of human law, the promulgation of a law makes known not only the order that the law prescribes, but also the authority that enacts the law. The king's command without the king's seal carries no weight. Granted, some regulative power perhaps belongs to the first principles of practical reason by the very fact that men naturally understand them to be true. But is this understanding, without the additional awareness that they originate from the will and command of the Author of nature, sufficient to give them the full obligatory force of law? For Thomas, law is nothing if not obligatory. The very starting-point that he adopts in constructing his definition of law is an etymology according to which the term *lex*, law, is derived from the term *ligare*, to bind or to oblige.[13] If people are inculpably ignorant of having been commanded

---

10. See *ST* I–II.90.2.

11. This becomes clear a littler later, when he says that "law is a declaration of reason in the mode of commanding" (*ST* I–II.92.2).

12. See *ST* I–II.17.3*ad*1; II–II.47.8.

13. *ST* I–II.90.1.

by a legitimate authority to do something, then even if they truly believe or know that they ought to do it, can they properly be said to be under an obligation to do it?

There seems to be a certain tension between the terms that comprise the expression *natural law*. The naturalness of natural law—the fact that its precepts are naturally known—seems to invite a merely "philosophical" conception of it, with no reference to its divine Author. But it is difficult to conceive natural law in this way and at the same time to ascribe a fully legal character to it. Natural law does not seem able to function as a law in the full sense except insofar as it is known to have been instituted and promulgated by God. But on Thomas's view, such knowledge is not natural; at least, not in the way that the knowledge of the first principles of practical reason is.

In light of such considerations, it should come as little surprise that the question of the legal character of Aquinas's natural law has received a number of different answers. In the rest of this chapter I shall look at representatives of what I take to be the main ones. To simplify the procedure, I divide them into four groups. On certain subordinate issues, however, authors placed in the same group will sometimes differ significantly, and authors in different groups will sometimes agree.

NATURAL LAW AS A LAW IN A QUALIFIED SENSE

A very detailed and rather extreme claim for the need to consider natural law in isolation from anything extrinsic to man, including the eternal law, was put forth in the mid-twentieth century by the Benedictine scholar Dom Odon Lottin.[14] On Lottin's view, the consideration of the eternal law is not merely incidental to the understanding of natural law. It is positively detrimental. In his view, the real function of the doctrine of natural law in Aquinas's thought is to provide the foundation for what Lottin calls an "intrinsic morality." This would be a system of principles or standards of human conduct that proceed from the light of man's own reason and not from any extrinsic impositions, such as the commands of a divine lawgiver. The truth and the normative character of these principles is intrinsic to them. Their status as true norms can and, in the first instance, must be seen independently of any external authority. In this setting, connecting natural law with the eternal law only obscures the proper function of natural law. Indeed, Lottin says, it is hard to see in any case what can be learned from such a connection. No one in this life knows the eternal law as it is in itself, whereas everyone knows natural law. To explain natural law in terms of

---

14. See especially Lottin, "La valeur."

eternal law is to explain the more known by the less known. It is not necessary to have recourse to such an explanation in order to grasp that natural law is a genuine moral standard and carries genuine obligation. The object of natural law consists in those things that are "commanded because [intrinsically] good, and prohibited because [intrinsically] evil."[15] Lottin stresses the absence of the eternal law from the discussion of natural law in *ST* I–II.94.[16] In his judgment, the reason why natural law is called a participation of the eternal law is simply that the eternal law is the supreme rule of all good and the ultimate source of any other rule.[17]

Lottin acknowledges that it is not surprising to find a theological study of the various kinds of law placing the eternal law first, and that doing so provides a way of unifying the study of all the other kinds of law that apply to us. Nevertheless, according to his historical findings, the thematic discussion of the eternal law made only a very late entry into the mainstream of scholastic theology, and Aquinas himself felt no need to take it up until he became acquainted with one or the other of two Franciscan works that treat it.[18] To Lottin, this suggests that the presentation of natural law in the setting of the eternal law does not spring from the inner tendency of Thomas's thought on natural law. This tendency is to focus on reason's natural capacity to grasp a moral order that is intrinsically applicable to human action. That the eternal law should be the ultimate origin of this order serves only to underscore the respect that is due to natural reason itself, as to an imprint of the mind of God. "One can therefore organize the treatment of natural law without starting from the concept of eternal law."[19] And this is a better way to organize it.

> When one studies the eternal law prior to natural law, one undoubtedly respects the objective order of things; but one does not follow the logical order of our apprehensions, which goes from the more known to the less known; now, the eternal law is not known to us except by way of analogy, whereas we grasp the natural law in ourselves. Moreover, when one places the Thomistic definition [of law] at the beginning of the treatise on laws, certain readers are tempted to understand the natural law in the light of positive law, since it is in positive law that the Thomistic definition is perfectly embodied. Now, it is not in

---

15. Lottin, "La valeur," 367.
16. Lottin, "La valeur," 369.
17. Lottin, "La valeur," 377.
18. Lottin, *Psychologie et Morale*, 63–67. See below, 33.
19. Lottin, "La valeur," 377.

> this light that one should consider it [viz., natural law]; for that which must be inculcated above all, in teaching natural law, is the intrinsic character of this law, or if one wishes, of the dictate of natural reason that defines it; now, the reader runs the risk of not grasping this essential mark of the natural law, when he considers the *ordinatio* of natural reason, immanent to man, in the perspective of the *ordinatio* of a lawgiver, even a divine one, imposing itself from the outside.[20]

Lottin's insistence upon presenting natural law entirely in terms of what is intrinsic to its human subject thus leads him to separate the account of it not only from the eternal law, but also from Aquinas's definition of law in general. While nearly all the interpreters judge that Thomas generates his definition of law chiefly in light of the experience of human positive law, Lottin goes further. For him, positive law is the only kind of law that fully satisfies the definition. Since reference to the work of a lawgiver is in no way necessary for understanding the precepts of natural law as genuine norms, it is neither necessary nor even suitable to study natural law in light of the general definition of law as something imposed or promulgated by governing authority. Only positive law requires reference to the promulgation and sanction of a governor to establish its normative status. If natural law, properly considered, is nothing other than the principles of action existing naturally in each individual's reason, then its notion does not include the note of a conclusion drawn by practical reason for the direction of action; nor that of something essentially brought forth in view of a common good; nor that of something instituted by someone who has charge of a community; nor even that of something promulgated. It realizes none of the attributes that Aquinas judges to be essential to any true law, except imperfectly and by some sort of analogy.

> Does this definition [of law in general] help to understand natural law better? We do not think so; for, in order to apply it to natural law, all of its terms have to be taken in an analogical sense. . . . Moreover, let us see how Saint Thomas himself handles this. Certainly, he sees in natural law an act of reason, *aliquid per rationem constitutum, quoddam opus rationis* (I–II q. 94 a. 1); but nowhere does he exploit the more precise concept of an *ordinatio rationis* with which he had defined law in general (I–II q. 90 a. 1). Saint Thomas certainly also addresses the promulgation of natural law; but it is to conclude that this law does not need promulgation (I–II q. 90 a. 4, ad 1). As for the other

---

20. Lottin, *Principes de Morale*, 220–21n2.

two elements of the definition of law in general, regarding the law's author and end, nowhere, in his entire Question devoted to natural law, does Thomas even dream of applying them.[21]

Elsewhere Lottin even denies that the eternal law perfectly fulfills the nature of law as defined in *ST* I-II.90.[22] For Lottin, this definition is not properly applicable to anything other than human positive law. Aquinas, however, can hardly hold this view. Within his treatment of the eternal law, he lays down the principle that "the conception of one who governs the acts of his subjects takes on the nature of law, assuming the other conditions that we ascribed above to the nature of law," and then he shows that the eternal conception of the divine wisdom fulfills these conditions and can therefore be called an eternal law.[23]

It is also difficult to understand how Lottin can read *ST* I-II.90.4*ad*1 to mean that no promulgation pertains to natural law.[24] In one place he does qualify this, saying that natural law has no promulgation "from without" and that its promulgation is "internal."[25] But this seems no less odd. Surely if it is God who promulgates natural law, then its promulgation is originally "from without." Lottin tries to argue the point on the basis of *ST* I-II.100.4*ad*1, where Thomas likens the precept of faith to the first precepts of natural law, which are self-evident and "do not need promulgation."[26] However, that passage does not end here, and its concluding remark is almost exactly the same as what *ST* I-II.90.4*ad*1 says about the promulgation of natural law. The precept of faith "does not need any promulgation other than the infusion of faith."

In any case, from the manner in which he qualifies the general definition of law when applying it to natural law, the analogy that Lottin has in mind seems to be what is sometimes called analogy of improper proportionality. In Thomas's language, this is metaphor. The thought would be that, in some respects, the natural dictates of each man's reason function in relation to his actions as laws function in relation to the actions of the members of a community. Perhaps it would be similar to the metaphor by which, according to Aquinas, the right subordination of the other powers of the soul to reason is called justice.[27]

21. Lottin, "La valeur," 367–69.
22. Lottin, *Principes de Morale*, 219–20.
23. *ST* I-II.93.1.
24. He says the same in Lottin, *Le droit naturel*, 70–71.
25. Lottin, *Psychologie et Morale*, 38.
26. Lottin, *Psychologie et Morale*, 38n2.
27. *ST* I-II.100.2*ad*2; II-II.58.2. See the quotation from Gregory Stevens below, 15–16.

Germain Grisez's famous article on the first principle of practical reason also insists that natural law cannot be understood in the first instance as a command imposed upon man by God. Grisez does not deny that the first principles of practical reason are in fact derived from the eternal law. But this is not how they first or naturally present themselves to the human intellect. In fact, he says, according to their original and natural existence in man's mind, they are not commands at all, divine or human. "From man's point of view, the principles of natural law are neither received from without nor posited by his own choice; they are naturally and necessarily known, and a knowledge of God is by no means a condition for forming self-evident principles, unless those principles happen to be ones that especially concern God."[28]

Grisez calls these principles *precepts* or *prescriptions*, to distinguish them from the kind of declaration called *command*. The difference is that command carries a certain impulse derived from the commander's will. This impulse gives the declaration a moving force or a power of "promoting the execution of the work to which reason directs."[29] Grisez thus draws a sharp distinction between natural law and human or divine positive law. "Human and divine [i.e., revealed] law are in fact not merely prescriptive but also imperative, and when precepts of the law of nature were incorporated into the divine law they became imperatives whose violation is contrary to the divine will as well as to right reason."[30] Grisez does not develop further the question of the sense in which natural law, as he presents it, constitutes a law. He stresses the directive and rational quality of law and treats the dimension of moving force almost as accidental to it.[31] As a result, one might infer that he sees no obstacle to calling the first principles of practical reason, taken just in themselves, a law in the full sense. But this would only be a conjecture.

---

28. Grisez, "First Principle," 192–93.
29. Grisez, "First Principle," 192.
30. Grisez, "First Principle," 192.

31. "Those who misunderstand Aquinas's theory often seem to assume, as if it were obvious, that law is a transient action of an efficient cause physically moving passive objects; for Aquinas, law always belongs to reason, is never considered an efficient cause, and cannot possibly terminate in motion" (Grisez, "First Principle," 193n66). This sounds as though no law of any sort can possibly be a command, and it is hard to square with his remark that human and divine law are imperative. Perhaps he only means that law cannot be an efficient cause per se, but only in conjunction with an act of will. Thomas does hold that knowledge is a cause of things only when functioning together with will. See *ST* I.14.8.

In fact, Grisez's collaborator, John Finnis, asserts without hesitation that natural law is "only analogically law."[32] There would be no loss of meaning, he says, if one were to speak of "natural right," "intrinsic morality," or "natural reason or right reason in action," instead of "natural law." In this regard Finnis refers, evidently with approval, to an article by Mortimer Adler. Adler argues that natural law is law "only by analogy of attribution . . . to the primary analogate, which is human positive law."[33] What this means is that natural law is called law in the same way that medicine is called healthy. Medicine is called healthy only because it is a principle of health in animals. It does not have the nature of health in it. Similarly, natural law provides an understanding that precedes and directs any human work of legislation, expressing those basic human needs that human laws seek to address. But it does not have in itself the nature of law. In another article Adler argues in detail that natural law, philosophically understood, is neither promulgated in the proper sense, nor received from an extrinsic and dominating authority, nor fully coercive, nor relative to the constitution of any actual community.

> Natural law is law only if we look to God as its maker, because, as St Thomas says, it proceeds from the will as well as from the reason of God. But if you consider natural law purely on the human level, whereon it is simply discovered by reason, with no aid from the will, then, being entirely a work of man's reason, natural law does not meet St Thomas's definition of law.[34]

As this quotation indicates, Adler's discussion is restricted to that notion of natural law which he considers to be possible within the limits of philosophy; that is, without reference to divine legislation. For my purposes, the real question would be whether such a notion is possible for Aquinas. Finnis has no doubt that it is. To him, Aquinas's presentation of natural law in light of the eternal law is "no more than a straightforward application of his general theory of the cause and operation of human understanding in any field of inquiry."[35] As a merely theoretical reflection, this application does not enter into the proper, suitably practical account of natural law.[36]

Wolfgang Kluxen presents a comparable view. He grants that it is only by reference to the eternal law that the first principles of practical reason

---

32. Finnis, *Natural Law and Natural Rights*, 280.

33. Finnis, *Natural Law and Natural Rights*, 294. The reference is to Adler, "Question about Law."

34. Adler, "Doctrine of Natural Law," 78.

35. Finnis, *Natural Law and Natural Rights*, 399.

36. See Finnis, *Natural Law and Natural Rights*, 390.

can be understood to have the full nature of law. Apart from that reference, natural law can be known materially, but not formally. He also argues that even if natural law's divine origin is philosophically knowable, it is only in metaphysics, and that such knowledge has a practical significance only within revealed theology. Only revealed theology is a knowledge of God that is both theoretical and practical.[37] But Kluxen considers moral philosophy to be independent both of metaphysics and of revealed theology. Treating moral phenomena simply as they immediately show themselves in human experience, moral philosophy judges everything in the light of the first principles of practical reason, and it does not have or need any further foundation for these principles. The principles of practical reason are understood as true directives of human conduct in virtue of themselves. Moral philosophy has little or no interest in the question of their divine origin or of their legal character, or in the formal consideration of natural law as law.[38]

A number of other authors can be found who are in explicit or implicit agreement with Lottin's basic position.[39] For them, treating natural law without reference to the eternal law would be fully in accordance with the inner tendency of Thomas's thought. The notion of natural law is nothing other than the notion of principles of "intrinsic morality," and this notion contains only an imperfect or "analogical" realization of Thomas's criteria of law. Those who wish to be true to the spirit of Aquinas's ethics are urged to rethink the theory of natural law in a way that sets aside the connotations of *law* and places the notion of right reason at the center of the discussion.

NATURAL LAW AS A SELF-STANDING LAW

Not all of the interpreters who agree with the position of Lottin, that the eternal law is not pertinent to the proper account of Thomistic natural law, draw the conclusion that, within the limits of this account, natural law falls short of the full nature of law. According to some, Thomas's natural law can be seen as a law in the proper sense of the term even when it is considered just in itself and not in relation to the eternal law. They see the reference to the eternal law only as an indication of the ultimate source of natural law's legality. In other words, the first principles of practical reason, considered simply according to themselves, can be called laws in the full sense. The eternal law enters into the account of natural law only because all legislation

---

37. See *ST* I.1.4; II-II.4.2*ad*3; II-II.9.3; II-II.45.3.
38. Kluxen, *Philosophische Ethik*, 233–37.
39. See, for example, Leclercq, *La philosophie morale*, 386–88; Turienzo, "La doctrina tomista," 11–14; Bourke, "Is Thomas Aquinas"; Brown, *Natural Rectitude and Divine Law*, 30–52, esp. 38–39n22.

is ultimately derived from the legislation of God. The eternal law "does not enter into the doctrine of natural law precisely as such, but is of paramount importance in what may be termed the ontological perspective in which the full perfection of the part is seen in its relation to the whole."[40]

An extensive version of this interpretation is presented by Dermot O'Donoghue.[41] According to him, "St Thomas does not provide a direct definition of Natural Law, but he defines it indirectly, as a participation in Eternal Law."[42] O'Donoghue finds that although knowledge of the eternal law sheds much light on the function of natural law in the economy of the universe, approaching natural law by way of the eternal law is not required by the intrinsic intelligibility of natural law. He sees no reason to set the eternal law aside when treating of natural law, but neither does he think it necessary to follow Thomas's procedure and start from the eternal law.

O'Donoghue criticizes Lottin for denying that natural law is a law in the proper sense of the term.[43] He cites Thomas's explicit statement that natural law is a law in the proper sense.[44] This is how Aquinas distinguishes between man's participation of the eternal law and the participation found in irrational creatures. At the same time, and for the same reason, O'Donoghue criticizes those who make the legality of natural law depend solely upon the eternal law. To present natural law in this way, he holds, is to say that it is nothing but a portion of the eternal law passively received in man.[45] In his view, to call natural law a passive participation of the eternal law is to confuse it with the kind of subjection to eternal law that is common to man and other creatures, the kind that Aquinas calls subjection *per modum actionis et passionis*.[46] It is to locate natural law in appetitive inclinations. These are passive principles, by which something is attracted toward some action or end. But natural law must be understood as an object of knowledge, which is prior to appetite. It serves as an active principle, ordering and attracting something to an action and an end. Existing as an object of reason, natural law can be said to be a law in the proper sense. So if human beings have a natural law, it is because they naturally participate in the eternal law in an active way.

---

40. Farrell, "Sources," 277–78n160.
41. O'Donoghue, "Thomist Concept."
42. O'Donoghue, "Thomist Concept," 92.
43. O'Donoghue, "Thomist Concept," 90–91.
44. *ST* I-II.91.2*ad*3.
45. For this sort of view, see below, 21–30.
46. *ST* I-II.93.6.

For O'Donoghue, this means that they must naturally participate in the very work of enacting law. Even though natural law shares in the nature of law only to the extent that man participates in the eternal law, the participation in question must be a participation in the very act of legislating. Natural law must be a law naturally instituted by a command of man's own reason. It must receive all of the conditions of legality from reason itself. It must be a law promulgated not only "to" man but also "by" man.[47] Its dependence upon the eternal law cannot be essentially different from the dependence of any other law, for example human law, on the eternal law. To be sure, in stating precepts of natural law, we are in fact also stating precepts of the eternal law.[48] But we are not at first aware of this fact.[49] And nevertheless the obligatory and legal nature of these precepts is evident to us right from the start, because it is something for which our own reason is also responsible.[50] O'Donoghue grants Lottin's point that natural law, insofar as it is considered a dictate of mere reason, cannot be seen as issued by a public authority for a common good. But he cites texts from the *Summa theologiae* to argue that in some cases the full nature of law can be attributed to privately issued dictates and to dictates that are concerned with individual goods.[51] Natural law would be a law that one naturally imposes on oneself.

In short, O'Donoghue understands Aquinas's teaching on natural law to entail a doctrine of man's natural autonomy. Whereas the beasts are naturally determined to act in accordance with the eternal law, man's acts are brought into accordance with the eternal law through a law which man himself originates. It is for this reason that man's compliance with the eternal law can be said to be free or self-determined.

O'Donoghue is by no means alone in holding such a position. For instance, Frederick Copleston offers a similar argument:

> For Aquinas . . . it is the human reason which is the proximate or immediate promulgator of the natural moral law. This law is not without a relation to something above itself; for it is . . . the reflection of or a participation of the eternal law. But inasmuch as it is immediately promulgated by the human reason we can speak of a certain autonomy of the practical reason. This does not mean that man can alter the natural moral law which is

---

47. O'Donoghue, "Thomist Concept," 103.
48. O'Donoghue, "Thomist Concept," 103.
49. O'Donoghue, "Thomist Concept," 96.
50. See O'Donoghue, "Thomist Concept," 105–7.
51. See O'Donoghue, "Thomist Concept," 104, citing *ST* I–II.90.2*ad*1; I–II.96.1*ad*1; I–II.97.4.

founded on his nature. But it means that the human being does not receive the moral law simply as an imposition from above; he recognizes or can recognize its inherent rationality and binding force, and he promulgates it to himself.[52]

This notion of natural law as an expression of man's autonomy or self-legislation, then, is not meant to imply that we have any control over the natural law that we possess. Natural law is not the fruit of our own deliberation and choice. Rather, the thought is that what natural law requires of us is always and, from our point of view, first of all something that we require of ourselves. Our own hearts utter its precepts, and it is because these are so deeply engrained in us that we have no power to change or uproot them. This is why the binding or obligatory character of its precepts is immediately apparent to us, even before we become aware of their original derivation from a higher personal authority, outside ourselves, to which we are subject.

It seems in fact that the existence of something called moral obligation is central to this line of interpretation. By *moral obligation* I mean a kind of necessity or absolute requirement to which we are subject, and know ourselves to be subject, by the very fact of having reason, and independently of any advertence to external authority, even that of God. Lottin does not deny the existence of such obligation. It is one aspect of what he calls the "intrinsic" character of natural law. He simply will not allow that, taken by itself, it fully warrants giving the name of law to the rules determining that obligation. O'Donoghue and Copleston do allow this.

So does Alan Donagan. As mentioned earlier, Donagan finds in Thomas a distinction between two points of view. "From the point of view of moral philosophy, the natural law is a set of precepts the binding force of which can be ascertained by human reason; from the point of view of theology, it is that part of what God eternally and rationally wills that can be grasped by human reason as binding upon human beings."[53] Donagan criticizes Elizabeth Anscombe for holding that "morality can intelligibly be treated as a system of law only by presupposing a divine lawgiver."[54]

Evidently, in this line of interpretation, the question of the legality of natural law is framed not so much in terms of the four elements of Aquinas's final definition of law, as in terms of the attribute from which he begins his study of the essence of law. "*Law* (*lex*) is derived from *binding* (*ligando*),

---

52. Copleston, *Aquinas*, 214. See Farrell, *Natural Law*, 80–82, 102–3; Lazure, "La loi naturelle," 12; Manser, *Das Naturrecht*, 67–74.

53. Donagan, "Scholastic Theory," 330. See also Donagan, *Theory of Morality*, 6.

54. Donagan, *Theory of Morality*, 3. See also Donagan, "Scholastic Theory," 328. For Anscombe's view, see below, 29.

because it obliges (*obligat*) one to act."⁵⁵ The decisive consideration is that man acknowledges the obligatory force of natural law's precepts immediately upon understanding them. For this reason, the light of man's own intellect can be regarded as the immediate source of natural law's obligatory force, and hence also of its legality. Thomas does say that obligatory force is something proper to law.⁵⁶

Gregory Stevens has given clear expression to this view:

> Because the necessity of this [first] principle [of practical reason] is the result of the meaning of the subject and predicate, it does not have to be supported by any outside authority, but is, in a true sense self-sustaining. In fact, the acceptance of authority by the human, moral agent is governed by this principle, and authority is accepted because it shares in the nature of the good, which is asserted in this judgment. Of course, neither this judgment and its necessity, nor anything at all in man and in creation can be fully explained without reference to the Creator, but rationally and philosophically, the necessity of this principle can be discovered and supported without direct recourse to the authority of God.... When this ordination is seen as joined with the will in actually moving to operation, the law is designated as a precept, as actually inducing and leading to action.⁵⁷

However, Stevens goes on in the same article to distinguish between what he calls the "inner necessity" of natural law, which is its force of "moral" obligation, and obligation in the strictest sense of the term. In fact he applies the same analogy to the obligatory force of natural law as that which Lottin applies to its legality. Evidently he is led to do so because, for Aquinas, law in the full sense is something constraining, indeed coercive. "Law by its nature has two features: first, that it is a rule of human acts; second, that it has coercive power."⁵⁸ Stevens says:

> It may be helpful to distinguish the inner necessity of this principle from the more exact use of the term *obligation*. This latter involves the notion of being bound, of being under constraint, and brings with it the notions of a superior and inferior, in such a way that the action of the inferior is seen as regulated by the will of the superior. Strictly and formally speaking, this subjection of

---

55. *ST* I–II.90.1.

56. *ST* I–II.90.4.

57. Stevens, "Relation of Law," 200–203. See Lazure, "La loi naturelle," 24.

58. *ST* I–II.96.5. What Lottin says may sound as though obligation and coercion are the same thing. On this question, see chapter 6 below.

one's action to the will and determination of another is applicable only to the field of justice.... When the terminology of justice is used in regard to the forms of justice other than distributive, the notions of what is due and just are used in a proper analogical sense. When, however, these terms are applied in other contexts, they are to be seen as used in a metaphorical sense, as St Thomas notes. Such would be the case of applying the notions of justice to man's higher, rational self, seen as the superior with rights, and to his lower self, seen as the inferior with duties; or to the relations of intellect and will. Such would also be the case if the terms of justice are used to describe the psychological reaction to objective facts and reality. While in these cases it may be quite true to say that man feels constrained, or under obligation, this does not in any way authorize the philosophical conclusion that the moral law, as such, is a constraint, imposed from without on man's freedom and reason.[59]

It seems, then, that this position treats natural law as a law in the full sense only because it abstracts from certain aspects of Aquinas's complete understanding of law. So at least in some crucial respects, this position is not very different, after all, from the one represented by Lottin and others. By treating natural law in abstraction from the eternal law, both positions are led to qualify the legal character of natural law somewhat, in comparison with Aquinas's definition of law. In fact, in a slightly later article, Stevens concedes this point explicitly.[60]

NATURAL LAW AS A NOT QUITE NATURAL LAW

A somewhat qualified conception of natural law's legal character seems to result from removing the eternal law from the account of natural law. It is therefore not surprising to find other interpreters insisting that reference to the eternal law is an essential factor in Aquinas's understanding of natural law. Some of them also go so far as to maintain that the legal force of the first principles of practical reason is not fully actualized except insofar as the divine institution sanctioning them is recognized.

This position, however, makes it difficult to preserve the strictly natural character of natural law. It does so for the same reason that the previous interpretation tended to qualify its legal character. The reason is that the first principles of practical reason are naturally self-evident to everyone, whereas the existence and legislative work of God are not.

---

59. Stevens, "Relation of Law," 204–5.
60. Stevens, "Moral Obligation," 17–21.

The Question of the Legal Character of Natural Law

A very forthright statement of this position is offered by Ernest Fortin.[61] Explicitly criticizing Finnis, Fortin insists that Aquinas conceives natural law to be a law in the strict and proper sense of the term, and that Thomas's notion of law includes not only the element of rationality but also the elements of will, moving force, and coercion or sanction. He then makes the following claim:

> What the Thomistic theory essentially requires is not only that the content of the natural law be naturally known to all human beings but that it be known precisely as belonging to the natural law, that is to say, to a law which is both promulgated and enforced by God as the author of nature and hence indispensably binding on everyone.[62]

Disappointingly, Fortin supplies no arguments in support of this contention. In a sense, however, it does not matter, because in fact what he goes on to argue is that Thomas himself does not hold the "Thomistic theory." That is, Thomas does not think that the truth of God's promulgating and enforcing the precepts of natural law is naturally known. This means that he does not really think that it is a natural law after all.

Fortin reaches this conclusion through more than a little reading between Thomas's lines. His argument starts from a reflection on Thomas's view of how the First Table of the Decalogue is known:

> Since all laws draw their effective power from the will of the lawgiver, such a view [of God as legislator] clearly presupposes that the divine nature is characterized by will no less than intellect. It becomes intelligible only within the framework of a providential order in which the thoughts, words and deeds of individual human beings fall under God's supervision and are duly rewarded or punished by Him. Here precisely is the difficulty to which on its own ground the argument is exposed; for, the truth of the proposition that the God of nature is a solicitous God, entitled to and demanding the love and worship of all rational creatures, would appear to be secured only through the precepts of the First Table, which, by Thomas's own admission, are not universally accessible without the aid of divine revelation.[63]

---

61. Fortin, "New Rights Theory," 590–612, esp. 605–611. See also Fortin, "On the Naturalness" (portions of which are reworkings of passages in Fortin, "Augustine, Aquinas, and the Problem").

62. Fortin, "New Rights Theory," 608–9.

63. Fortin, "New Rights Theory," 609. The "admission" by Aquinas is found in ST I–II.100.1.

Since, Fortin concludes, the precepts of the Second Table of the Decalogue depend on those of the First for full legal efficacy, it is difficult to see how they can be regarded as fully natural. Yet according to Aquinas, these precepts belong to natural law taken "absolutely."[64] The knowledge of their truth requires no help from revelation. Fortin therefore suggests the need to distinguish between the knowledge of the precepts of natural law merely as true, and the knowledge that they are genuinely legal precepts. It is with respect to the latter knowledge that the naturalness of natural law is doubtful. It is true, we may note, that Aquinas regards the precepts of the Second Table as only secondary precepts of natural law; that is, as precepts that require some reasoning (though not very much) from those that are primary and self-evident. But the same sort of doubt could be raised also about the primary precepts.[65]

Fortin also calls attention to that accompaniment of law which is called punishment or sanction. Although Aquinas's definition of law does not mention sanctions, Fortin observes, this does not mean that law need not carry sanctions. Even if carrying sanctions is not strictly a constitutive factor of law, it is still one of law's essential effects or accompaniments.[66] But Fortin finds that, in Aquinas's treatment, the subject of the sanctions proper to natural law is conspicuous by its absence. Aquinas does hold that violations of natural law are punishable, and that natural law itself calls for such punishment; but he says that the specification of the punishment called for by natural law belongs to positive law.[67] In other words, Thomas does not seem to think that natural law brings with it any punishment of its own for such violations.

Fortin suggests an explanation for this silence. Perhaps Aquinas wants to indicate natural reason's unawareness, or at least uncertainty, not only of what natural law's proper sanctions are, but even of whether the violations of it are punished in any way at all, in each and every case.[68] This reading would corroborate the thought that Thomas regards natural reason as not fully aware, or not fully certain, that the practical truths that it knows are genuine laws. Reason may be unable to discern the existence, or at least the universality and inescapability, of sanctions for violating natural law. This inability would correspond to its uncertainty as to whether the universe is governed by an omnipotent and provident governor from whose justice

---

64. *ST* I–II.100.1.
65. See *ST* I–II.100.3.
66. *ST* I–II.92.2. See also *ST* I–II.100.9.
67. *ST* I–II.95.2.
68. Fortin, "New Rights Theory," 609–610.

no one can escape. This uncertainty in turn leaves reason in doubt as to whether the common practical principles are a law at all. While everyone knows the common principles of the natural law, not everyone seems to know of the existence of the eternal law from which these principles derive and obtain their legal force. And so the principles do not naturally function as laws; that is, as rules carrying the force of the authority and the coercive power of their framer.

"To put the matter in more concrete terms, human reason, left to itself, cannot be absolutely certain that crime never pays and that in the end the only people who are happy are the ones who deserve to be happy."[69] There may be wrongdoers who "get away with it" in this life, and "short of appealing to retributions in an afterlife, on which the unaided human reason is unable to pronounce itself, the strict natural law theorist has no option but to deny that such a person can ever be at peace with himself."[70] But, Fortin says, it is neither demonstrable nor empirically verifiable that all undetected criminals are afflicted with remorse of conscience.[71] Yet punishment for each and every wrongdoing would be an essential requirement of any theory of natural law as a genuine law. For it is a genuine law only if it is a law of God.

Thus Fortin's doubt as to the naturalness of Thomistic natural law is not only a doubt about the ability of all people to know its legal character in a wholly natural or immediate way. It is also a doubt about whether this knowledge can be attained even by the few who make full use of natural reason; that is, by philosophers. Fortin finds it highly suggestive that Aquinas should say about sin that it "is viewed by theologians principally as a punishable [sic] offense against God, but by philosophers only [sic] as something that is contrary to reason."[72] This inability of natural reason to be certain of sufficient sanctions would explain why some thinkers, holding to its naturalness, have wanted to identify natural law altogether with the natural principles of practical reason, presenting it independently of God and of the strict notion of law, and making it a mere *lex indicans* rather than a true *lex praecipiens*.[73]

69. Fortin, "New Rights Theory," 610.
70. Fortin, "New Rights Theory," 611.
71. Fortin, "On the Naturalness," 448.

72. Fortin, "New Rights Theory," 609. Fortin is quoting *ST* I-II.71.6ad5. That passage has nothing corresponding to the words *punishable* and *only*; they are Fortin's additions.

73. Cf. Strauss, "Natural Law," 83. According to Suárez, this view was held by Gregory of Rimini, Hugh of St. Victor, Gabriel Biel, and others. See Suárez, *De lege naturali*, 79–80 (*De legibus* II.vi.3, lines 7–13; the line numbers are those of the edition cited).

Fortin's interpretation is directed against the contention of some historians of political philosophy, with whom he is in agreement on certain basic tenets, that Aquinas's natural law doctrine is a modification, and a misunderstanding, of the ancient, especially Aristotelian notion of natural right. The fullest statement of this position is by Harry Jaffa.[74] Jaffa and Fortin agree that natural law can function as a law only insofar as it is known to be promulgated and sanctioned by God, and that natural reason can never be fully certain of divine providence.[75] (Jaffa offers no more support of these claims than Fortin does.) They also agree that a clear sign of the difference between Aquinas's natural law and Aristotle's natural right is the fact that Aquinas attributes universality to the first precepts of natural law. Aristotle attributes some variability, according to time and place, to all of natural right. Moreover—for Fortin this seems to be the most important point—the natural right that Aristotle discusses is entirely within the sphere of political right.[76] It refers to that portion of political right that tends to be common to the various kinds of regime and does not depend on explicit agreement or institution.[77] It makes no reference to a universal, supra-political order. Aristotle does speak of a single form of regime that is by nature best.[78] But he does not seem to mean that it would be suitable always and everywhere, under any and all circumstances.

Where Fortin differs from Jaffa is in holding that Aquinas is perfectly aware of this difference and has not misunderstood Aristotle. Fortin's Thomas understands Aristotle's natural right to be altogether natural, but he does not understand his own natural law to be so. Natural law somehow contains natural right, and in that sense it is natural, but it is not natural with respect to its form as law or to its indispensability. The only sort of law whose existence men are naturally certain of, and which therefore naturally functions as a law, is human law. If there is any sense in which the legal character of natural law is natural, for Fortin's Aquinas, it would be only as something that has been revealed for all men everywhere, Jew and Gentile alike. Even though he says the contrary, what Fortin's Aquinas really thinks is that natural law is a kind of revealed law.

---

74. See Jaffa, *Thomism and Aristotelianism*, esp. chapter 7.
75. See Jaffa, *Thomism and Aristotelianism*, 169, 221n9.
76. See Aristotle, *Nicomachean Ethics* V.10, 1134a24–26, 1134b17–19.
77. See Aristotle, *Rhetoric* I, 1368b7–9, 1373b1–18.
78. Aristotle, *Nicomachean Ethics* V.10, 1135a5.

NATURAL LAW AS A NATURAL DIVINE LAW

The positions so far considered may be summed up as follows. The first is that natural law is a law only in a qualified sense, either by its partial resemblance to true law, which is human positive law, or by its causal relation to true law. The second position is that it is a law unqualifiedly, and this without reference to the eternal law, because its legal character is manifest according to its intrinsic nature as the set of first principles of man's practical reason. The third position is that natural law is law unqualifiedly, but only insofar as it derives from the eternal law; that it functions as a law only insofar as derivation from the eternal law is known; and that, since this derivation is not known naturally, natural law is natural only in a qualified sense.

The mere permutation of the terms would suggest another conceivable interpretation. This would be that natural law is a law in the full sense, that its legal character is owing exclusively to its divine origin, and that it is naturally known because its divine origin is self-evident to us. However, I have found no one who adopts such a view. Evidently the interpreters are too aware of Aquinas's rejection of the proposition that God's existence is naturally self-evident to us.[79]

Nevertheless it is still possible to hold that natural law is a law in the full sense only on account of its divine origin, and that it is also fully natural, in the sense of naturally known. This is possible in two ways. One is by holding that although the divine origin of natural law is not self-evident, there is a valid sense in which it is naturally known, or at least knowable, by all. This is Suárez's view:

> Natural law, as it is in man, has the force of a divine mandate as indicating it [that mandate] and not the mere nature of the thing. . . . So natural reason, which indicates what is per se bad and good for man, consequently indicates that it is according to the divine will that the one be done and the other avoided. . . . Hence the natural law existing in us is a sign of some will of God. Therefore, above all, [it is a sign] of that [will] by which He wills to oblige us to the observance of that law. Therefore natural law includes this will of God.[80]

---

79. See *ST* I.2.1.

80. *Lex naturalis, prout in homine est, habet vim divini mandati tanquam indicans illud, et non solam rei naturam. . . . Ergo ratio naturalis quae indicat quid sit per se malum vel bonum homini, consequenter indicat esse secundum divinam voluntatem ut unum fiat et aliud vitetur. . . . Ergo lex naturalis in nobis existens est signum alicuius voluntatis Dei. Ergo maxime illius qua vult nos obligare ad legem illam servandam. Ergo lex naturalis includit hanc Dei voluntatem* (Suárez, *De lege naturali*, 88–89, 92 [*De legibus* II.vi.7, lines 30–32; II.vi.8, line 17–19; II.vi.10, lines 21–24]). Perhaps I should apologize for

This is how, for Suárez, the natural light of reason constitutes a "sufficient promulgation" of natural law.[81] It is not enough to know the precepts of natural law in themselves. What they show in themselves is only that certain actions are intrinsically due or undue. One must also see the precepts as signs of God's legislative will. But natural reason can see them in this way. Although their being such signs is not self-evident, it can be easily inferred. It requires neither revelation nor sophisticated philosophical inquiry.

However, on Suárez's view, it is also not enough to infer that God has caused the precepts to exist in man's mind. For this is not the work of God's *legislative* will. Properly speaking, for Suárez, what causes the light of reason and the precepts of natural law to exist in man's mind is God's mere *creative* will. His legislative will presupposes this, but it is something else. It is His will to oblige us to the precepts, or in other words, to be offended by our doing what is intrinsically undue.[82] Hence, even if we grant that natural reason can know of God's production of human nature and of reason's natural light, Suárez still has to explain how reason can know of His properly legislative action. This may seem to be a problem, because God's will concerning creatures is free. But Suárez argues that, by one free act of His will, God can, as it were, bind Himself to others. "I say that, on the supposition of one free act, the divine will can be necessitated to another."[83] Given His will to create man with the light of reason, His legislative will concerning the precepts of natural law follows necessarily: "On the supposition of a will to create rational nature with sufficient knowledge for doing good and bad and with a sufficient cooperation on God's part for both, God could not have not willed to prohibit to such a creature the intrinsically bad acts or willed not to command the necessary noble (*honestos*) acts. For just as God cannot lie, so too He cannot govern foolishly or unjustly."[84] And "on the supposition

---

taking up one reader of Thomas who lived more than four centuries ago, when all of the others whom I discuss are from within the last hundred years. My excuse is threefold: no reading of Thomas on natural law has had more influence than Suárez's; it has something in common with Fortin's position and enters into the discussion of Farrell's; and, most importantly, having it in view will help me, in chapter 3, to bring out a really crucial element, and one that is rather neglected, in Thomas's own teaching.

81. Suárez, *De lege naturali*, 107 (*De legibus* II.vi.24, lines 19–31).

82. Suárez, *De lege naturali*, 107 (*De legibus* II.vi.24, lines 19–31).

83. *Dico . . . divinam voluntatem . . . ex suppositione unius actus liberi posse necessitari ad alium* (Suárez, *De lege naturali*, 105 [*De legibus* II.vi.23, lines 2–3]).

84. *Supposita voluntate creandi naturam rationalem cum sufficienti cognitione ad operandum bonum et malum et cum sufficienti concursu ex parte Dei ad utrumque, non potuisse Deum non velle prohibere tali creaturae actus intrinsece malos vel nolle praecipere honestos necessarios. Quia sicut non potest Deus mentiri, ita non potest insipienter vel iniuste gubernare* (Suárez, *De lege naturali*, 105–6 [*De legibus* II.vi.23, lines 10–16]).

that He wanted to have subjects using reason, He was not able not to be their legislator, at least in those things that are necessary for the natural honesty (*honestatem*) of morals."[85] It is through such a consideration as this that natural reason serves to notify man not only of the things that are intrinsically due and undue but also of God's legislative will commanding what is due and prohibiting what is undue.

Suárez thus recognizes that the knowledge of natural law as a genuine law requires some reasoning. But he considers the reasoning easy and within everyone's power.[86] In that sense the knowledge is natural.

Recently, Lawrence Dewan has expressed agreement with Suárez's position and argued that it fits with Aquinas.[87] Like Suárez, Dewan judges that the full promulgation of a law must include the notification of its expressing the lawgiver's will. Dewan finds Thomas teaching that some knowledge of God, as orderer of the world and source of help and guidance, is commonly accessible to people through a spontaneous and—in that sense—natural reasoning process, with failure to reach such knowledge normally being culpable.[88] This, Dewan reasons, would explain how Thomas can hold that the love of God above all things is a naturally known primary precept of natural law.[89] And it would explain how natural law is naturally known to be a divine law.

The other possible way in which to hold that natural law is at once fully a law, dependent upon divine institution for its legal character, and fully natural, is to deny that its functioning as a law requires knowledge of its divine origin. All that would be required is the knowledge of the first principles of practical reason, considered in themselves. These would constitute a purely natural participation, in the sense of an originally unconscious one, in the eternal law. They would still function as a law, inasmuch as they would be understood as normative and obligatory. But this understanding would not depend on knowing their derivation from the eternal law, even though the eternal law is in fact their origin and the source of their obligatory force and legal quality. Likewise, even though all the elements of Thomas's definition

---

85. *Ex suppositione quod voluit habere subditos ratione utentes, non potuit non esse legislator eorum, saltem in his quae ad honestatem naturalem morum necessaria sunt* (Suárez, *De lege naturali*, 106 [*De legibus* II.vi.23, lines 20–23]).

86. See Suárez, *Tractatus quinque* tract. 5 (*De vitiis et peccatis*), disp. 5, sect. 3, 558–60, esp. no. 6, 559.

87. Dewan, "St. Thomas and the Divine Origin," esp. 126. See also Dewan, "St. Thomas and the Divinity," 229n53.

88. Dewan, "St. Thomas and the Divine Origin," 128–29, cites *ScG* III.38; *ST* II–II.85.1; and the commentaries on Psalm 8 and on the Apostle's Creed.

89. *ST* I–II.100.3*ad*1.

of law do in fact apply to them, knowing them and understanding them to be obligatory would not depend on having grasped this about them. In short, on this view, it is not necessary for people to have formed the very concept of natural law, as a full-fledged law consisting in a participation of the eternal law, in order for the natural law to have been fully promulgated to them and to have begun to function as a true law measuring their conduct. Natural law is natural simply because it belongs naturally to us and rests upon an understanding of human nature and what is due to it.

Walter Farrell lays out this view in some detail. On his account, natural law fulfills the definition of law only by reason of its divine origin. Nevertheless natural human reason is a principle of the obligation that the precepts carry with them, because reason is what inflicts the punishment for violating them; namely, the remorse of conscience. This is why the obligation is naturally known, even though it is instituted by God and not by reason itself.[90] Farrell does not address the problems raised by Fortin regarding the insufficiency of remorse of conscience as the sanction proper to a law of God. What he does address, at some length, is how obligation is related to the legislator's will.

According to Farrell, it is the rational or normative aspect that is really constitutive of the nature of law and of precepts generally.[91] He takes the law's obligatory force to be the same as its coercive force—its carrying sanctions—and he sees this as a mere corollary or a consequence of its normativity. The distinction and relation between the normative and obligatory aspects of law corresponds to the distinction and relation between the roles of intellect and will in the act of issuing a precept, which is command (*imperium*).[92] Command is primarily an act of the intellect, because it is essentially a kind of intimation, and because it consists in ordering something toward action. Both intimating and ordering are works of reason. What the will contributes to the formation of a command is a certain moving force. It gives reason's intimation of an order the power to initiate or stimulate execution of the action ordained. This is its obligatory force. The dictate of the commander's reason measures conduct by virtue of itself, but it carries obligatory force by the influence of an act of the commander's will. This act is the commander's choice of the action to be ordained.

Farrell insists that human reason is in no way the legislator of natural law. Natural law is strictly a law of God, instituted not by man or nature or

---

90. Farrell, *Natural Law*, 138–41, 154–55.
91. Farrell, *Natural Law*, 7, 55.
92. Farrell, *Natural Law*, 56–61.

reason but only by eternal divine providence.⁹³ Its obligatory force originates in God's will. Nevertheless the way in which it carries this force is not by serving as a sign of God's will. It is rather that the precepts of natural law are a participation in the dictate of God's reason, which has the moving and obligatory force of command by virtue of the impulse of God's will, and that man's own will naturally shares in this impulse, through its own natural inclinations. Farrell likens their role to that of choice in the formation of commands.⁹⁴ The natural inclinations function together with the natural light of reason to constitute the proximate source of reason's natural practical dictates. This explains the human mind's natural tendency to inflict remorse of conscience for violation of the dictates. According to Thomas, the natural inclinations too are participations of the eternal law.⁹⁵ Hence the precepts of natural law can be said to owe their whole force to the eternal law. Yet their force does not depend on knowing their derivation from the eternal law. Rather, the eternal law's force is naturally brought to bear on human conduct by the mediation of human reason and will.

Farrell's opponent on this point is Suárez. As we saw, according to Suárez, natural law conveys legal obligation only by serving as a sign of the legislative will of God.⁹⁶ In Farrell's view, Suárez's teaching might be valid if precept or command were, as Suárez holds, essentially an act of will, the legislator's choice to oblige his subjects to a course of action. But since it is essentially an act of intellect, there is no reason why the natural dictates of the human intellect should not be precepts, carrying obligatory force, by their own nature. They can be, even though the only agent instituting them and giving them their force is God. He makes them be intrinsically preceptive and intrinsically obligatory. No advertence to His will is needed in order to appreciate their obligatory force. It is needed only in order to fully account for that force.

Actually Suárez's understanding of the obligatory force of the precepts of natural law is somewhat more complicated than Farrell's discussion makes it seem. This is because Suárez does ascribe to the precepts of natural law a certain intrinsic force of obligation, one that does not involve reference to God's legislative will. Of themselves, the precepts convey duties toward man's own nature and establish certain natural obligations, obligations in conscience.⁹⁷ What is proper to God's legislative will, for Suárez, is

---

93. Farrell, *Natural Law*, 138–41, 150–55.
94. Farrell, *Natural Law*, 100–101. See also Stevens, "Relations," 202.
95. *ST* I-II.91.2; I-II.93.6.
96. See above, 21.
97. See Suárez, *De lege naturali*, 139, 141 (*De legibus* II.ix.4, lines 10–13; II.ix.6,

to add a *further* obligatory force to them. This consists in His being offended by what runs contrary to them. This is the properly *legal* force of natural law, and it comes into effect only insofar as the precepts are understood as signs of that will. It is because the light of reason suffices to present the precepts as such signs that it constitutes a sufficient promulgation of natural law *as* law. So the precepts do, for Suárez, have a force of their own. However, on his view, this force does not depend on God's legislative will. Clearly Farrell would disagree with this. Farrell makes even the intrinsic force of the precepts of natural law to be the effect of the eternal law.

Now, although Farrell is careful to observe the Thomistic criteria of law in his way of ascribing the nature of law to the natural dictates of reason, his position is still exposed to some of the difficulties raised in relation to the second interpretation presented above, that of natural law as a law just in itself. For one thing, it is not clear that the intrinsic obligatory force of the natural dictates has an efficacy that is sufficient to suit a law of God. This is Fortin's objection. For another, the very notion of obligation, especially if it is understood as a kind of coercive force, seems to involve reference to an extrinsic agent imposing it. This is why Stevens held that the natural dictates of reason, taken in themselves, can be called obligatory only in a metaphorical sense.

Farrell does not address these difficulties. However, the well-known British philosopher, Peter Geach, offers what is in effect a response to both of them.[98] Geach does not refer his view to Aquinas. But he is recognized as a serious reader of Thomas and as one of the initiators of what is called analytical Thomism, and I think the very fact that he holds this view should make us consider the possibility that Aquinas does too.

Geach frames his discussion in terms of something like the *Euthyphro* question. Are the things that God commands morally obligatory because God commands them, or does God command them because they are already obligatory? Geach argues for the former. God's commandments can "generate moral obligation."[99] They do so by virtue of His sheer overweening power to enforce them and to order things in such a way that compliance with them always turns out for the best. Geach in fact grants that his position is "plain power worship."[100]

---

lines 14–24).

98. Geach, *God and the Soul*, 117–29.

99. The phrase is from Geach, *God and the Soul*, xix (where the Analytical Table of Contents describes p. 117 of the volume).

100. Geach, *God and the Soul*, 127.

At the same time, Geach argues that it is possible to be under such divine commands without knowing of their divine origin:

> The rational recognition that a practice is generally undesirable and that it is best for people on the whole not even to think of resorting to it is . . . *in fact* a promulgation to a man of the Divine law forbidding the practice, even if he does not realise that this is a promulgation of the Divine law, even if he does not believe there is a God. . . . This means that the Divine law is in some instances promulgated to all men of sound understanding. No man can sincerely plead ignorance that lying, for example, is generally objectionable. I am *not* saying that a sane and honest man must see that lying is *absolutely excluded*; but he must have some knowledge of the *general objectionableness* of lying, and this is in fact a promulgation to him of the Divine law against lying. And he can advance from this knowledge to recognition of the Divine law as such, by a purely rational process. . . . As Hobbes said: "These dictates of reason men use to call by the name of laws, but improperly: for they are but conclusions or theorems concerning what conduceth to the conservation and defence of themselves: whereas law, properly, is the word of him that by right hath command over others. But yet if we consider the same theorems as delivered in the word of God that by right commandeth over all things, then are they properly called laws."[101]

The promulgation of God's law does not, in the first instance, require an indication of its divine origin. Geach does think that its divine origin can be known philosophically, in natural theology.[102] But as far as I can tell, he does not think that this knowledge has to be naturally accessible to everyone in order for the promulgation to be considered sufficient.

Geach's distinction between the simply natural knowledge that a certain form of conduct is generally objectionable, and the reasoned or revealed knowledge that it is absolutely forbidden, could serve as a response to Fortin's and Jaffa's argument that the exceptionlessness of the precepts of natural law casts doubt on the naturalness of their promulgation. People do not have to know their exceptionlessness in order to be said to have had the precepts promulgated to them.[103] Evidently Geach is making even the

---

101. Geach, *God and the Soul*, 124–26. Geach's only real argument for this assertion takes the form of an imaginary example. I discuss it below, 78.

102. Geach, *God and the Soul*, 123.

103. Thomas does seem to hold that, unlike such specific precepts as the prohibition against lying, the primary, common precepts of natural law are naturally understood

conduct's general objectionableness, and not just the exceptionlessness of the prohibition of it, to be the effect of God's action of prohibiting it. Unfortunately Geach does not take up the question of how God's action causes either that objectionableness or the knowledge of it. Still, Geach's position does at least address Stevens's concern. It means that the natural dictates of reason are obligatory, from the start, by virtue of an extrinsic imposition and in more than a merely metaphorical sense, even though their being an effect of that imposition is not itself known from the start.

As regards the law's sanctions, Geach does not speak of the remorse of conscience, but he does say that "an act's being a good or bad thing for a human being to do is of itself a fact calculated to touch an agent's inclinations."[104] Perhaps he would grant that at least this power to touch one's inclinations would be a necessary part of the law's promulgation. But clearly, on his account, the fact that the remorse of conscience does not necessarily present itself as the effect of a divine influence, and that by itself it is not fully proportioned to the exigencies of a divine law, does not prevent it from being sufficient as the sanction that accompanies the natural promulgation of that law. For in any case, that promulgation itself is enough to render one liable to whatever other sanctions God may attach to the law. One need not know about them in order to be liable to them.

Another philosopher regarded as one of the initiators of analytical Thomism is Elizabeth Anscombe. In a famous article, Anscombe presents a view that is in a sense the other side of Geach's coin.[105] She argues that the notion of a moral law, or of moral obligation, or of a special, peremptory "moral" sense of the term *ought*, is simply meaningless outside the perspective of an ethics somehow based on a divine law.[106] Apart from such a perspective, the notion has no intelligible content. It has only a kind of "mesmeric force." She dismisses the idea that conscience itself could be the proper source of such obligation or play the role of the moral lawgiver or the moral authority, because conscience can dictate "the vilest things."[107] And she finds the notion of moral obligation, as it is understood in modern moral philosophy, completely absent in Aristotle. On her view, this is as it

---

to be exceptionless. But this is incidental to Geach's point. The exceptionlessness of the first, common precepts is a function of their mere generality, not of any reference to God's legislation. See *ST* I-II.97.1ad1. On how the derived or secondary precepts of natural law become more susceptible of exceptions, the less common or more specific they are, see Flannery, *Acts Amid Precepts*, 50–83.

104. Geach, *God and the Soul*, 122.
105. Anscombe, *Ethics, Religion, and Politics*, 26–42.
106. Geach also says things to this effect in Geach, *God and the Soul*, 122.
107. Anscombe, *Ethics, Religion, and Politics*, 27.

should be, since his ethics is not based on a divine law. What she does find in Aristotle is only the notion of what makes a man bad *qua* man:

> To have a *law* conception of ethics is to hold that what is needed for conformity with the virtues failure in which is the mark of being bad *qua* man (and not merely, say *qua* craftsman or logician)—that what is needed for *this*, is required by divine law. Naturally it is not possible to have such a conception unless you believe in God as a lawgiver; like Jews, Stoics and Christians. But if such a conception is dominant for many centuries, and then is given up, it is a natural result that the concepts of "obligation," of being bound or required as by a law, should remain though they had lost their root; and if the word "right" has become invested in certain contexts with the sense of "obligation," it too will remain to be spoken with a special emphasis and a special feeling in these contexts.[108]

The consideration of this mere psychological survival, Anscombe says, shows what sense there is to be found in Hume's argument against inferring *morally ought* from *is*. To the extent that the "moral" use of *ought* has no meaning anyway, it certainly cannot be inferred from *is*, or, for that matter, from any other real predicate. If moral philosophers are not prepared to adopt an ethics based on divine law, they should jettison such terms as *illicit*, *prohibited*, *morally wrong*, etc. and instead speak of actions as being conformed or opposed to specific moral virtues. The virtues could in turn be derived from factual statements about what man is and what his excellence consists in. Even if, in the end, there is a divine law that gives the notion of moral obligation or moral duty its validity, this notion would not be what is uppermost or most formal in ethical thinking, not the very lens through which morality as such or as a whole would be primarily envisioned.

Anscombe thus agrees with Geach, that divine law or divine command generates moral obligation.[109] And like Geach, even though she does not think that the requirements of reason or virtue are naturally understood by everyone to express divine precepts, she clearly does not consider the notion of a natural moral law to be incoherent. For she does not think that such a notion requires that men naturally apprehend either the legality or the strict obligatory force of such a law. Observing that "the thinkers who believed in 'natural divine law' held that it was promulgated to every grown man in

---

108. Anscombe, *Ethics, Religion, and Politics*, 30.

109. Anscombe, *Ethics, Religion, and Politics*, 41. See Geach, *God and the Soul*, 117, 126.

his knowledge of good and evil,"[110] so that they satisfied the stipulation that "you cannot be under a law unless it has been promulgated to you," she goes on simply to assert that "it is clear that you can be subject to a law that you do not acknowledge and have not thought of as law."[111]

Evidently, however, not everyone thinks it so clear.

SYNOPSIS AND PLAN

To sum up, there seem to be four basic positions on the question of the legal character of natural law. In the first two, it is approached with the assumption that natural law can be adequately treated without reference to God or to the eternal law. Of these, the first concedes that natural law, so treated, falls short of the full nature of law as Aquinas understands it. This position is asserted most strongly by Odon Lottin. Other adherents are Germain Grisez, John Finnis, Mortimer Adler, and Wolfgang Kluxen. According to the second position, the precepts of natural law retain the full nature of law even when seen independently of the eternal law. Their status as first principles of practical reason immediately endows them with a legal character. Alan Donagan's interpretation is placed here, as are those of Frederick Copleston and Gregory Stevens. The most extended interpretation along this line, and the one to which I have given most attention, is that of Dermot O'Donoghue.

The other two positions make the account of natural law inseparable from the doctrine of the eternal law. Understanding natural law in this way makes possible a straightforward attribution of full legality to it. The issue that divides these two positions is whether the legal character of the precepts of natural law is as natural as is the understanding of the precepts in themselves. Ernest Fortin answers negatively. Like Harry Jaffa, Fortin thinks that natural law can be natural only in a very weak sense. Against Jaffa, Fortin argues that Aquinas himself, read discerningly, thinks so too.

Fortin's basic assumption, which is that natural law functions as a law only insofar as its divine origin is known (or at least knowable), can already be found in Francisco Suárez. But unlike Fortin, Suárez insists that this knowledge is natural in a quite valid and satisfactory sense, because it can be grasped by an inference that is naturally within people's reach. Suárez's view is thus a version of the fourth and final position, which is that natural law cannot be adequately treated apart from the eternal law, and that it is nevertheless both fully legal and fully natural. Also falling under the fourth heading are Walter Farrell, Peter Geach, and Elizabeth Anscombe. These

---

110. Anscombe, *Ethics, Religion, and Politics*, 37.
111. Anscombe, *Ethics, Religion, and Politics*, 38.

authors, however, differ from Suárez in a significant way, in that they do not think the sufficient promulgation of natural law requires the notification of its divine origin. On their view, it cannot be understood as a law without reference to that origin, but it does not have to be understood as a law in order to function as one.

The plan for the rest of the book is as follows. In chapter 2, I take up the question of Aquinas's understanding of the relation between natural law and the eternal law. I bring some historical considerations to bear on the question, and then I try to resolve it through a detailed analysis of the relevant texts of the *Summa theologiae*, especially the *quaestio* on the nature of law in general, which is *ST* I–II.90, and the article in which the existence of natural law is demonstrated, which is *ST* I–II.91.2. The conclusion that I shall draw is that the formulation "participation of the eternal law in the rational creature" is meant to express the formal notion of natural law, and that therefore, in Aquinas's doctrine, the concept of natural law is inseparable from the concept of eternal law.

What will remain, then, is the question of the naturalness of natural law, as law. The question is whether the legal character of its precepts is actual from the very moment that their truth is first understood, or whether they become fully legal only when seen precisely as a participation of the eternal law. This amounts to the question of whether the precepts of natural law become full-fledged laws in the same manner as do precepts of human positive law, namely, by way of the notification of their authoritative institution. This forms the concern of chapter 3. The answer that I reach there is negative.

Chapters 4 and 5 are concerned with what sort of knowledge natural law does require in order to function as a law; in particular, what sort of knowledge of natural things it requires. A very common view is that it rests on knowledge of man's natural inclinations. This is the focus of chapter 4. There I argue that this is a misreading, and that in fact the natural inclinations are rather the result of the knowledge of natural law, or at least of the knowledge of the goods with which natural law is concerned, than its basis. Then in chapter 5, I lay out what I think is Thomas's view of the sort of knowledge of nature that natural law does suppose.

If natural law is a law in the full sense, it must be obligatory. And if its legal character is natural to it, so must be its obligatory force. The proper, natural obligatory force of natural law is the object of chapter 6. Drawing partly on a passage from Thomas's *De veritate*, I try to lay out how he understands the general nature of legal obligation. Part of this consists in determining how, on his view, legal obligation is related to sanction. What I find is that obligation is not primarily a function of sanction, but of the law's very normativity with respect to human conduct. Nevertheless sanction does play a secondary role, and I therefore try to identify what he regards as the sanctions proper to natural law. From there I go on to address how natural law establishes obligations before the divine lawgiver and makes its subjects liable to His sanctions.

In the final chapter, to round out the account, I gather together some of the other things that are natural, in one sense or another, about Thomas's natural law. These are five: the natural scope of the duties that it enjoins; its overall natural tendency; its consisting of principles that are first in our apprehension but that ultimately have to be seen as effects of what is first simply; the philosophical accessibility of the understanding of natural law as a participation in the eternal law, and how this might be of interest to moral philosophy; and the way in which, for Thomas, natural law seems to underlie not only the dictates of any sound body of positive law but also the very concept of law, as he defines it. Along the way, I offer more or less summary assessments of the positions surveyed in chapter 1, with special attention, in the third section, to the position of Francisco Suárez.

2

The Relation between Natural Law and Eternal Law

In relation to the various positions surveyed in the previous chapter on the question of the legal character of Aquinas's natural law, the issue that needs to be resolved first concerns his understanding of the relationship between natural law and eternal law. The issue is what significance to attach to his judgment that "natural law is nothing other than a participation of the eternal law in the rational creature." Is this a strict definition of natural law? Or is it only a certain characterization of natural law, one that is brought to light when natural law is eventually viewed in the setting of the doctrine of the eternal law? Once this issue is resolved, we can go on to consider how the legal character of natural law is to be understood. This chapter will attempt to resolve the issue, first through certain historical considerations, and then through a detailed examination of the text in which Thomas arrives at his formulation of natural law as a participation of the eternal law in the rational creature.

THE QUESTION OF THE FRANCISCAN INFLUENCE

As we saw in the previous chapter, Odon Lottin is one of the strongest proponents of the view that Aquinas does not mean for the expression *participation of the eternal law in the rational creature* to be taken as a definition of natural law. Lottin's defense of this view is of special interest. He has to explain why Aquinas nevertheless presents natural law in terms of the eternal law. His explanation is not only theoretical, but also, and even chiefly, historical. In his judgment, the narrow connection between natural law and the eternal law that appears to be drawn in the *Summa theologiae* is for the most part the result of a rather alien historical influence: a certain Franciscan tract on law. I propose to examine whether the actual comparison between the two works shows Thomas to be moving with or against his source. This inquiry will serve as background for the analysis of Aquinas's own texts. The comparison will be restricted to points immediately pertinent to the present question.

As mentioned in chapter 1, Lottin's research showed that the formal treatment of the eternal law entered into the mainstream of scholastic theology only rather late. Its first appearance seems to have been in an anonymous, mid-thirteenth-century Franciscan treatise on law entitled *De legibus et praeceptis*. This treatise was evidently a major source for the treatise on law, now attributed to Jean de la Rochelle, found in the so-called *Summa fratris Alexandri*. In Lottin's judgment, the subsequent influence of the Franciscan treatment upon the *Summa theologiae* of Thomas is shown by two things. The first is the nearly complete absence of any mention of the eternal law in the earlier works of Aquinas. This suggests that perhaps he began to give it serious consideration only after encountering the Franciscan tract. The second thing, which is more decisive, is the degree to which the account of the eternal law in his *Summa theologiae* resembles that of the Franciscan treatment. Aquinas preserves both the bulk of the questions on the eternal law raised in the earlier work, and a good measure of their order. His location of the study of natural law immediately after that of the eternal law also follows the Franciscan procedure.[1] For Lottin, the evidence of heavy borrowing from a Franciscan (read Augustinian) source confirms the impression that the setting of natural law in the *Summa theologiae* is at least somewhat at odds with the inner tendency of Aquinas's thought on natural law. "A synthetic exposition is uneasy."[2]

It is hard to quarrel with Lottin as to the influence of the Franciscan tract on law upon Aquinas's *Summa theologiae*. Still, clear differences between the two treatments remain. And precisely because the evidence for the influence is so strong, these differences can be considered all the more revealing as to what is really proper and characteristic of Aquinas's thought.

Chapter 7 of the section on the eternal law in the *Summa fratris Alexandri* concerns the "derivation of laws from the eternal law." This chapter is

---

1. Lottin, *Psychologie et Morale*, 63–67.
2. Lottin, "La valeur," 345.

divided into four articles, each showing the derivation of one specific type of law from the eternal law. The specific types of law are unjust law, the *lex fomitis*, human law, and natural law.[3] What corresponds to this chapter in Thomas's *Summa* is I–II.93.3. Or rather, it almost corresponds. The title of Aquinas's article is "Whether every law is derived from the eternal law." Here we find him in agreement with the overall position of the *Summa fratris Alexandri*, that laws are derived from the eternal law to the extent that they are right and just; that is, to the extent that they are true laws. Nevertheless Thomas's treatment of the question differs from that of the *Summa fratris Alexandri*. One minor difference is that he has collapsed several specific questions, about specific laws, into one general one, about the derivation of all law from the eternal law. But the really striking difference is that, on the particular issue of the derivation of natural law from eternal law, he is completely silent. The body of his article is concerned exclusively with human law. There are also three objections, but they are concerned only with the *lex fomitis*, unjust law, and human law. There is no mention of natural law at all.

It is inconceivable that Aquinas's silence about natural law in this article is owing to some conception of natural law as wholly independent of the eternal law. Besides, even if he did think natural law independent of the eternal law, that would still not explain why he does not even apply the question of derivation from the eternal law to the case of natural law. The explanation for this silence must be sought, instead, in the general nature of the things to which he does apply the question. These things are what the article calls "other laws besides the eternal law": *aliae leges praeter legem aeternam*, and more precisely, "conceptions of governance in inferior governors": *rationes gubernationis in inferioribus gubernantibus*.

The reason why natural law is not treated in this article, then, seems to be that even to ask whether natural law is derived from the eternal law would imply that natural law constitutes a law diverse from the eternal law, "another law besides the eternal law." This implication would evidently run contrary to the account that Aquinas had already given of the relation between natural law and eternal law. In his earlier proof of the existence of natural law, in *ST* I–II.91.2, he had insisted that natural law is not "diverse from the eternal law," being nothing but "a certain participation of it."

The laws described in *ST* I–II.93.3, as "other laws besides the eternal law" are laws existing in the minds of governors or lawgivers other than God. Now, law existing in the mind of the governor is what Thomas calls

---

3. *Summa theologica seu sic ab origine dicta "Summa fratris Alexandri"* (hereafter *Summa fratris Alexandri*) III, pars 2, inq. 1, c. 7 (4.1:323–29).

law as it exists in one ruling and measuring: *lex sicut in regulante et mensurante*. But in the proof for the existence of natural law in *ST* I–II.91.2, he was careful to present natural law only as law existing in the mind of someone subject to the government of law, someone ruled and measured: *lex sicut in regulato et mensurato*.[4] Natural law, so understood, is not a new law issued by some governor distinct from and subordinate to the author of the eternal law. It is nothing but a derivative expression of the very same law enacted by God from eternity, the expression naturally impressed by God upon His rational subjects. It is not another law besides the eternal law. It is only another promulgation of God's law, besides the first and eternal promulgation of that law. It is a promulgation of the eternal law considered on its passive side; that is, seen as terminating in the mind of the rational creature through the natural light of reason.

Not surprisingly, Lottin accounts for the absence of natural law in *ST* I–II.93.3 somewhat differently. Rather than saying that Aquinas nowhere raises the question raised by the Franciscan tract, whether natural law is derived from the eternal law, he makes this question correspond to *ST* I–II.91.2; that is, to the very demonstration of the existence of natural law. But this does not seem right. Besides the fact that this reading has Aquinas asking two questions at the same time, the exact title of this article is "Whether there be any natural law in us"; and surely what this corresponds to in the *Summa fratris Alexandri* is the first chapter in the section on natural law, the one entitled "Whether a natural law be instilled in the rational creature."[5] In contrast to Aquinas's order, this article of the *Summa fratris Alexandri* does not precede, but follows, the question of the derivation of laws from the eternal law.

How does the author of the *Summa fratris Alexandri* demonstrate the existence of natural law? Not as Aquinas does, by showing that a share in the eternal law is in some way naturally instilled in man. Rather, he does so simply by citing what he calls "a rule innate to the moving part" of man, analogous to the "principles of truth" innate to the cognitive part. (Presumably these would be what Thomas calls the first principles of speculative reason.[6]) "Just as the cognitive part has principles of truth inborn in it, and a notion of these principles, such as this: *every whole is greater than its part*, and, *anything must be either affirmed or denied*; in the same way, the moving

---

4. He introduced this notion in *ST* I–II.90.1*ad*1. It also appears in *ST* I–II.90.3*ad*1.
5. *Summa fratris Alexandri* III, pars 2, inq. 2, q. 1 (4.1:338–40).
6. See *ST* I–II.94.2.

part has a rule inborn in it, through which it is ruled in the direction of the good; and this rule we call natural law."[7]

What we should notice is that the argument makes not the slightest mention of the eternal law. It is only in replying to an objection, one which to some extent anticipates Aquinas's first objection in *ST* I-II.91.2, that the author of the *Summa fratris Alexandri* comes to identify natural law with what he calls the "notion of the eternal law impressed on every soul." This impression of the eternal law is in fact something that he had demonstrated earlier—but, significantly, without calling it a natural law. In other words, he seems to treat *natural law* and *impression of the eternal law* as expressions that are only materially identical, or convertible. Their formal significations differ. The formal notion of natural law, for him, seems to be simply the notion of the innate principles of practical reason. His formulation is almost the exact inverse of Aquinas's: "That notion . . . of the eternal law impressed on the soul is nothing other than the natural law itself in the soul, which is indeed a likeness and image of the divine law itself and of the divine goodness in the soul."[8]

Aquinas's proof for the existence of natural law, by contrast, is dominated by the thought of divine providence and the eternal law from start to finish. For him, the demonstration of an impression of the eternal law upon man is simply identical with the demonstration of a natural law. To affirm the one is immediately to affirm the other. The formulation *participation of the eternal law in the rational creature* seems to signify the very object held in view when the existence of a natural law is first affirmed. The reality corresponding to each of these expressions is demonstrated in one and the same argument.

Moreover, although Aquinas will go on to identify the reality of natural law with the first principles of practical reason, he does not treat this identity as simply immediate or formal. Even after he has demonstrated the existence of natural law, he finds it necessary to inquire into which one of the things naturally existing in the human soul properly merits the name of natural law. He makes this inquiry in the first article of Question 94, where he asks whether natural law is the same thing as the habit of *synderesis*. Also, when he comes to reject the identification of natural law with *synderesis*, the

---

7. *Sicut cognitiva habet principia veri sibi innata et notionem illorum, sicut hoc: 'omne totum est maius sua parte et 'de quolibet affirmatio vel negatio,' ita et motiva regulam habet sibi innatam, per quam regulatur in bonum; hanc autem legem appellamus naturalem* (Summa fratris Alexandri III, pars 2, inq. 2, q. 1, solutio [4.1:339]).

8. *Notio . . . illa legis aeternae impressa animae nihil aliud est quam ipsa lex naturalis in anima, quae quidem est similitudo et imago ipsius divinae legis et divinae bonitatis in anima* (Summa fratris Alexandri III, pars 2, inq. 2, q. 1, ad 2 [4.1:340]).

basis upon which he does so is the fact that *synderesis*, a habit, cannot possibly be a law in the strict sense of the term. A law, being a work of reason, *quoddam opus rationis*, cannot be a habit, but only the object of a habit, an object such as the first principles of practical reason. In Aquinas, then, the identification between natural law and first principles of practical reason is only a mediated or reasoned identification. And the middle term is precisely something belonging to the strict definition of law, the fact that it is a work of reason. Thomas proceeds as though the legality of natural law were its most evident feature, something contained in the very meaning of its name.

This same point can be reached from the opposite direction. Readers of the *Summa theologiae* will recall that *ST* I–II.94 is by no means the first place in which the first principles of practical reason are discussed. Their existence, together with that of the habit by which they are held, *synderesis*, is shown considerably earlier, in the *Prima pars*: I.79.12. Neither in this article, nor in the one following it, on conscience, is the term *natural law* to be found. By contrast, the more or less corresponding part of the *Summa fratris Alexandri*, which also comes much earlier than the section on law, does invoke the notion of natural law.[9] There, the fifth chapter in the part on conscience asks whether conscience is the same as natural law. And the answer treats natural law as simply identical with principles of practical reason.

Unlike the author of the section on law in the *Summa fratris Alexandri*, then, Thomas evidently regards the proof of the existence of first principles of practical reason, by itself, as somewhat inadequate for a disclosure of something answering to the name *natural law*. It is, in fact, a rather striking feature of the *Summa theologiae* that neither in the treatise on man in the *Prima pars*,[10] nor anywhere in the *Prima secundae* prior to the treatise on law, is *natural law* mentioned under that name even so much as once.[11] This restraint is certainly not for want of opportunities. There are several places prior to the Treatise on Law where one might have expected him to speak of natural law, and where he uses other, convertible expressions

---

9. *Summa fratris Alexandri* I, lib. 2, inq. 4, tract. 1, sect. 2, q. 3, tit. iv, mem. ii, c. 5 (2:499).

10. *ST* I.75–102.

11. In *ST* I.96.3, he speaks of "laws of nature," but he is referring to the condition of the human body. He does speak of natural law in the moral sense in *ST* I.60.5*sc*; I shall return to this article, which is about natural love in the angels, at several points below. He also speaks of natural law in the moral sense in *ST* I.113.1*obj*1/*ad*1; there he is talking about men's need of guardian angels to help make up for their manifold deficiency in applying the "universal principles of right" to particular actions. Perhaps Thomas is seeing the existence of a natural law as rather more evident from an angelic perspective than from the human.

instead: expressions such as *true and immutable rules and seeds of virtues*,[12] *first* or *common principles of practical reason*,[13] *principles of common right*,[14] *natural right* as contained in the *natural forum of reason*,[15] *natural reason* understood as *derived from the eternal law as its proper image*,[16] *the natural rule that man, according to his nature, ought to observe*,[17] and even *the rule of human reason that is gathered from created things that man naturally apprehends*.[18] Thomas even adheres to expressions such as these, instead of using the term *natural law*, when he is explicitly discussing other kinds of law—human, eternal, or divine.[19] He begins to use *natural law* regularly only when he is able to show, in light of the definition of law and the proof of the existence of eternal law, that there is something natural to man that fully satisfies the criteria of law. And the very first use of the term *natural law* in the treatise on law is in the assertion that "natural law has the nature of law to the highest degree."

What is the general conclusion to be drawn from the comparison between the *Summa theologiae* and the *Summa fratris Alexandri* on the question of the relationship between eternal law and natural law? Where Aquinas departs from the plan of the other work, it never seems to be in the direction of a more independent or self-contained status for natural law. On the contrary, it is often toward an even stricter connection between natural law and eternal law, as well as between natural law and the nature of law in general. The mere fact that he was writing under the influence of the Franciscan work, then, hardly warrants the judgment that Aquinas's presentation of natural law in the *Summa theologiae* is in any way at odds with the spirit of his own thought on the matter. Far from showing signs of resisting the influence, he seems to have embraced it gladly, and even to have carried it further.

I do not mean to suggest that between Aquinas and the author of the section on law in the *Summa fratris Alexandri* there is any serious disagreement about the substance of the relation between eternal law and natural law. Thus, the latter states with great clarity that "natural law is in us without

---

12. *regulae et semina virtutum et vera et incommutabilia* (ST I.79.12obj3).
13. ST I.79.12; I.79.13; I-II.58.4; I-II.58.5; I-II.62.4; I-II.63.1.
14. *principia iuris communis* (ST I-II.51.1).
15. *ius naturale ... in naturali iudicatorio rationis* (ST I-II.71.6ad4).
16. ST I-II.19.4ad3.
17. ST I-II.75.2ad3.
18. ST I-II.74.7.
19. See, for example, *ST* I-II.19.4; I-II.19.6; I-II.21.1; I-II.71.2ad4; I-II.71.6 (esp. ad4); I-II.74.7; I-II.75.1; I-II.75.2ad3; I-II.78.1; I-II.87.1.

our cooperation, but from the edict and impression of God . . . but in temporal law we cooperate in its coming to be in us."[20] The differences lie in how each organizes the account of that relation.

Perhaps the most fundamental difference has to do with what is the most striking departure by Thomas from the plan of the section on law in the *Summa fratris Alexandri*. This departure is his insertion, prior to his study of each type of law in its own right, of two new *quaestiones*: one "on law in general," in which he constructs his definition of law, and the other "on the division of law," in which he proves the existence of each of the main types of law.[21] By contrast, the treatise on law in the *Summa fratris Alexandri* consists entirely in the study of each particular type of law. There is no prior study of law in general, and the questions concerning the existence of each type are not grouped together into a preliminary, general overview of the division of law. The existence of each type of law is shown within the section devoted to that type in its own right.

This is not to say that the *Summa fratris Alexandri* tells us nothing about the nature of law in general. It tells us a great deal.[22] And what it tells us fits well with Aquinas's own *quaestio* on law in general. But it seems to me that by organizing his material on law in general into a separate and prior *quaestio*, and by following up that *quaestio* with an overview of the whole division of law, Aquinas shows himself to be more at pains to make clear the way in which the common nature and definition of law belongs to each kind of law. When he asks whether a given type of law exists, what he seems to be asking is whether there is anything existing in the manner specified by the name of that type to which the definition of law applies, either absolutely or with some qualification.[23] This consideration is particularly relevant to the question of the existence of natural law, because it is all too easy for us to

---

20. *Lex naturalis est in nobis sine nostra cooperatione, sed ex Dei inditione et impressione; . . . sed in lege temporali nos cooperamur ad hoc quod sit in nobis* (*Summa fratris Alexandri* III, pars 2, inq. 1, q. un., c. 7, a. 4, ad l [4.1:329]).

21. *ST* I-II.90–91.

22. For instance, "three things concur in any law, namely, authority, truth, goodness" (*ad quamlibet legem concurrunt tria, scilicet auctoritas, veritas, bonitas*) (*Summa fratris Alexandri* III, pars 2, inq. 1, q. un., c. 4 [4.1:319]). That pretty well sums up the first three elements in Thomas's definition of law. And the fourth certainly comes to mind when we read that "law has being in promulgation, and then it merits the name of law, because it then binds" (*lex habet esse in promulgatione, et tunc meretur nomen legis, quia tunc ligat*) (*Summa fratris Alexandri* III, pars 2, inq. 1, q. un., c. 1, obj. 2 [4.1:314]). The author also employs the distinction between law as it exists in the ruler and law as it exists in his subjects (*Summa fratris Alexandri* III, pars 2, inq. 1, q. un., c. 1, ad 1 & ad 2 [4.1:315]). See Ignatius Brady, "Law in the *Summa fratris Alexandri*," 133–47.

23. The *lex fomitis* is law only in an extended sense and has the definition only in a qualified way: *ST* I-II.91.6.

take the meaning of the expression *natural law* for granted, rather than to let his way of arguing for its existence show what he means by it. In the case of things whose existence can or needs to be proved, it is a typical procedure of his to take the proof itself as the basis for the meaning of its name.[24]

THE MEANING OF THE QUESTION POSED IN *SUMMA THEOLOGIAE* I-II.91.2

So let us turn to Thomas's proof of the existence of natural law, as presented in *ST* I-II.91.2. It is here that he describes natural law as a participation of the eternal law in the rational creature. Analyzing the proof seems to be the most promising way of getting at the function that he means to assign to this description.

The question posed in this article is "Whether there be in us any natural law (*aliqua lex naturalis*)." This formulation gives a clear indication of the kind of inquiry pursued in the article. Following Aristotle, Thomas distinguishes four basic kinds of questions that can be answered through scientific reasoning. Two of them are asked about a subject, and two about something existing in a subject. About a subject, it may be asked *an sit*, whether it exists; and if it does, then *quid sit*, what it is. About something existing in a subject, it may be asked *utrum insit rei*, whether it belongs to a given subject; and if it does, then *propter quid*, why it does. Clearly the question from which the present article begins is of the form *utrum insit rei*. It is asking whether something called *natural law* exists in a certain subject, man.

It is especially significant that the formulation of the question contains the indefinite determiner *any* or *some* (*aliqua*). This suggests that the article does not even presuppose that the term *natural law* expresses something real. It is not asking whether man is one of the subjects to which the reality called *natural law* belongs. It is asking whether anything existing in man is fit to be called a natural law. This means that no definite conception of natural law, no substantive notion of "the" natural law, can be assumed.

Of course the article does assume the meaning of the term *law*; defining law was the task of the immediately preceding *quaestio*. What is not yet clear is how the term *natural* is supposed to qualify the term *law*. This is unclear because the term *natural* is notoriously polysemic. What does it mean in this case? The full answer will emerge only as a result of the proof itself. However, some preliminary help can be got from considering

---

24. He is quite explicit about this in the most famous case, that of proving the existence of a God: *ST* I.2.2; I.2.3.

the overall *quaestio* to which the article belongs. That can already tell us something about what Thomas means by *natural* here. I–II.91 is concerned with the "diversity of laws." Natural law is one of the divisions of law. Now, any proper division of a subject is made according to some element of the subject's nature. Therefore, by ascertaining the element of the nature of law according to which law is divided in I–II.91, it may be possible to determine the way in which the term *natural* qualifies the notion of law in general. Since the most proper division of a subject is made according to the ultimate differentiating element of its own nature, we may conjecture that Aquinas has divided law according to that particular element, at least in the cases of the types that are laws in the proper sense, as natural law clearly is.[25] Once it is determined which feature this is, the expectation that it forms the basis of his division can be verified.

NATURAL LAW AS ONE OF THE DIVISIONS OF LAW

Thomas analyzes the nature of law in I–II.90. He does so by a reflection on a pair of common features that fall under the meaning of the term *law*.[26] One is that it is a certain rule and measure of human acts, *quaedam regula et mensura actuum*. The other is that it is something according to which one is effectively led toward or restrained from action, *secundum quam inducitur aliquis ad agendum vel ab agendo retrahitur*. Neither of these features by itself is sufficient to constitute a law. Not every measure of acts carries its own inducement to comply with it, and not every inducement that people follow is a genuine rule, or principle of rectitude, in their acts.[27] For instance, the deliverances of moral philosophers can be true rules and measures of human acts, but in themselves they have very limited power to induce compliance. On the other hand, the impulses of sensuality are strong inducements, but they are not principles of rectitude.

The evidence that Thomas cites in support of this description of law is an etymology of the Latin word for law: "*Law (lex) is derived from binding (ligando), because it obliges (obligat) one to act.*"[28] I shall go into Thomas's

---

25. *ST* I–II.91.2ad3. The *lex fomitis* is law only in an extended sense. That itself distinguishes it from the other types.

26. This is one way to arrive at a definition. See *In Post. an.* II.13–14, 220–25 (on Aristotle, *Posterior Analytics* II.13, 96a22–97a6).

27. On a rule as a measure and a principle of rectitude, see *ST* I–II.21.1. On the use of the terms *inducere* and *retrahere* to indicate how law moves, see *ST* I.103.5ad2; *ST* I–II.92.2.

28. On the use of this etymology by Aquinas's predecessors, see Lio, "Annotazioni al testo," 372–95. Albert the Great says that the *ratio nominis* of *lex*—its nominal definition, as opposed to the definition declaring its essence—is *ligatio*: Albertus Magnus,

concept of obligation at some length in chapter 6. What we will see is that obligatory force, in the strict and primary sense, is something proper to law, and that it consists in a kind of power to induce people to act (or not to act) that only a true rule and measure of human acts can have. If we want a short formula for the working conception of law from which Aquinas begins his inquiry into its substance or essential definition, we can say simply that it is the conception of an obligatory rule of action.

The first element of the definition of law that Thomas brings forth, as immediately implied by its function of regulating and measuring human acts, is its belonging to reason. Reason is the first proper principle of human acts, and the first principle of a genus is that by which everything in the genus is measured. Of course not everything that belongs to reason is a law. Reason has speculative or theoretical functions, whereas law is something practical. And it is practical, not only as being about actions, but also as ruling and directing them in an efficacious way. Thomas's general term for this sort of work of practical reason is *ordination*. An ordination that is given or applied to people in such a way as to incline them to act according to it is called a precept or command.[29] Naturally it is possible for a command to fail to convey a true measure of someone's acts or to constitute a genuine principle of their rectitude. Even though all commands proceed from reason, they can fail in this way because they can fail to be fully reasonable or rational. And then they are not laws. In calling law an ordination of reason, then, Thomas is neither lapsing into redundancy, nor merely reiterating his teaching that the power from which a command flows is reason. He means that law is a command that flows, not simply from the power of reason, as does all command, but from right reason, reason hitting truth in its judgment of the suitability of the order of action that the command enjoins.[30]

Now in saying that law is a work of reason, Thomas does not mean to exclude a role for the lawgiver's will in the work of legislation. "All law proceeds from the reason and will of the lawgiver."[31] Quite generally, command involves the commander's will. Command has a certain "moving force," and

---

De bono, tract. 5, q. 2, a. 2, obj. 17, 285 line 14; ad 1, 285 lines 17–20; cf. ad 17, 288 lines 24–29. Interestingly, in these texts Albert is explaining how the *lex membrorum* or the *lex peccati*—Thomas's *lex fomitis*—is a law. Albert grants that it does not have the essence of law, but he argues that in a way even it binds: not as a precept does, but as inclining habits and dispositions do. Thomas by contrast will not apply the notion of binding to the *lex fomitis* at all. It is law only in the sense of an effect of the just ordination of God's law. See *ST* I-II.91.6.

29. *ST* I-II.17.1; I-II.17.2.
30. See *ST* I-II.90.1*ad*3. This is spelled out somewhat in *ST* I-II.96.4.
31. *ST* I-II.97.3.

this derives from an act of will. The will adopts the order that the commander has conceived and tends toward applying it to the agents that are supposed to comply with it.[32] And it uses reason to convey the order to the agents, and to do so in a way that leads them to execute it. I shall say more about command in chapter 3.[33] But here the point is that a command, an ordination, is a law, properly speaking, only if it is truly rational. Otherwise it can be called a law only in some qualified and extended sense.[34]

We are looking at Thomas's definition of law with a view to his way of dividing law into different kinds in I-II.91. At this point, we can ask whether law can properly be divided according to its nature as an ordination of reason. It seems not. There are many reasonable ordinations and many reasonable precepts that are not laws. For instance, Thomas points out that although the head of a household can make precepts or statutes for the family, these are not laws, properly speaking.[35] To be an ordination of reason is only a generic feature of law. The most proper division of law cannot be a division of the class of ordinations of reason. Law is itself one of the divisions of that class.

The next element of the nature of law is determined through a further reflection on law's character as a rule or measure of human acts. Law belongs to reason in virtue of the fact that reason is a measure, the first proper measure, of human acts. But there is a primary principle in virtue of which reason functions as measure of human acts. The natural starting-point of practical reason as a whole is man's last end, which is called happiness. And since an individual man is a part of a complete community—a city (*civitas*)—the primary happiness is that of the community as a whole. Hence reason's work of measuring people's acts starts from the ultimate common good, the common happiness, of the complete community to which they belong. What primarily has the nature of law, then, is a dictate ordering action to the common good.[36] "Nothing stands firmly according to practical reason except by ordination to the last end, which is a common good."[37] And since what primarily has some perfection is that in virtue of which other things have it, nothing belonging to reason can have the nature of law unless it share somehow in the work of ordering things to the common good. An ordination that runs against the common good cannot have the

---

32. *ST* I-II.17.1; I-II.90.1*ad*3.
33. See below, 74–79.
34. *ST* I-II.92.1*ad*4.
35. *ST* I-II.90.3*ad*3.
36. *ST* I-II.90.2.
37. *ST* I-II.90.2*ad*3.

character of a strict measure of human acts at all, and a dictate whose immediate object is some merely private good can have the nature of law only in a derivative or secondary way, insofar as it is in accordance with the order to the common good.[38]

Is the division of law made according to law's common feature of ordering toward the common good? Again, it seems not. Not every rational intimation of order toward the common good is a law. Private citizens can exhort each other to do what is for the public good, but their exhortations are not laws.[39] This is because a private citizen, as private, only shares in the common good and is not its owner. It belongs to private citizens only insofar as they are parts of the whole community and are ordered to the whole. What the common good primarily belongs to is the whole community or the "public person"—the individual or group—that has care of the whole community. Only the whole community or its overseer has an agency that is fully proportioned to the end to which acts subject to law are primarily ordered. "To order things to an end pertains to the one to whom that end properly belongs."[40] This then is the third essential component of law: its origin in public authority. This feature reflects both the regulating and the moving character of law. Only the mind of one working in the capacity of overseeing a community is in every respect sufficiently informed to determine a reasonable ordering of movements toward its overall good, and only someone with power over the common good and its distribution is able to enforce this arrangement adequately, to impose it upon others as something from which they cannot happily escape. That is, only public authority can make the order obligatory and compelling.[41]

However, even a public authority's conception and adoption of an order toward the common good may not yet be a law. For it may not yet exist in the manner required to direct or induce action. That is, it may not yet be a command. Although the directive and moving force proper to law depends on its origin in public authority, something further is required in order for it to exercise that force. What is to be moved by an agent must be acted upon by the agent and receive something from the agent. Law must be applied to those whom it is supposed to rule.[42] It "is imposed upon others" (*imponitur aliis*). Thomas had already remarked that it belongs to the nature of law, by the very fact that it is a rule and measure, to be able to exist in things in two

---

38. See *ST* I–II.90.2*ad*1.
39. *ST* I–II.90.3*ad*2; cf. I–II.92.2*ad*2.
40. *ST* I–II.90.3.
41. See *ST* I–II.90.3*ad*2; I–II.92.2*ad*3; *In Eth.*, X.14, 600, lines 204–223.
42. *ST* I–II.90.4. See *ST* I.103.5*ad*2.

ways: either as in the one ruling and measuring, or as in the one ruled and measured.[43] Here, he is indicating that it is not just possible, but necessary, that a law be determined to exist in both of these ways, in order that it possess the ruling and moving force proper to law.

The way in which the law moves those subject to it, or the way in which it is imposed upon them, is not in the manner of something physically compelling. Again, it moves as something obligatory, which means in the manner in which a rule and measure is said to move. "Law is imposed on others in the mode of a rule and measure." The moving work proper to law is the work of regulating or measuring. Now, an agent's acts are regulated when the inner source of its acts is somehow conformed or proportioned to the rule. To apply a rule to something's acts is to impress upon it "a certain interior principle of its acts."[44] Furthermore, since the first inner principle of men's acts is their own reason, the way in which a rule and measure is imposed upon them is as something they know, and know in a way that wins their assent or inclines them to judge it as something obligatory or necessary to obey.[45] It is by way of the very knowledge of the law that men are "led toward" or "restrained from" action by the law, as by a principle of direction or guidance in their self-directed movements.

Here I would like to insert a parenthetical remark. This need for the law to be applied to and interiorized by those subject to it, has a bearing on the understanding of the whole treatise on law in the *Summa*. Not infrequently, it is said that Thomas regards law as an "extrinsic principle" of human acts. This would be in contrast to such intrinsic principles as habits and virtues and vices.[46] But this is something of a misunderstanding. In the *Prima secundae*, after treating of those intrinsic principles,[47] and on the threshold of the treatise on law, Thomas says that now the extrinsic principles of human acts may be considered. But, he goes on, the extrinsic principle leading to evil—the Devil—has already been discussed in the *Prima pars*. So there only remains to consider the extrinsic principle leading to good. This principle is God, "who instructs us by His law and helps by grace."[48] Now, no one takes Thomas to hold that grace is a merely extrinsic principle of human acts. It "posits something" in the human soul.[49] Only its source, God, is extrinsic.

---

43. *ST* I–II.90.1*ad*1; I–II.90.3*ad*1.
44. *ST* I–II.93.5. See *ST* I–II.21.1.
45. See *ST* I–II.92.2.
46. See *ST* I–II.49, *proem.*
47. *ST* I–II.49–89.
48. *ST* I–II.90, *proem.*
49. *ST* I–II.110.1.

The Relation between Natural Law and Eternal Law

But God's law, too, is something existing in the human soul. Naturally it exists first in God. What exists in Him exists *as* law, however, only because it is ordered toward existing also in those who are to be ruled by it. Even the eternal law is law only because it is eternally promulgated.[50] In fact, already in the discussion of the intrinsic principles of human acts, Thomas had to refer to the reality that constitutes natural law, even if it was not under that name, but as the object of the natural habit of the understanding of practical principles.[51] And in an article on the eternal law, he asserts quite explicitly that even a human governor impresses "a certain interior principle of acts" on the people subject to him, and that God does this for all of nature.[52] In short, law is *both* an extrinsic and an intrinsic principle of human acts. This is why the eternal law, in God, and natural law, in man, can be considered the same law.[53] A principle of action that is not apt to be interiorized somehow by the action's subject is not a law. It is mere physical force or violence. This is true not only of natural law but also of positive law, divine or human.

So then—returning to law in general—"in order that it obtain the power of obliging, which is proper to law, it is necessary that it be applied to the men who are to be ruled according to it," and "such application comes about by its being brought to their knowledge from its very promulgation."[54] Presuming that an ordination has the other three features that law requires, it is finally made into a full command, and so into an actual law, only through a proportionately general and effective enunciation, which is the solemn public proclamation called *promulgation*. This is the fourth and finishing element of the general nature of law. Promulgation is the act by which a law first becomes a law in act and not merely in the lawgiver's intention. "Laws are instituted when they are promulgated."[55]

Here at last is something that seems to be proper to law. Every law is something promulgated, and there is nothing that is promulgated, in the proper sense of the term, except law. Promulgation is not just any act of public notification. It is the public notification, and imposition, of a law.[56]

---

50. *ST* I-II.91.1ad2.

51. See, for example, *ST* I-II.51.1; I-II.58.4; I-II.62.3; I-II.63.1.

52. *ST* I-II.93.5.

53. *ST* I-II.91.2ad1.

54. *ST* I-II.90.4.

55. *ST* I-II.90.4sc. All of this is just what the *Summa fratris Alexandri* said. See above, 40n22.

56. On the public character of promulgation, the *Epitome* of Julius Paulus on the *De verborum significatu* of Festus, the Roman grammarian, finds a verbal connection. "Laws are said to be promulgated (*promulgari*) when they are first set forth before the public (*vulgus*), as though being 'provulgated' (*provulgari*)" (Festus, *De verborum*, 251).

It seems reasonable to conclude, then, that the division of law carried out in I–II.91 is made according to certain differences among the promulgations of law. This conclusion is confirmed by simple inspection of Thomas's way of defending the need for human and divine law as laws distinct from the eternal law. His defense gives precision to the proper difference between these various laws. One of the objections to the existence of divine law is that eternal law is itself divine law, and that natural law, from which human law is derived, is a participation of it. Since a divine law has therefore already been given to man, in the form of natural law, there seems to be no need for another divine law.[57] Thomas's reply focuses on the way in which the special divine law that he wants to establish is promulgated. Although it is not unique in having its origin in eternal law, this kind of law is the only one that is "divinely given" (*divinitus data*) to man.[58] Divine law was given first through God's angels and then through His own Son become man.[59]

Similarly, the distinctive character of human law is that it is "humanly posited."[60] In order for a dictate of human reason to become a law, its being derived from natural law is not sufficient. It requires the "other conditions of law," and these are summed up in its character of something promulgated by a human authority.[61]

Promulgation seems to be the only possible basis for a consistent distinction between the kinds of law treated in I–II.91. At least in the cases of eternal and divine law, there seems to be no difference between them with respect to the other features of law. The reason that ordains each of these laws, and natural law as well, is divine. The common good in view of which they are instituted is also divine. And they are imposed by a divine governor. It is only in the modes of their promulgation that a difference appears. For although eternal law is certainly promulgated by God, the promulgation of divine, revealed law is not eternal. The Old Law was first promulgated at the time of Moses, and the New Law was promulgated at the time of Christ.[62]

As for the restriction of promulgation to the publication of a law—that is, of something obligatory—Suárez argues that "this term [*promulgated*] indicates an order toward inducing obligation" (*haec vox* [*promulgata*] *indicat ordinem ad obligationem inducendam*) (Suárez, *De legis obligatione*, 69 [*De legibus* I.xii.4, lines 26–27]; the line numbers are those of the edition cited).

57. *ST* I–II.91.4*obj*1.
58. *ST* I–II.91.4*ad*1.
59. *ST* I–II.98.3.
60. *ST* I–II.91.4; I–II.95.2; I–II.95.3; etc.
61. *ST* I–II.91.3.
62. *ST* I–II.98.6; I–II.106.3.

This is not an objection to the divine status of these laws. There are many acts of God *ad extra* that are attributed to Him temporally.[63]

Somewhat more accurately, then, I-II.91 seems to proceed as follows. First it divides law into law in the proper sense and law by extension (the *lex fomitis*). It subdivides law in the proper sense into law eternally promulgated and law promulgated in time.[64] It subdivides law promulgated in time into law promulgated naturally, humanly, and supernaturally or divinely. And finally, it subdivides law promulgated divinely into the Old Law and the New Law.[65]

Evidently, then, *natural law* means nothing other than law promulgated to man in a natural way. This conclusion also finds support in Aquinas's text. The very first objection to the thesis that promulgation is essential to law is that although natural law most fully possesses the nature of law, it seems to be in no need of promulgation. His reply is that, far from having had no promulgation, natural law is promulgated through God's very "insertion" of it into people's minds so that it come to be known naturally: *ex hoc ipso quod Deus eam mentibus hominum inseruit naturaliter cognoscendam*.[66] The expression *ex hoc ipso* suggests that natural law gets its very name from the manner in which its promulgation is accomplished. It is by this that it is distinguished from the other kinds of law. If we ask *by whom* this law is promulgated, the answer is the same as for what are called eternal law and divine law. It is promulgated by God. In that sense it is a divine law, just as the eternal law is.[67] But in I-II.91, the expression *divine law* is reserved for law promulgated by God in a supernatural or divine way.

It is not yet clear what a natural promulgation of law might consist in. This requires study. But it is now possible to follow the argument of I-II.91.2,

---

63. *ST* I.13.7. Still, not everything said of God implying a relation to creatures is said temporally; see I.22.1*ad*2 (on His providence); I.34.3*ad*2 (on His Word). Lottin seems to neglect this point when he says that no true law can be eternal (Lottin, *Morale fondamentale*, 220).

64. This is not quite the same as Augustine's famous division of law into eternal and temporal. By *temporal law* Augustine means law that can be justly changed in the course of time. See *De libero arbitrio* 1.6.14–15; cf. *ST* I-II.97.1. Obviously natural law, especially in its primary precepts, does not fall into this category; and not every supernaturally revealed law is variable either. This is not to say that Thomas denies the validity of Augustine's distinction. He simply does not take it as a proper division of kinds of law.

65. Later we learn that the promulgation of the Old Law was through the mediation of angels (*ST* I-II.98.3). The New Law was given by Christ.

66. *ST* I-II.90.4*ad*1.

67. In *De malo* 2.4, he speaks of reason "informed by divine law, either naturally or by teaching or by infusion."

with a view to determining the significance of the expression *participation of the eternal law in the rational creature*. It may be hoped that in the process, the meaning of the expression *natural law* itself, as signifying a law naturally promulgated to man, will also gain in precision.

THE DEMONSTRATION OF THE EXISTENCE OF NATURAL LAW

Thomas begins the argument by recalling once again the distinction made in *ST* I.90.1*ad*1, between law as it exists in one who rules by law, and law as it exists in one who is ruled by it. "Since law is a rule and measure, it can exist in something in two ways: in one way, as in the one ruling and measuring; in another way, as in the one ruled and measured; for it is ruled or measured insofar as it shares in something of the rule or measure." As was seen in the discussion of promulgation, it is necessary that law come to exist in this twofold way, in order that it have the effect proper to law.

We may ask why the question raised in *ST* I–II.91.2 leads Aquinas to turn immediately to the distinction between the two modes in which law can exist. Perhaps this distinction is called for by the consideration of something in the very notion of a natural law. A natural law is a law naturally promulgated. Through promulgation, the legislator makes an ordination exist in the agents who are to be ruled by it and function as a directive principle of their action. In the case of human subjects, this means making the ordination to be something that they know, and know as something to which they need to conform their conduct—as a rule and measure of it. As the act through which the law comes to be imposed upon those who are to be ruled by it, promulgation thus constitutes the act through which the governor begins to exercise his characteristic action upon his subjects, which is to order them to the common good.

The rule of a community according to law can be accomplished by its governor either immediately or through mediators or instruments.[68] Consequently, if the term *promulgation* names the act through which the rule of law is initiated, nothing prevents attributing promulgation not only to the governor, as to the primary agent, but also to any instruments that he uses to complete the imposition of the law upon his subjects. The initial promulgation, or the institution, of law must be an action of the governor

---

68. See *ST* I.103.6, on the distinction between the plan of governance (*ratio gubernationis*), which in God's case is providence, and its execution. Forming the plan, which includes framing the laws, belongs to the governor. See also *ST* I.22.3. But evidently communicating the law to its subjects pertains to execution, and this can involve mediators.

himself, since the law is issued from his own mind and finds its principal seat there.[69] But the process by which it comes to exist in the minds of his subjects may involve certain further, intermediate acts of promulgation or publication on the part of his ministers. "It belongs to the ruler alone to institute law by his authority, but sometimes he promulgates an instituted law through others."[70]

What can be concluded from the twofold existence of law, then, is that a distinction in promulgations need not entail a diversity in the thing promulgated. It does not imply that a new order has been instituted. One and the same law can have several promulgations, although they must all be ordered to one primary promulgation, by which the law first issues from the mind of the governor. The secondary promulgations do not establish the law as something by which the lawgiver rules. They only distribute it to the subjects, as something by which they are ruled. It is one and the same law that is the object of these various promulgations; the same, that is, as regards the order that has come to be legally sanctioned, and as regards its author and its end.[71]

The very first objection in I-II.91.2 shows the importance of this consideration.[72] Failure to observe the distinction between the one law promulgated and the manifold acts of promulgating it would lead to the rejection of any natural law. A natural law is a law promulgated "by nature." But this cannot mean a law that nature herself frames, as opposed to a law framed by God.[73] The framing of law is essentially a work of reason and will, not of nature.[74] At most, nature can be only a secondary and instrumental source

69. This does not contradict the quotation from Gratian invoked in *ST* I-II.90.4sc: "Laws are instituted when they are promulgated" (*leges instituuntur cum promulgantur*) (Gratian, *Decretum*, I, d iv, pars iii, ad can. 3, *In istis*, col. 6). Simultaneity, even if it is necessary, does not entail identity.

70. *ST* I-II.98.3ad3.

71. Thomas makes a somewhat similar point in his discussion of teaching: "The same knowledge is in disciple and teacher, if its identity is considered with respect to the unity of the thing known" (*ST* I.117.1). However, that same knowledge could also be in other disciples and other teachers. By contrast, it does not seem right to say that laws instituted by different governors or for different communities are the same law, even if they express the same order. In comparison with a piece of pure knowledge, a law is more practical, more tied to particulars—those whose actions it regulates.

72. *ST* I-II.91.2obj1.

73. Notice that the sort of objection raised in *ST* I-II.98.3obj3 is nowhere raised about natural law. One might mistakenly think that, in promulgating the Old Law, the angels were its very authors. Thomas does not imagine anyone thinking that a law promulgated by nature is a law that nature institutes.

74. A law, in the proper sense, is a sort of proposition, and quite generally, propositions are not works of nature but of reason and intellect. See *In De an*. III.5, lines 81–86.

of law, something promulgating law only in a secondary way. It can only mediate the promulgation. Since God is the only voluntary agent whose work precedes nature, any law promulgated through nature must be His law. But neither can natural law consist in a law that God first institutes through His act of producing nature, as distinct from and added to the law that He institutes from eternity. For, as Augustine teaches, the most perfect order of things is instituted by God in the eternal law. There is no further order left for Him to institute. A further law instituted by Him at creation—a new law, pertaining to nature—would be superfluous. But nothing pertaining to nature is superfluous.

This objection, Thomas says in his reply, would be valid "if natural law were something diverse from the eternal law." Only by distinguishing between modes of promulgation without diversifying the things promulgated can the existence of a natural law be affirmed. The natural promulgation of a law cannot be the first promulgation, the very institution, of the order contained in that law. It can only be an act through which that order, already promulgated and instituted by the governor of nature, is transmitted to those who are to be ruled by it.

Returning to the body of the article, we find that, immediately after distinguishing between law in the ruler and law in the ruled, Aquinas turns to a reflection on divine providence. The reason for this move must be that, as just seen, the proper mode of existence of any natural law is as in something ruled by eternal law. A natural law can exist only in what is ruled by the eternal law and has the eternal law somehow imposed upon it through the instrumentality of nature. As concluded in the previous article, everything governed by divine providence is ruled by eternal law, which is the plan (*ratio*) of divine governance. Because the eternal law is the rule and measure of everything ruled by divine providence, it must somehow be impressed upon, or made to exist in, everything subject to divine providence. But things are subject to divine providence just insofar as they participate in being.[75] So too, insofar as they first participate in being and exist by nature, they must possess an impression of the eternal law.

What is the effect of this impression? It must be the rule and measure naturally existing within each thing, inclining it toward its own acts and ends, or constituting within it a tendency or order toward the acts and ends that are suited to it. "Since all things which are subject to divine providence are ruled and measured by the eternal law . . . it is manifest that all things

---

Law is also a work of the legislator's will. See *ST* I–II.97.3.

75. *ST* I.22.2.

participate somehow in the eternal law, namely, insofar as from the impression of it they have inclinations toward their own acts and ends."

The term *somehow* (*aliqualiter*) in this sentence suggests that Aquinas does not conceive of this impression, or the inclination that it yields, as taking exactly the same form in all creatures, any more than their ways of acting are the same. This is important in relation to a second objection to the existence of natural law.[76] The objection is that man does not act for an end by mere natural appetite, as irrational creatures do, but by reason and will, and that therefore no ordering of him to his end by law can be something natural. Thomas's answer, in effect, is that while man does not act for an end by natural inclination *alone*, even the acts of reason and will start from naturally known principles and a natural inclination to the last end.[77] And so the law through which the acts that originate from man's reason and will are first directed to the last end must also belong to him naturally.[78] The naturally existing determinations of man's reason and will are not principles of merely natural or purely physical acts, but natural principles of voluntary acts. The natural inclination that arises from natural law need be nothing other than an inclination to act voluntarily in a manner conformed with eternal law.

However, this advertence to the peculiar nature of man's acts, as originating from reason and will, seems to raise a third doubt about the existence of any natural law in man.[79] Through reason and will, man has *liberum arbitrium*, free decision, something found in no other animal. But this suggests that man should be less subject to law than the other animals are. For the free is what exists and acts for its own sake.[80] Beings that are subject to law, however, are governed by another, for the sake of the common good. So what is more free would seem to be less subject to law, not more. Yet natural law is assumed to be something to which man alone might be subject. None of the other animals is said to be under a natural law. If they are not, then a fortiori neither is man.

It is once again through the principle of the twofold existence of law that this objection is met. The presumed uniqueness of man's subjection to a natural law would indeed conflict with man's greater freedom, if natural law were understood to be law as it exists in the lawgiver rather than law as it exists in his subjects. This would mean that there is some law of God

---

76. *ST* I–II.91.2*obj*2.
77. Cf. *ST* I–II.10.1.
78. *ST* I–II.91.2*ad*2; cf. *ST* I.103.5*ad*3.
79. *ST* I–II.91.2*obj*3.
80. See *ST* I.21.1*ad*3.

to which human beings alone are naturally subject, a law from which the other animals are exempt. But because a natural law must be law as it exists in those ruled by a law, no such inconvenience is entailed. The reason why a natural law is not attributed to the other animals is not that they are not naturally subject to any law, but that what their natural subjection to the eternal law produces in them cannot be called a law in the proper sense of the term.

In the proper sense of the term, law is *aliquid rationis*. But although what exists in the ruler under the name *law* must be something of reason, since to rule is to order things to an end, which is proper to reason, the required share in this law on the part of the ruler's subjects may or may not have a rational mode of being. It may be something that can be called a law only in the sense of deriving from a law and bearing some proportion to it. It can be any sort of inclining principle that originates from the lawgiver's imposition of the law.[81] The instincts of beasts are such principles. But in man's case, the inner inclining principle does retain a rational mode of being, and hence, too, the proper name of law. And this form of subjection to the eternal law is the very thing suited to man's greater freedom. The first principle of freedom is reason, which makes it possible to deliberate about practical matters and to decide for oneself what (if anything) to do about them. And insofar as people share in the law in a rational way, it is even left up to them to decide whether and how to apply the law to their actions. It makes them free subjects of the eternal law, subjects whose acts are conformed to it only through choice, not through a natural determination.[82] The use of their natural inclinations rests with them, because these are inclinations of their reason and rational appetite. In short, all creatures, rational and irrational, are naturally subject to the eternal law. And precisely because man's specific natural subjection to the eternal law takes the form of something that can properly bear the name of law, the government exercised over man by the eternal law, in view of the common good of the universe, can be said to be for man's own sake, as befits those who have free choice and mastery of their acts.[83]

In order to complete the demonstration that there is naturally in man a genuine law, then, it is only necessary to show that something naturally impressed upon man from the imposition of the eternal law exists in the mode of reason. This is the aim of the rest of the argument of I–II.91.2. It is first shown on the basis of visible evidence, and then from Scripture.

---

81. Cf. *ST* I–II.90.1*ad*1.
82. See *ST* II–II.47.12; II–II.50.2; *ScG* III.114.
83. *ST* I.22.2*ad*4/*ad*5; I.103.5*ad*2/*ad*3; *ScG* III.112–14.

The visible evidence is the superior way in which man is subject to divine providence, as compared with other creatures. It is proper to man to become a participant in the very work of providence, "being provident for himself and others." The natural aptitude in man for becoming capable of exercising providence is something that Thomas seems simply to take for granted here. It is nothing mysterious. Providence, he tells us elsewhere, is nothing but the chief part of prudence, the part by which people order the doable things presently at hand to the future attainment or conservation of their due end.[84] All people, insofar as they have reason—insofar as they are human—have at least some basic disposition or aptitude for such activity.

How is it, then, that people's natural aptitude for sharing in the work of providence shows that they naturally possess a rational participation of the eternal law? It implies that they naturally possess a likeness of the principle according to which providence is exercised. This principle is a certain intelligible object, a *ratio*; and the *ratio providentiae divinae*, the plan of divine providence, is nothing other than the eternal law. Hence man's natural impression of the eternal law must include a rational participation in it. It is this sort of participation that inclines people to share in providence. And they must have this participation from the imposition of the eternal law itself, since it is from the imposition of the eternal law that each thing is naturally inclined to its own acts and ends.[85]

That the principle of man's share in the work of providence is a rational share in the eternal law becomes even clearer through considering the nature of providence's operation: to order something to its due end and to the action that is due to it by reason of its end. To say that man's proper work is to exercise providence is to say that man "has a natural inclination toward his due act and end" (*debitum actum et finem*). It seems to me that Thomas means this formally: an inclination to his due act and end, as due. In favor of this reading is the fact that he uses the singular rather than the plural, saying "act and end" rather than "acts and ends." This contrasts with what he said two sentences previously about creatures generally: that they have inclinations toward their proper acts and ends (*proprios actus et fines*). If *due* here is taken only materially, no difference between man and other creatures is signaled, and neither the need for the participation's rational character, nor the significance of man's sharing in providence, is explained. Moreover, the article goes on to connect natural law in man with knowledge of the "works of justice." The inclination is toward acts and ends apprehended as just or

---

84. On providence as the principal part of prudence, see *ST* I.22.1; II–II.49.6. On the due end as principle of practical reasoning, see *ST* I–II.58.4c/ad3; I–II.65.1.

85. On reason as "inclining" us, see *ST* I.79.12; II–II.22.1ad1; II–II.136.3ad1.

as due. For Thomas, the notions of the just and the due are very closely connected.[86]

Such an inclination presupposes or involves the capacity to relate to things or to be affected by them according to their dueness. The due or the owing is what belongs to someone, and this is what is ordered to them as to an end.[87] Order to an end is determined according to a rule or measure.[88] Hence this capacity must be something pertaining to reason. It is proper to reason to grasp order, to formulate measures, and to compare things with their measure. This capacity must originate from a rational apprehension of a measure of human actions and ends.

Now the primary measure of all created things is the eternal law. The eternal law is the first principle through which anything is due or right or just in creation. It is, as Augustine says, "that through which it is just that all things be most ordered"—*qua iustum est ut omnia sint ordinatissima*.[89] Nothing else can serve as a measure for anything except insofar as it somehow shares in the order instituted by the eternal law. Hence, if man's "inclination toward the due" is essentially rational, then it must be a natural impression of the eternal law that attains to a specific likeness of the eternal law as rational or intellectual. As Thomas had already told us, "the eternal law is in a way known to us by natural reason, which is derived from it as its proper image."[90] To say that it shares in the rational or intellectual character of the eternal law is to say that it retains the full form of law. And so, since it is also something natural, it fully answers to the name *natural law*.

We might wonder why, if Thomas means to present natural law as a law in the full sense, there is no mention of its ordering to common good. Perhaps one answer is that if natural law is not something diverse from the eternal law, then neither is its ordering to common good anything diverse from that of the eternal law. The primary common good toward which the eternal law orders is indicated in I–II.91.1*ad*3: God himself.[91] So there is no need for I–II.91.2 to mention it. However, this article does at least gesture toward the common good, in speaking of the rational creature's being provident for himself *and others*. The article does not explain how natural law makes this possible, but the explanation will become clear a little later, in I–II.94.2: what pertain to natural law are things that practical reason

---

86. See *ST* I.21.1*ad*3; cf. II–II.58.11.
87. *ST* I.21.1*ad*3.
88. *ST* I–II.21.1*c*.
89. *ST* I–II.91.2*obj*1.
90. *ST* I–II.19.4*ad*3. On the image of God in man, see *ST* I.93.
91. On natural law as ordering to God, see chapters 3 and 7 below.

natural apprehends "as human goods." It does not say "as one's own goods." The goods and what they are the goods of—human beings—are grasped universally, and the precepts of natural law express things to be done and avoided for the sake not only of the good that is proper to oneself but also of other people's good. Natural law orders toward common human good. The very universality of the precepts thus constitutes an ordering toward common good. And actually this universality was already signaled in one of the articles in the *Prima pars* where Thomas did mention natural law. There he identified natural law with the "universal principles of right."[92] Moreover, in the other *Prima pars* article where he mentioned natural law, he insisted that everything is naturally inclined toward common good—especially the universal good which is God—even more toward its own singular good.[93] In chapters 3 and 7, I shall go more into how natural law orders toward common good and toward God.

ST I–II.91.2 also invokes Scriptural support for the existence of a natural law. The *Sed contra*, appealing to the *Glossa ordinaria*, reads Romans 2.14—"the Gentiles do naturally the things that are of the Law"—as an indication of a natural law, "by which everyone understands and is aware in himself of what is good and what is bad." (This foreshadows the famous discussion of the precepts of natural law *ST* I–II.94.2, where the very first precept is said to be the one based on the notions of good and bad.) Then at the end of the corpus of I–II.91.2, Thomas returns to our understanding of good and bad, and he relates it to verses 5 and 6 of the Fourth Psalm:

> After the Psalmist has said, "Offer up the sacrifice of justice," he adds, as if someone were asking what the works of justice are, "Many say, 'Who shows us good things?'" In reply to this question he says, "The light of Your countenance, Lord, is imprinted on us," as if to say, the light of natural reason, by which we discern what is good and what is bad—which pertains to natural law—is nothing other than the imprint of divine light in us. Whence it is clear that natural law is nothing other than the participation of the eternal law in the rational creature.[94]

---

92. *ST* I.113.1obj1/ad1.

93. *ST* I.60.5sc/ad1/ad3/ad5. Also pertinent is *ST* I.60.4.

94. Thomas is not the first to invoke the fourth Psalm to show the existence of a natural law. See Albertus Magnus, *De bono* tract. 5, q. 1, a. 2, obj. 8, 269 line 83–270 line 6; cf. ad 8, 271 lines 59–62.

ETERNAL LAW AS A COMPONENT OF THE FORMAL DEFINITION OF NATURAL LAW

In light of the analysis of I-II.91.2, there appears to be little doubt that Thomas takes *participation of the eternal law in the rational creature* to be a strict definition of natural law. In fact, he seems to regard this expression as natural law's one formal definition. By this I mean the definition expressing why that which is natural law answers to the meaning of the very name *natural law*. Thomas does not proceed as though the existence of natural law were already acknowledged, asking whether it is somehow derived from the eternal law. Nor does he proceed as though the verification of its derivation from the eternal law were merely a removal of obstacles to its retaining the name *natural law*; that is, as though something had already been affirmed to be a natural law and then doubt had been cast on this affirmation by the consideration that all law must somehow be derived from eternal law. From the start, his argument proceeds as an investigation into something whose existence can only be affirmed by reference to the eternal law. This must be because he understands *natural law* to signify something that is a law in an unqualified sense, and because nothing that is strictly natural can be an unqualified law unless it be a law of God existing in certain beings ruled by God. No reality existing in man can be judged to answer to the name of natural law unless it be considered in the light of the eternal law and of the manner in which the eternal law is first communicated to man.

Surely this explains why, until he arrives at I-II.91.2, Thomas tends to avoid the expression *natural law* in the *Summa theologiae*, almost always using some other expression to designate what turns out to be the same reality.[95] This restraint is all the more noteworthy, in view of his frequent use of the passage from the fourth Psalm earlier in the *Summa*. In the *Prima pars*, he uses it to show that the light of the agent intellect is derived from the divine light (I.79.4); that the human intellect apprehends all things "in the eternal reasons" (I.84.5); that everyone possesses an image of God, inasmuch as the very nature of the human mind constitutes a certain aptitude for knowing and loving God (I.93.4); and that God is man's principal teacher (I.117.1*ad*1). And earlier in the *Prima secundae*, he uses the fourth Psalm in showing that the goodness of the human will is measured primarily by the eternal law, insofar as it causes reason's own power to measure the will (I-II.19.4). Yet even here, in a practical setting, he refrains from using the expression *natural law*. So the study of the nature of law in general, and the determination of the existence of the eternal law, seem to be crucial, in Thomas's judgment, for establishing the existence of natural law. I would

---

95. See above, 38–39.

say that he locates the notion of natural law squarely within the framework of the doctrine of man as in the image of God.[96] It is no more possible to consider natural law, as law, apart from the eternal law, than to consider an image, as image, apart from its original.

There can also be no doubt now about whether Thomas takes the question of natural law to be a question about something that is a law in the unqualified sense, *maxime habens rationem legis*. Despite the thoroughness of his earlier investigations of the things pertaining to the mind of God, he raises the question of the existence of the eternal law only following a rigorous analysis of the nature of law in general. In view of such a preparation, one would certainly expect that if he meant anything to be understood as a law only according to some partial likeness or in some extended sense, he would say so explicitly—as indeed he does in the case of the *lex fomitis*.[97] By contrast, Aquinas is at pains to verify the presence of all the elements of the nature of law in the eternal law.[98] And in the case of natural law, the presence of all of the elements of the nature of law is not even questioned. What is questioned is only the suitability of there being such a law, in view of the exhaustiveness of the eternal law and in view of the intellectual and free nature of man.

This is not to say that the definition of natural law as a participation of the eternal law tells us everything there is to know about natural law. On the contrary, as I shall argue in the next chapter, the inquiry into the specific properties of natural law need not, or perhaps even should not, refer to the eternal law. But reference to the eternal law is certainly required for attributing to it the nature of law without qualification. What is intrinsic to natural law is not sufficient, by itself, to account for its possession of the full nature of law. What is intrinsic to something in a subject is determined according to the nature of the subject, and human nature is no more cause of the legality of natural law than it is cause of the eternal law.

It may not be necessary simply to dismiss Donagan's distinction between "theological" and "philosophical" definitions of natural law, one in terms of God and the eternal law, and one remaining entirely on the level of human nature.[99] But these cannot be definitions serving the same logical purpose, and it is the "theological" definition that gives the proper explanation of the name given to the thing defined. A definition that leaves God and the eternal law out of the picture cannot express the formal nature of natural

---

96. See especially *ST* I.93.4; I–II.19.4*ad*3.
97. *ST* I–II.91.6.
98. *ST* I–II.91.1; I–II.93.1.
99. See above, 3.

law. At most, such a definition—for instance, *first principles of practical reason*—can only express what is material and differentiating in this nature.[100] And there is a definite order between these definitions. Only through the formal definition can the material definition be understood to be a definition of a natural law.

---

100. When an act involves the coordination of two powers, its formal notion is taken from the superior or governing power, while its material notion is taken from the inferior, which is the act's immediate source and subject. See *ST* I–II.13.1; I–II.17.4.

3

Natural Law, God's Will, and Positive Law

The study of Thomas's argument for the existence of natural law leaves little doubt as to what he wishes the reader of the *Summa theologiae* to understand by the expression *natural law* and by the formula *participation of the eternal law in the rational creature*. Both the procedure and the setting of the argument indicate that the object of this formula is what must be held in view when the existence of a natural law is affirmed in a scientific way. This would not be necessary if *natural law* meant nothing more than first principles of practical reason, or naturally known rules of human conduct, or anything else whose notion did not embrace the full set of conditions for a law. The argument gives as much support as could be desired for defining natural law in terms of the definition of law in general, in the way proposed at the beginning of chapter 1. Natural law is an ordination of divine reason, for the common good of the universe, promulgated to man, through the instilling of the natural light of his intellect, by God, the author and governor of the universe. The formal nature of such a law is what *participation of the eternal law in the rational creature* is meant to express.

It therefore becomes necessary to resolve the questions that were seen to arise from this way of understanding natural law. These are, first, how natural law, so understood, can remain something fully natural; and second, whether and how such a natural law possesses the obligatory and compelling force of law. The second question will be the concern of chapter 6. The present chapter and the two following address the first question.

The analysis of *ST* I–II.91.2 immediately raises the first question, by indicating that the basic meaning of the expression *natural law* for Aquinas is law naturally promulgated. The issue is whether, or in what way, man's strictly natural practical knowledge, the knowledge of the first principles of practical reason, constitutes a sufficient promulgation or notification of God's law. What casts doubt on its sufficiency is that it seems not to include explicit knowledge of the authority promulgating the law, His purpose in promulgating it, or the fact of the promulgation. In short, it seems to exclude the very knowledge that these principles are laws.

This feature of the natural knowledge of the first principles of practical reason was what led to Lottin's complaint about defining natural law in terms of the eternal law and in terms of the definition of law in general.[1] It is only in the case of positive law, he says, that knowledge of the lawgiver's institution of the law is an essential element in the subjects' understanding of the law's precepts as genuine norms of action. That is, if a law is merely positive, its subjects know the law in such a way that it actually rules and measures their acts only when they know that it is the law; and this amounts to knowing that competent authority has instituted it. Lottin's complaint is that to define natural law in terms of the definition of law in general is to assimilate it too much to positive law, which in his view is the only law that perfectly fulfills the general definition. Nor is it only for Lottin that the difference between the principles of practical reason and the precepts of positive law is problematic. According to the position at the other extreme, that of Fortin, it is only by becoming like precepts of positive law, through the revelation of their origin in divine authority and of their divine sanction, that the first principles of practical reason take on the character of a true law.[2] Thus, common to both positions is the judgment that, according to their original and strictly natural existence in the human mind, the first principles of practical reason cannot be termed laws in the full sense of Thomas's definition of law.

Now if the account of the basis of the Thomistic division of law given in chapter 2 was accurate, and if a natural law is a law naturally promulgated, then there is already good reason to doubt whether Aquinas would accept this judgment. The difference just described, between the principles of practical reason and the precepts of positive law, is not by itself a sufficient ground for considering the former to be, in themselves, laws in only

1. See above, 5–8.
2. See above, 17–20.

a qualified sense. If the various laws enumerated in *ST* I–II.91.1–4 are properly distinguished by their modes of promulgation, then we cannot simply assume that the specific mode of promulgation which is proper to positive law is the only truly legal one. Perhaps the peculiar mark of the law promulgated naturally is the very fact that its promulgation does not essentially require a notification of the promulgating authority. Perhaps, that is, the very naturalness of the knowledge of these precepts somehow suffices to give them the degree of force that is secured for other laws only through their formal presentation as laws, that is, as decrees issued or posited by competent authority. At the very least, it seems safe to say that if Aquinas understands *natural law* to mean law naturally promulgated, then his affirmation of the existence of a natural law is not easy to square with an intention to suggest that natural law is not really quite natural after all.

Still, it remains to be seen exactly how the full nature of law can belong to rules that are not made known in the way that positive law is made known. This will be the object of the last three sections of this chapter. In the first two sections, I shall try to verify the proposition that, for Aquinas, the original or natural assent given to the precepts of natural law comes about independently of advertence to divine authority. Hitherto I have simply taken this proposition for granted.

THE DEFINITION OF NATURAL LAW AND THE NATURAL KNOWLEDGE OF ITS PRECEPTS

The clearest evidence that Aquinas does not think the understanding of first practical principles involves advertence to divine authority would be the two points adduced by Donagan and others in support of a purely "philosophical" definition of natural law. The first is that Aquinas attributes the understanding of the common principles of natural law to all people, whereas he denies that all people know God's existence and attributes. The second is that there is no reference at all to divine legislation or to the eternal law in the *quaestio* of the *Summa theologiae* devoted to natural law, I–II.94; and in particular, that there is no mention of knowledge of God's authority as part of reason's natural understanding of the precepts of natural law, which is discussed at length in I–II.94.2. The obvious inference is that Aquinas does not think that the legal character of natural law, considered according to the existence in man's mind that is proper to it, depends in any way upon either divine revelation or upon rational knowledge of God as its legislator. He thinks that it is already a law for man, "by the very fact that God has inserted it into the minds of men as something to be naturally known." This means that man is subject to natural law—is ruled and measured by it—even before he has the knowledge by which to judge it to be a natural law. We grasp the truth of its precepts, and hence their normative quality, before we attain any clear knowledge of their authoritative origin. The application of natural law to man is already brought to completion in this apprehension.

This line of reasoning is so compelling that what is really required is to show that it nevertheless does not compromise the account of the definition of natural law already given. This may be shown on the basis of a certain distinction. Natural law is a certain set of rational propositions or dictates. It is the expression of a certain body of knowledge. But the *knowledge of natural law* may mean one of two clearly distinct things. It may mean the practical knowledge that natural law is itself the expression of; or it may mean the rather more theoretical knowledge about this very expression, according to which, among other things, it receives the name *natural law*. The propositions that constitute natural law are one thing. Propositions about those propositions, such as that they constitute a natural law, are another. The former are norms of action. The latter are theoretical reflections on these norms. Natural law and the theory of natural law are not the same thing, even though both are objects of knowledge.

This distinction is important in more than one way. For one thing, as Finnis observes, the theory of natural law may have had, and in fact has had, a long and uneven history; but if any such thing as natural law exists, it cannot have had much of a history at all.[3] For another, and more importantly for us, this distinction must surely be at least part of what allows Aquinas to define natural law as a participation of the eternal law in the rational creature, while at the same time asserting that all people know the common principles of the natural law, and deriving the various precepts of natural law without any reference to the eternal law. The "theological" definition of natural law, as a participation of the eternal law, obviously belongs to the theory of natural law, which perhaps not everyone possesses. But the constituents of natural law are nevertheless, by definition, within everyone's grasp.

At the same time, some reflection on the distinction casts further doubt upon the claim for the existence of a purely "philosophical" definition of natural law, in Donagan's sense; that is, a definition that makes no

---

3. See Finnis, *Natural Law and Natural Rights*, 23–25. I would not say that natural law cannot have had *any* history. There is some variability in the knowledge of its precepts (*ST* I–II.94.4; I–II.94.6). This is one reason why they were included in the Old Law (see *ST* I–II.99.2*ad*2; I–II.100.5*ad*1; and esp. I–II.98.6—"when the natural law began to be obscured on account of the exuberance of sinners"). And even the rectitude of the application of the secondary precepts to particular situations is somewhat variable (*ST* I–II.94.4; I–II.94.5). An important case would be the lawfulness of polygamy under the Old Law (*ST Suppl.* 65.1–2 [*In Sent.* IV.33.1.1–2]).

reference to the eternal law. If we can grant that Aquinas does not think everyone knows the "theological" definition of natural law, we should also grant that he gives no indication of thinking that everyone knows any definition of natural law at all. Knowing any definition would require some reflection on the first principles of practical reason or on the moral order generally, and not everyone undertakes such reflection. Everyone knows the principles, but not everyone knows that they know them. Some may even try to deny it. Even a "philosophical" definition of natural law would belong to the theory of natural law and would fall outside the scope of what all men know about natural law. There is no reason to think that everyone has a concept of first principles of practical reason, any more than that everyone has a concept of first principles of theoretical reason—even though everyone somehow knows those principles. The definition of natural law is not obliged to express only those things that everyone knows about natural law. What the definition of natural law is obliged to express is the essential nature of natural law. Knowing its precepts and knowing the existence and nature of those precepts are not the same thing.

The universality of the knowledge of the principles that make up natural law thus says absolutely nothing about the presence or absence of eternal law in the definition of natural law. Does the fact that all people know the existence of some things created by God, without knowing of God, imply that creation or createdness can be defined without reference to God? Surely just as this fact implies only that these people do not know that the things whose existence they know are also God's creatures, so the other implies only that some people do not know that the primary practical principles are also God's laws. It is a confusion between theory and practice, of the very kind that Finnis flags, to say (as he does) that because the first principles of practical reason are self-evident, whereas God's existence is not, the theory of natural law does not belong to theology, even natural theology.[4] As I mentioned early on, for Thomas all theory of first principles belongs to metaphysics; and on his view, metaphysics and natural theology are the same science.

The question as to the place of the eternal law in the definition of natural law is entirely a question about the relation between the various elements of the theory of natural law. It cannot be answered by way of appeal to the contents of natural law itself or to the practical knowledge that natural law expresses. Is there, then, any reason to doubt whether the study of natural law in *ST* I–II.94 remains within the theological perspective in which natural law is understood as a participation of the eternal law? Has Aquinas

---

4. Finnis, *Natural Law and Natural Rights*, 48.

suddenly shifted from theology to philosophy, or from theological ethics to philosophical ethics, or to the perspective of what Lottin calls "intrinsic morality"? Does Thomas in fact have an equivocal notion of natural law, one that allows for two more or less independent definitions of it? Would he not have said so?

If the eternal law is not explicitly mentioned in *ST* I–II.94, I think the reason is simply that Aquinas has turned from a consideration of natural law according to what makes it law—its being a rational participation in the eternal law—to a consideration of it according to what is distinctive of it or specific about it, which is its being something natural to man. The focus of this second way of considering it is already indicated in *ST* I–II.91.2. Natural law is something natural to man because the immediate or proximate cause of its existence in him is something pertaining to his nature, indeed something distinctively human: the natural light of reason. But the natural light of reason can be considered in two ways: simply on its own terms—according to its own form—or in comparison with the extrinsic source in which it participates. It is the second way of considering it that presents it as resulting in a natural law in man, because natural law itself is something whose legal character is manifested by reference to its extrinsic origin, the eternal law. Nevertheless, whatever is special or proper to the natural light of reason and to its effects will be determined according to the first way of considering it, namely, on its own terms.

As Thomas often says, "whatever is received in a thing is received in it according to the mode of the receiver."[5] It is true that natural law exists and is named according to man's subjection to an extrinsic principle, and that it is only for this reason that natural law can be called a law without qualification. Nevertheless the properties of natural law will not directly follow upon the nature of the extrinsic principle from which it derives, but upon the nature of the principle intrinsic to its proper subject, through which its generation in man is terminated. In other words, its relation to the eternal law is what places natural law in the genus of law, but natural law's proper subject, natural human reason, is what differentiates or specifies it.

Once it is determined that a derivation of the eternal law naturally exists in man, through the instrumentality of his own intellect, the closer investigation of this reality must proceed in the light of what is known about the natural operation of reason. The inquiry into the special nature of natural law must be an inquiry in which natural law is considered as a certain natural perfection of the rational soul. *ST* I–II.94, is exactly such an inquiry. This is why it begins with the question of which one among the perfections

---

5. For instance, *ST* I.75.5.

already known to belong naturally to the rational soul can properly be said to constitute a law. This question seeks, as it were, the material rather than the formal definition of natural law. Once it is determined that natural law consists in the object of *synderesis*, the rest of the inquiry will only differ from an inquiry into the first principles of practical reason as such in that it is undertaken in the light of the judgment that these principles constitute a natural law. While *ST* I–II.91.2 provides the original disclosure of the reality of natural law, according to the criteria for law established in I–II.90, I–II.94 goes on to study this reality according to what is distinctive of it, or insofar as it is natural. A brief survey of the articles in I–II.94 confirms the judgment that the function of this question is to determine what can be said about natural law according to what distinguishes it from other laws, which is its being natural.

In I–II.94.1, it is asked whether natural law is a habit. The only habit even considered is a natural one, *synderesis*. The answer is negative. Law is a work (*opus*) of reason, something constituted by its operation, in the way a proposition is.[6] Hence natural law cannot be a habit. For a habit is not something that one does (*quod quis agit*). It is that by which one does something (*quo quis agit*). Thomas does grant that natural law can be called a habit in the sense of something held by a habit. For sometimes its precepts are actually considered (*considerantur in actu*) by reason, and sometimes they exist in reason only habitually. And in fact this is how natural law exists naturally: as something held by a natural habit.

Notice, by the way, that he does not say that the precepts are instituted by reason, as though reason were their legislator. (Obviously he is talking about human reason here.) He only says that they are considered by it. That is how they are its work. Propositions, whether practical or speculative, exist only through reason's consideration; more precisely, through its act of judging, "composing or dividing."[7] But this does not mean that reason has any control over their validity, or even over its own assent to them.[8]

I–II.94.2 asks whether the precepts of natural law are one or many. This article presents special issues which will be considered in the next two chapters. Here it is sufficient to note that the question is answered entirely by way of an account of the objects of man's natural understanding and natural inclinations.

I–II.94.3 asks whether natural law commands all acts of virtue. Once again, the answer is made by way of appeal to what is natural to reason.

---

6. Cf. *ST* I–II.90.1*ad*2.
7. *ST* I.16.2.
8. See *ST* I–II.17.6.

Because reason is man's proper form and the principal source of properly human inclinations, it naturally inclines him to follow its direction. At the same time, the directives that it is naturally disposed to form only give general guidelines for virtuous or rational activity. They do not define each act of virtue in its specific nature.

Finally, articles 4, 5, and 6 of I–II.94 ask, respectively, whether natural law is the same for all men, whether it can change, and whether it can be deleted from people's hearts. All of these questions pertain to the naturalness of natural law. The answers all invoke the distinction between primary precepts—those which are naturally known in the strictest sense, being self-evident to all—and other, secondary precepts that are derived from the first in the manner of nearby or easily known conclusions. Thomas holds that the primary precepts are absolutely the same for everyone and, taken universally or in themselves, cannot be deleted from the human heart. The secondary precepts can sometimes fail, as to their validity and as to the knowledge of them. But they do so only rarely, and so they too are natural, inasmuch as the natural is what is *either* always *or* for the most part.

In sum, the absence of any reference to the eternal law in *ST* I–II.94 in no way implies that Aquinas's formulation of natural law as a participation of the eternal law is anything less than the formal definition of natural law. Nor does it suggest that he employs the term *natural law* in an equivocal way, such that its application to the first principles of practical reason constitutes a shift to a different definition. He is simply focusing on what pertains to the natural existence of natural law in the human mind. The intention of I–II.94 gives no reason to expect any appeal to the eternal law or to God as author of natural law.

Such an appeal might even serve to obscure the treatment, by adding superfluous detail. For example, reference to the eternal law, might lead someone to think that the exceptionlessness of the primary precepts of natural law rests only on their being divinely instituted. It might give the impression that, in the mere light of reason, the precepts appear to be valid only for the most part, and that, unless they are referred to God, treating them as exceptionless would be unreasonable. Of course God is the cause of the basic sameness of nature. But natural law is the same everywhere only because nature is, and only to the same extent.[9]

---

9. See *ST* I–II.97.1*ad*1; II–II.57.2*ad*1.

THE GRASP OF THE PRECEPTS OF NATURAL LAW AS RULES AND MEASURES: *EX IPSA RATIONE BONI*

Even more importantly, reference to the eternal law might make it seem that the precepts of natural law come to be understood as obligatory—as true rules and measures of human action—in the same manner that precepts of positive law do, namely, by way of the awareness of the authoritative act, and the coercive power, of the governor instituting them. In Aquinas's view, it is simply impossible that practical reason form its first truths in this way.

A text that shows this last point very decisively, I believe, is presented in the course of Thomas's negative answer to the question, "whether precepts about having faith ought to have been given in the Old Law":

> Law is not imposed by any ruler except upon those subject to him. And therefore the precepts of any law presuppose the subjection of the one who receives the law to him who gives the law. But the first subjection of man to God is by faith. . . . And therefore faith is presupposed to the precepts of the law.[10]

In saying that the first subjection of man to God is through faith, Aquinas is evidently speaking about subjections that come about voluntarily, self-subjections. After all, the question concerns precepts about faith.[11] Precepts given to rational beings are about voluntary operations. The act of faith is a voluntary operation. Obviously, even prior to having faith, man is somehow subject to God. He is so by the very fact of being created. But it would be silly to ask whether there are precepts given to man about being created. Precepts given to man are about voluntary operations. Being created is not an operation on the creature's part at all, let alone a voluntary one.

Now, Thomas does not mean that there can be no precept at all given to man by God until man comes to submit voluntarily to His authority by faith. In that case there could be no precepts of natural law. But the text is talking about precepts of the Old Law, which is to say, precepts given in the mode of positive law. Any precept by God that governs man in the manner of a positive law presupposes man's subjection to God by faith. And therefore there is no positive precept of faith itself.

What we should notice, however, is that Aquinas is far from thinking that there is simply no such thing as a precept of faith. In treating of the distinction of the precepts of the Decalogue, he says that

> the precept of faith is presupposed to the precepts of the Decalogue, as is the precept of charity. For just as the primary,

10. *ST* II–II.16.1.
11. On faith or belief as voluntary, see *ST* II–II.1.4; II–II.1.6*obj*3/*ad*3.

> common precepts of the law of nature are known in virtue of themselves to one who has natural reason, and are not in need of promulgation; so also this [precept], to believe in God, is primary and self-evident to one who has faith.... And therefore it needs no other promulgation than the infusion of faith.[12]

Notice that he does not say that the precepts of natural law have no promulgation. He says that they do not "need" promulgation. This is because, to whomever has natural reason, they have been promulgated already.

So it is not that there is no precept about faith at all. It is that there is no positive divine precept about it.[13] This is because all positive divine precepts presuppose it. But they also presuppose the self-evident precept of faith. Assent to precepts as obligatory on the grounds of their divine authority depends upon a prior assent to the precept that God is to be believed and obeyed—assent to the very precept that God's authority is to be accepted. And more generally, all positive precepts—that is, precepts that are understood to be obligatory in light of their institution by a governing authority—presuppose some dictate of reason urging subjection to that authority, such as a judgment of the suitability of belonging to this or that regime. And Thomas is saying right here that the precepts of natural law are of this sort. The assent to them is not based on consideration of their authoritative origin. Yet they do have such an origin, just as the precept of faith does.

Reason's grasp of the precepts of natural law as obligatory—its first, natural grasp of them, in accordance with which they constitute a natural law—cannot be based on the consideration of God's authority, or for that matter, of any authority at all. To say otherwise would be to initiate a mere infinite regress. The precepts of natural law would have to presuppose other precepts, and those in turn would presuppose still others, and so on indefinitely. And then the precepts of natural law would not be precepts of natural law after all. They would not be the *first* direction of our acts to the last end.[14] There would be no first direction—which means that there would be no direction at all.

Reason's first grasp of the rules that are connatural to it cannot come about under a consideration of their authoritative institution. In addition to the infinite regress problem, this is also shown by the very fact that their derivation from God is not immediately evident to reason. And even if it were, that cannot be reason's first basis for acknowledging them. To

---

12. *ST* I–II.100.4*ad*1. On the precept of charity, see *ST* I–II.100.3*ad*1.

13. At least, not in the "mode of precept," as a command. See the related discussions of precepts of hope and fear in *ST* II–II.22.1; II–II.22.2.

14. *ST* I–II.91.2*ad*2.

acknowledge precepts on the basis of the duty to comply with the authority issuing them is to consider them in relation to a certain specific good or specific virtue. It is to consider them as pertaining to the virtue of *obedience*. But obedience is only one virtue among many, and not the first. This is true even if it is understood as obedience to God. This virtue too presupposes faith.

> All acts of virtue pertain to obedience, insofar as they fall under precepts. . . . Yet it does not follow that obedience is absolutely prior to all [other] virtues. . . . For even granting that an act of virtue falls under a precept, someone can perform the act of virtue without giving thought to the precept. Hence if there is any virtue whose object is naturally prior to the precept, that virtue is naturally prior to obedience; as is evidently the case with faith, through which is made known to us the sublimity of divine authority, by reason of which He has the power of commanding.[15]

Now, elsewhere Thomas does grant that, even when the agent is not "giving thought to the precept," acts of virtue do involve obedience in a broad sense. They do so inasmuch as all acts of virtue fall under precepts of divine law. The virtuous agent's will can be said to be inclined to fulfill the precepts, and such an inclination can be called obedience. But compliance with the mandates precisely through consideration of the lawgiver's authority and of the duty in justice to obey one's superior, he says, is obedience in a special sense. And when it is a case of obedience to God, it presupposes, rather than being presupposed by, the virtue of faith.[16] But if this is so, then a fortiori, both it and any sort of obedience in the special sense, out of consideration of one's duty toward one's superior, presuppose the precepts of natural law.

Thomas is really quite explicit about the fact that it is not in light of any superior authority instituting them that the precepts of natural law first seem obligatory—even though, again, they *are* instituted by a superior authority. This is simply to say that their original obligatory force is not that of a positive law. Even if they, or some of them, are included in a positive law or are known to be prescribed by a superior authority, that is not what first makes it seem a duty or a necessity to comply with them.

> Some of the precepts of any law have obligatory force from the very dictate of reason, because natural reason dictates that this ought to be done or avoided. And precepts of this sort are called

---

15. *ST* II-II.104.3*ad*2.
16. See *ST* II-II.4.7*ad*3.

moral.... But there are other precepts that do not have obligatory force from the dictate of reason itself, because, considered in themselves, they do not absolutely have the quality of due or undue. But they have obligatory force from some divine or human institution.[17]

Or again, "Written law contains natural right (*ius naturale*), but does not institute it; for it [natural right] does not have force (*robur*) from law but from nature. But written law both contains and institutes positive right, giving it the force (*robur*) of authority."[18] And more succinctly: "Moral precepts have efficacy from the very dictate of natural reason, even if they never be instituted in a law."[19]

How then do the precepts of natural law present themselves as obligatory and win reason's assent? It must be out of the very understanding of what good and evil are, as manifested by the natural light of reason. As Albert says, the precepts of natural law are rules and measures that reason dictates "out of the very notion of the good"—*ex ipsa ratione boni*.[20] Their original force does not depend on reason's grasping God as their author. Its eventually doing so may very well give them an even greater force: that of a duty, in justice, toward God as rightful governor. But prior to that, they already have an intrinsic force of their own. Since they are called moral precepts, I think that we may very well call this moral obligation. I shall discuss this notion in greater detail in chapter 6.

But it is significant that Thomas is willing to call compliance with such precepts, on account of their intrinsic force, a case of obedience in the broad sense, inasmuch as the precepts do express divine mandates, so that the will to comply with them is in fact an inclination to fulfill the mandates. Indeed, Thomas says explicitly that the natural inclination toward virtue *is*

---

17. *ST* I-II.104.1. See also *ST* I-II.100.11. I do not mean that, for Thomas, all the precepts that oblige "by the dictate of reason" are properly precepts of natural law. Thus, in the reply to the third objection in *ST* I-II.104.1, he speaks of things dictated by reason "informed by faith," such as the love and worship of God, and he contrasts these with things that oblige by "divine institution." Still, what belongs to reason informed by faith presupposes what belongs to it by nature.

18. *ST* II-II.60.5.

19. *ST* I-II.100.11.

20. "That is strictly called natural right (*ius naturale*) which an innate power has inserted ... and nothing pertains to that natural right other than the universal [principles] of morals, which conscience dictates out of the very notion of the good" (*stricte dicitur ius naturale quod 'innata vis inseruit' . . . et nihil est de illo iure naturali nisi universalia morum, quae dictat conscientia ex ipsa ratione boni*) (Albertus Magnus, *De bono* tract. 5, q. 1, a. 1, ad 16, 266, lines 39–43).

itself an inclination toward what is consonant with the eternal law.[21] This is not because it involves any consideration of the relation between virtue, or the dictates of reason concerning virtue, and the eternal law.

This is true, I take it, even of the precepts of natural law concerning God. Their original force does not rest on their being understood to have been instituted by Him. Natural law is a law instituted by God, but He gives it a force that does not depend on the consideration of its institution. It has its force in itself, immediately.

The conclusion to be drawn seems very simple. We should not think of the eternal law as an eternal positive law. In that case, even its force would presuppose that of the dictates of natural law, and these would not consist in a participation in it. It is rather their very source. It is the source of their *intrinsic* force, the force that they have when "considered in themselves"— their *natural* force. This, I would say, pertains to the very strength of this lawgiver's action. It is a unique strength. No creature has it. It extends to the very "institution of nature" itself.[22]

This thought is not easy to grasp. In the next two sections I shall try to show how Thomas can explain it.

THE QUESTION OF THE ROLE OF GOD'S WILL IN NATURAL LAW

In the previous section we observed a similarity between the precept of faith and the precepts of natural law. Understanding the truth and normativity of these precepts does not consist in knowing them to have been enjoined by a superior to whom one owes obedience. At least the understanding of that very debt of obedience cannot consist in such knowledge. However, there is also a difference between faith, as a presupposition of divine positive law, and natural law, as a presupposition of positive law generally. The object of faith is the very Word of God. By faith, one apprehends certain things as truths spoken by God Himself, expressions of the First Truth. This apprehension includes an awareness of God's authority and of the duty to obey whatever precepts He issues. That is how faith serves as a presupposition of divine positive law. By contrast, although the natural light of reason and the precepts of natural law come from God, the precepts are not immediately apprehended as having been spoken or issued by God. The object of natural reason is not the Word of God. It is the truth that can be reached starting from natural experience. The rule of human reason "is gathered

---

21. *ST* I–II.93.6.
22. See, for example, *ST* I.22.2ad3.

from the created things that man naturally knows."²³ Whereas faith enables one to perceive certain truths as expressions of God's own truth and certain precepts as binding with His own authority, the light of reason enables one to perceive certain truths simply as true in their own right, and certain precepts simply as normative or binding or obligatory—as rules and measures of one's action—in their own right.

Nevertheless these truths and these precepts are in fact a participation in God's truth and in the eternal law, and to know them is not only to have received something from God, but also to be subject to Him as to a lawgiver and to have received a genuine law from Him. He is the source not only of the knowledge of the precepts of natural law but also of their obligatory force. It is He who *makes* them binding. In conveying them to us, He is acting not only as a teacher guiding us toward the understanding of certain things, but also as a commander, inducing us to act or not to act in certain ways. In chapter 6, I shall discuss in more detail what the obligatory force of natural law consists in. But what I wish to address here is a question that arises from the consideration of God as the lawgiver and commander from whom the precepts of natural law get their force. The question is how the precepts of natural law depend on God's will. For as we have already seen, Thomas does hold that the legislator's will is involved in making law, and that God's will is involved in natural law. "Every law proceeds from the reason and will of the legislator: natural and divine law, from the reasonable will of God, and human law from the will of man ruled by reason."²⁴

We can put the question in terms of the nature of the act of commanding. In Thomas's language, the terms *praeceptum* (whence *precept*) and *imperium* (command), like the corresponding verbs, are synonymous.²⁵ In the *Summa theologiae*, as part of his investigation of the nature of human or voluntary action, Thomas devotes an entire question to the act of command.²⁶ He says that it is an act concerned with things that are "for the sake of an end" (*ad finem*).²⁷ It follows upon the choice (*electio*) of those things,

---

23. *ST* I–II.74.7.

24. *ST* I–II.97.3. The reply to this article's first objection speaks only of will: "Natural and divine law proceeds from the divine will."

25. *ST* I–II.92.2c/obj1; II–II.47.8obj3. See Schultz, "Necessary Moral Principles," 150n3. It unnecessary to distinguish, as Grisez does, between precept and command, in order to avoid making the first principles of practical reason depend on an act of the human will. See above, 9. Grisez is right to want to avoid that. But in order to do so, it is only necessary to distinguish between the precept or the command and the act of commanding, and between how the precept or the command exists in the commander and how it exists in those who are under his command.

26. *ST* I–II.17.

27. See *ST* I–II.17.1.

and precedes and governs their actual execution or bringing about (*usus*). It consists in "ordering someone toward doing something," by way of a certain "intimation" or "declaration."[28] Since intimating something to another belongs to reason, command is "essentially an act of reason." Reason is the power from which the act of command immediately proceeds or is elicited.

However, the "intimation" proper to command serves not only to convey information about something, but also to move or order someone in a certain way. Aquinas's use of the verb *ordinare* in *ST* I-II.17.1 is evidently meant to express more than the mere apprehension or conception of order. Naturally it involves having such a conception. But *ordinare* means to apply an order to things, to move them or dispose them to be moved, in accordance with that order. It is a kind of action. Aquinas makes this clear in discussing another way in which reason orders, that of petition or request: "Both of these, commanding and petitioning or requesting, involve a certain ordination, namely, insofar as a man disposes for something to be done by some other agent."[29] To dispose for something is in some way to cause it. It therefore belongs only to practical reason, not to speculative, as he says earlier in the same article. The difference between command and petition is that command moves and orders with a certain necessity, the one commanded being under the commander's power.

Now since the act of command not only intimates but also moves and orders, the commander's will must also be involved in bringing it about. For by *will* is understood the dominant moving power in the soul. The will "moves the commanding reason."[30] That is, a command intimates reason's conception of an order between an agent and some action to be performed; but it intimates this conception in a manner that not only causes the agent to understand the order, but also gives the agent a certain "impetus" to follow it.[31] To command (*imperare*) is to order the person commanded to act, or to impose (*imponere*) upon the person commanded the order toward the act.[32] In commanding, reason operates as a mover of action, not only by presenting the order to the agent or to the power that executes it, but also as an agent in its own right, through its very way of presenting the order. Commanders are responsible for what is done at their command, and in such a way that the act of command and the act commanded, insofar as

28. *ST* I-II.17.1; I-II.17.2. Notice that the action commanded is one thing, and the end that the commander aims to achieve by means of it may be something else. The end of the precept is not the same as what the precept is about. See *ST* I-II.100.9ad2.

29. *ST* II-II.83.1.

30. *ST* I-II.17.2ad1.

31. *ST* I-II.17.2ad2.

32. *Imperare est imponere ordinem* (Ramírez, *De actibus humanis*, 400).

it proceeds from the command, constitute a single act.[33] It is simply a fact that people can sometimes speak in a manner that exerts a kind of forceful control over their hearers' actions, and that they can think in a manner that exerts such control over their own actions as well. However, among the powers of the soul, operating as an agent belongs primarily to the will. Reason's operating in that way must therefore derive from the will. It is the will that moves reason to intimate the order conceived in a manner that actually orders toward its execution. The act of command emerges from reason, both because the proximate source of the imposition or impression of order must be whatever it is that contains the order, and it is proper to reason to grasp order, and because it belongs to reason to convey or intimate what the soul contains. Nevertheless, in order to move effectively, reason's command must share in an impulse of the will.

It is important to be clear about the precise role played by the will in the work of commanding. A command is not the same as a proposition expressing or signifying one's will. Saying "I want you to do this" does not necessarily constitute a command to do it. It may only be a sort of request. To be sure, if it is said by a superior to a subordinate, it may very well constitute a command. And normally, in the case of a human commander, even if the command does not make explicit reference to his will—even if he simply says "Do this"—one may reasonably infer that he wants the subordinate to do it. Or at least, it may normally be inferred that he wants the subordinate to have the need to do it, inasmuch as the very act of saying "Do this" creates (or is meant to create) such a need. But the essential role of the commander's will in the act of command is not that of what the command makes known. What the command essentially makes known is a certain order of action to be executed by the one to whom the command is addressed. The role of the commander's will is to give the conveyance of the order its moving force, its power to make the one commanded be ruled by the order and somehow bound to execute it.

This does, however, mean that even if it does not necessarily signify the commander's own will, a command is something more than the mere expression of a certain order that the one commanded ought to carry out. Someone's saying "you ought to do this" does not necessarily constitute a command.[34] It may not do so, even if they say it voluntarily, and it is true, and you are genuinely bound or obliged to do the thing. This is because their saying it may not be the very thing that *makes* you bound or obliged to do the thing. It may not be what gives the order its power over you. It

---

33. *ST* I–II.17.4; cf. *ST* I–II.20.6*ad*3.
34. See *ST* I–II.17.1.

may be only an indication of an obligation that you are under, an obligation that originates, not from the one who says it to you, but (for example) from someone else's command, which the one who says it is only reminding you of. The distinction between the imperative and the indicative moods reflects this difference. But a genuine command need not be in the imperative mood. It can be in any mood: deprecative, optative, or even indicative.[35] Speaking of human legislation, Thomas says that a person "can impose a law upon the rational beings that are subject to him, insofar as by his precept, *or by any sort of pronouncement*, he imprints upon their mind a rule that is a principle of acting."[36] The way in which the rule is formulated is incidental. The point is that the commander, by pronouncing it, makes it be the rule. The utterance establishes or institutes some intelligible order of action as a rule for the agent or agents to whom it is issued, and imprints the rule on them so that it actually rule them. But what I am arguing is that, in order to rule, this imprint does not need to convey knowledge of the act of the commander's will, nor does it need to convey knowledge of the commander's act of uttering the command.

One sign that this is Thomas's view is his being perfectly happy to speak of God's commanding irrational beings and even of His legislating about them. God does not just move these beings. He impresses upon them a certain order—a work of His reason—in such a way that they themselves are inclined to act according to it.[37] We can come to understand these inclinations as signs of His command, but obviously the irrational beings themselves cannot do so, and they do not need to do so in order for their inclinations to regulate their actions.[38] If these inclinations cannot be called laws in the proper sense, this is simply because they are not themselves rational conceptions.[39] It is not because they do not function as signs of God's command. In the case of human beings, the first impression of the command of the eternal law is a rational conception of the very order contained in the command, together with a natural inclination to act according to this conception.[40] That is enough to make it a law in the full sense.[41]

---

35. The deprecative and optative moods express request or petition. See *In Peryerm.* I.7, 37, lines 78–88.

36. *ST* I-II.93.5 (emphasis added).

37. *ST* I-II.93.5. Likewise, Thomas speaks of a "confining" or "restraining" (*cohibitio*) of irrational things analogous to the obliging of men (*ST* I-II.93.4*ad*4; cf. I.22.2*obj*3/*ad*3).

38. On the inclinations in irrational beings as rules of their actions, see *ST* I-II.21.1.

39. See *ST* I-II.91.2*ad*3.

40. *ST* I-II.93.6.

41. Again, see *ST* I-II.91.2*ad*3.

The conception only needs to present the order as something that it is good and due for human beings to follow. That is how it induces them to comply with it. It does not need to include an indication of the order's having been commanded or of its being the object of a superior's will. It need involve nothing more than the knowledge of the order as something good and due to be observed.

It is also difficult to see how it could involve anything less. I say this because Geach, in trying to show how man may be said to have had a law promulgated to him by God even without his being aware of God and His government, proposes a solution that seems less than satisfactory. According to him, "You have had a city's parking regulation promulgated to you by a No Parking notice, even if you are under the illusion that you may ignore the notice and think it has been put up by a neighbour who dislikes cars."[42] But surely if this illusion were not your fault—if you could not reasonably have been expected to think otherwise—then even if the regulation in question had been generally promulgated, it would not yet have been promulgated *to you*; and you surely would be under no true obligation to abide by it. To the extent that a person is led to consider a dictate as nothing more than the expression of the whim of someone with no authority, how can that dictate be said to rule and measure the person's actions? In Geach's example, you apprehend the regulation and understand its meaning, but you do not apprehend it as a true regulation. You do not understand parking in this place to be in any way wrong or undue, and you cannot be expected to. How then are you obliged to avoid it? Surely the genuine promulgation of a law must bring it about that those subject to it understand it as a measure of their conduct, or at least that they can be blamed if they do not. Seeing the "general objectionableness of lying"[43] is not like seeing a No Parking notice that you think a neighbor has put up. It is like seeing the objectionableness of parking where the notice is posted. You may see that in light of the No Parking notice itself, but only if you take the notice as a sign of an authoritative rule. Geach wants to say that our seeing the objectionableness of lying does not depend on taking anything as a sign of God's institution of a rule prohibiting lying, and surely this is correct. But he does not explain how it is nevertheless the effect of such an institution, a promulgation of God's law. This is what I hope to have explained by the end of this chapter.

At this point, we can at least say that, for Thomas, there can be obedience to a governor's command, either out of instinct or out of deliberate

---

42. Geach, *God and the Soul*, 125.
43. See above, 27.

choice, without advertence to the governor's act of command itself.[44] Thomas is quite happy to speak of the understanding of the common principles of natural law as a sort of knowledge of the eternal law, even though it is not knowledge of the eternal law as it is in itself or as God's work, but only as in a "radiation" of it, a radiation of the "unchangeable truth."[45] Man judges things according to this truth, "insofar as he resolves them into it as into a mirror, according to the first intelligibles."[46] The good is itself one of these intelligibles, "among the firsts."[47]

Positive law given to human beings, whether by other human beings or by God, functions as law and carries its proper obligatory force only insofar as it is joined to the notification of the lawgiver's institution of it. But the precepts of natural law, as first and naturally understood, do not convey or constitute knowledge of God's institution of them. They do not need to, in order to serve as "rules that are principles of action." Human reason naturally understands them as true and as genuine rules measuring our actions, and they have their own aptitude to function as principles of action, inasmuch as the human will—the appetitive source of human action—is naturally inclined to comply with reason's dictates.

But the question remains, what role God's will plays in constituting the precepts of natural law as genuine rules that are principles of human action.

Now, in Thomas's view, man is God's creature, and the light of human reason is a concreated participation in the divine light.[48] So it is clear that the precepts of natural law do come from God somehow and that they somehow depend on His will. For it is by His will that He creates. However, it is still not quite clear whether or how the precepts are to be understood as laws that God voluntarily institutes, laws whose force depends on His will. For their power to function as principles of human action seems to consist simply in their being understood as true rules of human action; that is, as expressing an order that human action must comply with if it is to be right and good. It is by being so understood that they engage the human will's natural inclination to follow reason.

---

44. See above, 71. Irrational creatures participate in the eternal law precisely *per modum obedientiae* (*ST* I–II.93.5*ad*2).

45. *ST* I–II.93.2.

46. *ST* I.16.6*ad*1.

47. *In Eth.* I.1, 5, lines 150–51.

48. For Thomas, the light of reason is the power of the soul that he calls the "agent intellect." To call it concreated is not to deny that it is truly natural to man. It flows from human nature, which is to say, from the human form, the rational soul (*ST* I.77.6). That it is concreated only means that it accompanies the soul's creation (*ST* I.77.7*obj*1/*ad*1) and flows from the soul by virtue of God's creative influence.

To be sure, the human will is also concreated, and indeed it is itself a kind of likeness of the divine will.[49] But its natural inclination is not what makes the precepts true or the order that they express obligatory. It is not what makes them be the rule. The human will does not share in the action of instituting natural law, even in a secondary way. Natural law's force depends on the human will, not as what it is *from*, but only as what it is *over*.

This is clear, if for no other reason, because the precepts of natural law are *universal* truths. Each person naturally understand them to apply to all human conduct, as such, not just to his or her own case. Thomas does think that one can command oneself, and that sometimes one human being can command a whole group of human beings. But he certainly does not think that an individual human being can legislate for all human action, or even mediate such legislation. Nor does he think that the precepts of natural law are instituted by an agreement that all the members of mankind have reached. At most, one's will can be the source of commands given to oneself or to the particular group of individuals who do happen to be subject to one's will, to perform particular acts of compliance with the precepts of natural law. It cannot be the source of the precepts themselves, taken in the universal scope that they are naturally understood to have.

But if the force of the precepts of natural law consists simply in their being understood as true rules of human action, what role does God's will play in effecting it? Does their very truth depend on His will? Granted, our understanding them to be true depends on His will, insofar as it depends on His wanting to create us and to give us the light of reason. But this point applies to all of our understanding of truth, whether practical or speculative. It seems to present God, not as the commander and lawgiver who institutes a natural law, but only as the creator who brings us into being and the teacher who guides us on the path that naturally suits us. God "shows us good things." He is the Father of lights. He understands human nature and the rule of action that befits it, as directing toward its full perfection, or toward the good that is proportioned to it; and He has wanted to make a share in that understanding connatural to us, because such a share itself befits our nature. But it does not seem to be by His will that this order of action befits our nature. It does so on its own, in virtue of what it is and what human nature is. His communicating it to us only seems to be the production of an indication of an obligation that we are under, not by any voluntary institution of His, but simply as a natural consequence of our being what He has made us to be.

---

49. *ST* I.59.1.

This is how Suárez views the precepts of natural law. He grants that, even when they are considered simply as truths that a person understands, they do convey a certain obligation.[50] But it is not the obligation of a divine law. They obtain the force of a divine law only insofar as the person also understands them, or at least could and should understand them, as signs of God's legislative will—His very will to establish an obligation or a duty toward Him, as governor of the universe, to comply with them. What they convey on their own are only duties toward the person's own nature.[51] And even if the understanding of them as true must be seen as an effect of God's *creative* will, the notion of His *legislative* will—His will to establish obligations toward Himself—adds something to the notion of His creative will. By creation, man is given a share in the light of the divine intellect, but this relation to the divine intellect does not add any special obligation to the precepts of natural law beyond that which is intrinsic to them.[52] The notion of God as Father of lights does not of itself imply the notion of God as Lawgiver establishing obligations by His will and command.[53] "This will, prohibition, or precept of God is not the whole reason of the goodness or malice which is in the observance or transgression of natural law, but supposes in the acts themselves a certain necessary honesty or turpitude, and joins to them a special obligation of divine law. This assertion is gathered from Saint Thomas in the passages cited above."[54]

I think, however, that Thomas provides a way to see the precepts of natural as having, just in themselves, an obligatory force from God's will, as from a genuine lawgiver.[55] This will take some explaining, especially in the face of a certain objection, which I shall raise in a moment.

50. See above, 25–26.

51. See above, 25n97.

52. See Suárez, *De lege naturali*, 104–5 (*De legibus* II.vi.22, lines 20–30).

53. See Suárez, *De lege naturali*, 77–79, 92–94, 100 (*De legibus* II.vi.2; II.vi.11; II.vi.17).

54. *Haec Dei voluntas, prohibitio, aut praeceptio non est tota ratio bonitatis et malitiae quae est in observatione vel transgressione legis naturalis, sed supponit in ipsis actibus necessariam quamdam honestatem vel turpitudinem et illis adjungit specialem legis divinae obligationem. Haec assertio sumiter ex divo Thoma locis supra citatis* (Suárez, *De lege naturali*, 92 [*De legibus* II.vi.11, lines 1–5]). The "passages cited above" seem to be *ST* I–II.71.6*ad*4 and I–II.100.8*ad*2, which Suárez cites in *De lege naturali*, 84 (*De legibus* II.vi.5, lines 3–14). In that place he does not really explain how either passage supports his view, but he does give a reading of *ST* I–II.71.6*ad*4 in Suárez, *De lege naturali*, 101 (*De legibus* II.vi.18, lines 1–24). I discuss this reading below, 88.

55. Irwin, *Development of Ethics*, 553–56, offers what seems to me to be a quite Suárezian reading of Aquinas on this matter. In my opinion, the texts that Irwin cites do not bear it out.

First of all, man is after all only a part of God's creation. *If* natural law is a true law, this is only insofar as it is a share in the eternal law, which rules everything. The eternal law orders all things to the common good of the universe. Can we not then see the precepts of natural law as voluntarily instituted by God, as by a true commander and governor and lawgiver, in view of the common good of the universe? Even if it is not by signifying His will that these precepts direct man toward his own proper good, it would be by virtue of His will that the order toward man's proper good is required for the good of the universe in the first place. God was not bound to create man. He wanted to do so, Thomas insists, not as a matter of justice toward man or any creature or even the universe as a whole, but out of the sheer goodness of His will.[56] But He also, out of His goodness, wanted man's existence and good to be integrated into the order toward the good of the universe as a whole. God's will to create man and to convey the precepts of natural law to him, then, could be seen as part of His will to institute the order toward the common good of the universe, which on the whole would be His will to institute the eternal law. The precepts of natural law could then be seen as the effects of that institution.

To this account, however, someone might object that not even it seems to succeed in showing the proper obligatory force of the precepts of natural law, which is nothing but their truth, to be the effect of any legal institution, even a divine one. It only shows how they might carry additional force by divine institution. The argument for this objection would run as follows.

Any ordination that a lawgiver institutes logically presupposes certain things. Most fundamentally, it presupposes the common good toward which the ordination directs those to whom it is given. The ultimate common good is the absolutely ultimate end, and as such, its own nature is the very first principle upon which the whole ordination of law depends. But if the law presupposes what the common good is, then it also seems to presuppose what the community is that the lawgiver governs for the sake of that good. God's will to create man, however, does not seem to presuppose any of these things. For His will to create man is simply a part of His will to create the whole universe, and obviously this will does not *presuppose* what the community is that He governs. It rather constitutes that community. What it presupposes is only the goodness of His own will. Creation itself, God's will to create, and even His will to govern the universe of His creatures, seem to be pre-legislative or pre-governmental determinations, determinations that any genuine legislation on His part logically presupposes.

---

56. *ST* I.21.4.

For the same reason, the essential constitution of the common good of the universe does not seem to be something that God's will to create the universe presupposes. In its essentials, the constitution of the common good of the universe seems to be a direct function of the constitution of the universe itself. It is the good that is directly proportioned to the universe as a whole. Hence it is itself determined by the very will to create the universe. And given the constitution of the universe and its proportionate common good, there is a certain determinate rule or order of it, toward that good, that naturally befits it. This rule does not seem to depend on any additional determination of God's will, any properly legislative determination. He may order the world to some *further* end or ends, beyond what its own makeup requires, and there may be various particular ways of ordering it to its essential good; and these orders may depend on His legislative will. But the essential good itself and the essentials of the order to it do not seem to depend on that.

Moreover, the common good of the universe is what it is, in part, just *because* man is part of the universe. So even if man exists only by God's will for the good of the universe, it does not seem to be by this will that either man's good, or the naturally suitable order of man's actions to it, are what they are. Rather, this will seems to presuppose these things. But the truth of the precepts of natural law consists in their expressing these very things. Granted, God eternally knows that truth, and if this knowledge, or His conception of it, is what is meant by the "eternal law," then it would pertain to the eternal law. But then the eternal law itself is not being taken as a full-fledged law, one that He has instituted voluntarily in view of a common good. Any true law, voluntarily instituted by Him, would seem to be a kind of positive law. It would presuppose the constitution of the community that it governs and the essential order of the community's members to the community's good, and it would merely confirm that order and add further determinations to it.

In short, the objection is that the precepts of natural law do not seem to get their first, intrinsic force from God's legislative will. At most, it seems, God's legislative will only adds a further obligatoriness to them, a further respect in which man's compliance with them is required or due. In addition to being required for the sake of the good of conformity with his own reason, compliance with them is also required for the sake of obedience to God's will as the governor of the universe. By willing to govern the universe, and to govern man as a part of it, God makes man's compliance with natural law a matter of justice toward Himself. God can justly punish man for not complying with it, just as human legislators can justly punish citizens for not complying with certain portions of natural law. Even though they did not institute natural law, they can add a certain force to it, by issuing their own precepts to observe the things that it requires.[57] But then, as in the case of human legislators, this additional obligation to observe the precepts of natural law, as a matter of justice toward the divine legislator, evidently requires knowing that He exists, that He governs the universe, and that the precepts of natural law are included in the requirements of His governance. This knowledge involves considerable additions to the understanding of the precepts just in themselves. If it is only in respect of this obligation toward God that the precepts of natural law can properly be called laws, then the naturalness of the promulgation of natural law becomes a question and needs to be argued for—as Suárez saw plainly.[58]

Nevertheless I think it is clear that this is not Thomas's view. He wants to say that the eternal law is a full-fledged law, and that it is the source even of the intrinsic force of the precepts of natural law. It is the source of the obligation that they carry just by being understood by us as true, their moral obligation. It is the source of their very truth. First I shall call attention to a text that explains why I say that this must be Thomas's position, and then I shall try to show how he can answer the objection just presented.

ETERNAL LAW AND POSITIVE LAW

The text appears in the *Summa theologiae* prior to the treatise on law, near the start of the treatise on sin. It refers explicitly to the eternal law, and implicitly to natural law. In the article to which it belongs, I–II.71.6, Thomas asks whether Augustine has suitably defined sin as "a word or deed or desire contrary to the eternal law." The passage that interests me is a reply to one of the article's objections. But first let me lay out the reasoning in the corpus. There Thomas explains Augustine's definition in such a way as to show its suitability. A sin, Thomas says, is nothing other than a bad human act. A human act is a voluntary act, either elicited from the will or commanded by it. It is bad "insofar as it lacks due commensuration." This is to say that it does not measure up to its rule. The rule of the human will is twofold. Its proximate and homogeneous rule is human reason itself. But its primary rule is the eternal law, which is, as it were, the reason of God. And thus Augustine's definition posits two factors. One, which is the "word or deed or desire," pertains to the substance of the human act and has a material role in sin. It is the subject of which sin is predicated. The other factor is being

---

57. See *ST* I–II.95.2.
58. See above, 21–23 and 81.

against the eternal law. This pertains to the sin's badness, its *ratio mali*. It has a formal role. It is what constitutes the sin's sinfulness.

What we should especially notice about this discussion is how Thomas understands the badness of sin. It essentially consists in the sin's failing to measure up to its rule. This failure is not the result of the sin's being bad. It is rather the very cause, in the sense of the formal principle, of the sin's being bad.

With this point in mind, consider the article's fourth objection and its reply.

> *Objection*: Something is said to be forbidden by the fact that it is against the law. Not all sins, however, are bad because they are forbidden, but rather some are forbidden because they are bad. So in the general definition of sin it should not say that sin is against the law of God.
>
> *Reply*: When it is said that not every sin is bad because it is forbidden, this is understood of a prohibition that is made according to positive right (*ius positivum*). But if one refers to natural right (*ius naturale*), which is primarily contained in the eternal law, and secondarily in the natural forum (*naturale iudicatorium*) of human reason, then every sin is bad because it is forbidden. For by the very fact that it is disordered (*ex hoc enim ipso quod est inordinatum, iuri naturali repugnat*), it is repugnant to natural right (*iuri naturali repugnat*).[59]

Let me gloss this, starting with the notions of positive right and natural right. These are not quite the same as positive law and natural law. They are rather things that are regulated by such laws. They are things that are right or well adjusted, things that are just—hence the term *ius*.[60] Law, properly speaking, is a certain conception (*ratio*) of what is right or just, by which reason determines a work that is just. It is a kind of rule of prudence.[61] But there are two ways of being right or just.[62] One is by being according to a rule established by a common agreement, either private or public. This is

---

59. *ST* I-II.71.6obj4/ad4. Aquinas's discussion here appears to express, in very condensed form, the thought running through Augustine's *De libero arbitrio*, 1.3.6–1.6.15. Augustine begins by observing that certain things are not evil because "temporal law" (law that can justly be changed in the course of time) forbids them, but rather they are forbidden because they are evil; and he concludes by affirming the existence of another, atemporal or eternal law from which everything just and lawful in temporal law is derived.

60. See *ST* II-II.57.1.

61. *ST* II-II.57.1ad2.

62. *ST* II-II.57.2.

positive right. Another way of being right or just is "by the very nature of the thing." I shall consider what this means shortly. Notice, however, that Thomas follows Aristotle in holding that what is naturally right, among human beings, is not altogether immutable. This, remarkably, is because human nature itself is not always right. The human will is part of human nature, and its disposition can be either right or wrong. And when a person's will goes wrong, the right or just way to treat him changes.[63] Nevertheless, Thomas insists, there are some forms of action that are always wrong, such as theft or adultery.[64] Human agreement or institution cannot make what is repugnant to the very essence of the just or the right be right.[65] It cannot run contrary to natural right, making right what is naturally wrong. It can only make right or wrong things that in their own nature are indifferent. This power is not itself the effect of human agreement. Not to comply with a valid human law is itself contrary to natural right.

However, not everything dictated by humanly posited law is *merely* positive right. Human law can also dictate things that are naturally right and prohibit things that are naturally wrong. This is clear because it can add its own sanctions to such things. Its doing so is itself naturally right. And thus, as the reply about the definition of sin says, of the things that are contrary to positive right, some are bad only because they are prohibited—only by virtue of the common agreement or institution—while others are prohibited by that institution because they are already bad. They are already contrary to natural right.

This last point, moreover, applies also to divine law, in the sense of law divinely promulgated. Some things are bad because they are prohibited by this law—merely *ex institutione*, as matters of purely positive right—while others are prohibited by it because they are already bad, contrary to natural right.[66] However, the rectitude of some things that pertain to natural right in divine law is hidden to man.[67] These things require "divine instruction"

---

63. *ST* II-II.57.2*ad*1. Thomas does not mean that an essential principle of man, something pertaining to man's very definition, can change or go wrong. The will is not identical with man's soul or substantial form. But it flows necessarily from his soul, and in this sense it pertains to his nature.

64. *ST* II-II.57.2*ad*2.

65. See *In Eth.* V.12, 306–7, lines 197–207: there is such a thing as the essence (*ratio*) of justice, and what belongs to this cannot change. Thomas certainly finds Aristotle judging some kinds of action to be bad under any circumstances whatever. See *In Eth.* II.7, 99–100, lines 146–90 (on Aristotle, *Nicomachean Ethics* II.6, 1107a8–27).

66. *ST* II-II.57.2*ad*3; I-II.99.3*ad*2.

67. *ST* II-II.57.2*ad*3.

and must be taken on faith.⁶⁸ Evidently, with respect to this, divine law is a revelation of eternal law that goes beyond natural law. By it we can have recourse to the eternal law in matters that mere natural reason cannot determine.⁶⁹ Natural law, properly speaking, covers only that portion of natural right which natural reason can determine.

I mention natural law because I-II.71.6ad4 implicitly refers to it. It speaks of what is contained "in the natural forum"—*in naturali iudicatorio*—of human reason. Thomas takes the expression *naturale iudicatorium* as a way of referring to *synderesis*.⁷⁰ This is the intellectual habit of first principles of practical reason. It is that which contains the precepts of natural law.

But now consider what the reply about the definition of sin says about the things that are repugnant to natural right. These things, *all* of them, are bad because prohibited. This is because each of them is bad, repugnant to natural right, "by the very fact that it is disordered." This is just another way of saying that its badness consists in its being wrong, which in turn consists in its not measuring up to its rule. That is what Thomas said in the body of the article. He also said it earlier in the *Summa*, when he asked whether a human act, insofar as it is good or bad, has the nature of rectitude or sin. "Every voluntary act is bad by the fact that it falls short of the order of reason and the eternal law, and every good act agrees with reason and the eternal law."⁷¹

This is an absolutely crucial point. Natural right is what is right "according to the nature of the thing." There is also what is wrong "according to the nature of thing." There are "intrinsically good acts" and "intrinsically bad acts." But this does not mean a goodness or a badness that does not consist in a relation to a rule. The goodness or badness of all human acts—their proper goodness or badness, which is moral goodness and badness—consists in their relation to their twofold rule of human reason and the eternal law.⁷² Natural right is what is "contained in" or determined by this rule. An intrinsically good act is one which, just by virtue of what it is in itself, agrees

---

68. For the expression "divine instruction" and some examples, see *ST* I-II.100.1 (quoted below, 220–21). The precept of faith is of this sort; see above, 70.

69. See *ST* I-II.19.4; I-II.71.6ad5.

70. See *ST* I.79.12obj3/ad3; I.79.13; *De ver.* 16.1obj9/ad9; 16.1obj.15/ad15; 17.1obj5/ad5; 17.2obj1/ad1. I suppose that he uses this expression in *ST* I-II.71.6ad4 because of the verbal connection between *iudicatorium* and *ius*. Notice, in any case, that this expression puts reason in the position, not of a lawgiver, but of a judge, with the task of applying or using the law as a principle of judgment.

71. *ST* I-II.21.1.

72. See also *ST* I-II.18.5; I-II.19.3.

with the rule. An intrinsically bad one is one which, by virtue of what it is in itself, falls short of the rule. When Thomas speaks of positive law making what is originally indifferent be right or wrong, what "originally indifferent" means is what is originally, in itself, neither required nor prohibited by eternal and natural law.

At this point I wish to call particular attention to the fact that Suárez thinks the reasoning in *ST* I-II.71.6*ad*4, taken at face value, actually proves the contrary of what Thomas says. Suárez thinks this passage makes even the things repugnant to natural right be prohibited because they are wrong and bad.[73] He reads the last sentence—*ex hoc enim ipso quod est inordinatum, iuri naturali repugnat*—as saying that because a sin is bad (*inordinatum*), it is repugnant to natural and eternal law (*ius naturale*). This fits with Suárez's own view, that the eternal law supposes an order of human morality—of the *honestum* and *inhonestum* for man—that it does not institute.[74] Suárez argues that what Thomas really means is that the prohibitions of eternal law only add a further badness and disorder to immoral things, making them also offenses and injustices toward God.

Suárez's reading of that last sentence of I-II.71.6*ad*4, however, seems forced. For one thing, Thomas does not make *ius* synonymous with *lex*. What *ius* properly means is a certain "thing," a right or just thing, *res iusta*. *Lex*, properly speaking, is an intelligible conception that establishes or measures or determines *ius*—a kind of formulation of it, a *ratio iuris*.[75] And more importantly, as just discussed, Thomas makes even the intrinsic moral badness of certain acts a matter of their relation to their rule, the rule that they are fit to be measured by, just because they are human acts. A human act's being disordered just is its lacking the order prescribed by the eternal law and by natural reason. That makes it a bad act, one contrary to that which is naturally due or a matter of justice, *ius naturale*.[76]

Human acts are naturally measured by reason because reason is their very source. This is why those that deviate from the rule of reason are truly bad, deviating from the direction inherent in their own principle. There is no such thing as a human act that does not depend on reason or presuppose reason's naturally understood principles. And human acts are also naturally apt to be measured by the eternal law, inasmuch as the eternal law is the very

---

73. See Suárez, *De lege naturali*, 101 (*De legibus* II.vi.18, lines 1–24); cf. Suárez, *De lege naturali*, 92–94 (*De legibus* II.vi.11, lines 1–42). Notice that this is also how Lottin views the things prohibited by natural law. See above, 6.

74. See above, 25–26.

75. *ST* II-II.57.1*ad*2.

76. Cf. *ST* I.21.1*ad*3.

source of human reason and its rule.[77] The rule of human reason truly rules because and insofar as it is a share in the eternal law. This is how it has its intrinsic obligatory force, its force of moral obligation, which is nothing other than its declaring truly how we ought and ought not to act, such that our acts cannot be good, or avoid being bad, except by conformity with it. I shall have more to say about the obligatory force of the precepts of natural law in chapter 6. But what I now want to try to show is how, on Aquinas's view, the eternal law so considered—as the source from which the precepts of natural law have their truth and intrinsic obligatory force—can be understood as a genuine law, proceeding from God's reasonable will as governor of the universe directing all things toward the common good of the universe.

The objection that I laid out, in the previous section of this chapter, against this way of understanding the eternal law, comes down to this: even though the precepts of natural law come from God, and indeed from His will to create man and to show him the order of conduct that suits him according to his nature, this cannot by itself be understood as the promulgation of a genuine law. This is because God's will, so considered, is prior to anything that He does or institutes as the governor directing toward the common good of the universe. For it is prior to the very constitution of the universe and hence prior even to the determination of the essential nature of the universe's good. Any directing toward that good presupposes the determination of the universe's nature. God's willing that good supposes His having preconceived it; and this supposes His having preconceived the community that it would be the good of. But it is only out of the sheer goodness of His will, freely willing to bring this community into being, that He establishes Himself as its governor and makes its proportionate good a genuine end toward which to direct the actions of anything in it. This determination of His will (so the objection runs) is not itself a legislative act. Only the directives issued by Him on the supposition of this community, its good, and His authority over it, would be full-fledged laws. But that very supposition brings with it, independently of any directive issued by Him as governor, certain naturally valid rules for the community's activities, rules entailed by its own nature and the nature of its proportionate good. In His role as governor, He may issue dictates that confirm these rules, or to their intrinsic validity the force of His authority; and in Him those dictates are indeed eternal, and can be called an eternal law. But they would not be what first make the naturally valid rules valid. They would not be what make the precepts of natural law true and obligatory. They would only add the force of His governing authority. This force would accrue to the dictates of reason insofar as these are seen

77. See *ST* I–II.19.4.

as signs of His legislative will. On this account, the eternal law would indeed function in the same way as any positive law does.[78] Its dictates would oblige only insofar as their authoritative institution is known or at least knowable.

The fundamental flaw in this objection, it seems to me, is its way of understanding God's will to create. I do not mean that He does not create freely or out of the sheer goodness of His will. Of course He does. But what *is* the sheer goodness of His will? For Thomas, it is His perfect love of His own goodness. It is a love that both rejoices in that good and tends toward communicating it to others, not in order to receive anything back from them, but simply because that goodness is so good and because that love is so intense. That goodness is the entire reason for His love of whatever else He loves. And what is more—here is the decisive point, which I think is far too neglected in discussions of law in Aquinas—God's perfect goodness is itself the primary and highest good of the universe. It is the common good *par excellence*. Thomas could hardly be clearer about this. God is "absolutely the universal good," which it is natural for all things to love more than they love themselves, as that to which they primarily belong.[79] And thus, "the end of divine governance is God Himself, nor is His law other than Himself."[80]

This, by the way, is not solely Thomas the theologian speaking:

> Since the origin of things is something extrinsic to the whole universe, namely God, the end of things must likewise be a certain extrinsic good. And this is clear from reason. For it is manifest that the good has the character of an end. Hence, the end of any given particular thing is a certain particular good, whereas the universal end of all things is a certain universal good. But a universal good is that which is good per se and through its essence; that is, it is the very essence of goodness, whereas a particular good is a good by participation (*est participative bonum*). Now it is clear that within the whole universe of creatures there is no good which is not a good by participation. Hence the good that is the end of the whole universe must be extrinsic to the whole universe.[81]

---

78. Irwin simply takes it for granted that, for Aquinas, what God's prescription establishes is positive right and presupposes natural right. See Irwin, *Development of Ethics*, 554.

79. *ST* I.60.5.

80. *ST* I.91.1*ad*3. On God as the highest common good, see Dewan, "Divinity of the Common Good," 228–32.

81. *ST* I.103.2.

Thomas finds this view presented quite explicitly in Book XII of Aristotle's *Metaphysics*.[82] On Thomas's reading, Aristotle's first unmoved mover, which Aristotle himself calls a God, relates to the world as a commander and lord exercising providence over all things.[83] To be sure, Thomas goes beyond Aristotle in explicitly asserting the immediacy of God's providence over contingent particulars and the freedom with which He institutes the world. But Thomas thinks these points too are within the scope of philosophy, specifically of metaphysics.[84]

Now there is no distinction, in God, between His substance and His common or universal goodness.[85] And it is this goodness of His that is the reason for His love of whatever He loves. "The good of the whole universe is what is apprehended by God, who is the maker and governor of the universe, whence it is that whatever He wills, He wills under the aspect of the common good that is His goodness, which is the good of the whole universe."[86] *Whatever* He wills, He wills by reason of the common good that is His goodness. God's will for His goodness, the goodness that is maximally common, in no way presupposes His willing something else.

What this implies, I believe, is that, with respect to creatures, there is no such thing as God's pre-legislative or pre-governmental will. His will as maker and His will as governor are one and the same. "It is according to the same intelligibility (*secundum eandem rationem*) that it belongs to God to be the governor of things and to be their cause, because it belongs to the same being to produce a thing and to give it perfection, which pertains to a governor."[87] Again, God's governance is the execution of His providence, which is "nothing other than the plan of the order of things toward their end"; and "it is necessary that all things, just insofar as they participate in being, be subject to divine providence."[88] And the eternal law is nothing other than the plan of providence insofar as it regulates the inclinations of creatures toward their proper acts and ends. This means that it regulates the very essences of creatures. For the most elementary end and good of a creature is its existence, and it is inclined to its existence by the very principles of its essence, the production of which goes hand in hand with the creation

---

82. See *In Meta.* XII, lect. 12, §2628–31.
83. See *De sub. sep.* cap. 3 (near the end).
84. See *In Peryerm.* I.14, 76–79, lines 321–461; *In Meta.* VI, lect. 3; XII, lect. 7.
85. *ST* I.60.5*ad*5.
86. *ST* I–II.19.10.
87. *ST* I.103.5.
88. *ST* I.22.2.

of it.[89] The command by which things are brought into being, God's creative fiat, must be understood not only as the work of an artist or a maker but also as the work of a governor and legislator. Every effect of His in creatures, even their very being, falls under His providence, and hence under the eternal law ordering things to the highest common good, the absolutely last end, which is Himself.

> Since every agent acts for the sake of an end, the ordering of effects toward their end extends as far as the first agent's causality does. . . . But the causality of God, who is the first agent, extends to all beings. . . . Hence, everything that has being in any way must be ordered by God toward its end, in accordance with what the Apostle says in Romans 13.1: "The things that are from God are ordered by God." Therefore, since, as has been explained, God's providence is nothing other than a plan for ordering things toward their end, it must be the case that all things, insofar as they participate in being, are to that extent subject to God's providence.[90]

Surely it is clear that, on Thomas's view, what God has planned for the universe as a whole does not merely presuppose the constitutions of various components of it that He has planned to make. The components, the parts, are planned in view of the constitution of the whole. The form that He primarily intends *in* things is the good of the order of the whole universe.[91] But that in turn is intended for the sake of the good that is beyond the universe, the divine good.[92]

Moreover, insofar as it regards creatures, the rule contained in the eternal law is not only something conceived by God's intellect, but also something that He voluntary and freely institutes.[93] The world and its order do not flow from His will by necessity. His determination to create rather than not to create, and to create what He actually has created rather than something else, is one that He freely gives to Himself.[94] It is a choice, an eternal one. To be sure, whatever God wills concerning creatures must be

---

89. On the principles of a thing's essence—its matter and form—as inclinations toward its being, see *ST* I.59.2. On creation as the production of a thing in being together with all of its principles, see *ST* I.45.4*ad*2. (Creatures receive their being through their forms: *De ver.* 27.1*ad*3.)

90. *ST* I.22.2.

91. *ST* I.49.2.

92. *ST* I.103.2.

93. *ST* I.19.3,5,10.

94. On God's will as "self-determining," see *ST* I.19.3*ad*5.

Natural Law, God's Will, and Positive Law

in accordance with His own goodness and with His wisdom. It must be "reasonable."[95] But His goodness is out of all proportion to every possible creature and order of creatures. So His wisdom allows for alternatives in what He creates. It is in the nature of His will to be able to determine itself to any (or none) of them.[96]

> The order which is imposed on things by God's wisdom, and in which the nature of justice consists, does not exhaust God's wisdom in such a way that the divine wisdom is limited to just this order. For it is clear that the whole conception of the order which someone who is wise imposes on the things he has made is taken from the end. Therefore, when an end is exactly proportioned to the things that have been made for the sake of that end, the wisdom of the maker is restricted to some determinate order. But God's goodness is an end that immeasurably exceeds created things. Hence, God's wisdom is not determined to any particular order of things in such a way that no other course of things could flow from it.[97]

The order naturally found in the things that actually exist is exactly the one suited to them. It is required by or due to them according to their own natures. Nevertheless God could have instituted any one of indefinitely many different sets of things, to which a different order would have been due, and He would have impressed that order upon them.[98] But whatever He chose would be for the sake of His own goodness. Whatever order He instituted would itself be, by that very institution, ordered to that goodness. God's goodness, which is God, is the primary common good. He is the "universal good without qualification" (*bonum universale simpliciter*).[99] The order that is inherent in the universe is also a common good and end toward which He directs things, but it is a strictly secondary end.[100] It is itself ordered toward His goodness, by a wise dictate of His reasonable will.

> There is a twofold order to be considered in things. One is that by which something created is ordered to something else created. ... Another order is that by which all created things are ordered to God. ... Thus therefore the due in God's work can be taken in two ways: either according as something is owed to God, or

---

95. *ST* I–II.93.4*ad*1.
96. See *ST* I.19.3*ad*5.
97. *ST* I.25.5.
98. *ST* I.25.5*ad*2/*ad*3.
99. *ST* I.60.5*ad*3.
100. See *In Meta.* XII, lect. 12, §2630–31.

according as something is owed to a created thing... according to the proportion (*rationem*) of its nature and condition. But this due depends on the first; for that is due to each which is ordered to it according to the order of divine wisdom.[101]

We can say, then, that the very command by which God institutes the community of the universe, all the way down to the very natures or essences of its members, is an "ordination of reason, for the common good, by the one who has care of the community."

Now, I grant that His goodness can actually be considered a "common" good only relative to some community that it is the good of. And it is only by His free determination that such a community exists. But this is a trivial point. For one thing, even if calling His goodness a common good requires considering it in relation to a multitude of beings, even considered just in itself it can hardly be regarded as a "private" good. It is eminently, supereminently, communicable. And more importantly, His decision to institute a community does not in any way determine the constitution of this highest common good.[102] Its own nature—the divine nature—is in no way a function of the natures of the many things that it is the good of. What is a function of their natures is only the suitable order among them. This too is a common good, but it is secondary. The common good that the eternal law must be understood to presuppose is the divine good alone. It does not itself suppose any creaturely nature or creaturely good. The dictate of the eternal law does not presuppose the natures of things. It institutes them. Hence, the natures of things and the orders toward the ends that are proportioned to their natures, singly and as a community, can be seen as the effect of the eternal law, understood as a law enacted by the reasonable will of God for the common good—the common good of the very universe that is ordained to exist by that law.

We can even say this: it is only by virtue of the eternal law that anything good in creatures is unqualifiedly good, and anything bad, unqualifiedly bad. God's goodness is the primary goodness—the very essence of goodness. It

---

101. *ST* I.21.1*ad*3. See *ST* I.105.6, esp. *obj*2/*ad*2.

102. God's own nature is in no way a function of anything in any way distinct from it. He is not only the "universal overseer (*provisor*) of all being" (*ST* I.22.2*ad*2), but also the cause of the very "nature of being" that created things commonly share in (*ST* I.45.5*ad*1). He does not share in it. He has, and is, His own nature of being; this is proper to Him, containing in a supereminent way all the perfection of being and, without detriment to its simplicity, every other perfection as well (*ST* I.4.2). It is the *cause* of the common nature of being. Thus His will can "be understood as standing outside the order of beings (*extra ordinem entium*), as a cause pouring forth the whole of being (*totum ens*) and all its differences" (*In Peryerm.* I.14, 78, lines 438–41).

is therefore the measure of the goodness of everything else. Nothing else is truly good except insofar as it is ordered to His goodness. And creatures are ordered to His goodness only by His own voluntary ordination.

This is not to say that creatures, considered just in themselves, have no goodness. It is not that a creature's goodness consists in nothing but its relation to God's goodness and God's will. Creatures have goodness just insofar as they have being. Their being is a likeness of the divine goodness. But even this goodness is the effect of God's ordination. Creatures are unqualifiedly good, and not bad, only insofar as they proceed from the will of the highest good, for the sake of the highest good.[103] Whatever is contrary to God's will and God's law is by that very fact not in order toward the highest good and is therefore bad.

Thomas says that God does not love things because they are good; rather, they are good because He loves them.[104] The good is what all desire. What everything desires is its perfection.[105] Perfection is desirable on its own account. It is intrinsically apt to be desired. Nevertheless it is apt to be desired on its own account only by what it is the perfection of, what has the nature to which it is proportioned. God does not desire or will the perfection of a creature simply on its own account. He wills it entirely on account of His own goodness and perfection, of which it constitutes a certain likeness. But He also wills that it be desirable on its own account, as His is; which is to say, He wills that there be something that it is or can be the perfection of, something by which it is fit and apt and due to be desired on its own account. And He wills that things actually do love and desire their proportionate goods, as He loves His. All things have inclination toward their own perfection, because they are effects of the divine will and therefore resemble it.[106] Inclination to its good pertains to every nature, insofar as it is a nature. But nothing is actually a nature independently of God's will. What is independent of His will is only His conception of the nature. The object of this conception has no actual perfection and no actual inclination except through His will. Thomas quotes Augustine: "All natures have it from God that they are natures."[107] And so, as Thomas says, God is the very reason why the creature's good is good.[108]

---

103. See *ST* I.6.4.
104. *ST* I.20.2; I.20.3.
105. *ST* I.5.1.
106. See *ST* I.59.1; I.19.1.
107. *ST* I–II.71.2ad4; Augustine, *De libero arbitrio* 3.15.42.
108. *ST* I.60.5ad1.

If this holds generally for the intrinsic perfection and goodness of things, it also holds for their actions. No action would be right or good if it were not according to the order toward God's goodness, as freely determined by His will. This is not to say that the consideration of an action just in itself offers no basis for judging it right or good, wrong or bad. But again, even to judge an action in itself is to judge it in relation to its agent. To consider an action in itself just is to consider it as proceeding from its agent.[109] If, so considered, it can be judged right or wrong, good or bad, it is because there is something in its agent that functions as a measure or rule by which to judge it. In irrational agents, this rule is their natural inclination. In rational agents, it is the practical truth that they have grasped (or ought to have grasped), starting from the practical truths that they naturally understand in light of their natural understanding of their due good, which is the good proportioned to their nature. In both cases, then, the rule is a function of the agent's nature. But the nature determines a rule only because God has instituted the nature. Without His institution, the natural inclination would not be actually right, nor would the natural understanding be actually true. Neither would they be actually wrong or false, or even actually indifferent. They would not exist. They would not be actually anything, but only possibilities that He discerns in His own actuality. The principles that naturally measure the actions of things do so only by God's voluntary institution of the natures that underlie those principles, such as the nature of man and of human reason.

To say that actions contrary to a creature's natural principles are wrong and bad because they are prohibited by God does not mean that, even given those principles, He could just as well have permitted or even commanded the creature to act contrary to them. The principles themselves already *are* certain participations in His eternal law, applications of the order dictated by it. God's legislative action is really the *cause* of nature and of nature's own intrinsic causality and order. It is not a superimposed, alien influence. This way of understanding God—as cause of the natures of things—is so front and center in Thomas's mind that, on his view, the denial of natural right can lead to the conclusion that there is no such thing as sin against God. "There were some, as the Philosopher says, who believed that nothing is naturally just or, consequently, unjust, but only as posited by human law. And accordingly no sin was imputed as being against God."[110]

---

109. See *ST* III.13.1*ad*2.

110. *In Rom.* V, lect. 4, §428. The reference is to Aristotle, *Nicomachean Ethics* V.10, 1134b18–27.

Perhaps the most crucial point, however, is this: the eternal law's being the work of God's free will does not mean that it is a kind of positive law. The order that it establishes is not an order of positive right. The actions that the eternal law prohibits, considered in themselves and apart from the law, are not merely indifferent. They are not indifferent in themselves, because they are contrary to the order of the natures of their own agents. The eternal law determines even the things that pertain to natural right. It is true that none of the things that the eternal law prohibits are prohibited because they are already bad in themselves. All are bad because the eternal law prohibits them. But the thought is not that, in themselves, they are indifferent and that the eternal law makes them bad. It is that the eternal law makes them be bad in themselves. It is true that we consider them and see their badness before we are even aware of their relation to the eternal law. But this does not mean that their badness is not the effect of the eternal law's prohibition. It only means that what is prior in our understanding is not prior in the nature of things or from the standpoint of wisdom.

Suárez, however, does treat what is prior to us as though it were also prior in the nature of things. He takes the intrinsic goodness or badness of action to be something that God's legislative will and God's law merely presuppose. It is Suárez who is making the eternal law a kind of positive law. And he is also making the precepts of natural law, considered precisely as true laws, to function in the way that positive laws function in those who are subject to them. He makes their legality consist in their serving as signs of the legislator's will.

As I shall discuss in greater detail in chapter 5, for Thomas the precepts of natural law are naturally formed in light of man's natural understanding of the common nature of the good and the specific nature of the human good. The precepts are immediately understood as true, and as measuring human actions, in virtue of themselves. And there are human actions that by their very nature comply with these precepts, and others that by their nature violate them. The former are thereby naturally right and good, and the latter are naturally wrong and bad. Of themselves, these precepts truly oblige, and human actions are truly measured by them. But it is the divine institution itself that gives them their intrinsic power to oblige and to measure. Only a divine institution can have this effect, because only God can institute the very natures and natural principles of things. In doing so, He instills something of His institution's own directing and moving power. It is in this way that all natural things, rational and irrational, are subject to the eternal law.[111] In man's case, He instills it as a kind of intelligible light,

---

111. See *ST* I–II.93.5.

a light that binds. It binds just by showing us truth about what is right and wrong, good and bad, in our conduct. But that truth ultimately depends on God's will. Even the truth of the first principles of practical reason depends on His will.

It does so even though the principles cannot be false. They are naturally, necessarily true. Even the natural, absolute necessities in creatures are the effect of God's will and of the eternal law.[112] The fact that the principles are self-evident, known to be true in virtue of themselves, does not mean that their truth has no other cause. Their truth depends, immediately, on the intelligibilities signified by the terms of which the principles are composed. These intelligibilities are in turn gathered from natural things—things created by God. The primary intelligibilities, those which underlie the most common principles, are those of being and its attendants (which include the good). The common nature of being is God's proper effect. It has no other cause.[113] And He is a cause that produces its effect voluntarily and freely.

It is clear, I hope, that I do not mean that God could have made the truths that naturally rule and measure human action—the action of beings that have human nature—be other than they are. Now on Suárez's view, these truths are necessary, and therefore, although they do flow from God's intellect, their truth is not the effect of His free will. "The dictates of natural reason . . . are intrinsically necessary, and independent of all will, even the divine, and prior in intelligibility (*secundum rationem*) to that [will] by which He freely wills anything."[114] This means that what He freely wills does not account for those dictates; rather, they account for at least some of what He freely wills—and not only for particular actions or events that He wills, but also, as we saw earlier, for what He wills as legislator.[115] Thomas would surely agree that these dictates are intrinsically necessary. But I do not think he would accept the conclusion. The dictates of natural reason are propositions. They are necessarily true; they cannot be false. Their not being false does not depend on God's free will. However, this does not entail that the propositions themselves, or even their being true, does not depend on His

---

112. See *ST* I-II.93.4, esp. *ad*4; *ST* I.22.2*ad*3; I.44.1*ad*2; I.50.5*ad*3; *In Peryerm*. I.14, 78, lines 437–54.

113. *ST* I-II.66.5*ad*4. In one place Thomas presents the principle of non-contradiction as the effect of God's providence, inasmuch as it supposes the existence of things whose natures are distinct from their own negations—which is to say, things that have the nature of *beings* (*De ver*. 5.2*ad*7). Pertinent is *ST* I.16.1*obj*1/*ad*1.

114. *Dictamina rationis naturalis . . . sunt intrinsece necessaria et independentia ab omni voluntate, etiam divina, et priora secundum rationem qua illa libere aliquid velit* (Suárez, *De lege naturali*, 76–77 [*De legibus* II.vi.1, lines 8–11]). See also Suárez, *De lege naturali*, 104 (*De legibus* II.vi.22, lines 7–24).

115. See above, 22.

free will. For they are not *actually* true unless and until they actually exist in the human mind, and their actually existing in a human mind depends on His free will.[116] This is not because He could have willed that these dictates not be self-evident to the human mind; that would be a disorder, contrary to what is due to human nature.[117] It is because He could have willed that no human being and no human mind exist at all. Its being *right* that any human being exists depends on His free will, the will by which He orders things to His good. This is a legislative will. And it is only when a human being exists, with a human mind that knows the dictates, that the dictates actually rule and measure human action.

Really there can hardly be any question that Thomas regards God's legislative will and the eternal law as the original source of reason's natural dictates. He says that "the eternal law is related to the order of human reason in the way that a craft is related to an artifact."[118] The craftsman uses the craft, and produces the artifact, voluntarily. And it is immediately after this that Thomas quotes Augustine saying that "all natures have it from God that they are natures." The quotation continues, "and they [the natures] are vicious to the extent that they depart from that craft by which they were made." That craft is the eternal law. It is the source of the natures themselves.

It is also worth observing that even the positive precepts of good human laws—those that constitute valid determinations of the common precepts of natural law—are "contained in the eternal law."[119] So are the precepts of divinely promulgated law.[120] All just laws are contained in the eternal law *determinately*. The eternity of the eternal law is not like the immutability of the common precepts of natural law. These are immutable in the way that universal abstractions are. They are merely indeterminate with respect to what they are abstracted from.[121] God is immutable, not by being an abstraction, but by being utterly simple and utterly perfect.[122] Eternity is

---

116. That the natural dictates of reason are necessarily true and cannot change from being true to being false does not mean that they are eternal truths. The only eternal truth is God's. See *ST* I.10.3*ad*3; I.16.7. Even though natural law is a participation in the eternal law, which is the eternal truth (*ST* I-II.93.2), we should not think of it as literally a part of the eternal law. It hardly could be, since the eternal law is identical with God (*ST* I-II.93.4), and He is simple and has no parts. Rather, natural law is a likeness of the eternal law, an imperfect one, and in that sense a partial one.

117. Cf. *ST* I.21.1*ad*3.
118. *ST* I-II.71.2*ad*4.
119. *ST* I-II.91.3*ad*1.
120. *ST* I-II.91.4*ad*1.
121. See *ST* I.16.7*ad*2.
122. *ST* I.9.1.

the successionless duration of an actuality that embraces and contains every thing and every feature of things.[123]

So there are ways in which the eternal law is like positive law. But on the whole it is not a positive law. Nor is it merely abstract and general, as natural law is. It contains both the principles of natural right that are common to human kind and the determinations of positive right that are proper to particular human communities. It stands above the distinction between natural law and positive law. Its regulative power is unique, just as God's causality is unique. What I have especially wanted to underscore is the uniqueness of His *final* causality, His goodness. It is the end of all other ends, the goodness on which both the existence and the goodness of all other goods depends.

THE ANALOGY OF LAW AND THE PRIMACY OF NATURAL LAW

To sum up: on Aquinas's account, man's natural knowledge of the first principles of practical reason, just in themselves, without any addition of further knowledge about them such as their expressing God's command or God's will, can be understood as knowledge of a genuine law that has been promulgated to him, the object and effect of an act of command issuing from God's reasonable will. In God, that act constitutes the eternal law. The first principles of practical reason are therefore, essentially, a participation of the eternal law in the rational creature, and one that has the proper nature of law. They lack none of the features ascribed to law in *ST* I–II.90.[124] This is so even though they do not have the nature of law in the way that positive law does. Positive law has its proper force, its power to regulate action, solely in light of its relation to its institution—its relation to the lawgiver's act of commanding it. Its sufficient promulgation involves a notification of that institution. Natural law does have its force from God's command, but not solely in light of its relation to that command; for the command itself gives it an intrinsic force. Its force is its truth. That truth depends on God's command, but it does not consist in a relation to that command.

So the precepts of natural law are a law in the proper sense of the term. They fully satisfy the definition of law. Still, even when a term is said properly of several things, nothing prevents its being said more properly of some

---

123. *ST* I.10.2*ad*4; I.13.1*ad*3; I.14.9.

124. There remains the question of sanction or punishment, which for Thomas is not of the essence of law but rather one of its effects (*ST* I–II.92.2). I shall address this in chapter 6.

than of others.[125] The nature that it signifies may somehow belong to all of them, and yet it may not belong equally to them. There may be an order in which it belongs to them. It may apply primarily and immediately to one of them, and only secondarily or derivatively to the others, with the secondary applications containing a reference or a relation to the primary one. This means that its definition is not exactly the same in each case. It is not said univocally of them, but analogically, according to some proportion. As said of the derivative instances, the term signifies the common nature as existing in a form that is quite diverse from the form in which it exists in the primary instance, but that is nonetheless proportioned thereto.

Now, our formation of a common notion that applies to various things by analogy does not always arise from the understanding of the one to which it primarily applies. Sometimes it arises from derivative instances. Here the most prominent examples in Thomas are those of the terms said commonly, and properly, of both God and creatures; for instance, the term *good*.[126] Our first encounter with goodness is in the experience of creatures, and creatures are what we first call good. In Thomas's terminology, it is in order to signify something about creatures that we first "impose" or institute the term *good*. Only later do we become aware of God and His goodness. Nevertheless, insofar as what we are aware of is the true God, we understand that when we call Him good, the nature of goodness that we thereby ascribe to Him is not the same as that which we ascribe to creatures. And we understand that it has priority, as goodness, over that of creatures. Forming a true conception of the goodness of God goes hand in hand with understanding the goodness of creatures as something intrinsically derivative from it, proportioned to it, a function of it. Our conception of goodness comes from creatures, but when we move on to conceive *creaturely* goodness, as such—as distinct from divine goodness—we conceive it as a secondary goodness.

How then does it stand with law? If both natural law and positive law are properly called laws, is it equally or according to some analogy? And if it is by analogy, which has priority?

Here a preliminary observation is needed. Unlike the notion of good, the very notion of a law is as of something that has a twofold mode of existence. To be a law is to be apt to exist both in the one who rules by it, the lawgiver, and in those who are ruled by it. This is simply to say that to be

---

125. See *ST* I.13.2. What is directly opposed to *proper* is not *analogical* but *improper*. What are called laws only in an improper way, as not having in themselves the full nature of law, are the inclinations of irrational creatures (*ST* I–II.91.2ad3; I–II.93.5ad1) and also the *lex fomitis* in man (*ST* I–II.91.6).

126. See *ST* I.13.5; I.13.6. Another good example is presented in *ST* I.34.1: the term *word* (*verbum*).

a law is to be promulgated. Obviously a law's primary existence is in the lawgiver. What exists in those who are ruled by it is derivative from and proportioned to what exists in the lawgiver. It should be clear that even though natural law is properly a law, it is only law as it exists in those who are ruled by law and not as it exists in the lawgiver. In this respect, natural law is law in a secondary sense. What is primary is the eternal law. Natural law is essentially something derivative from, and proportioned to, the eternal law. For Thomas, this is what *natural law* itself means. To be a natural law is nothing other than to be a participation of the eternal law. The notion of natural law is formed in light of the notion of the eternal law. The term *law* is applied to the eternal law before it is applied to the natural law. This is so even though we grasp the reality to which the term *natural law* is applied—the first principles of practical reason—before we grasp the reality of the eternal law. Nevertheless, that original grasp of the principles is sufficient for them to function as a true law, by which the eternal law rules us. We should keep all this in mind when comparing natural law and positive law as laws.

First, as regards the "imposition" of the term *law*, Thomas's approach to the definition of law suggests rather strongly that he thinks the term was originally imposed to signify human law. That is what the second and third articles in his treatment of the common definition of law refer to: the law of the political community, the city.[127] This is hard to quarrel with. When we speak simply of "the law" and of actions that are according to it or against it, do we not usually mean humanly posited law? We do not normally add the qualifier *human* to refer to it. It is when we want to refer to other kinds of law that we add qualifiers: divine, eternal, natural, and so forth.

Nevertheless it is equally clear, even within his exposition of the general definition of law, that Thomas does not consider human law to be what is primarily or most properly law. In the article on promulgation, even before he has presented his argument for the existence of natural law, he says that natural law "has the nature of law to the highest degree" (*maxime habet rationem legis*).[128] Now this can hardly mean that it has the nature of law to a higher degree even than the eternal law. He must rather be thinking of natural law in the way he says when he does argue for its existence, as not "something diverse" from the eternal law, but simply as a participation in it.[129] Natural law is law to the highest degree because the eternal law is so.

Clearly what it is to be a law is not the same in the case of human and eternal law. For the eternal law *is* the common good that it directs toward

---

127. *ST* I–II.90.2; I–II.90.3*ad*3.
128. *ST* I–II.90.4*obj*1.
129. *ST* I–II.91.2*ad*1.

Natural Law, God's Will, and Positive Law

and *is* the governor that rules by it.[130] And it consists in a truth that is identical with the intellect that conceives it, one that is true in virtue of itself and not by its conformity to anything other than itself.[131] In Thomas's account, it is really quite obvious that human law is law in a secondary way, by reason of its proportion, its analogy, to the eternal law. Human law has to be in accordance with the eternal law in order to be a law at all. So does any other law. All law is derived from the eternal law.[132] In fact all of it is some sort of participation in the eternal law.[133] But human law does not participate immediately in the eternal law. It does so through natural law. It is a "ruled rule" and a "measured measure" of human acts, and its measure is twofold: divine law and natural law.[134]

Natural law also has priority, as law, over human law. This is the case, whether human law be considered as it is in those who are ruled by it, or as in those who rule by it. In those who are ruled by it, human law obliges only by virtue of, and in accordance with, natural law.[135] And natural law is prior to human law even as it exists in those who rule by it. Their statutes are not true laws, not "legal," unless they comply with natural law.[136] "In the nature (*ratio*) of human law is first of all that it be derived from the law of nature."[137]

We could even say that insofar as the common definition of law in *ST* I-II.90 has mere human law in view, it implicitly refers to natural law. It is only by compliance with natural law that human law is rational or reasonable; that it directs toward the common good, since this is itself an essential requirement of rationality and so of natural law; and that it is promulgated by one who truly has care of the community, since there are natural principles regulating the assumption of authority. It is entirely on account of the precepts of natural law that the human mind is able to generate any true

---

130. *ST* I-II.91.1*ad*3.

131. *ST* I-II.93.1*ad*3. Even though "true" is said properly both of God's intellect and of the human intellect—both have the nature of truth in them—that nature is not altogether the same in both cases. See *ST* I.16.5, esp. *ad*2.

132. *ST* I-II.93.3.

133. See *ST* I-II.91.3*ad*1; *ST* I-II.96.4 (concerning human law); *ST* I-II.91.4*ad*1 (concerning law divinely given). Also, even though human law is a participation in the eternal law, it "falls short" of the eternal law in a way that natural law does not. See below, 195.

134. *ST* I-II.95.3.

135. Indeed, even the obligation of supernatural or divinely promulgated law, as it exists in those ruled by it, supposes natural law. Acting contrary to divine law would not be a sin if it did not also constitute the violation of a precept of natural law. See *ST* II-II.10.1*ad*1.

136. See *ST* I-II.96.4 and the expression *leges legales*, "legal laws."

137. *ST* I-II.95.4.

rules of its own. Thomas poses an objection to the existence of human law, which is that law is a measure, whereas human reason is not a measure of things but is rather measured by them. His answer is that "human reason just in itself is not a measure of things, but the principles naturally instilled in it are certain general rules and measures of all those things that are to be done by man; of these, natural reason is a measure, granted that it is not a measure of the things that are by nature."[138]

At the same time, the thought is not that the first principles of practical reason must be understood to derive from the eternal law and so to be laws in the full sense, before they can be understood as measures of positive law. Not all measures are properly called by the name of what they measure. Thus, natural things measure the truth of the human intellect's propositions, but they are not properly called true.[139] And even though the cause of their measuring our truth is something that is true properly and to a higher degree, namely the divine truth that measures them, we do not need to know this in order to know them to be measures of our truth. Similarly, the first principles that we naturally understand, whether speculative or practical, measure all of our other truths, but we do not have to see them as effects of the first, divine truth in order to see them as such measures.[140] To be sure, we do have to see them as true, whereas we do not have to see the practical ones as laws. But this is only because the definition of *truth* does not, of itself, imply a twofold existence, in measurer and measured or ruler and ruled, as the definition of *law* does.

Perhaps, then, we could even argue therefore that natural law displays a fuller share in the nature of law than does human positive law, not only insofar as it is seen as proceeding from the supreme law, but also in virtue of the very fact that it wins the mind's assent without need of any advertence

---

138. *ST* I–II.91.3*ad*2. Evidently by "natural reason" (*ratio naturalis*) here he means something other than "human reason just in itself" (*ratio humana secundum se*). Human reason just in itself is only in potency to knowing any truth, and it measures nothing. "Natural reason" must mean something like reason working in accordance with the naturally instilled principles. (The passage is about the existence of human laws.) Notice also that reason is in no way a measure of the things that are by nature—even though the eternal law is. Natural law is a share in the eternal law, but it does not measure everything that the eternal law measures. It only measures human acts. How the understanding of the precepts of natural law is related to the understanding of things that are by nature will be discussed in chapter 5.

139. *ST* I.16.1*c*/*ad*3.

140. The way in which "things" measure the truth of human propositions is different from that in which first principles do so. The truth of the propositions consists in their conformity to the thing. But we sometimes judge their truth in light of other propositions. These are principles from which we conclude them. First principles are principles whose truth is grasped immediately.

to its authoritative institution. The first principles of practical reason are not subject to any kind of practical judgment on man's part; that is, judgment as to whether they ought to be so or not.[141] We cannot really ask whether or not these principles are right and ought to be obeyed, for the simple reason that in asking it we could only be appealing to the principles themselves for an answer. To ask, for instance, why we ought to do good and avoid evil would be merely to ask why it is good for us to do so and evil not to. It is the strength of these principles, not their weakness, that they are not originally accompanied by evidence of their authoritative source. They need no such evidence, owing to the efficacy with which their author has instituted them.

Even taken in abstraction from their origin in divine institution, the first principles of practical reason are more fundamental and more efficacious measures of human conduct than any humanly posited rule. If some reference to authority is needed in order for these principles to receive the name *law*, according to its full definition, no such reference is needed for them to be understood as normative or obligatory. When Thomas defines natural law as the participation of the eternal law in the rational creature, he is not intending to give an answer to the question "Why is it right to obey the first principles of practical reason?" What his definition gives is the full explanation for their existence and for the regulative force that is intrinsic to them.

So long as the term *law* is restricted to human laws, then, the first principles of practical reason will have to be considered, not as falling short of the nature of law, but as supra-legal rules. Or perhaps, instead of objecting to their being called laws, it would be more reasonable to say that there is, or can be, a common conception of law that does not include reference to a lawgiver.[142] It would simply be the conception of a true universal rule and measure of human acts. According to this conception, the first principles of practical reason are *more* properly laws than human laws, because they are more perfect measures. In fact they are measures of a higher order, higher by as much as what exists by nature is higher than what exists by the human will.

This point seems to suggest a certain qualification of the earlier conclusion, that the existence of a natural law cannot be affirmed except in light of the discovery of divine providence and in relation to the eternal law. This is true insofar as what is at stake is the existence of something natural that answers to the full definition of law. But it is not true with respect to what

---

141. See *ST* I–II.93.2*ad*3.

142. Notice that Augustine, in *De libero arbitrio*, posits an eternal law—a rule superior to human law, always and everywhere the same—prior to, and in preparation for, his argument for the existence of a God (*De libero arbitrio* 1.6.14–1.6.15; 2.12.33–2.15.40).

is uppermost in the notion of law; that is, the quality of law on which its proper effects most immediately depend. This is its quality of a rule or measure of acts that men are inclined or induced to follow. To know this about the first principles of practical reason, there is no need to advert to God. Their original power in the human mind does not depend on the mind's having referred them to God's authority. This is so even though accounting for it does depend on that, and even though complying fully with it will quickly lead one to make the reference.[143]

But the fundamental point is that God's governance is not ruled by them and does not in any way presuppose them. His legislation as a whole is in no way subject to or constrained by the precepts of natural law. The only sense in which it is subject to any law is with respect to what it determines about creatures, this being subject to the eternal law as it is in itself and as really identical with God's goodness, God's wisdom, and God's will.[144] Natural law supposes human nature and the common nature of the good. God's legislation, as a whole, supposes neither. It institutes both. The common nature of the good, as what all desire, is not something that God's goodness shares in. It is itself a likeness of His goodness. He institutes the common nature of the good itself, ordering it toward His goodness. His legislation is not ruled by the merely general truth that the good is to be done and sought, and the bad avoided. It is only ruled by His own goodness and by the wisdom according to which He directs everything else toward it. The general truth is an effect of this wisdom, not a principle of it. There is no absolute moral law that stands above even His goodness or His work of ordering things to it. The highest common good is not an ideal projection of reason, even God's. It is the actual good of His nature, which is His nature. What is originally a projection of His reason, becoming real through a determination of His will, is created nature and its intrinsic good. How the precepts of natural law relate to that nature and that good will be the concern of the next two chapters.

---

143. See below, 235.
144. See *ST* I–II.93.4.

4

Natural Inclinations in the Promulgation of Natural Law

THE QUESTION OF THE ROLE OF NATURAL INCLINATIONS IN NATURAL LAW

Natural law is a law naturally promulgated to man, a natural participation in the eternal law. In the previous chapter, I argued that the eternal law institutes the very natures of things. By the eternal law, human nature is ordained to exist for the sake of the divine common good. Clearly Thomas also thinks that the eternal law ordains human nature to be a principle of the reception of natural law, inasmuch as the precepts of natural law come to be known through the natural light of reason, which flows from the principal part of human nature, the rational soul.[1] But a further question readily presents itself. To what extent, for Thomas, does the promulgation of the precepts of natural law, their being made known, involve knowledge of human nature itself? Does he think that the fundamental truths about how we ought to act are a function of truths about nature? It is often assumed that he does, both by his supporters and by his critics.

One of the critics is Alan Donagan. He thinks that Thomas gives nature too much of a role in the constitution of the moral order, and he suspects that this is precisely because of Thomas's belief that nature is instituted by God.

---

1. See above, 79n48.

> St Thomas was mistaken in looking to Aristotelian natural philosophy for a way of specifying the goods that the natural law bids us seek, and the evils it bids us avoid.... I am inclined to conjecture that he was led to make it by his belief in creation: accepting Aristotle's views about natural teleology, and believing that the natural world was created by God, it may have seemed reasonable to treat the ends of natural things and processes not only as divinely appointed, but as divinely sanctioned.[2]

Donagan judges Aquinas's procedure mistaken in two ways. First, he says, not everything that Aquinas treats as the object of a natural inclination really is one. For example, Aquinas judges that since words are naturally signs of the speaker's thoughts, lying is wrong. But, says Donagan, "from the point of view of natural science, a lying speech act is not, *per se*, either defective or interfered with.... For a thing tends towards its natural end provided there is no impediment, and a lying speech act does not in the least tend towards truth."[3] Secondly, and more fundamentally, Donagan argues that it is simply not evident that because nature seeks something, we should seek it too. Man, a rational and free agent, is not the servant of mere nature. Donagan approvingly quotes Richard Robinson: "Let nature look to her own purposes, if she has any. *We* will look to *ours*."[4]

These two criticisms are not too difficult to rebut. Regarding lying, there are two points. First, although it is true that a lying speech act does not tend toward truth, but toward falsehood, one can still ask whether its doing so is not a deviation from the natural tendency of speech itself. And surely it is. Even though lying is a fairly common practice, for the most part people's utterances are truthful. Lying is the exception. As Kant says, if lying were a downright "law of nature," it would self-destruct. Speech would not have the general, natural credibility upon which lying's own efficacy depends. And surely, ceteris paribus, telling the truth comes easier to us. Without practice, lying takes a special effort, and most people do it clumsily and with signs of unease. That is what polygraphs are about. Granted, with practice, lying can become easy and smooth, but this only shows that people can acquire habits opposed to their natural tendencies. A habit is only a "second" nature. Taking *natural* in the Aristotelian sense, of what is "always or for the most part," and *unnatural* as its contrary, lying is indeed unnatural.

The second point, which is more important, is an anticipation of a later discussion in this chapter. It is that lying's being contrary to a natural

---

2. Donagan, "Scholastic Theory," 336.
3. Donagan, "Scholastic Theory," 334.
4. Donagan, "Scholastic Theory," 335.

tendency, or unnatural in the sense just considered, is not quite Thomas's reason for judging it wrong. He does not think that an action's being right consists merely in its being an instance of what that kind of agent usually does, or that its being wrong consists in its being contrary to that. In the case of irrational kinds of agents, he does think that they usually do what is right for them to do, and that they seldom do what is wrong. But the usual thing's being usual is not what makes it right. Rather—again, speaking of irrational agents—its being right explains why it is usual, and the contrary's being wrong explains why the contrary is rare. This is Thomas's "natural teleology": goodness has its own causality, final causality, and natural tendencies are among its effects. And he thinks that this can be fully explained only by divine providence. When he argues that lying is always sin, however, his stated reason is that it has an "undue object." Spoken words are by nature signs of what is in the speaker's mind. Using words to signify something that is not in one's mind—to signify one's holding some proposition that one does not hold—is therefore "unnatural and undue."[5] But what he means by calling it "unnatural" is that it is contrary to the *order* that follows upon the nature of speech.[6] It lacks something that the perfection and goodness of speech requires, just insofar as it is speech. And this suffices to make it bad and undue. This is a different sense of *unnatural* from the one that Donagan seizes upon. As it happens, lying is unnatural in both senses. It is contrary to what usually happens, and it is contrary to what suits a thing according to its nature. But as we shall see, in the case of human action, as opposed to that of irrational things, Thomas does not think that the two always go together. In the human sphere, something can be contrary to nature and nevertheless be pretty common, and something can be due to nature and yet rather rare. Thomas is not taking natural tendency, in the sense of what is for the most part, to be the proper measure of right and wrong in human conduct.

As for Donagan's insistence that nature's purposes need not be ours, the response is surely that the natural law centers, not just on any nature, but on human nature. "Pertaining to natural law," Thomas says, "are all those things to be done or avoided that practical reason naturally apprehends to be human goods."[7] The human good is the good that suits man as man; that is, as having human nature. Earlier Thomas had laid it down that "the

---

5. *ST* II–II.110.3.

6. On this notion, see *ST* I–II.18.5, and below, 165. To say that speech is naturally a sign of the human mind is to say that the human mind naturally represents itself in speech. So we could also say that the lie, which misrepresents the speaker's mind, is contrary to the order that follows on the nature of the human mind itself. It lacks something that the nature of reason requires.

7. *ST* I–II.94.2.

goodness of each and every thing consists in this, that it be fittingly disposed according to the mode of its nature."[8] Perhaps the goods of other natures need not concern me. But my own nature is not something alien to me or merely attached to me. It is what I most fundamentally am. What is a good of human nature is not something that may or may not be my good too. For I do not just happen to be human, any more than I just happen to be myself. What suits me according to my nature suits me in a more fundamental way than what suits me according to some feature that does not pertain to my nature, taken in this sense. Thomas thinks that reason naturally gives priority to what is according to nature, taken in this sense. "The principles of [practical] reason are those things that are according to nature; for, with the things that are determined by nature presupposed, reason disposes other things as is fitting."[9] By "the things that are determined by nature," he does not mean the things that exist or come about by nature (which are things that come about for the most part) rather than voluntarily; he means the things that are determinately fitting or unfitting, by comparison with nature. They are the things that are naturally right or due, wrong or undue. Practical reason begins from such things, simply because fittingness is relative to a form, and because the primary form of a thing is its nature. The purposes of human nature are reason's *first* purposes.

So Donagan's specific criticisms may not really impact Thomas's position. However, there is at least one other issue that Donagan might have raised. It has to do with the fact that natural law is supposed to be a set of moral principles known by everyone, or at least by everyone who reaches the use of reason. They are known naturally. And the knowledge is true. Thomas says, "Just as natural cognition is always true, so natural love is always right, since natural love is nothing other than the inclination of nature instilled by the Author of nature; hence, to say that natural inclination is not right is to disparage the Author of nature."[10] Presumably it would be a similar disparagement to say that natural cognition is not always true. But if the precepts of natural law are a function of human nature, then knowing them would seem to suppose some knowledge of human nature, true knowledge. How can Thomas be so sure that people have such knowledge? Could it perhaps be simply—along the lines of Donagan's conjecture—that he thinks that to say otherwise would be to disparage the Author and Legislator of nature, in whom he believes? Is such a view philosophically defensible?

---

8. *ST* I–II.71.1.
9. *ST* II–II.154.12.
10. *ST* I.60.1*ad*3.

Natural Inclinations in the Promulgation of Natural Law

It is not a purely hypothetical question. There is a brief remark in Thomas's most famous passage about natural law—*ST* I-II.94.2 (hereafter 94.2)—that is often interpreted as indicating what he thinks the common knowledge of human nature underlying the precepts of natural law consists in. And, so interpreted, it also seems to be open to serious objections. In that passage, after treating the very first precept of natural law, which rests on the universal notion of good—"the good is to be done and sought, and the bad, avoided"[11]—Thomas goes on to speak of other precepts, which concern specific goods, goods that practical reason apprehends "as human goods." And here he lays it down, quite unconditionally, that

> all the things toward which man has natural inclination, reason naturally apprehends as good, and consequently as things to be pursued by action, and their contraries as bad and to be avoided.[12]

In what follows I shall be referring to this passage repeatedly. I shall call it simply the natural inclination text.

Quite commonly, this text is taken to be presenting us with Thomas's way of grounding the precepts of natural law upon knowledge of human nature.[13] On this reading, the natural way in which a person comes to judge things as human goods—and therefore as due to be pursued, and so forth—would be by his seeing them as the objects of natural human inclinations. What seeing them as good consists in would be just that: seeing them as the objects of these inclinations.

I think it is a mistake to understand the natural inclination text in this way. A few other interpreters—few but eminent—do too. The situation is complicated, however, because those of us who agree that it is mistaken do not agree among ourselves as to what the correct reading of the text is. Nor do we agree as to how, or even whether, Thomas does ground the natural knowledge of the precepts of natural law on knowledge of human nature. I shall proceed as follows. First, drawing on things that he says elsewhere, I shall indicate just one problem that the common way of understanding the natural inclination text raises. (Other problems will emerge in the subsequent discussion.) I shall then consider two alternative ways of taking it that have been proposed. After that I shall present my own interpretation of it,

11. *ST* I-II.94.2.

12. *Omnia illa ad quae homo habet naturalem inclinationem ratio naturaliter apprehendit ut bona* (*ST* I-II.94.2).

13. For just a few example's of this reading, see van Overbeke, "La loi naturelle," 65; Elders, "Nature as the Basis of Moral Actions," 576–77; Cahalan, "Natural Obligation," 126.

together with my responses to the other alternative proposals. Then, finally, having laid out my own interpretation, in the next chapter I shall try to explain how Thomas does ground the precepts of natural law on knowledge of nature. That will be a rather lengthy discussion, because he does so in several ways. But only then will I be in a position to say something about whether or not his belief in creation has unduly influenced his natural law theory.

So let me proceed to the one problem that I wish to raise at this point for the common way of taking the natural inclination text. The problem is as follows. On that reading, by "natural inclination" Thomas must mean something that exists, and can be apprehended, independently of reason's judgment that its object is good. Otherwise it could not serve, without circularity, as the ground of that judgment. It must simply mean an inclination that human beings have in common, an inborn tendency in them to act in a certain way. Presumably it would show itself in the way that, for Aristotle, what is natural shows itself: by the fact that people always or for the most part do act in that way. But now, if that is what Thomas means, then it is very hard to see how he could hold that natural human inclination, or the natural human cognition that would (on this reading) be founded upon it, is always right and never wrong. For in fact he thinks there is an inclination of this sort that is not always right (or even sometimes). It is what he calls *fomes peccati*, the fuel of sin that is inherited along with original sin. This is chiefly an inborn disposition of the sensitive appetite, by which the appetite tends to transgress the boundaries of right reason.[14] By it, the appetite is ordered, not to the common good, but rather to private good.[15] It makes the sensitive appetite selfish.

Moreover, this selfishness or rebelliousness of the sense-appetite is not entirely, for Thomas, the effect of original sin. In his *Sentences* commentary, he indicates that there is a genuine, though evidently qualified, sense in which it is natural. He says that if man had been created in a purely natural condition, there would have been such defects as mortality, passibility, and the "struggle of concupiscence against reason." These would not have had the character of sin or punishment, since they would not have been the effect of man's will, but would have "followed on the principles of nature."[16] These principles are man's matter and form. Presumably the proper source of the defects would be on the side of the matter.[17] The animal or sensitive

---

14. See *ST* I–II.82.3*ad*1.
15. See *ST* I–II.91.6*obj*3/*ad*3.
16. *In Sent.* II.31.1.2*ad*3. See also below, 130n75.
17. Cf. *De malo* 4.7*ad*5; *ST* I.97.1.

part of man's nature is material relative to the rational part.[18] This is why I say that it is only in a sense that the struggle would be natural, namely, with respect to the condition of the matter. In another sense—with respect to what is due to the form, which is the rational soul—it would be against nature.[19] And this would be the more proper sense, because nature is more form than matter, the form being what provides the differentia that completes the nature of the species. But the point is that the rebelliousness of the sense-appetite is an effect of original sin in the sense that original sin is the lack of the gift of original justice, which kept the sense-appetite in check.[20] The loss of original justice also brought a weakening of the will's own natural inclination to follow reason.[21] As a result, the will is more prone to follow the sense-appetite. It is because of this that the sense-appetite's rebelliousness is frequently a source of sin.[22] For Thomas does thinks that, for the most part, people follow the sense-appetite and its selfish tendency against reason.

This comes out in a defense of the thesis that vice is "contrary to nature." An objection says that it is not, because "vices are found in men for the most part." In his reply, Thomas does not at all reject this unflattering judgment. Rather, he explains why it is true.

> In man there is a twofold nature, namely, rational and sensitive. And because man arrives at the act of reason through the operation of the sensory power, more people follow the inclinations of the sensitive nature than the order of reason; for those who reach the beginning of something are more than those who attain its consummation. But vices and sins come about among people because they follow the inclination of sensitive nature against the order of reason.[23]

Thomas is saying that vice is contrary, in the sense of unsuited, to man's rational nature. And since, as he explains in the body of this article, what constitutes man as man is rational nature, vice can be said without qualification

18. *ST* I.76.3*ad*4; I.77.7.
19. See *ST* I–II.82.3*ad*1; I–II.85.3*ad*3.
20. See *ST* I–II.82.1*ad*3.
21. *ST* I–II.85.1; I–II.85.3.
22. Thomas does not think that it is absolutely necessary for the sense-appetite to be bent on private good to the detriment of the common good. In beasts it is quite naturally ordered to the common good, and in man it can be disposed to be so ordered, insofar as it does have an aptitude to be ruled by reason (*ST* I–II.91.6*ad*3).
23. *ST* I–II.71.2*ad*3. Similarly, "only among men does the bad seem to be for the most part, because the good of man according to sense is not the good of man as man, that is, according to reason; and more follow sense than reason" (*ST* I.49.3*ad*5).

to be contrary to man's nature. But this is not because it is contrary to how people tend to act, in the sense of how they usually act. People do not usually act virtuously. And they certainly do not do so "by nature." In this same article, Thomas readily grants that even though virtue—the contrary of vice—is "according" to man's nature, inasmuch as it inclines toward what is according to the order of reason and so suits rational nature, it does not exist by nature.[24] Bad conduct is unnatural, not in the sense of rare—it is the usual thing—but only in the sense that it is unsuited to its subject's natural constitution. But thus it is clear that Thomas cannot think that the order of reason itself, whose principles are the precepts of natural law, is founded merely upon the ways in which people usually act or tend to act. This would mean that it is founded, at least in part, upon things that are contrary to it.

The question then is how, on Thomas's view, the order of reason itself is constituted. It cannot be by reason's merely identifying the things that people for the most part actually do or pursue and declaring them good and right. And indeed, would it not be hard to take such a view very seriously? The inclinations that Thomas is speaking of in the natural inclination text must be inclinations that are always right. But since we also have other inclinations, even inborn ones, that are not always right, how is it that reason would naturally use only the right ones as the basis for judging the human goods and thereby constituting its order? What will set the right inclinations apart, if it is not the very fact that they are according to an order that reason has already conceived? Thomas is really rather explicit about this. The inclinations of the various parts of man's nature, he says, "pertain to natural law" only "insofar as they are ruled by reason."[25] As we considered in the previous chapter, what is dictated by natural reason is not so *because* it is naturally right. It is naturally right because it is dictated by the eternal law and natural reason.

A remark by Etienne Gilson displays the problem in a nutshell: "Since it is eternal law that makes us what we are, we have only to yield to the *legitimate* inclinations of our nature in order to obey it."[26] The question is precisely how it is that we can possibly distinguish between the inclinations that are legitimate and those that are not, if it is not in light of our natural knowledge of human goods. But if that is how we can do so, then the inclinations themselves cannot be what show us the goods, and the natural inclination text in 94.2 must mean something else.

---

24. *ST* I–II.71.2*ad*1.
25. *ST* I–II.94.2*ad*2.
26. Gilson, *Thomism*, 303 (emphasis added).

SOME ALTERNATIVE READINGS OF THE NATURAL INCLINATION TEXT

As I said, on the most common reading, the natural inclination text makes reason's natural apprehension of the human goods that pertain to natural law be a direct function of man's natural inclinations. The natural or spontaneous way in which reason apprehends things as human goods would be by apprehending them as objects of natural human inclinations. Some interpreters, however, do not take the text this way. They assign some different role to the natural inclinations in the apprehension of the goods.

Probably the best known interpretation of this sort, at least in the English-speaking world, is the one initially proposed by Germain Grisez and subsequently adopted by John Finnis.

Now, Grisez and Finnis do grant that the precepts of natural law somehow follow man's natural inclinations. But their explanation for this correspondence is not that the inclinations function as standards to which reason looks in the formation of its precepts or in its judgments of the human goods. Indeed they eschew all mere objects of observation or of speculative knowledge, such as natural inclinations or even human nature itself, as criteria for the practical understanding of the goods toward which the precepts of natural law direct human agents. On their view, such criteria are ruled out in 94.2 itself. This is because there, Thomas presents the precepts as *per se nota*, self-evident. The precepts are first principles, grasped immediately, not by the application of other principles or other criteria.

As for the natural inclination text, Grisez takes it to be referring to the "felt inclinations" of "sense spontaneity" that emerge in man prior to the advent of intelligence. The function that he attributes to these inclinations in the formation of precepts of natural law appears to be twofold. First, they call reason's attention to their objects. Reason cannot direct action toward the objects if it does not consider them. The inclinations provide the data in which they are grasped. Secondly, the inclinations serve to display their objects as potential goals of action, real practical opportunities. They do so inasmuch as they are essential factors in man's very capacity to have the objects as goals at all.[27] Nevertheless, reason's apprehension of the objects as good is not mediated by any comparison with the inclinations. It is immediate. The inclinations do not serve as its criteria. Here is how Grisez puts all of this.

> Is reason merely an instrument in the service of nature, accepting what nature indicates as good by moving us toward it?

---

27. See Grisez, "First Principle," 357–58.

> No, the derivation is not direct, and the position of reason in relation to inclination not merely passive. Using the primary principle [that good is to be done and sought, etc.], reason reflects on experience in which the natural inclinations are found pointing to goods appropriate to themselves. But why does reason take these goods as its own? Not because they are given, but because reason's good, which is intelligible, contains the aspect of end, and the goods to which the inclinations point are prospective ends. Reason prescribes according to the order of natural inclinations because reason directs to possible actions, and the possible patterns of human action are determined by the natural inclinations, for man cannot act on account of that toward which he has no basis for affinity in his inclinations.[28]

For Grisez, then, the formation of the precepts of natural law follows man's natural inclinations only in the sense that the latter serve as the occasion for it and provide conditions without which man would not be pliant to the direction of reason. Reason is not taking the inclinations as the very criteria of good and bad.

Several other authors, although disagreeing with Grisez and among themselves about natural law in other respects, offer comparable interpretations of the role of the inclinations.[29] Let me consider just two of them, John Finnis and Jacques Maritain.

Finnis accepts Grisez's argument and develops it. Like Grisez, Finnis insists that the self-evidence of the precepts of natural law excludes their derivation from any prior understanding of nature.[30] Also like Grisez, Finnis takes Aquinas's expression *natural inclination* to refer to spontaneous, pre-rational urges or drives. These inclinations are immediately "felt" or experienced by the one who has them; and "by a simple act of non-inferential understanding one grasps that the object of the inclination which one experiences is an instance of a general form of good, for oneself (and others

---

28. Grisez, "First Principle," 357–58. See Finnis, *Natural Law and Natural Rights*, 34, 402.

29. For instance, see Flippen, "Natural Law and Natural Inclinations," 290, 312. Flippen differs sharply from Grisez, however, in holding that reason's specification of the human goods comes about by way of a comparison between the objects of inclination and human nature. Through this comparison are understood the basic elements of man's true perfection "according to the kind of being he is." As I shall explain, it is right to see the specification of the human goods as grounded on the understanding of man's perfection according to his nature. But I shall argue for a different relation between this understanding and the natural inclinations.

30. Finnis, *Natural Law and Natural Rights*, 33.

like one)."[31] Finnis insists that when Thomas speaks of moral good and evil as conformity or repugnance to nature, this is only as it were a conclusion from the fact that moral good and evil consist in conformity or repugnance to reason, and that reason is what specifies man's nature. The proper measure of moral good and evil is thus reason, not nature, and what is according to nature can be determined only in light of the account of what is rational, not prior to it or independently of it.[32] Thus, "the *underived* first principles of practical reasonableness ... make no reference at all to human nature, but only to human good."[33]

Finnis in fact criticizes Aquinas for speaking, in 94.2, of an "order of precepts of natural law" that follows the "order of natural inclinations." Natural law precepts may certainly be seen in the setting of the hierarchical universe of being; but such a metaphysical reflection has no practical value, Finnis judges, and it might even lead to the conclusion, which he considers erroneous, that there is some practical ranking among the precepts of natural law. For Finnis, there is no practical ranking among the precepts, because the "basic human goods" are "equally self-evidently good," irreducible, and each is capable of being regarded as "most important." In fact, he says, Aquinas's three-fold ordering "plays no part in his practical (ethical) elaboration of the significance and consequences of the primary precepts of natural law."[34] It is an "irrelevant schematization."[35] Finnis goes so far as to suggest that there is nothing intrinsically necessary about the "parallelism" or "fit" between man's felt inclinations and the intelligible human goods (or what Finnis calls "valuable aspects of human well-being"). The parallelism's only cause, if it has one, would be the providence of God, giving man a set of urges or drives that serves to direct his attention to the data in which he grasps his "basic goods."[36]

---

31. Finnis, *Natural Law and Natural Rights*, 34.

32. Finnis, *Natural Law and Natural Rights*, 35–36.

33. Finnis, *Natural Law and Natural Rights*, 36. Finnis seems to qualify this somewhat in his *Aquinas*; here he remarks on the close association between the notions of "good" and "perfection" (91), and he suggests that the practical knowledge of the first practical principles does "amount to an understanding however informal," of human nature (92). However, what he seems to mean is that this understanding of human nature would be a result of the practical knowledge, not a principle of it. Thus he says that "the epistemic source of the first practical principles is not human nature or a prior, theoretical understanding of human nature.... Rather, the epistemic relationship is the reverse" (91).

34. Finnis, *Natural Law and Natural Rights*, 94.

35. Finnis, *Natural Law and Natural Rights*, 95.

36. Finnis, *Natural Law and Natural Rights*, 403.

A few doubts might be raised about this interpretation. Certainly, as I argued earlier, if the natural inclinations that Aquinas is speaking about in the corpus of 94.2 are pre-rational urges, drives of man's sensitive part, it would be difficult to think that he is holding them up as proper standards of human conduct, since he regards such urges as often disordered and standing in need of direction by reason. But for this very reason, it seems possible to doubt whether the impulses of the senses are really what Aquinas has in mind, or even part of it.[37] For, whatever he means by *natural inclinations*, and even if he does think of them as no more than occasions for the formation of the primary precepts of natural law, he treats them as in perfect harmony with the precepts. Indeed, there is at least one text in which Aquinas seems to treat natural inclination as a measure of virtue itself. "Granted that the completion of virtue is through habituation or some other cause, the aptitude for virtue is in us by nature. Whence it is clear that the virtues perfect us for following the natural inclinations, which pertain to natural right, in the due way. And therefore, toward every determinate natural inclination whatsoever, there is ordered some special virtue."[38] If man's natural inclinations only happened to be in harmony with the precepts of natural law, the virtues could hardly be "ordered" to them. Rather, the inclinations do somehow "pertain" to natural right after all. Moreover, it seems obvious that at least some of the inclinations cited in 94.2 do not fit under the heading of "felt inclinations" or "sense spontaneity." For instance, the inclinations to know the truth about God and to live in society are said to be proper to rational nature. They cannot be sense-inclinations.

Another doubt concerns Grisez's suggestion as to why Thomas refers to the inclinations. This is that "man cannot act on account of that toward which he has no basis for affinity in his inclinations." Taking *inclinations* generally, as including those of the will, this is true. But if we confine the term to the inclinations of the sense-appetite, then for Thomas it is simply not true. "We will and do many things without passion, by choice alone, as is most evident in those in whom reason resists passion."[39]

One might also doubt whether Aquinas would accept Finnis's dismissal of his effort to show an order in the precepts in 94.2. I shall discuss this further on.

---

37. Finnis, *Aquinas*, 92–93, offers an interesting and well documented set of observations which show him to be uneasy with some of its implications. He is clearly worried about what sort of inclination it is that Thomas could have in mind in our passage. As he explains in considerable detail, there are several types of human inclination that are in some sense "natural" for Thomas but cannot possibly fit the bill.

38. *ST* II–II.108.2.

39. *ST* I–II.10.3*ad*3. See also *ST* I–II.59.5.

Natural Inclinations in the Promulgation of Natural Law 119

Another way of explaining the relation between natural inclinations and the precepts of natural law is that of Jacques Maritain. He presents it with reference to 94.2. However, what he regards as the key notion is not explicit there, or anywhere else in I–II.94. It is what Aquinas calls "knowledge by connaturality" or "judgment through inclination."[40] Although Aquinas does not appeal to this in his account of natural law, Maritain thinks that it provides the only way to make sense of the texts. On this account, the harmony between the inclinations and the precepts is far from accidental. Yet it does not hold in virtue of any conscious or theoretical reflection on the inclinations, any conceptualization of them as a foundation for practical reason's primary judgments. The inclinations do in a way inform these judgments, but not as objects of apprehension on which the judgments are based. Instead, the function of the inclinations is to move or incline the intellect itself, in the manner in which it can be inclined, toward these judgments. The natural knowledge of the precepts of natural law is, in Maritain's metaphorical language, a knowledge "in which the intellect, in order to bear judgment, consults and listens to the inner melody that the vibrating strings of abiding tendencies make present to the subject."[41] Shifting the metaphor, the inclinations might be said to cast a certain light on the objects of the mind's consideration, and the mind judges them in this light.

This interpretation seems to avoid the difficulties faced by that of Grisez and Finnis. It preserves the intrinsic connection that Aquinas seems to want to draw between the natural inclinations and the primary precepts. Also, Maritain's interpretation could be developed in such a way as to avoid the problem that sometimes the spontaneous impulses of the senses are bad. For since the natural inclinations in question are supposed to be moving reason itself, they would presumably be inclinations of the appetitive power that is "in reason," namely the will. And Aquinas's view does seem to be that the natural inclinations of the will are always right and toward what is good according to reason.[42]

This last point, however, raises a new problem. If the relevant natural inclinations are those of the will, then it is difficult to see how, in accordance with Thomas's psychology, they could possibly explain the formation of the first principles of practical reason. It is a basic tenet for Aquinas that people cannot actually will or want anything except what they understand to be

---

40. See Maritain, *Man and the State*, 89–94; "On Knowledge through Connaturality," esp. 477–80; "Du savoir moral."

41. Maritain, *Man and the State*, 92.

42. See below, 130.

somehow good. The proper object of the will is the understood good.[43] And more precisely, what presents the will with its object is practical intellect, intellect directing action in light of the good. "Just as imagining a form without appreciating it as suitable or harmful does not move the sense-appetite, so neither does apprehending a truth without the thought of good and desirable; whence it is not the speculative intellect that moves, but the practical intellect, as *De anima* III says."[44] There is no act of the will that does not suppose an act of the intellect presenting its object.[45] The intellect presents the will's object by apprehending something under the *ratio* of good.[46] This is not to say that the natural inclinations of the will do not exist in any way prior to the intellect's first apprehensions. In fact the will itself exists prior to those apprehensions, and the will just is a sort of inclination.[47] But until the intellect apprehends things as good, the will and its inclinations are only in potency.[48] It is not easy to see how the intellect could "consult" something existing only potentially or how it could be moved by such a thing. Things are knowable and able to cause movement only insofar as they are in act.

These considerations would explain why Thomas speaks of judgment by connaturality only in connection with certain acquired or infused dispositions of the intellect. The acts pertaining to such dispositions, in contrast with those of the intellect's primordial or natural dispositions, may in some cases be preceded and moved by acts of the will. Thus prudence depends on moral virtue, which makes it connatural to man to judge rightly about

---

43. See *ST* I.80.2; I.21.1*ad*2; I.82.4*obj*3/*ad*3; I–II.8.1; etc.

44. *ST* I–II.9.1*ad*2.

45. *ST* I.82.4*ad*3.

46. Kossel, "Natural Law and Human Law," 174, speaks of a "first act of the will which is its natural and spontaneous reaction to common being as apprehended by intellect." On his view, it would be by apprehending this act that the intellect first grasps the *ratio* of the good. Now, Thomas grants that the will's inclination can extend to all being. But it does so only inasmuch as being is apprehended by the intellect as good. The proper object of the intellect is being and truth, and the will's object falls under this as a less absolute, more conditioned object (*ST* I.82.3), one whose *ratio* is less common (*ST* I.82.4*ad*1). The intellect grasps the very *ratio* of good, and it is only by the intellect's applying the *ratio* of good to anything (even to being) that the will can be actually inclined to that thing (*ST* I.82.3). The intellect functions in relation to the will in the way that the agent intellect itself functions in relation to intellect (*ST* I.83.4*ad*3). The agent intellect makes the natures of things "actually intelligible," that is, able to move the intellect, by freeing them from matter; the intellect itself makes things "actually willable," able to move the will, by presenting them under the *ratio* of good.

47. See *ST* I–II.51.1, near the end of the corpus.

48. See *ST* I–II.10.1*obj*2/*ad*2. Another way to say this is that the human will is essentially a moved mover (*ST* I.82.4*obj*2). See also *ST* I.80.2; I.82.3*ad*2.

Natural Inclinations in the Promulgation of Natural Law

particular ends of action.[49] The gift of wisdom depends on charity, through which it is connatural to judge according to divine truth.[50] And the "declaration of what is just" depends on the virtue of justice, through which it is connatural to judge justly.[51] Nevertheless, charity presupposes faith, and both prudence and moral virtue presuppose *synderesis*.[52]

I conclude that neither the common way of reading the natural inclination text nor the alternative readings just considered are satisfactory. Now let me present the reading that I endorse. It is not my invention; I learned the essentials of it from two very important and far too neglected articles by Lawrence Dewan.[53] In what follows I do try to flesh it out somewhat. I hope I do not stray too far from what Dewan had in mind.

NATURAL INCLINATION IN THE ARGUMENT OF I–II.94.2

Despite the serious differences existing among the positions so far considered, there is one assumption that they all share, although they are not always explicit about it. This is that the natural inclination text is talking about inclinations that are pre-rational. That is, they would exist independently of reason's apprehension of their objects as good. The apprehension would only follow on them somehow.

I do not wish to deny that, taken in isolation, the text can sound like this. And the ensuing discussion in 94.2 gives some prima facie support to the assumption. From the fact that "all the things toward which man has natural inclination, reason naturally apprehends as good, and consequently as things to be pursued by action, and their contraries as bad and to be avoided," Thomas draws a conclusion. "Therefore, the order of the precepts of the law of nature is according to the order of the natural inclinations." He then goes on to use a certain order that he finds in man's natural inclinations as a basis for determining the order of the precepts. (This is the order that Finnis judges irrelevant.) It does sound as though the inclinations are prior to the precepts and, by extension, even to reason's natural apprehension of the human goods.

---

49. *ST* I–II.58.5; cf. I–II.56.3.

50. *ST* II–II.45.2.

51. *ST* II–II.60.1.

52. *ST* II–II.47.6; I–II.58.4; I–II.62.4. See II–II.45.1*ad*2. It is true that the assent of faith is moved by an act of the will, "a certain choice" (*ST* II–II.1.4; II–II.4.1). But this does not make it a judgment by connaturality. Connaturality with the object of faith comes precisely through charity (*ST* II–II.45.2), which supposes faith (*ST* II–II.4.7*ad*5).

53. Dewan, *Wisdom, Law, and Virtue*, 199–212, 213–20. Also quite pertinent is Dewan, *Wisdom, Law, and Virtue*, 125–50.

Nevertheless Thomas does not actually say this in so many words. He does not say that reason naturally apprehends certain things as good because, or even on the occasion, of man's natural inclinations to them. Nor does he say that the precepts themselves follow the inclinations. He only says that the order of the precepts is according to the order of the inclinations. This does not entail that, in themselves, the inclinations are prior to the precepts. It may only indicate that, as I shall explain further on, the order of the inclinations is in some way better known to us than the order of the precepts, so that we can infer the latter from the former, as he does in the continuation of the article. This way of taking it is more faithful to the overall thrust of the argument in 94.2, and also to its context. To show this, I need to rehearse the argument in some detail.

The question addressed in 94.2 is whether natural law contains one precept or many precepts. Aquinas's answer is that it contains many—just as man's natural inclinations are many—but that there is one overarching precept that all the others fall under. This is that "the good is to be done and sought, and the bad avoided." He argues for this answer in three broad stages.

First he lays it down that the precepts of natural law are certain practical principles that are self-evident.[54] Here he is picking up on what he had said in the previous article, that natural law is something constituted by reason, as a proposition is, and that it is held by the habit called *synderesis*, which is the habit of understanding first practical principles, comparable to the habit of understanding indemonstrable speculative principles.[55] Earlier Thomas had explained that a habit of principles is a habitual knowledge of truths that are "perceived at once" as true by the intellect. Insofar as they are so perceived, these truths are said to be self-evident.[56] They are opposed to truths that are perceived only through inquiry and known in light of something other than themselves, *per aliud*. From other passages we learn that, even though it is a sort of perception, the knowledge of truth is not an entirely passive affair, even in the case of self-evident truths. For one thing, the light by which the mind perceives these truths is its own. It is the light of the agent intellect. Thomas insists that the agent intellect is a power of the human soul.[57] The agent intellect is first of all the soul's power to abstract the intelligible forms of things from the matter represented in their sensible

---

54. For a magisterial discussion of the general topic of the self-evident, see Tuninetti, "Per se notum."

55. In the *Summa theologiae,* he introduces the notion of *synderesis* in ST I.79.12.

56. ST I–II.57.2.

57. That the light by which we discern good and evil is the agent intellect is explicit in *De spir. creat.* a. 10.

images. The abstracted forms themselves also "illumine" the mind. Through them, the mind discerns truth about the things that they are the forms of.[58] But it is only by the agent intellect's abstracting the forms that their illuminative power is actualized. Moreover it is in judgment—composition and division, or in other words affirmation and denial, by which propositions are formed—that the mind grasps truth.[59] Propositions are very definitely things that the mind makes or "constitutes."[60] And so Thomas can say that "from the very nature of the intellectual soul, it belongs to man that, having grasped what a whole is and what a part is, he immediately grasps that every whole is greater than its part; and likewise with the others"—the "others" being the other truths pertaining to the understanding of principles, whether speculative or practical.[61]

I mention these earlier discussions in the *Summa* as a way of stressing that the precepts of natural law are quite similar to speculative principles. They are propositions, with subject and predicate. Their truth is perceived immediately, by the fact that the predicate pertains to the concept or the intelligibility of the subject. And, it should be added, what truth is for them is the very same as what it is for speculative principles. It is their correspondence with the things that they are about, saying the things to be as they are, or not to be as they are not. Quite generally, what truth is or what it is to be true for speculative thought is the same as what it is for practical thought.[62] These similarities do not sit very well with Maritain's view of the knowledge of the precepts of natural law as knowledge by connaturality. Nor do they sit well with the theory of Grisez and Finnis, according to which precepts have a radically different nature from that of speculative propositions, and the nature of their truth differs no less radically.[63] The importance of the similarities for my own view should become apparent as we proceed.

Back in 94.2, Thomas draws a broad distinction among self-evident principles. Some are self-evident in themselves but not to us. Others are also self-evident to us. A proposition is self-evident in itself if the predicate is contained in the intelligibility of the subject. But not every proposition of this sort is self-evident to us, because in some cases we do not grasp, or grasp fully, the intelligibilities of the subject and the predicate. Thomas makes it clear, however, that the precepts of natural law consist in principles

58. See *ST* I.84.5; cf. I–II.3.6.
59. *ST* I.16.2.
60. See *In De an.* III.5, lines 81–86.
61. *ST* I–II.51.1.
62. See *ST* I–II.64.3.
63. I discuss this in Brock, "Practical Truth."

that are self-evident not only in themselves but also commonly or naturally to all men. This does not mean that the knowledge of them is innate, but that the process of apprehending their terms requires no special instruction or effort, and that even the most uncultivated minds are apt to know them. If their faculties are not stunted, they will know them. One of his examples is *whole is greater than part*. Here he also observes that among the things that fall into everyone's apprehension, there is an order in which they do so. Thus there is one very first object of apprehension, being, the grasp of which is included in the grasp of anything else, and upon it is founded one first truth, which evidently is included in the constitution of any other truth: to affirm and to deny [the same thing] do not go together.

In the second stage of the argument in 94.2, Thomas explains why the precept to do and seek the good and to avoid the bad must be regarded as the very first or most common principle of practical reason. Why is it that nothing falls under the consideration of practical reason except insofar as it is seen in light of the notion of the good, and hence also of its contrary, the bad? It is that practical reason is reason directing action. Since every agent acts for an end, the starting-point of the direction of action is the consideration of the end to be acted for. But nothing can be understood as an end except what is understood to be good. "End has the intelligibility (*ratio*) of good." To relate to something as an end is to desire it, and "the good is what all desire." Notice that Aquinas is not here explaining why it is that the proposition that the good is to be done and sought, and the bad avoided, is self-evident. He is only arguing, *a posteriori*, for the primacy of this proposition in practical reason. He means to show that reason is practical, or operates for an end, only to the extent that it operates according to its understanding of what good and bad are. This is *a posteriori*, because reason's being practical at all depends on the notions of good and bad. Reason can act for an end only because and insofar as it understands good and bad, just as it can grasp truth only because and insofar as it understands being and non-being.

As I read it, however, in the third stage of the argument Aquinas does, in effect, go on to provide an explanation of why the precept to do the good and avoid the bad is self-evident. It is a remark that he offers with a view to showing how it is that there are many other self-evident precepts founded upon the first one, and doing so in a way that sets up his subsequent presentation of the order among the precepts according to the order of man's natural inclinations. It is within this stage that the natural inclination text appears, and so I wish to dwell upon it at some length.

The stage begins in this way:

> And upon this [first precept] are founded all other precepts of the law of nature, in such a way, to wit, that all those things to be done or avoided will pertain to natural law, which practical reason naturally apprehends to be human goods. And since the good has the intelligibility (*ratio*) of end, and the bad the intelligibility of the contrary, it follows that all the things to which man has natural inclination, reason naturally apprehends as good, and consequently as things to be pursued by action, and their contraries as bad and to be avoided. Therefore, the order of the precepts of natural law is according to the order of natural inclinations.

The second sentence here has quite a complicated structure. At first glance, it seems to draw two conclusions from the same premise. The premise is that good has the *ratio* of end, and bad the *ratio* of the contrary. The first conclusion, presented as a conclusion by the words *it follows that*, is that all the things to which man is naturally inclined, reason naturally apprehends as good. The second, presented by the word *consequently*, is that the things naturally apprehended as good are also apprehended as things to be done and sought, and their contraries as bad and to be avoided.

One way to avoid reading this as drawing two conclusions from the same premise might be to see the second conclusion as making an implicit appeal to the formulation, in the argument's second stage, of the first principle of practical reason.[64] The sentence would then mean that because good has the *ratio* of end, and bad the *ratio* of the contrary, everything to which man is naturally inclined, reason naturally apprehends as good; and because (in light of the first precept) reason naturally knows that the good is to be done and sought, and the bad avoided, reason also naturally apprehends all of these things as to be done and sought, and their contraries as bad and to be avoided. However, this reading is unsatisfactory, for at least three reasons.

First, it is not at all clear how it follows, from the fact that good has the *ratio* of an end, and bad the *ratio* of the contrary, that reason naturally apprehends as good all the things to which man is naturally inclined. It does not follow even if being inclined to something is the same as having it as an end.[65] For the supposed premise means that every good is an end, whereas the supposed conclusion implies only that every end is a good. Nor does the supposed premise even imply that everything to which man is naturally

---

64. This is how Grisez reads it. See Grisez, "First Principle," 356–58.
65. See *ST* I.5.4*ad*1. Appetite is as though a certain motion toward a thing.

inclined is something that reason naturally apprehends at all—let alone as an end and as good.

Secondly, this reading overlooks the fact that the second stage of the argument said nothing in the way of explaining the first precept; that is, of showing why reason must naturally understand the good as to be done and sought, and the bad as to be avoided. It only showed why this understanding must come first in any operation of practical reason. Hence it does not really explain why the things that reason naturally apprehends as good, it naturally apprehends as to be done and sought, and the contraries as bad and to be avoided. An explanation of that would have to be an explanation of the first precept itself.

The third reason is that Thomas does after all provide such an explanation. It is precisely the statement that the good has the *ratio* of an end and the bad the *ratio* of the contrary. This shows why the proposition that the good is to be done and sought, and the bad avoided, is self-evident; and, likewise, why whatever is apprehended as good is apprehended as to be pursued by action, and its contrary as bad and to be avoided.[66] To say that the *ratio* of an end is in the *ratio* of good is to say that whatever is apprehended as good is apprehended as an end. And to be an end just is to be something that is to be pursued by action, and something whose contrary is to be avoided. In other words, the first clause of the sentence functions by itself as the premise for the third. This is supported by the presence of the terms *good*, *bad* and *contrary* in both clauses.

On this view, then, the sentence would mean, in part, that because good has the *ratio* of end, and bad the *ratio* of the contrary, all the things that reason naturally apprehends as good, it naturally apprehends as to be pursued by action, and the contraries as bad and to be avoided. This is simply to say that all such things are matters of precepts of natural law, precepts that fall under the very first precept as particular truths whose intelligibility contains that of one common truth. But what about the middle clause, which is precisely our natural inclination text? How does it figure in the argument? Does it not in fact constitute another premise? It provides a way of identifying the things mentioned in the previous sentence, the things that practical reason naturally apprehends as human goods. It tells us that the things to which man is naturally inclined are such things. This, taken together with the next clause, which says that all such things are matters of precepts of natural law, leads directly to the conclusion that Thomas wants, regarding the order of the precepts. This conclusion is the next sentence:

---

66. On what it means to explain a proposition's self-evidence, see above, 98.

"Therefore, the order of the precepts of natural law is according to the order of natural inclinations."

NATURAL INCLINATIONS FOLLOWING UPON NATURAL UNDERSTANDING

So we are back to the natural inclination text. In 94.2 it functions as a premise. What, for Thomas, is its own status as a truth? Must he not be taking it to be self-evident? Otherwise, in so fundamental a discussion, would he not have argued for it? But if it is self-evident, then its truth should be easy to see. If, however, we assume, as most readers do, that what it is referring to are pre-rational inclinations, then its truth is anything but easy to see. There are many non-rational inclinations existing in us by nature whose objects do not become known to us except after much investigation, if at all—certainly not "naturally." Think of some strictly physiological inclination, such as the natural tendency for our brain synapses to fire. Their firing is certainly a good thing. But it is hardly something that we are naturally aware of. Thomas did not even know that brains have synapses.

Or is it that the natural inclination text is to be understood as a conclusion from the principle laid down in the previous stage, that an end—an object of inclination—has the *ratio* of good? But in the previous stage, that principle was intended only to show that whatever reason takes as an end, it takes as a good; this is why the first principle of practical reason, which is reason reasoning for an end, is founded on the notion of the good. From this it can hardly be inferred that everything which is an end of some pre-rational process, every object of a pre-rational inclination, is something that reason itself naturally takes as an end or as a good.

I maintain that Thomas is taking the natural inclination text to be self-evident, and that its truth is even easy to perceive—once the meanings of its terms are rightly understood. To take *natural inclination* to mean pre-rational inclination, however, is to misunderstand it. The text is talking about the things to which *man* has natural inclination. Earlier in 94.2 Thomas had said that "he who says *man*, says *rational*." The natural inclination text is talking about the things to which man *as man* is naturally inclined, which is to say, the things to which *reason* naturally inclines man. It is just what he had said years before, in his *Sentences* commentary: "Natural inclination is from natural reason."[67]

So taken, the text needs no explanation or defense. It is talking about natural inclinations of the will. Reason does incline us to things. It does so

---

67. *In Sent.* III.33.2.3.

precisely by apprehending them as good, as desirable. What reason naturally apprehends as good, the rational appetite—the will—naturally desires. The very notion of a natural inclination of the will includes the notion of its object's being naturally apprehended by reason as good. Man, as man, is naturally inclined to certain things, *because* reason naturally apprehends them as good. To say that all the things to which man has natural inclination, reason naturally apprehends as good, is simply to say that all the things to which reason naturally inclines man are things that it naturally apprehends as good.

In a moment I shall undertake to argue for this reading of the natural inclination text. First, let me restate the third stage of 94.2 in a way that makes more visible how I understand the logic of its argument.

> And upon this [first precept] are founded all other precepts of the law of nature, in such a way, to wit, that all those things to be done or avoided will pertain to natural law, which practical reason naturally apprehends to be human goods. And since the good has the intelligibility of an end, and the bad the intelligibility of the contrary, everything that reason naturally apprehends as good, it consequently naturally apprehends as to be pursued in action, and the contrary as bad and to be avoided. And because everything to which man, as man—man as rational—is naturally inclined, reason naturally apprehends as good, the order of the precepts of natural law is according to the order of man's natural inclinations.

This reading can be defended in as many as five or six ways.

First, it establishes a direct connection between 94.2 and the proof of the existence of natural law in *ST* I–II.91.2. There, as we saw, it was argued that man "shares in the eternal reason (*ratio*) through which he has natural inclination toward due act and end." Notice the "through which." Man partakes in the *ratio*, the intelligible conception, that is the very source of natural inclination in him. Thomas goes on to trace this share in the eternal reason to the light of man's own natural reason, "by which we discern what good is and what bad is." The natural apprehension of things as good, and their contraries as bad, is a *source* of natural inclinations. Moreover, that article's second objection argues that there is no natural law for man, because the function of a law is to order acts to an end, and the ordination of human acts to an end cannot be through the sort of natural desire by which irrational creatures act for an end. This is because man acts for an end by reason and will. The objector is taking *natural* in the sense of something pre-rational. But Thomas's reply makes no appeal to anything in us that is natural in this sense. Instead, he simply reminds us that reason and will themselves have a natural dimension. "All reasoning derives from principles naturally known, and all appetite of things that are for the end derive from the natural appetite of the last end. And so likewise, the first direction of our acts toward the end must come about through a natural law." Surely this already precludes taking the natural inclination text in 94.2 as referring to pre-rational inclinations. It is referring to inclinations pertaining to reason and will, inclinations that are at the root of the order of *human* actions.[68] These are the actions that pertain to man *as* man. "Because a man is what he is on account of reason, only that operation which proceeds from reason through the will, which is the rational appetite, is said to be human without qualification."[69]

What Thomas says about operation is also true of inclination. We see this in an earlier passage in the *Prima secundae*. The topic is the theological virtues, which order us to a supernatural end. Thomas draws a comparison with our order toward our "connatural" end, which is through a certain "natural inclination."

> But this [inclination] comes about in function of two factors. First, in function of reason or intellect, insofar as it [intellect] contains first universal principles known to us by the natural light of the intellect, from which reason proceeds both in speculable and in practical matters. Second, through the rectitude of the will naturally tending toward the good of reason.[70]

The tendency, the inclination, belongs to the will. And it is very definitely the understanding of principles that is the source of the inclination to the end, not the other way around.

Furthermore, the inclinations in question here must be inclinations common to all people or natural to them according to the nature of the human species.[71] This is implied in the indication given in *ST* I–II.91.2, that natural law is that through which man is first disposed to participate in providence, to provide "for himself *and others*." The power to provide not only for oneself but also for other men requires some grasp of what is due to any human being, as human, to do, seek and avoid. It is also implied by

---

68. See *ST* I–II.1.1.

69. *ST* III.19.2.

70. *ST* I–II.62.3. See also I–II.63.2*ad*3. Thomas's early *Sentences* commentary is already very clear about this. "In every nature there is instilled a certain natural inclination toward its end, and therefore in reason there is a certain natural rectitude, through which it is inclined to the end" (*In Sent*. II.42.2.5). See also *De ver*. 14.2.

71. Finnis himself makes this point in Finnis, *Aquinas*, 93n150.

the fact that the precepts immediately corresponding to these inclinations are described as common to everyone, immutable in themselves, and indelibly written on the human heart.[72] Precepts with such characteristics do not fit inclinations peculiar to this or that individual or part of mankind, even peculiar inclinations that are natural. But according to Aquinas, one's pre-rational inclinations, inasmuch as they arise from the nature of one's body, pertain to one's individual nature, not to one's common, human nature. The inclinations that are natural according to the nature of the species are those that arise from the rational soul, which is the form through which one is a human being.[73] This, as we saw, is why Aquinas can say unqualifiedly that those who follow the "inclinations of sensitive nature" rather than the "order of reason" act "contrary to nature."[74] They act "contrary to the nature of man insofar as he is man," whereas it is "what is according to reason" that is "according to the nature of man insofar as he is man."[75] Unreasoned feeling may be right or wrong.[76] The inclinations proper to individuals, pertaining to their bodily powers, do not pertain per se to natural law. With respect to them, what pertains to natural law is only the common principle that all of our inclinations be ruled by reason.[77]

Thus this reading does not face the problem that I originally raised about the common reading of the natural inclination text. We do not need to find pre-rational natural inclinations that are always right and that can be identified independently of reason's apprehension of their objects as good. The passage in which Thomas says that natural inclination is always right is about the natural love of angels. *All* of their natural inclination is intellectual inclination, inclination of will. And the natural inclination of man as man, too, is inclination of will. The other inclinations in a man are only inclinations of this or that part.[78] These inclinations, Thomas says, pertain

---

72. *ST* I-II.94.4-6.

73. See *ST* I-II.51.1; I-II.63.1; I.83.1*ad*5.

74. *ST* I-II.71.2*ad*3.

75. *ST* I-II.71.2c. In the *Sentences* commentary he puts it very strongly: "The will of sensuality naturally inclines toward that which pleases the flesh, which is suitable to it, and which is an evil of man, insofar as he is man; but the rational will, according as it is the nature of man, or according as it follows the natural apprehension of the universal principles of right, is that which inclines to good" (*In Sent.* II.39.2.2c; cf. *ad*1, where he says that the will of sensuality naturally tends toward an evil of man, insofar as he is man, chiefly insofar as it is corrupted by the *fomes*).

76. In addition to the passages already cited, see *ST* I-II.78.3; I.81.3*ad*1/*ad*2; I-II.91.6; I-II.94.4; *In Eth.* VI.11, 375, lines 42–51; *In Meta.* XII, lect. 7, §2522; *De malo* 16.2.

77. *ST* I-II.94.4*ad*3.

78. "The will is the essential appetite of the whole man, insofar as he is a man,

to natural law only "insofar as they are ruled by reason."⁷⁹ They are not *principles* of reason's rule.

This is not to say that the ends proper to each of the powers are not things that reason naturally apprehends as good. They are. That is why the will itself is naturally inclined to them.⁸⁰ But the apprehension of them as good does not consist simply in seeing them as the objects of the powers' natural inclinations toward them. It involves seeing them as perfective of and suitable to the powers' operations, this being *why* the powers are inclined toward them; *and* it involves seeing them as suitable to the whole person.⁸¹ The inclinations of the powers toward their proper objects (which is by divine ordination) are right, but they are right *because* the objects are good, and if reason judges them to be right, it is in light of its understanding the objects as good. But the inclinations that "pertain to natural law" are those that are moved or ruled by reason's understanding itself. And the will's own natural inclination is right only because it is moved by intellect's natural cognition of the good, and because intellect's natural cognition—which is nothing other than its natural understanding of principles, speculative and practical—is always right.⁸² In voluntary matters, Thomas says, even if the rectitude of reasoning about the things that are for an end depends on the rectitude of the appetite of the end, nevertheless the rectitude of the appetite of the end itself depends upon the right apprehension of the end, which is through reason.⁸³ Even as regards the last end considered merely

---

because it follows upon the human soul, which is the proper form of the whole man, as he is a man. . . . Therefore man naturally wants to be and to live according to the threefold classification of vegetative, sensitive, and rational life" (Ramírez, *De actibus humanis*, 224).

79. See *ST* I–II.94.2*ad*2.

80. *ST* I–II.10.1.

81. See *ST* I.80.1*ad*3; I–II.10.1 (quoted below, 158). Also, it is not clear to me that Thomas thinks that the understanding of the goodness of the object to which a particular power is naturally inclined always gives rise to a *primary* precept of natural law, one that cannot be deleted from the heart. Consider what *ST* I–II.94.6 says about the so-called "sins against nature" (cf. *ST* II–II.154.12). The *universal* prohibition of lying does not seem to be primary either, or even secondary (involving only a little reasoning). See *ST* I–II.100.11. However, perhaps the precept to avoid ignorance (see 94.2*c*) cannot be deleted, since the intellect's understanding of itself and of its own perfection, truth, is presupposed to the understanding of the good itself. See *ST* I–II.16.4. Practical reason's apprehension of the human good, as human, can hardly fail to include an apprehension of reason's proper good.

82. See *ST* I.17.3*ad*2; *In De an.* III.9, 246, lines 101–110.

83. *ST* I–II.19.3*ad*2. See also *ST* I–II.58.4; II–II.47.6.

formally or abstractly—*beatitudo in communi*—the desire of it depends on the apprehension of it.[84]

Another consideration is that, in 94.2 itself, Thomas says that the things which pertain to natural law are those that practical reason naturally apprehends as human goods. Evidently the inclination belonging to man from the nature of the human species is also an inclination whose very object is presented as good according to the species, or as what is good for the human being as human. This would be impossible, were it not an inclination arising from intellect. Only the intellect apprehends the species of things. Only through intellect can we grasp something *as* human.

Someone might object that really the inclination of man as man is neither the inclination of any bodily power nor that of the will, but simply the inclination of human nature itself, that is, man's very essence. The powers are only accidents, qualities.[85] Now, Thomas does teach that the components of a subject's essence—its substantial form and matter—are already a sort of inclination.[86] And no doubt he thinks such inclination always right. However, as he explains in the same place, its range is rather limited. It is only toward what is included within the subject's own substantial being.[87] Any inclinations toward objects that extend outside the subject's being must be distinct from its essence. They must be accidents. Most of the objects of inclination mentioned in 94.2 are clearly not included in man's substantial being. Many of them cannot be objects of the sense-appetite either. But all of them are objects of the will, objects of its natural inclination. This comes out quite clearly in *ST* I–II.10.1, which finds a number of clear echoes in 94.2.

This reading also does not face the problem of the possibility of natural inclinations that are not naturally apprehended. Inclinations of the will cannot fail to be apprehended by the intellect of the person who has them. I shall discuss the intellect's apprehension of the will in more detail below.

Finally, Thomas is quite ready to speak of reason itself as a source of inclination, as "inclining" man toward things. In discussing *synderesis*, for instance, he says that it "is not open to opposites, but inclines to good alone."[88] Again, in explaining how matrimony is natural or something toward which nature inclines, he says that it is natural "because natural reason inclines (*inclinat*) toward it."[89] Speaking of reason as inclining is not incompatible with

---

84. See *ST* I–II.5.8c/obj1/ad1; I–II.10.2.
85. *ST* I.77.1.
86. *ST* I.59.2.
87. Cf. Lisska, *Aquinas's Theory*, 96–100.
88. *ST* I.79.12sc.
89. *ST Suppl.* 41.1 (*In Sent.* IV.26.1.1).

the understanding of the will as the dominant moving power in the soul. It means merely that practical intellect inclines, "not as executing movement, but as directing toward movement."[90] The will has primacy as an agent, applying the powers of the soul to the exercise of their acts. But it actually does this only insofar as it is actually inclined to do so, and its inclination always follows some direction provided by the intellect.[91] Since every agent acts for an end, the will cannot move anything until it is actually inclined toward something. It is through the intellect that the soul first takes on a likeness of the end and is thereby first fully capable of inclinations proportioned to the end.

This is not to say that the will adds nothing of its own and is nothing but an instrument of the intellect. The intellect moves it by presenting its object. This serves to specify its act, as an act of willing this or that (or of nilling it, if the object is presented as bad). Without an object the will cannot will. In addition to a principle of specification, however, the will also needs a principle of the very exercise of its act, since it passes from not willing to willing. Once it is moved to something, it can move itself to the act of willing something else for the sake of it; but its first act, which is its willing of the last end, has to be moved by something else. This can only be God.[92] But God's moving of the will, in this respect, is nothing other than His creating and conserving it in its own nature, in such a way that it is naturally moved to will the last end—*when* that end is presented to it by the intellect. We might say that the understanding of good and bad releases, and at the same time directs, that energy for willing with which the human soul is naturally endowed.

GETTING AT THE NATURAL INCLINATIONS

However, there still remains a question. If man's natural understanding of the human goods and of the precepts regarding them is prior to his natural inclination toward them, why is it that Thomas goes on to say that "the order of the precepts of natural law is according to the order of the natural inclinations," and to lay out the order of the precepts by reference to the order of the inclinations? Does this not imply that the inclinations are prior to the precepts and that the precepts are a function of them?

It implies only that the inclinations enjoy a certain priority of consideration, within the perspective from which Thomas approaches the precepts

---

90. *ST* I.79.11*ad*1.
91. See *ST* I.80.2.
92. *ST* I-II.9.4; I-II.9.6.

of natural law in 94.2. The inclinations are effects of the precepts, not principles, but they are quite proportionate effects, and for that reason they can be used to get at the precepts. Why does he adopt this approach? Because he thinks that these particular natural inclinations—those of man—can in turn be gotten at by starting from the consideration of the natural inclinations of irrational things. This is how he proceeds in 94.2. I would like to suggest that he has good reasons for adopting this strategy.

First of all, whether or not the presentation of an *order* of the precepts of natural law is of any relevance here, Finnis is certainly right to say that it is metaphysical. The whole perspective of 94.2 is metaphysical. It takes us back to the consideration of being itself and the principle of non-contradiction. And this is hardly a mere sudden burst of speculative fervor on Thomas's part. The perspective from which he first introduced natural law, in *ST* I–II.91.2, was already quite metaphysical. He presented natural law in the setting of God's universal providence and of its common effect in all creatures, which is their possession of natural inclinations toward their proper acts and ends. All beings, insofar as they are beings, have natural inclination. On the whole, natural inclination is more common than natural understanding. Not all things have knowledge of precepts, but all have inclinations. This is itself a reason for starting from inclinations. The move from inclinations to precepts is a move from the more common to the more particular. This sort of move is extremely typical of Thomas. 94.2 itself is filled with such moves. The very order that he presents, among the inclinations and among the precepts, is from the more common to the more particular. It starts from inclination toward a good of the nature common to all substances, the conservation of their natural being, and ends with inclination toward the good of man's proper nature, the nature of reason.

In the next chapter I shall look at this order more closely, and I shall argue that it is after all quite relevant to the intention of 94.2. But there is more to consider here regarding Thomas's use of irrational things to get at the natural inclinations of the human will. It says a good deal about how he understands these inclinations. And this is very important for understanding his conception of natural law. Even if, as I am arguing, the natural inclinations of man are not sources of the precepts of natural law, they do go hand in hand with the promulgation of the precepts. God's object in promulgating the precepts is not just that we know them, but that we be inclined to comply with them or "induced to act" according to them through our knowledge of them. Natural inclination is a universal effect of the promulgation of the eternal law. In man's case, it is brought about with and through knowledge of precepts, but it is no less integral to the promulgation's effect. We naturally participate in the eternal law both by way of cognition and by way of inclination.

> Because rational nature, together with what is common to all creatures, has something proper to it insofar as it is rational, it is subject to the eternal law in both ways. For in some way it has a notion of the eternal law, and, in addition, within each rational creature is a natural inclination toward what is consonant with the eternal law; for as *Ethics* 2 says, we are naturally prone toward having the virtues.[93]

Now 94.2 is not the first place in the *Summa* where Thomas gets at natural inclinations of the will by way of the inclinations of irrational things. He first does so in the *Prima pars*, and in fact there he tells us why he does so. The topic is not the human will, but the angelic. (This is where he says that natural inclination is always right, being instilled by the Author of nature.) With angels, there can be no talk of pre-rational inclinations. Yet, strikingly, in order to establish the existence of certain natural angelic inclinations, Thomas points to analogous natural inclinations in irrational things. There is natural inclination toward the good in oneself, or natural self-love; there is natural inclination toward the good of the others that share one's nature; there is natural love of God more than oneself.[94] In presenting this last love, Thomas also declares the general validity of this method. "For inclination in the things that are without reason shows the natural inclination in the will of an intellectual nature."[95]

Here Thomas is in the course of arguing that angels love God more than themselves, not only with "love of concupiscence," by which they want the divine good for themselves (as far as they can share in it), but also with "love of friendship," by which they want Him to have His own good.[96] Angels naturally want God to have His perfection and His good even more than they want themselves to have theirs. This is because they belong to Him more than to themselves. But Thomas argues for this love in the spiritual creatures by appealing to what irrational physical beings are

---

93. *ST* I–II.93.6. The reference is to Aristotle, *Nicomachean Ethics* II.1, 1103a25.
94. *ST* I.60.3–5.
95. *ST* I.60.5.
96. Thomas had offered a brief but highly metaphysical explanation of the difference between these kinds of love two articles earlier (*ST* I.60.3). They go together. Love of concupiscence is the love of the good that one wants some subject to have. Love of friendship is the love of the subject itself, as that for the benefit of which one wants the good. See *ST* I–II.26.4; II–II.25.3; *In De div. nom.* 4.9, §404. Very helpful discussions of the two loves can be found in Gallagher, "Desire for Beatitude"; "Person and Ethics"; "Thomas Aquinas on Self-Love."

naturally moved or inclined toward. He thinks this is fairly easy to discern. The natural inclination of such beings "is shown from the way in which they naturally behave, because 'each one is naturally apt to behave in the way that it naturally does behave,' as it says in *Physics* II."[97] The example that he cites here is the hand. It will, without deliberation, expose itself to a blow in order to protect the whole body that it is essentially and entirely a part of.

At this point Thomas adds another striking remark: "And because reason imitates nature, we find inclination of this sort in political virtues; for a virtuous citizen will expose himself to the danger of death for the conservation of the whole polity; and if a man were a natural part of this city, this inclination would be natural."[98] Now by *reason* here, he means the specifically human intellect. That is what imitates nature, understood as the realm of natural irrational things. I think this idea, that reason imitates nature, is also at work, implicitly, in the account of the order of the precepts of natural law in 94.2. I shall want to discuss it at some length in the next chapter, where I shall try to explain how Thomas thinks knowledge of nature does after all function as a principle of the human knowledge of precepts of natural law. But the remark also serves to remind us that, unlike the inclinations of irrational beings, not all of the inclinations of the human will are natural. As we saw, virtue is "according to" nature, but it does not exist "by" nature. It is not something that people have, or exercise, always or for the most part. This is so even though they do, by nature, have inclination toward virtue and toward acting virtuously.[99]

Moreover, not even the natural inclinations that are common to rational and irrational beings are simply identical. Their very way of being differs. Thomas is quite explicit about this:

> What is prior is always preserved in what is posterior to it. But nature is prior to intellect, since the nature of each thing is its essence. Hence, that which belongs to nature must be preserved even in beings that have intellect. Now it is common to every nature to have a certain inclination that constitutes its natural appetite or love. Nevertheless this inclination is found in diverse ways (*diversimode*) in diverse natures, and in each according to its own mode. Hence, in an intellectual nature there is natural inclination in function of the will, whereas in a sentient nature there is natural inclination in function of the sentient appetite,

---

97. *ST* I.60.5; cf. *De virt.* 2.4ad2. The reference is to Aristotle, *Physics* II.8, 199a9–11.
98. *ST* I.60.5.
99. *ST* I–II.93.6; I–II.94.3.

and in a nature that lacks cognition there is only the nature's being ordered toward something.[100]

Thus Thomas distinguishes between natural inclination or love that is *merely* natural, and natural love that adds to naturalness the perfection of sense or intellect.[101]

What difference does an inclination's being intellectual make? In one respect, it does indeed add perfection. Such inclination relates to the good in a more perfect way—a more absolute or unconditioned way. The will tends toward the good just insofar as it is good.[102] This is because the intellect grasps the good in an absolute way. And the same holds for specific goods. For instance, in 94.2, the first natural inclination that Thomas posits is that of substances toward the conservation of their natural being. All substances, not just animals, have this. But the rational substance has it far more perfectly than inanimate beings and even other animals do. "Each thing naturally in its own way desires to exist. Now desire in things having cognition follows cognition. But sense does not know existence except as here and now, whereas intellect apprehends existence absolute and with respect to all time. Hence everything having intellect naturally desires to exist always."[103]

However, there is also a sense in which the natural inclinations of the human will, in themselves, are less perfect than those of other things. They are less determinate. Of course they are not totally indeterminate. They have objects that specify them. But their objects are things grasped by the intellect, and the human intellect's proper way of grasping things is universal or general. What it directly grasps are the natures of things. The direct grasp of particular individuals of a given nature pertains to sensation. But the way in which things really exist, outside the soul, is particular; and appetite is distinguished from cognition precisely by the fact that it tends toward things in their real existence outside the soul.[104]

---

100. *ST* I.60.1. See also *ST* I–II.10.1*ad*1.

101. *ST* I.60.1*ad*1.

102. *ST* I.59.1.

103. *ST* I.75.6. Also, by the way, Dewan is surely right to insist that the inclination toward conservation in being regards not only the individual's own being but also that of his species; see his "Natural Law and the First Act of Freedom: Maritain Revisited," in Dewan, *Wisdom, Law, and Virtue*, 238. See also Brock, "The Primacy of the Common Good," 252. Thomas is explicit on this point in *ST* II–II.152.2*obj*1, where he makes the conservation of the species a precept of natural law. And notice that the context is a defense of virginity. Clearly, the natural inclination that he is talking about in 94.2 is not an inclination of the sense-appetite. It is toward the conservation of the species, taken absolutely. That is, it leaves quite indeterminate what the one so inclined is to do for the sake of that end. No mere sense-inclination can be indeterminate in this way.

104. See *ST* I.59.2; I.78.1; I–II.16.4.

> The will stands between the intellect and exterior operation, since the intellect proposes the will's object to it, and the will itself causes exterior action. So, then, the beginning of the will's movement is taken on the side of the intellect, which apprehends something as good universally; but the completion or the perfection of the will's act is taken according to its order toward the operation by which one tends toward the attainment of the thing. For the will's movement is from the soul toward the thing.[105]

In order to be complete and a principle of action, then, the will's inclination needs to be determined or particularized. Actions are in particulars.[106]

I do not mean that the indeterminacy of the will's natural inclination is a downright defect. It is the universality of the will's object that makes free choice, *self*-determination, possible.[107] However, this indeterminacy also has other consequences. For one thing, it makes the natural inclination itself harder to isolate for consideration. In the case of irrational things lacking all cognition, their natural inclinations are in a way less determinate than the external operations that they carry out, but only inasmuch as the operations have accidental features resulting from the circumstances. These can easily be filtered out by considering the operations of a number of things of the same kind. "Each one is naturally apt to behave in the way that it naturally does behave." And even among irrational animals, fairly specific patterns of activity common to all the members of a kind can be discerned without much difficulty. But in the case of human beings, it is not at all easy to say, simply by observing their actions, what inclinations are truly common and natural to them. Even within oneself, while it may not always be difficult to know what one wants, it is not so easy to identify what is truly natural in one's wants, or what it is that one wants simply by virtue of being the kind of thing that one is.

There is also the further complication that sometimes we are inclined toward particulars that are opposed to what we ourselves, considering the matter universally, take to be our good. This is largely because the inclinations of the sense-appetite, the passions, are not always according to reason, and because they are already determinate, bearing immediately on particulars. This is why they can have a great influence on our actual conduct.[108] This was the problem that I originally raised for the common reading of the

---

105. *ST* I–II.13.5*ad*1.
106. *ST* I.29.1.
107. See *ST* I.59.3.
108. See *ST* I–II.9.2*ad*2.

natural inclination text. That reading seemed to lead to the conclusion that the things that people do for the most part, or (in a sense) naturally, must be the very things toward which the precepts of natural law direct them; whereas in fact, unlike irrational things, people for the most part go astray. The natural inclinations of the human will cannot simply be read off from human actions, as though the actions were nearly always, and seldom anything but, direct executions of the inclinations. Sometimes the inclination does not get executed at all. Thus notice that Thomas does *not* argue for the existence, in angels, of a natural love of God above all by appealing to how human beings typically behave toward God. He does not do so, even though he thinks that human beings too have a natural inclination to love Him above themselves. For he also thinks that, given original sin, and without the supernatural help of God's grace, they absolutely cannot put this inclination into practice in their deliberate conduct. Without grace, they inevitably prefer the "private good."[109]

These considerations, however, seem to suggest that the problem I raised for the common reading of the natural inclination text also bears in a way on my own. Mine skirts the difficulty of explaining how reason naturally knows which of our inclinations are natural, so as thereby to know naturally what our true goods are, because it makes the relevant inclinations derive from reason's natural knowledge of the goods themselves. This ensures that the inclinations are always right. But the question would be whether it is after all so clear that our natural knowledge of the good *does* elicit natural inclinations. If for the most part our conduct is not fully in accord with what the inclinations are supposed to be, what grounds are there for even positing them? Donagan might suggest that Thomas's grounds are theological: his belief in creation and divine providence. His belief in divine justice would also be pertinent. If human beings had no natural aptitude at all for complying with His law, how could it be just to judge them by it?

Perhaps Thomas's primary grounds are indeed theological. However, as we saw, he does think that he finds support in Aristotle for the view that "we are naturally prone toward having the virtues." He also finds Aristotle taking the order of human things, the ethical order, to be radically different from the order of irrational natural things. Its intelligibility is different.[110] The natural inclinations of irrational beings are principles of bodily processes and movements. That is where they show themselves. But the natural inclinations of human beings, as human, are rational inclinations, and

---

109. *ST* I–II.109.3.

110. A sign of this is that the two orders pertain not just to different sciences but to different *genera* of science—practical and theoretical.

where they show up is in the life of reason. Even if people do not, for the most part, fully comply with the order of reason in their actions, their lives do for the most part involve various sorts of exercise of reason, voluntary ones, and it is to these that Aristotle looks in the effort to determine the common ends toward which reason directs human conduct: prevailing opinions and practices, cultural forms, and perhaps above all, human laws and customs. Obviously it is not that these things turn out to be uniform, or even entirely consistent with each other. But common general patterns and tendencies do emerge.[111]

There are also phenomena in the rational life of individuals that are pertinent. Even if people often fail to comply with the order of reason, and even with their own considered opinion of what it requires, they are not indifferent about the fact. They will try to excuse the failure, or justify it, or ignore it. And when these dodges fail, they will be pained by it. There is such a thing as remorse. Thomas sees it as proof of a natural inclination to follow reason.[112]

I shall return to these effects of the natural inclinations of the will in chapter 6, within the discussion of the force of natural law. But I cannot yet close the question of Thomas's view of the role of nature in the promulgation of natural law. I have only taken a position on what it is not. The natural understanding of human goods and of the precepts pertaining to them is not the effect of natural inclinations. But nature can still be involved in it in other ways. The first thing to consider is its involvement in the understanding of the good itself.

---

111. For this reason, I think Flannery, *Acts Amid Precepts,* is quite right to look to human laws and common human practices for a path toward the disclosure of the common principles of natural law. This would be the suitable approach for ethical science. I do not think that Thomas's metaphysical approach in the *Summa* is meant as an alternative to that, let alone a substitute. Rather, he takes it for granted, just as he takes physical science for granted. His own task is the final, sapiential determination of the matter.

112. See below, 208.

5

Nature and Human Nature in the Promulgation of Natural Law

THE INTELLIGIBILITY OF THE GOOD

In the previous chapter, I briefly discussed the reading of Thomas on natural law put forth by Germain Grisez and John Finnis. I mentioned that, although they do assign a certain preliminary role to natural inclinations in the genesis of the understanding of the precepts of natural law, they do not want to see the precepts as direct functions of the inclinations. They insist that the goods toward which natural law directs us are intelligible goods. Goodness itself is something intelligible, and the goods all share in it. The intelligible goodness of a thing does not consist merely in its being the object of an inclination, whether sensitive or voluntary or purely natural. By understanding goodness, the intellect is able to guide and form inclination itself. To be good, or at least to be truly and intelligibly good, is not merely to be desired. It is to be desirable.

I think that Grisez and Finnis are right to insist on this point. The good has its own intelligibility. To understand something is to grasp its nature (more or less perfectly). There is such a thing as the nature of the good or what it is to be good. Reason's natural understanding of things as human goods does not consist in simply registering desires for those things, even natural desires. It consists, at least in part, in understanding that they share in the nature of the good. It also consists in understanding that they are goods of human beings. But if we want to determine what that understanding amounts to and what (if anything) it rests on, we should first consider what the understanding of the good itself amounts to and rests on. Thomas actually has a highly developed account of the good's nature and intelligibility. And as we shall see—pace Grisez and Finnis—the intelligibility of the good is, for him, very much a function of the intelligibility of nature itself. Likewise, that of human goods is a function of that of human nature.

In 94.2 itself, Thomas tells us that the first precept of natural law is founded upon the *ratio*—this can mean either the nature or the intelligibility, or both—of the good. And he tells us what it is. His formulation is one that he takes from the beginning of the *Nicomachean Ethics* and that he cites innumerable times. "The good is what all desire." Now, taken by itself, this may indeed sound as though to be good is nothing other than to be desired, to be an object of inclination. But elsewhere Thomas explains that this formulation gets at the good by way of its proper effect. The good is desired *because* it is good.[1] To say that it is desired because it is desired makes little sense. The good, in the primary sense, is what "has in itself that whence it is desired."[2] It is the desirable. It is what makes desire itself intelligible.

Thomas does allow that sometimes when we judge a thing good, it is because we find that it fits some desire that we already have. We are especially prone to deem good that which attracts the sense-appetite. But this is not the only way, or even the primary way, in which the intellect judges something good. There is a passage in his commentary on the *Metaphysics* where Thomas is very clear about this.[3] He is discussing Aristotle's argument that the first, highest cause of things must be a final cause—a desirable, a good—and that, as the first desirable, it must be an intelligible good. Not everything that we find desirable, he observes, is an intelligible good. He points to the incontinent person. "According to reason, he is moved by the intelligible good. But according to the concupiscible power, he is moved by something pleasant to the senses, which seems good, although it is not good unqualifiedly (*simpliciter*) but only in a certain respect (*secundum quid*)." Thomas goes on to indicate how different these two ways of seeming good are. "What is desired according to concupiscence seems good because it is desired. For concupiscence perverts the judgment of reason, such that what is pleasant seems good to it. But what is desired with intellectual appetite is desired because it seems good in itself (*secundum se*)."

---

1. See *In Eth.* I.1, 5, lines 148–60.
2. *ST* I.5.6c/ad2.
3. *In Meta.* XII, lect. 7, §2522.

That which is unqualifiedly good, then, is an intelligible good. This is the primary notion of the good. The unqualified is prior in notion to the qualified. And the intelligible good is not something that seems good to reason merely because it is already desired. It seems good, desirable, in itself. Things that are good in themselves are what Thomas elsewhere calls *bona honesta*, honorable or noble goods. These are the goods that "have in themselves that whence they are desired." They are genuine origins of desire. Neither reason's judgment that they are good, nor the will's resulting desire of them, supposes any prior appetitive response to them such as pleasure. To be sure, the *bona honesta* are pleasant. But the pleasure taken in them presupposes the judgment that they are good.[4]

So it certainly is not a judgment "through inclination." In fact, pleasure need not even accompany it. There is pleasure only when what is judged good is also judged to be present.[5] If we tend to think that judgments of good and bad must always be associated with pleasure and pain, perhaps it is because we do not always distinguish sufficiently between intellect and sense. Thomas brings out the relevant difference in his commentary on *De anima* III.7 (at 431a8–16). There Aristotle says that when what is sensed is pleasant or painful, the sensitive soul, "as it were affirming or denying," pursues or shuns it. Pleasure and pain, he explains, are "the operation of the sensitive mean with respect to the good or bad as such." Thomas remarks that although making an affirmation or a negation is proper to intellect, the sense-power makes something like it when it apprehends something as pleasant or painful.[6] A little further on, turning to the intellectual soul, Aristotle says simply that when it affirms or denies an object as good or bad, it pursues or shuns. Thomas picks up on the fact that this time there is no mention of pleasure or pain. In Aristotle's account of the sensitive part, Thomas says,

> desire or shunning did not follow at once from the grasp of that which is good or bad, as here with intellect; but pleasure and pain followed, and then from this, desire and shunning [followed]. The reason for this is that just as sense does not grasp universal good, so too the appetite of the sensitive part is not moved by universal good or bad, but by a certain determinate good which is pleasant to sense, and by a certain determinate bad which is painful to sense. But in the intellective part there is the grasp of universal good and bad; whence too, the appetite of

---

4. See *ST* I–II.4.2ad2.
5. *ST* I.20.1; I–II.30.2; I–II.31.1.
6. *In De an.* III.6, lines 52–61.

the intellective part is moved immediately by the apprehended good or bad.[7]

Intellect grasps "universal good and bad," the *ratio boni* and the *ratio mali*. As he says in *ST* I–II.91.2, it discerns "what good is and what bad is." It can move desire and shunning by simply applying the concepts of good and bad to the judgment of things. Neither the judgment, nor even the desire or shunning that the judgment moves, presupposes any prior appetitive response such as pleasure or pain.[8]

What may make all of this difficult to understand (besides our tendency to confuse intellect and sense) is that the *ratio* of good does after all contain a reference to appetite. To be good is to be desirable. So in order to grasp "what a good is" and to move desire, intellect must also grasp "what desire is." This might lead us back to thinking that its grasp of the good does somehow depend upon some sort of primordial experience of inclination or appetite.[9] Now I think that in fact it does. I shall explain this in the next section. But it would be a mistake to make the grasp of the good be a function of the experience of one's *own* appetite. For this could only be one's own prerational appetite, sense-appetite. Thomas is very clear that the experience of sense-appetite does not provide the basis for grasping the *ratio boni*. This is a point that Dewan has brought out especially forcefully.[10]

In the unqualified notion of the good, if there is any one kind of desire that is essentially implicated, it is not sense-desire. It is the desire that is proportioned to the intellect itself, intellectual desire—the desire of the will.[11] This is why, in order to grasp the good, the intellect must grasp *itself*:

> First, intellect apprehends just a being (*ipsum ens*); second, it apprehends itself understanding (*apprehendit se intelligere*) a being; and third, it apprehends itself desiring (*apprehendit se appetere*) a being. Whence, although the good is in things, there

---

7. *In De an.* III.6, lines 111–26.

8. In fact, even at the level of the senses, Thomas posits an apprehension of "suitable or harmful" prior to the response of pleasure or pain (*In De an.* III.6, lines 75–79; *ST* I–II.9.1*ad*2). If pleasure or pain must follow, I take it that this is because what is apprehended by sense is apprehended in or according to its own *presence* (perhaps as merely remembered or imagined). But the universal apprehension of something simply abstracts from its presence or absence. It bears absolutely on "what the thing is."

9. See Caldera, *Le jugement par inclination*, 34.

10. See Dewan, *Wisdom, Law, and Virtue*, 114–15, 293–97.

11. On the connection between the notion of the good and the will, see also *De ver.* 1.1, where he refers the good to the appetite of the soul that is "in a way all things," which is the intellectual soul.

comes first the *ratio* of a being; second the *ratio* of a true [which is in the mind]; and third the *ratio* of a good.[12]

This talk of intellect apprehending *itself* desiring is striking. In a way, it is only shorthand for the *person* apprehending himself desiring. But it is the person *qua* intellectual apprehending this; and, it is the person apprehending himself desiring *qua* intellectual. If the experience of sense-appetite sufficed to give rise to the notion of the good, apprehending oneself as intellectual would not be necessary. It would be sufficient to apprehend oneself as sensitive.

So the appetitive act relative to which intellect knows "what a good is"—the desire essentially associated with the *ratio boni*—is something intellectual. It is the operation of the intellectual appetite, the will. Yet this cannot mean that in order to know the *ratio boni*, one must first "experience" the will's operation, as though an operation of the will were already there to be experienced. For again, the will does not operate except through intellect. It bears on universal good and bad. There is no such thing as operation about universal objects that does not involve intellect.

But knowing the will's operation does not require that it already "be there." In general, even though it is true that what is known is always somehow "in act," it need not always be in act in itself. It suffices that its proper causes or principles be in act. This is how we can know some future events: by discerning them in their actual present causes. As for the acts of the will, the cause in which the intellect knows them is itself. Thomas says that the intellect knows the act of the will, not just once that act has its own existence, but insofar as it already "exists in" the intellect, "as the principled is in the principle, in which there is a notion of the principled."[13]

This is how intellect *first* knows the act of the will. This act *must* be known before it occurs, because its occurrence is caused by the practical intellect of the one who has it.[14] Practical intellect causes its effects by ordering or directing to them. It *always* pre-conceives them. It knows them, not as already existing, but as good or fit or due to exist.[15] This is how it knows, and causes, the will's desire for something: by judging the thing good, which is to say, fit to be desired, *conveniens ad appetendum*.[16]

Perhaps we can even say that when Thomas speaks of intellect apprehending itself desiring, he is speaking in the way in which he elsewhere

12. *ST* I.16.4*ad*2.
13. *ST* I.87.4*ad*3.
14. *ST* I–II.9.1*ad*2.
15. See *ST* I–II.93.2*ad*3.
16. *ST* I–II.19.1*ad*1.

speaks of practical intellect as "moving"; namely, as directing to movement.[17] Then it would truly be intellect knowing itself (though also knowing the movement of the will as what it is directing toward). In any case, we should not overlook the fact that prior to its knowledge of itself as practical, intellect knows itself absolutely, as understanding "a being." Thus it can grasp "a true." As Dewan says, "The intellect, in conceiving 'the true,' already knows itself as terminus of the 'movement' from being to the soul; its natural 'next thought' is of the 'movement' from the soul to being."[18]

We might also say that in knowing the true, the mind already knows itself as principle of a certain "ordering" of the soul's operation. For the very acts of affirming and denying are a sort of ordering, though one that terminates "in the soul itself." They are intellect ordering its own thoughts, applying conceptions to its consideration of things, or removing them, as it sees fit.[19] Knowing itself as a "soul-orderer," it can go on to conceive itself ordering the soul with respect to things "outside," directing appetite. Aristotle's comparison of appetitive acts to affirmations and denials would then be no mere afterthought. It might even be the most natural way to think of them.

At any rate the comparison is not confined to acts of sense-appetite. In his account of the principles of good choice in *Nicomachean Ethics* VI.2, Aristotle remarks that "what affirmation and denial are in intellect, pursuit and avoidance are in appetite" (1139a21). Thomas's comment ties the comparison to the very possibility of "intelligent desire."

> Intellect in judging has two acts, namely affirmation, by which it assents to the true, and negation, by which it dissents from the false. To these two there respond proportionally two [acts] in the appetitive power, namely pursuit, by which the appetite tends to a good and adheres to it, and shunning, by which it draws back from a bad and dissents from it. And accordingly, intellect and appetite can be conformed, insofar as what intellect affirms to be good, appetite pursues, and what intellect denies to be good, appetite shuns.[20]

So although *good* means desirable, grasping it need not be a function of pre-rational desire. Still, it must be a function of something. To understand a thing is to know its nature. There is such a thing as the nature of desirability, the "what good is" that the natural light of reason enables the

---

17. *ST* I.79.11ad1.
18. Dewan, *Wisdom, Law, and Virtue*, 205.
19. See *ST* I.16.2.
20. *In Eth.* VI.2, 336, lines 61–75. Cf. Plato, *Republic* IV, 437c.

rational creature to discern.[21] And there is more involved in it than what the merely abstract notion of desire—of "movement from the soul to things"—expresses. For not every possible object of such movement is something that even *seems* to have the "nature of the good." This was the point of the passage from the *Metaphysics* commentary. What seems to have the nature of the good is what seems to be good "in itself" or to "have in itself that whence it is desired." It is what seems *honestum*. But being pleasant to the senses also makes a thing seem to be a possible object of desire (indeed it makes it able to move the will), and yet it does not, by itself, make the thing seem *honestum*. It only makes it similar to the *honestum* in a certain effect: pleasure. The *honestum* is certainly pleasant. The good that is *only* pleasant and not *honestum*, however, is good only in a qualified, derivative sense. The unqualified sense is that of the good in itself, the *honestum*. Again, this is the primary sense, the one first understood, to which all others refer.[22] And the "that whence it is desired" which the *honestum* has in itself, whatever this is, will be what goodness or desirability primarily consists in.

In other words, from the very start, understanding what a good is means not only grasping a certain relation to desire, but also grasping the principle of this relation, that which the relation is a function of.[23] It is just as with grasping what a true is. In part, *true* signifies a certain relation to intellect. The true is that which intellect naturally tends toward and accepts.[24] But *true* also signifies the basis of this relation. There is something belonging to what is true that makes it acceptable: its conformity to what it is about. This is what its acceptability is a function of, and what its truth consists in. A brief look at what Thomas thinks desirability or goodness consists in can shed further light on his use of natural inclinations in 94.2.

We have already heard him saying that first the mind grasps a being, then it grasps itself understanding a being, and then it grasps itself desiring a being. So *a good* always means at least: a being. It also means something relative to the soul: an understood being. But there is something else as well that it also means (in the primary sense), something pertaining to the good

---

21. *ST* I–II.91.2.

22. *ST* I.5.6ad3. The *bonum delectabile*, taken as opposed to the *bonum honestum*, seems to coincide with what Thomas calls the *bonum apparens*, the "specious good." See *ST* I–II.19.1ad1; cf. I.5.6ad2; I.63.1ad4; *In Eth.* III.10, esp. 148, lines 92–100.

23. Jenkins, "Good and the Object of Natural Inclination," holds that while the real nature of the good is something more than merely being desired, our first and natural apprehension of it is only as what is desired. I think this is tantamount to saying that the only natural apprehension of the good is sense-apprehension, or in other words, that there is no natural *understanding* of it at all.

24. *ST* I.16.1.

thing in itself. Thomas explains this in the corpus of *ST* I.16.4. "A good," he says, is not quite as "close" (in intelligibility) to "a being" as "a true" is. For "the true regards being absolutely and immediately. But the *ratio* of good follows on being insofar as it is somehow perfect. For thus is it desirable."[25]

What goodness (in the primary sense) consists in is perfection.[26] It is so in the good thing, and it is also so in the mind's initial grasp of it. Thomas is arguing that good comes after true *in ratione*, in intelligibility. What this means, he says, is that it enters the mind later.[27] Its *ratio* supposes and includes the *ratio* of perfect. (Presumably the *ratio* of "a bad" includes that of "a defective.") The common notion of the good is by no means empty. It is not whatever you may happen to desire, nor even whatever reason may regard as something to direct action toward. It already has a certain content, though this is very general and common. Not just any way of grasping or signifying a thing allows the mind to judge it good, in the primary and unqualified sense. It must be grasped and signified as perfect.

What is it to be perfect? It is to be something "from which nothing is absent according to the mode of its perfection."[28] This is not circular. Thomas is presenting perfection as something related to a measure, which is that which sets a mode.[29] Elsewhere he calls perfection "fullness of being."[30] The fullness of a container is measured by its capacity, which is determined by its inner shape (its inner peri*meter*). What Thomas identifies as the measure of a being's fulfillment is "what it is," its nature. This is determined by its form.[31] And so, "for each thing, that is good which befits it according to its form, and bad, that which departs from the order of its form."[32] Again, "the goodness of each and every thing consists in this, that it be fittingly disposed according to the mode of its nature."[33] Moreover, "every existence and every good is *considered* through some form."[34]

A sign of how basic the *ratio* of perfect is, for the *ratio* of desirable, is that desire is understood, from the start, as movement from what is in the soul to what is in reality; that is, from a thing's being known to its simply

---

25. See *ST* I.5.1.
26. See *ScG* I.37, 111b, lines 10–24; *In Eth.* IX.11, 539, lines 50–67.
27. See *ST* I.16.4*ad*2.
28. *ST* I.4.1; I.5.5.
29. See *ST* I.5.5; I–II.85.4; *In Sent.* III.34.1.3c; III.34.2.1qc3c.
30. *ST* I–II.18.1; I–II.18.2.
31. *ST* I.5.5.
32. *ST* I–II.18.5. Other pertinent texts: *ST* I.21.1*ad*3; I.49.1; I–II.71.1; I–II.71.2.
33. *ST* I–II.71.1.
34. *ST* I–II.85.4.

being. If grasping goodness presupposes grasping truth, it is not only because the desire to which goodness is relative is intellectual, but also because grasping desirability involves comparing the two modes. Merely being known is a ghostly way of being—insubstantial, unfulfilling.

We should notice that the thought is not quite that goodness is implied in perfection, as though derivable from it by some kind of conceptual analysis. It is the *ratio* of the perfect that is included in the *ratio* of the good, not vice-versa. To say otherwise would be to fall into the so-called is-ought fallacy that Hume exposed, and that Finnis and Grisez are so wary of.[35] The *ratio* of a good adds something new to the *rationes* of a being, of the nature of a being, and of the fullness of a being according to its nature. It adds the relation to desire, the attractiveness, the final causality.

However, this novelty definitely has the status of an addition, an outgrowth. The *ratio* of the perfect is the matrix in which it is begotten (and apart from which it corrupts). In relation to Hume, this is very important. For even though what Hume exposed is a genuine fallacy, the larger argument that he was engaged in is itself nothing short of sophistry. He showed that the notion of what is according to nature does not contain the notion of good. But what he actually needed was the sophistical inference from this, which he leaves tacit, that the notion of good does not contain the notion of what is according to nature. For it is really only this inference that provides grounds for his main thesis, which is that the notion of good has no rational or intelligible basis at all—that it is a mere function of sentiment or feeling.[36]

Finnis and Grisez do reject this thesis. They *say* that reason grasps intelligible good. Yet they give every appearance of accepting that tacit inference. Its effect, I believe, is just what Hume wanted: to eviscerate the intelligibility of the good.

---

35. See, for example, Finnis, *Natural Law and Natural Rights*, 33–49; *Aquinas*, 90; Grisez et al., "Practical Principles," 127.

36. See Hume, *Treatise of Human Nature* Book III, Part I, Section i, esp. 469–70; Section ii, 470–76. (It is interesting to notice that for Thomas, even the mere *bonum delectabile*, to the extent that it retains something of the *ratio boni* and is capable of moving the intellectual appetite, also retains at least some appearance of being "according to nature." See *ST* I–II.6.4ad3.) Of course Hume does not depend only on this bit of sophistry to do the work of rendering the good unintelligible. Thomas makes the notion of the good depend on the notions of formal causality, as seen in substantial form, and of efficient causality, seen in the form's active power (*ST* I.5.4). But Hume's famous critique of causality leaves no room for active power or substantial form, or the distinction between potency and act, or even substance. On the formal cause, see Hume, *Treatise of Human Nature* Book I, Part III, Section xiv ("Of the Idea of Necessary Connexion"), 155–72; Book I, Part IV, Section vi ("Of Personal Identity"), 251–63; and on substance, see Book I, Part IV, Section iii ("Of the Antient Philosophy"), 222.

I suppose that the connection between goodness and perfection also explains the general priority, as to goodness, of the common good. This is an instance of the priority of the good of the whole relative to that of a part. The whole, as such, is more perfect than the part, as such. Not surprisingly, Hume denies the intelligible priority of the common good. "It is not contrary to reason to prefer the destruction of the whole world to the scratching of my finger."[37]

We might ask: why does the mind find the perfect fit to desire, and the defective fit to shun? Here I believe we reach a sheer beginning, something immediate. If we observe a desire for something—say, a desire for food, perhaps our own desire for it—but we do not see how the object desired perfects the desirer, we wonder why the desire exists. But when we see that the object enhances or favors or perfects the desirer's own being, we no longer wonder. We do not ask: why does it desire to enhance its being—what good is that? Rather, now its desire makes sense. We have traced the observed desire to something desirable *per se*. We might as well ask, why does the mind find acceptable the propositions that state the case as it is, and unacceptable the ones that do not? It is just the nature of mind.

KNOWING PERFECTION AND KNOWING DESIRE

I have been arguing that, for Thomas, if there is any one kind of desire that is essentially associated with the notion of the good, it is intellectual desire, and that the actual existence of this desire—that of the will—is not the source of the notion of the good, but rather its result. However, I do not mean to suggest that Thomas thinks that the formation of the concept of the good does not depend on the experience of any actual desire at all. It does. The good is "what all desire." This does not refer to any single kind of desire, even that of the will. It invokes only a general, common notion of desire. The notion of the good goes hand in hand with a common notion of desire, and forming this notion does depend on an experience of desire. But again, it is not one's own sense-desire. Not all desires are sense-desires either. Nor are all sense-desires desires for things that are unqualifiedly good, things that perfect the one desiring them. But Thomas does think that all beings desire things that are unqualifiedly good. This is how he can reason from the good as "what all desire" to the good as the perfect. Even if not all desires are for perfections, all beings do desire their own perfection. This is what it is *natural* for them to desire, each in its own way. I also think that his view must be that the intellect's formation of the notion of the good involves an experience of things

---

37. Hume, *Treatise of Human Nature* Book II, Part III, Section iii ("Of the Influencing Motives of the Will"), 416.

that is such as to disclose this common feature of things, their all somehow desiring their perfection. This would be the source of the common notion of desire that is involved in the notion of the good. And the experience which gives rise to it is the very same as the experience which gives rise to the notion of perfection itself. It is the ordinary experience of the movements and actions of things. This will take some explaining.

Before seeking for the origin of a concept, we need to make sure that we are clear about its content. What does *desire* mean? My dictionary calls it a type of feeling. Perhaps that does not quite fit the kind of desire called will. Nevertheless it is probably right that by *desire* we usually mean some type of psychological act or disposition, something that only beings with "inner awareness" have. Descartes calls all desires "thoughts"; Hume calls even willing an "impression." But taken generally, this is not at all what Thomas means by desire—*desiderium* or *appetitus*. The very formula of the good that he uses in 94.2 is an indication of this. *Bonum est quod omnia appetunt.* As is clear both from the neuter *omnia* and from other passages, what Thomas means by *all* in "what all desire" is not just all people. Nor is it just all animals. It is all beings.[38] Not all beings have will or sense-desire, or any sort of psychological activity at all. But all do have desire.[39] If for us this word inevitably conveys something psychological, then let us speak instead of inclination. We are supposed to see this as an inseparable feature of all things. And we are supposed to see that what is common to all things is inclination toward perfection.

For Thomas, desire or inclination is simply a certain sort of tendency, or effective order, toward something. Not every tendency is an inclination. Some tendencies are merely imposed upon a thing by something else and are incidental or even contrary to the thing's inclination. An inclination is a tendency rooted in the thing itself—ultimately in its nature, in what it is. It is somehow the thing's "own." This is not found only in animals. Plants are inclined to grow, to reproduce, and so on. Inanimate things have inclinations toward their proper activities. Thomas ascribes inclination or desire even to prime matter.[40]

Thomas's views of the constitution of these beings differ in many ways from those of modern natural science. Has modern science entirely dispensed with the notion of inclination? I doubt it. But for our purposes, the

---

38. See *ST* I.5.1; *In Eth.* I.1, 5, lines 165–73.

39. If the good does have a special association with the will, surely this is precisely because the will is the appetite of that which is itself "in a way all things." Again, see *De ver.* 1.1; *ScG* III.112, 356b, lines 10–20. In a way, the will's desire reflects or gathers up that of all things.

40. *ST* I.5.3*ad*3.

question is incidental. We are not talking about the scientific account of things, but about the common experience from which the common concept of the good originates. Our experience is of a world made up of things that all have inclinations—toward states, activities, and movements of various sorts. We find ourselves quite surrounded by desire. And we *observe* it in things. We do so all the time. It would be silly to say that you see a dog chasing a rabbit, but that you cannot tell whether the dog desires the rabbit—that only the dog can tell this (and he keeps it to himself). Granted, desire is not observable in the way that, say, color or sound is. It is "underneath" the sensible objects. But then, so are many kinds of action, such as "chasing." It is the very business of intellect to get underneath the sensible objects, to under-stand them.[41] If we cannot see a dog desiring a rabbit, then neither can we see a dog chasing a rabbit. We cannot even see *a dog*.

And to call something a dog, or even a tree or a rock, is already to attribute a host of inclinations to it. It is mostly in light of their regular activities and movements that we form our conceptions of what the things around us are. What they are and what they are inclined to be and to do enter our minds together. This is "a nature": an inner principle of both the existence and the activity of a thing. Even if, as with "a substance" (a subject of existence and activity), it takes a philosopher to formulate the general definition of "a nature," some confused concept of what a nature is comes quite naturally to us.

It is desire understood in this very broad sense, then, that for Thomas goes hand in hand with the notion of the good. Rather than with feelings, what we should associate desire with is movement and action. A desire is a tendency toward something, toward the real possession of something, and so it is typically a tendency toward receiving the thing, or conserving it, or bringing it about in others. This association of desire with action is just what the first precept of natural law expresses: the good, as "what all desire," is "to be done and sought." And its contrary, the bad, which would be "what all shun," is "to be avoided." Desire pertains to the very concept of the good, and action and movement pertain to the very concept of desire. This is why the first precept of natural law is a self-evident proposition.

But if the notion of desire is tied to that of action, so is the notion of perfection. The very term *perfect*, Thomas remarks, suggests *totaliter factum*, totally made or produced or formed.[42] And among natural things, which are the primary things, to be perfect—to be *mature*—is to be able to make one's

---

41. See *ST* I.18.2; II–II.8.1.
42. *ST* I.4.1*ad*1.

like.⁴³ This makes sense, inasmuch as likeness is "communication in form."⁴⁴ A thing has its "fullness of being," according to its form, when it can "overflow" and give such being to another. The more perfect things are the more active things. Living things, those whose activity is somehow self-sustaining and self-promoting, are more perfect than non-living things. The connection between perfection and action also indicates why the good is primarily "in things" and not "in the soul"—why desire is from the soul to things. Merely to be in the soul, to be known or conceived but not real, is to be only in potency. It is not to be "in act."⁴⁵ And neither is it to be active. "Heat in the mind does not heat," Thomas says, "but in the fire."⁴⁶ Thus the *ratio* of good presupposes not only that of the being of a thing according to its form or nature but also that of the active power of its form.⁴⁷ These together constitute the perfection of the thing. And desire is a principle of activity because its object is perfection. It is a principle of being moved toward perfection, of being "totally made" by that which can make it, and a principle of conserving and promoting the perfection received. And if we naturally understand that perfection is desirable, this is because we naturally perceive that it is in fact desired, quite universally, and because this immediately makes sense to us. We see the proportion between desire and perfection. The good is the perfect, seen as a principle of desire. Desire does not explain goodness. It is goodness that explains desire.

Now this is to say that the good does not enter our minds solely, or even primarily, as a practical notion. It does not first function to direct our own desires and actions. It first functions to explain the actions and desires of the things around us. The good is the final *cause*, the final explanation, and as such it refers to desire. "Just as the causality of the efficient cause is taken according to influence, the causality of the end is taken according to appetite."⁴⁸ The good causes by attraction. Goodness explains the being and the activity of things, inasmuch as it explains their inclination toward their being and their activity, the tendency of their own forms to keep them in their being and to communicate it.⁴⁹ This is the "diffusiveness" of the good,

---

43. *ST* I.5.4.
44. *ST* I.4.3.
45. See *ST* I.18.4*ad*3. I take it that grasping perfection supposes grasping the distinction between being in potency and being in act—between "can be but is not" and "is." We then see the proportion of potency to act, and we thereby see act as the perfection of potency.
46. *De ver.* 22.12. See *ST* I–II.5.6*ad*2.
47. *ST* I.5.4.
48. *ST* I–II.2.5*obj*3.
49. On form as "holding" a thing in being, see *ST* I.59.2.

its aptitude to be that which things tend to have and to hold on to and to promote. We might even say that it explains the substantiality of things. A substance is something stable, enduring, able to remain itself while undergoing change, and apt to be a source of change in other things. The good, then, is first of all an explanatory notion, one that governs an entire mode of explanation. It is primarily a speculative notion. In 94.2 Thomas says that the good is the first thing to fall into the apprehension of practical reason. He does not say, however, that what the good first falls into is the apprehension of practical reason.

I do not mean that the good's functioning as a practical notion, directing our own desires and actions, requires any further experience or even any reasoning. Once the notion of the good has been achieved in the course of the mind's natural process of sizing things up and understanding them, the practical way of apprehending the good comes as a natural result. This is why the understanding of the good involves the consideration of the mind itself and of its own inclination. In knowing "a true," the mind is knowing itself knowing "a being," and in so doing it is also knowing itself as a being— a knowing one. And in knowing "a good" it is knowing the desirability of the perfection of a being, the desirability of it *for* the being, as such, and therefore also for itself as a being, and as a being whose way of desiring is through its own knowledge of being and of its perfection and of the desirability of its perfection. What originally elicits our desire of the good is thus nothing other than our grasp of its goodness. This is all it takes for the good to move the will.

And it is what elicits the will's most fundamental inclination. Out of its experience of things that are beings in particular ways, the mind somehow forms a universal conception of being, one not contracted to any particular mode but regarding it absolutely. It also grasps perfection or fullness of being in this way. What the will primarily desires is just that: to attain all perfection, utter fullness of being, such as leaves nothing to be desired. This is the desire of the last end, beatitude. "Just as each and every thing desires its perfection, so intellectual nature naturally desires to be blissed (*beata*)."[50] And "all people desire to fulfill their perfection, which is the nature (*ratio*) of the last end."[51] Thomas sees this desire as belonging to the will in the way that the principle of non-contradiction belongs to the intellect. It is the first principle of all other willing.[52] All of man's other inclinations, including the natural ones, are under its sway.

50. *ST* I.26.2.
51. *ST* I-II.1.7.
52. *ST* I-II.10.1; I-II.91.2*ad*2.

This suggests that the first precept of natural law, the one founded upon the *ratio* of the good, constitutes an understanding that is proportioned to the desire of beatitude. Now, 94.2 does not make any explicit reference to beatitude or to happiness. However, in 91.2, Thomas did say that just as there is a natural desire of the last end, so "the first direction of our acts to the end" must be through a natural law.[53] And there is what he had said a little earlier about law in general: "The first principle in matters of action, which practical reason concerns, is the last end. The last end of human life is happiness or beatitude. Hence law must regard most of all the order that is toward beatitude."[54] To direct to the last end is the function of natural law as a whole, and natural law as a whole is founded upon the first precept. Insofar as it is practical, functioning to direct the human will and human action, it directs toward beatitude, our whole perfection and good.[55] Directing us toward beatitude, however, does not just mean inciting us to want beatitude. That we want beatitude is presupposed. It means showing us the *order* toward it and thereby making our voluntary pursuit of it *right*.

We can see this easily, if we simply do what sometimes is not done, which is to look at the whole first precept and not just its first clause. By its first clause, it directs toward doing and pursuing good. Taken by itself, however, this seems to provide no direction at all. The good, after all, is convertible with being. There is nothing that does not have some goodness about it.[56] What has no goodness at all, no perfection, is nothing. It is not even bad. And there is no voluntary action that is not somehow aimed at something which in some way shares in goodness, or which at least seems to do so. But even though the first precept is founded upon the good, it does not speak only of good. To reduce the first precept to "good is to be done and sought," cutting out what it says about bad, would be like taking the principle of non-contradiction, which is founded on the concept of a being, and cutting out what it says about non-being. It would provide no direction for thought. No thought would be ruled out by it. To understand a thing is also to understand its opposite. The principle that is founded on the concept of a being refers not only to being but also to its intelligible opposite, non-being (the concept of which is itself founded on that of being). And similarly the principle founded on the concept of the good also refers to the bad (the concept of which—namely, privation of good—is founded on

53. *ST* I–II.91.2ad2.
54. *ST* I–II.90.2.
55. I say "insofar as it is practical" because I do not think the sheer *truth* of the first precept, as Thomas formulates it, is confined to its practical function. On this, see below, 168.
56. *ST* I.5.3.

that of the good). But for this very reason, what the first precept means by *good* cannot be merely whatever has some goodness in it. For many things that have some goodness in them have some badness too, and yet the very same principle says that the bad is to be avoided. The principle can hardly be saying that some of what is to be done and sought is to be avoided. What *good* refers to, in the first precept of natural law, is not whatever has some goodness in it. It is what *unqualifiedly* good, which is the unqualifiedly perfect. In directing toward good *and* away from bad, the first precept is, in effect, directing toward total good, the good that lacks nothing. And for rational beings, this is the ultimate end, beatitude.

To be sure, understood only as answering to the first precept, beatitude or the ultimate end remains something very general and indeterminate. It is what Thomas calls the "common concept" of happiness: "a perfect overall good" (*bonum commune perfectum*).[57] The first precept does not suffice by itself to direct human action, far from it. It does not say determinately what things are good and what things are bad. It is only a beginning of reason's rule or reason's order, which is the moral order. But it is definitely a beginning of that. And alongside it there are other naturally understood precepts that already serve to begin to fill it in and to articulate the moral order, and thereby to render the true last end itself more determinate.

It is true that any voluntary action, as such, consists in doing or seeking something that is, or at least seems, somehow good. No one aims directly at the bad on its own account. No one acts purely for the sake of the privation of good. But the first precept does not say simply that the bad is not to be done or sought. It says that the bad is to be avoided. Some actions whose objects are good, apparent or even real, bring badness, privation of due good, with them. These are bad actions, actions that ought to be avoided.

True, even bad action consists in avoiding something that is or seems *somehow* bad, namely the very lack of whatever good it is that is the action's end. But this does not show that every voluntary action complies with the first precept. The precept does not say that *some* good, or what has some aspect of goodness, is to be done or sought, or that *some* bad, or what has some aspect of badness, is to be avoided. It says unqualifiedly that good is to be done and sought, and bad avoided. And this is supposed to be self-evidently

---

57. "It is the common notion of beatitude that it be a perfect overall good; and this [Boethius] signified when he says that it is 'a state that is perfect in the gathering of all goods,' by which is signified nothing other than that the blissed person is in the state of perfect good" (*ST* I–II.3.2*ad*2). Notice that whereas the Boethius formulation speaks of a "gathering of goods," Thomas's gloss presents happiness as more of a unity, "perfect good." We do not start from various specific "basic goods" and only subsequently see the need to "integrate" them. We start from the good as a whole, although we see at once that it has parts.

and unqualifiedly true. Must it not then be referring to what is truly and unqualifiedly good and to what is truly and unqualifiedly bad? Many things that have some aspect of goodness are not to be done or sought at all. This is because, speaking unqualifiedly, they are not good but bad. And the agents who do or pursue them may very well know this.[58] Likewise, many things that have some aspect of badness are not to be avoided, because, speaking unqualifiedly, they are good, and those who avoid them may very well know this. Such people are doing or pursuing the good and avoiding the bad only in some qualified sense. If they are complying with the first precept, it is rather in the way that a dead horse is being a horse; or (perhaps better) in the way that a black horse with white teeth is being white. Thomas says that the primary precepts of natural law, taken universally—in their own intelligibility—cannot be erased from the human heart. But as to their applicability to particular actions, they can be, on account of concupiscence or some other passion.[59] This is to say that particular actions can be in violation of them—voluntary and culpable violation. He does not make the very first precept an exception.

I do not mean that the good and bad to which the first precept refers are solely moral good and bad. It refers generally to the human good and bad. The precept of natural law that bears properly on moral goodness and its contrary is the one discussed in I-II.94.3: the precept to act virtuously or according to reason. Nevertheless the first precept is already a moral precept, in the sense that it does serve to discriminate between action that is according to reason and action that is contrary to reason. It is, after all, a dictate of reason. Action in compliance with it is by that very fact according to reason, and action that transgresses it is contrary to reason.[60] And any action contrary to reason violates it, because any such action is bad. To be fully in compliance with it is to be morally unimpeachable.

KNOWING HUMAN GOODS AND KNOWING HUMAN NATURE

The will's natural inclination toward beatitude is not its only natural inclination. It is the one that pertains to it just because it is a will, intellectual appetite, bearing on the good according to its own intelligible nature and as a whole. But there are also certain determinate goods toward which the

---

58. See *ST* I-II.19.1*ad*1.

59. *ST* I-II.94.6. See also I-II.99.2*ad*2. Here he calls all of the common, primary precepts of natural law "moral."

60. For a fuller discussion of the first precept as ordering to happiness and as moral, see Butera, "Moral Status."

human will is naturally inclined. For the will is not a complete entity or substance in its own right, but rather the appetitive power of a subject of a certain nature, by which the subject desires what is apprehended as suited to it.[61] And so the will naturally wills not only the good and the last end but also

> universally (*universaliter*) all the things that suit the willing subject according to his nature. For through the will we desire not only the things that pertain to the power of the will, but also those that pertain to each of the powers and to the whole human being. Hence a human being naturally wills not only the object of the will, but also the things that pertain to the other powers, such as the cognition of truth, which belongs to the intellect; and existing and living and other things of this sort that regard his natural constitution. All of these things are included under the will's object as certain particular goods.[62]

The term *universally* at the beginning of this quotation is interesting. We can take "all the things that suit the willing subject according to his nature" together, as a whole set, and we can say that the will naturally wills that whole. This of course would not be possible if the intellect did not naturally have a conception of such a set of things. It must naturally know what a nature is and what it is to suit a nature. And the will's naturally willing any particular thing, on account of its suiting the subject's nature, requires the subject's naturally knowing that the thing does so. This is corroborated rather explicitly in 94.2. For there we are told that all the things which pertain to natural law, all the things to which man is naturally inclined, are things that practical reason naturally apprehends "as human goods." What does *human* mean, if not pertaining to the nature of man?[63] What we natu-

---

61. See *ST* I.80.1*ad*3.

62. *ST* I–II.10.1.

63. Earlier, I quoted Finnis, saying that "the *underived* first principles of practical reasonableness . . . make no reference at all to human nature, but only to human good" (Finnis, *Natural Law and Natural Rights*, 36). I do not understand this. Does *human good* not mean precisely what is good for that which has a human nature? When we see that certain things are good for people and not for walruses, are we not seeing that they fit human nature and not walrus nature? I suspect that what Finnis really means is that the first precepts make no direct reference to the constitutive *principles* of human nature, such as the spiritual soul. I suppose that the consideration of the principles does pertain to some special speculative science. But this does not mean that the first precepts make no reference at all to human nature, any more than the fact that they do not specify the virtues that are principles of the human good (*ST* I–II.94.3) means that they make no reference at all to the human good.

rally apprehend as a human good is what we can all immediately see to be proportioned to human nature, as a perfection of it.

And notice that what is apprehending the goods in this way is practical reason. Evidently there is a consideration of human nature itself that enters into practical reason. This may seem odd, inasmuch as human nature, in itself, seems to be a speculative matter, not practical. The practical intellect causes what it understands.[64] Human practical intellect does not cause human nature. Reason's conception of the human form is not the original source of the human form's reality. However, on Thomas's view, not everything that enters into practical intellect's consideration is something that it causes. Counsel or deliberation—practical reasoning—takes many things on board: things grasped by the senses, things grasped universally by practical knowledge, and things grasped universally by speculative knowledge.[65] In its practical operation, reason uses natural things. It even uses human nature and what is natural to man, in the sense of what belongs to man per se.[66]

> Just as a man exists by nature, so do all of his per se attributes, such as being capable of laughter and capable of mental discipline. If then some cause does not make a man absolutely, but rather makes a man be such, it will not belong to that cause to constitute the things that are a man's per se attributes, but only to use them. Thus the statesman makes a man be civil; but he does not make him be capable of mental discipline, but rather uses this property of a man so that he become civil.[67]

Now the very idea of natural knowledge of human nature, even speculative natural knowledge, would make no sense, if all knowledge of nature had to be scientific knowledge. Scientific knowledge does not come naturally. It requires investigation and reasoning, and not everyone has it. The natural knowledge of natural law itself is not scientific knowledge. It is not the science of ethics or of politics. But this does not mean that it is not intellectual. It is an "understanding of principles." And as 94.2 itself makes clear, it certainly supposes the natural understanding of speculative principles, such as the principle of non-contradiction, the principle that whole is greater than part, and so forth. This understanding is not scientific either. The scientific understanding of the things that these principles regard—being, unity, whole and part, etc.—is metaphysics. So is the scientific

---

64. *ST* I–II.3.5obj1.
65. *ST* I–II.14.6.
66. This is the sense of *natural* that is at work in *ST* I–II.10.1.
67. *In Meta.* VI, lect. 3, §1219.

understanding of good and evil. But it would be ridiculous to say that therefore people do not naturally have any understanding at all of good and evil.

It seems obvious that the natural knowledge of the precepts of natural law does not suppose scientific knowledge of human nature. In order to understand the precepts of natural law, one does not need to be able to demonstrate all of man's per se attributes; perhaps not even the statesman who uses them can demonstrate them. Nor does one need to have formulated the principle of such demonstration, which is the orderly, scientific definition of man. Formulating such a definition would mean identifying the ultimate genus to which man belongs—substance—and dividing it by differentiae into species, all the way down to the proper differentia of the human species. Such definitions do not come naturally to our minds.

But this is not to say that no knowledge of human nature at all, no understanding of what a human being is, comes naturally to us. Not having scientific knowledge of something does not mean being altogether ignorant of it. On the contrary, the inquiry by which such knowledge is achieved must start from some pre-scientific knowledge of the thing. One must at least know that the thing exists.[68] And this means that one must somehow know something about its nature.[69] If one did not somehow know its nature, one would not know it at all, even that it exists. The very way in which a thing engages the intellect is through some grasp of what it is, just as the way in which a thing engages eyesight is through some perception of its color. Just as color is the proper object of eyesight, so "what a thing is" is the proper object of intellect.[70] And just as eyesight first perceives a thing confusedly, without distinguishing all of its facets and contours, so does the intellect first grasp what a thing is. "We know man by a certain confused cognition before we know how to distinguish all the things that belong to the definition of man."[71]

People who cannot define man scientifically may be perfectly aware that there are such things as human beings, perfectly able to distinguish beings that are human from beings that are not, and perfectly apt to think universally about those that are. They may also be fully aware of man's having certain attributes, such as mortality or the power of speech, without being able to demonstrate these in light of their causes in the principles of human nature. And they may be quite apt to make sound universal judgments about what is suited or unsuited to human beings, what is good or

---

68. See *In Post. an.* II.6, 194, lines 12–26.
69. See *In De Trin.* q. 6, a. 3, 167–68, lines 114–32.
70. See, for example, *ST* I.17.3; I.85.6.
71. *ST* I.85.3*ad*3.

bad for them. Such judgments, and the resulting practical precepts, may come quite naturally to them. And it may come quite naturally to them to understand that they themselves are human beings and that the judgments and precepts apply to them. Upon this, inclinations of their will, their intellectual appetite, naturally follow.

I do not mean that it is impossible for a person to be altogether ignorant of what a human being is. In 94.2, Thomas says that "this proposition, 'man is rational,' is self-evident in its own nature, since one who says *man* says *rational*; and yet this proposition is not self-evident to someone who does not know what man is (*quid sit homo*)." It is not a purely hypothetical example. A toddler might very well say the word *man* without knowing what concept it signifies, and even without having the concept. To say that something is naturally understood, and therefore "commonly known to all," does not mean that absolutely everyone understands it. It means that everyone has the natural aptitude to understand it, and that the process of actually coming to understand it is one that people undergo naturally, spontaneously, and "always or for the most part." A person's actually understanding anything at all takes time, because it requires some sense-perception and experience from which to gather intelligible notions by abstraction. Moreover, a person's stock of notions is not built up in an entirely random way. It naturally follows a certain order. For instance, the process tends to go from the more common or general to the more proper or specific. "It happens to our intellect to know animal before knowing man."[72] And the factors which enter into the definition of a specific nature are known in themselves before they are brought together and distinctly coordinated *as* parts of the definition. We can have some grasp of what it is to be rational even while we still understand man only in a confused way and do not understand that this is man's proper differentia.

In the previous chapter, I argued that Thomas does not take a human person's own natural inclinations to be the proper basis of the person's natural apprehension of human goods. It is the other way around. However, Thomas definitely does hold that the apprehension is based on something; namely, a natural—non-scientific but nonetheless truly intellectual—understanding of human nature. In fact, in the final portion 94.2 itself, where he lays out the order of the natural inclinations, he presents them as being toward things that are "good according to nature" (*bonum secundum naturam*), whether it be the nature that man shares with all substances, or that which is he shares with other animals, or the nature of reason that is proper to him. I see no reason at all to doubt that Thomas holds practical

---

72. *ST* I.85.3.

reason's natural understanding of human goods to be based on, and a very direct function of, reason's own natural understanding of human nature.

Surely this view is supported by his whole approach in 94.2. Quite explicit, and really quite prominent, is the concern for the order in which things "fall into the apprehension" of the human intellect, and especially "into the apprehension of all," as things naturally known. And the order is entirely from the more general or common to the more specific or proper. First he speaks of what is absolutely most common: being itself and the things associated with it. Then he speaks of the good.[73] And then he speaks of the specifically human good (the practical good), and he lays out the natural inclinations and the precepts corresponding to them in that same sort of order. First comes what pertains to the nature of substance, then what pertains to the nature of animal, then what pertains to the nature proper to man, reason. We could not understand its being good for man to be conserved in the being of human nature if we had no grasp of what it is to be a subject of natural being, that is, a substance. We could not understand the good for man of the bonding of male and female, or of the rearing of offspring, if we had no notion of our animal dimension. If we had no notion of man as having reason, we could not understand its being good for man to know the truth about God or to live in society; and we certainly could not know that it is good for us to act according to reason.[74] Are not such notions after all quite elementary, stock pieces in the mental repertoire of anyone capable of voluntary or moral action, anyone with the use of reason?

Someone may object that even a non-scientific knowledge of human nature would seem to require or to include some knowledge, also non-scientific, of man's natural inclinations. After all, on Thomas's view, we at the natures of things—natural things, such as human beings—very much by way of their activities, and these show their natures only inasmuch as they proceed from the inclinations rooted in their natures. I readily grant this. It is not in conflict with what I have been arguing. I have only been arguing that one's understanding of human goods is not the effect of one's *own* natural inclinations, either by some kind of introspection or by their somehow coloring one's apprehension of the goods. But if we grow up surrounded by natural, non-human things, we obviously also grow up surrounded by human beings. And if we grasp the nature of a thing by way of perceiving the inclinations that are common to things of that nature, the same holds for our grasp of human nature. The understanding of it does involve the perception

---

73. Even though being and the good are convertible, being is a more common intelligible, inasmuch as one can think of something as a being without thinking of it as good, and not vice-versa. See *ST* I.5.3*ad*4; I–II.9.1*ad*3.

74. *ST* I–II.94.3.

of natural human inclinations. But this is a perception of inclinations *common* to human beings, not of inclinations proper to oneself. One grasps those inclinations as characteristic of human beings. One goes on to form a notion of human nature, in its various dimensions, as the proportionate source of such inclinations and of the operations that result from them. And one also grasps the objects of those inclinations as perfections proportioned to human nature and therefore as constituting human goods, things that are suitable for human beings to be inclined toward and to act for.

I also grant that the understanding of human nature is a rather more complex affair than the understanding of other natures. This is not only because human nature itself is more complex, but also because of what we considered earlier: that human beings often do not act in conformity with the inclinations of the nature that is proper to them. They do not always act according to reason. How then can acting according to reason be perceived as something to which they are naturally inclined? Again, the answer is that, whereas a non-human nature shows its inclinations only by the ways of moving and resting that are common to things of that nature, human nature has other ways of showing itself and its inclinations: in speech, in institutions, in culture, and so forth. If we frequently act contrary to reason, we also frequently reprove ourselves for doing so and try to correct ourselves. Our needs show themselves not only in how we attend to them but also in how we deal with our failures to attend to them. And it is quite natural for us to learn to interpret all these distinctively human things, as natural as it is to learn to use language.

It is also quite natural to understand oneself to be a human being. We grasp that human nature is our own nature. By this I mean our own *nature*: we grasp it, not just as a feature that we happen to have, but as what we are, constitutive of our very being and identity. And we grasp the things that befit human nature as befitting ourselves. Clearly a very great deal of our understanding of ourselves is achieved in light of our understanding of the human world around us and of our belonging to that world. The same holds for our human inclinations, the inclinations of our wills. These are *always* toward things understood under some universal notion of goodness.[75] And the most natural ones are toward the things that are good according to our natural being, which is our human being. These presuppose some universal conception, some understanding, of human nature.

I do not mean that one naturally sets off, in a sharp and clear way, the things that are truly common to human beings, as human, from the things proper to one's own society and culture. But the common things

---

75. ST I.80.2ad2.

are somehow embedded in the culture, and it is in virtue of them that the culture can take hold of one's life. For instance, there is such a thing as the nature of language, common to all the particular languages.

The point also comes out, in a different way, in that *Prima pars* text on the love of God above all things.[76] *Because* reason imitates nature, a city's virtuous citizens will risk death for the preservation of the city, and *if* they were a natural part of this city, that inclination would be natural to them. Thomas is saying that there is a natural order of human inclination, pertaining to human reason, that is at the root of the inclinations proper to this or that community.

Finnis argues that the natural knowledge of natural law cannot rest on knowledge of human nature, because the knowledge of human nature supposes the exercise of the knowledge of natural law. This is because knowing human nature requires knowing reason, and knowing reason involves knowing its practical operation, and the very principles of that operation are the precepts of natural law.[77] I certainly grant that someone's having a complete, scientific knowledge of human nature presupposes his having the natural knowledge of the precepts of natural law. But Thomas says that "to each and every one, his own reason naturally dictates that he act virtuously," and by *virtuously* he means "according to reason."[78] So each one naturally has a universal conception of reason itself, indeed of practical reason—the reason according to which one should act—and at least this precept of natural law presupposes such a conception.

This should come as no surprise. For one thing, our ordinary experience of the human world obviously includes experience of the activity of practical reason. Moreover, this precept pertains to the nature proper to or distinctive of man. Prior to that—prior in practical reason's understanding—are the precepts pertaining to the more common dimensions of his nature. Our natural understanding of our nature, and of the goods proportioned to it, does not come all at once. It develops gradually, starting from the more common dimensions and proceeding toward those that are properly human such as the precept to act according to reason. So there can be a functioning of each one's practical reason, which one's own reason can grasp, regarding the goods pertaining to the common dimensions, prior to formation of the precept to act according to reason. Also, even prior to those common precepts is the very understanding of the good, which, as we saw, brings with it a functioning of practical reason, reason moving the

---

76. *ST* I.60.5.
77. Finnis, *Natural Law and Natural Rights*, 90–92.
78. *ST* I-II.94.3.

will. So, in a way, the understanding of *all* the precepts of natural law goes together with some apprehension of human nature, and not just according to some common dimension, but also according to what is proper to it, its rationality, and even its practical rationality.

Notice, by the way, that even Thomas's argument for the existence of a precept of natural law to act according to reason proceeds from the general to the particular. "Every thing is naturally inclined toward action that suits it according to its form, in the way that fire is naturally inclined toward heating. Hence, since the rational soul is the proper form of man, there is a natural inclination in every human being toward acting according to reason."[79] We might ask: for Thomas, is it right for a person to act according to reason because the rational soul is man's proper nature or form, or is it right for a person to act according to man's proper form because this form is the rational soul? Clearly it is the former. *Whatever* a thing's proper form is, that is what the thing ought to act according to. It measures the thing's good. "For each thing, that is good which suits it according to its form, and bad, that which departs from the order of its form."[80] This is an interesting notion, the "order of its form" (*ordinem suae formae*). Thomas does not say the *inclination* of the form, even though every form is a source of inclination.[81] Rather the inclination itself is according to the form's order. It would be "a certain order of exigency or necessity," a certain dueness, that is in function of the form.[82] The inclination would in turn be a function of that. In the case of non-rational form, the inclination is directly instilled by divine providence. In the case of that form which is reason, the inclination is mediated by reason's own conception of the order. This is the natural way for *this* sort of form to yield inclination. Again, "the [will's] very appetite of the due end presupposes the right apprehension of the end, which is through reason."[83]

This is why reason ought to govern all of the other parts of man's nature, such as the sensitive appetite. It is not just that reason happens to belong only to man and to no other kind of thing. It is that the rational soul is man's proper substantial form, which is to say, that which properly determines the unity and being, the very identity, of a human being. And even if not everyone has an accurate, scientific conception of the rational soul—as a substantial form, as spiritual, and so forth—nevertheless we naturally do have a perception of our minds and of the fact that rationality ought to rule.

79. *ST* I–II.94.3.
80. *ST* I–II.18.5.
81. *ST* I.5.5.
82. *ST* I.21.1*ad*3.
83. *ST* I–II.19.3*ad*2.

One is naturally aware that what one is, one's "self," is primarily the "interior man."[84]

As I mentioned earlier, Finnis judges Thomas's ordering of the inclinations and the precepts in 94.2 to be an irrelevant schematization. I think it is very relevant, both to the intention of 94.2 and to Thomas's conception of practical reason itself. The question raised in 94.2 is not, "What are the basic human goods?" If that were the question, then the article would be woefully incomplete. Thomas recognizes many other objects of natural human inclination, many other goods pertaining to natural law, besides those mentioned in 94.2. One of them, hardly a marginal one, appears in the very next article: acting virtuously. But the question raised in 94.2 is whether natural law contains one precept or many. The answer is that it contains many precepts, but there is one primary precept on which they all depend. They "communicate in one root" (94.2*ad*2). Thomas insists that the many precepts, insofar as they are referred to the primary one, constitute one "natural law" (94.2*ad*1).

This is why the schematization, the ordering of the precepts, is relevant to 94.2. Thomas wants us to see not only the multiplicity of the precepts of natural law, but also the way in which they constitute a unity. If they can all be traced to a single source, this is precisely because they flow from it in a certain order. "A multitude proceeds from one thing in a certain order."[85] He is showing us a *natural* ordering and *natural* unity of the precepts. This is because the type of order that he lays out is, as we have seen, the type that reason naturally follows: from the more general to the more special. I argued earlier that I–II.94 is all about the naturalness of natural law.[86] 94.2 is about its natural unity. The unity is not that of a single precept. They are many. But without the order among them, natural law would be a mere jumble. It would be nothing but a heap of precepts.[87] There would be many natural laws. They would be leading us in many directions. And then, how could they be giving us our first direction toward the last end, which must be one?[88] The presentation of the order among them is therefore relevant to Thomas's very conception of practical reason. It shows the natural unity of practical reason's direction. A direction that lacks unity can hardly be considered rational. If there were no intrinsic order among the precepts of natural law, then there would have to be yet another, special precept, telling

---

84. See *ST* II–II.25.7.
85. *ST* I.77.4.
86. See above, 66.
87. Cf. *ST* III.2.1; *In Meta.* VII, lect. 17, §1673.
88. *ST* I–II.91.2*ad*2; I–II.1.5.

us to unify them, and how to do so, and toward what. Thomas needs no such special precept. He only needs the unity of the nature of reason itself.[89]

THE IMITATION OF NATURE

Now I would like to return to that remark by Thomas in his discussion of the angels' natural love of God above all things: "Reason imitates nature." He invoked this idea to account for a certain virtue. It is by no means a casual remark or an isolated use of the idea. To some, the notion may smack of the sort of physicalism that Donagan criticizes Thomas for. But I do not see how to sweep the doctrine under the rug. Thomas actually has quite a principled account of reason's imitation of nature, and he makes considerable use of the idea in his moral teaching.[90] As we shall see, it confirms the suggestion made earlier in this chapter, that a certain knowledge of natural inclinations does after all underlie the precepts of natural law—not the inclinations of one's own will, nor the sensitive or pre-rational inclinations that one experiences in oneself, but the natural inclinations of the beings around us. We shall also see that Thomas's doctrine of the imitation of nature does have theological underpinnings. But I wish to examine it especially with an eye to Donagan's worry, that Thomas is assigning an unduly normative status to "mere nature," giving it too much of a role in the promulgation of natural law. I think we can see that the fear of physicalism is unfounded.

First let me pick up on something that I argued for earlier: that the good is primarily a speculative notion, and only secondarily (though naturally and immediately) practical.[91] It not only moves the natural inclination of our own wills, but also, and even first of all, explains the inclinations of natural non-human things. For this reason, it seems to me that we can also say that the first precept of natural law, which is founded upon the good, also applies to such things. True, our understanding of it does not function to direct the actions of such things. But surely its *truth* applies to them—indeed to all things whatsoever. For every being, it is true that it ought to do and pursue the good and avoid the bad, in the way of doing so that is suitable according to its nature. The first precept is already an irradiation and a participation of the eternal law, which is the law "by which it is just that *all things* be perfectly ordered." All due order of action and movement and inclination is toward the good and away from the bad. Anything that is not doing what the first precept says is going astray. For irrational beings, to go

89. See *ST* I–II.94ad2/ad3.

90. For a superb full-length study of the doctrine, see Golubiewski, "Imitation of Nature."

91. See above, 153.

astray is to deviate from their own natural inclination.[92] For rational beings, it is to deviate from the order of reason. The first precept expresses reason's grasp of a rule of order that measures all things and that, once grasped, also runs through all of its own ordering.

Is this a confusion of the speculative and practical domains? I do not see why. After all, the common principles that govern speculative thinking are not confined to speculative matters. In 94.2, Thomas says that being is what falls first into our apprehension "absolutely" and that it is included in everything whatsoever that anyone understands. So it is included in practical understanding too. Certainly practical thought has to respect the principle of non-contradiction. The other common principles that Thomas cites in 94.2 also play obvious roles in practical thought. That *whole is greater than part* is implicit in the understanding that the common good, as such, is greater than the private. And that *things that are equal to one same thing are equal to each other* has application in matters of justice. The equal distribution of goods is often achieved by measuring the shares against a single measure.

If only some principles are called practical, it must be because only they are intrinsically apt to direct action. They alone are rules of action, precepts. But must their truth be confined to the sphere of human action? For Thomas, the difference between practical intellect and speculative intellect is not a difference with respect to the nature of intellect.[93] Likewise, the difference between practical truth and speculative truth is not a difference with respect to the nature of truth.[94] It is only a difference in what the truth is used for, the end in view of which it is considered. Truth is speculative inasmuch as it is considered for its own sake, as satisfying the desire to understand something. It is practical inasmuch as it is considered for the sake of directing action according to it. But I see no reason why the same principle cannot be applicable to the consideration of both speculative and practical matters and used for either purpose.

Our understanding of a natural thing cannot be practical in the sense that it actually directs the natural activities of the thing. But surely it can give rise to what Thomas calls "certain practical judgment," as to "whether it ought to be so or not."[95] The good of anything whatsoever consists in the perfection that it "ought to have."[96] If it were not so, how could Thomas

---

92. ST I–II.21.1.
93. See ST I.79.11.
94. See ST I–II.64.3.
95. ST I–II.93.2ad3.
96. ST I.5.1ad1.

see fit to correlate many of the precepts of natural law with inclinations that man shares with non-human things? It may be that the precepts do not serve as principles for reasoning about such things, because we do not reason practically about such things. We naturally see that reasoning practically about things that are not in our power is otiose. So, again, it is only in relation to practical human things that the first precept of natural law functions practically. But that does not mean that its truth applies only to practical matters. It does not even mean that reason first grasps it in relation to practical matters. Thomas says that "human acts can be ruled by the rule of human reason, which is gathered from the created things that man naturally knows."[97] He says this quite generally. He does not make an exception of the first precept. Things of all kinds tend to do and pursue what is good for them and to avoid what is bad. We see this, and it immediately makes sense to us. We see that it is just what anything ought to do—ourselves included. And we tend to regulate our own conduct accordingly. This would be an example of reason imitating nature.

But let us look at Thomas's own understanding of the imitation of nature. Two passages, from his commentaries on Aristotle's *Physics* and *Politics*, present the theory of it. In the first, he is explaining Aristotle's own remark that craft imitates nature.[98] The reason for this, Thomas says, is that "the beginning of a work of craft is cognition; and all of our cognition is received through the senses from sensible and natural things; whence in matters of craft we work in a way similar to natural things."[99] Thomas is simply applying to practical cognition his general view of how human intellectual cognition begins. We are not angels, whose cognition starts from the apprehension of their own spiritual natures.[100] Our intellect's first and proportionate object is sensible, corporeal nature.[101] Whatever else it apprehends, it grasps somehow in terms of or in relation to sensible things. Thomas is saying that we somehow gather even practical principles from our understanding of natural sensible things. And by *practical* I mean not only principles of craft or production, but also principles of moral action or conduct, the sphere ruled by the virtue of prudence.[102] The passage on angelic love gave an example of that. It presented the imitation of nature

97. *ST* I–II.74.7.
98. Aristotle, *Physics* II.2, 194a21–22.
99. *In Phys.* II.4, 65, ¶6.
100. See *ST* I.84.7; I.87.3.
101. *ST* I.84.7.

102. Thomas even finds imitation of nature in the operation of reason itself, as falling under reason's own direction and constituting the domain of logic. See *In Post. an.* I, *proem.*, 5, lines 51–74.

as at the root of a specific political virtue. And in fact, in his commentary on the *Politics*, Thomas offers a much fuller theoretical foundation for the imitation of nature.

Before looking at that text, however, I would like to remark on how pervasive this doctrine is in Thomas's determinations of specific norms, virtues, and vices in the moral part of the *Summa*, especially the *Secunda secundae*. I shall not try to give anything like an exhaustive presentation of its appearances; that would take up far too much space.[103] But we should notice that the doctrine not only is connected to Thomas's conception of natural law, but also underlies a regularly recurring element in the methodology of his moral theology. This is so even though he often does not call attention to the fact that he is using it. Let me simply cite a few instances.

In some places, without providing any defense or rationale for the procedure, Thomas determines something about human conduct simply by way of appeal to an inclination, or to a way of acting, found commonly among irrational things. For example, one of his arguments for the sinfulness of suicide is that "everything naturally loves itself, the result being that everything naturally keeps itself in being, and resists corruptions so far as it can. Wherefore suicide is contrary to the inclination of nature, and to charity, whereby every man should love himself. Hence suicide is always a mortal sin, as being contrary to the natural law and to charity."[104] Again, consider his explanation of the sinfulness of pusillanimity: "What is contrary to natural inclination is a sin, because it is contrary to natural law.[105] But in each thing there is a natural inclination toward carrying out action commensurate with its power, as is evident in all natural things, both animate and inanimate."[106] Similarly, to show that there is such a thing as the virtue of *vindicatio*, he reasons that "the virtues perfect us for duly pursuing the natural inclinations, which pertain to natural right. And so some special virtue is ordered to each determinate natural inclination whatsoever. But there is a special natural inclination toward removing harmful things; whence the irascible power is given to animals separately from the

---

103. Golubiewski, "Imitation of Nature," has gathered together and classified a great many of its appearances. See especially chapter 6.

104. *ST* II–II.64.5. See also *ST* II–II.69.4*obj*1.

105. In this sentence, I take it, Thomas is talking about natural inclination in rational beings, since only they have natural law. Notice that it is the contrariety to natural law, not to natural inclination, that makes for sin. This makes sense if the inclination only follows the law and is itself right on that account.

106. *ST* II–II.133.1.

concupiscible power."[107] Notice the references to natural law and natural right in these passages.

In other places where he follows this sort of procedure, Thomas does justify it, on the grounds that the same divine source of the order naturally existing in irrational beings is also the measure of voluntary action. Thus, on there being such a thing as military prudence, he says that "things done through art and reason should be like those that are according to nature, which have been instituted by God's reason."[108] In a similar way, he argues that the order of natural and divine right requires a virtue by which one complies with divinely ordained authority—the virtue of obedience—and the basis of his argument is that, by a divinely instituted order, lower natural things need to be moved by higher things, according to the excellence of the natural power divinely conferred on the higher things.[109] And here too he refers the matter to natural right.

On still other occasions, Thomas indicates that the correspondence between the natural rules of man's practical reason, together with the natural inclinations that result from them, and the natural inclinations of physical things, has an even more immediate basis than their common derivation from the eternal law. It is reason's grasp of the physical things themselves. One example, from the *Prima secundae*, is a passage that I quoted just a moment ago: "Human acts can be ruled by the rule of human reason, which is gathered from the created things that man naturally knows."[110] The same idea, expressed in terms of natural inclinations, is found a little later in the *Prima secundae*, where he explains that one effect of sin is to deserve punishment. I shall discuss this text in the next chapter.[111]

In the passages considered so far, Thomas does not say explicitly that natural things convey to us a knowledge that conforms to or shares in God's law. But it is safe to assume that this is ultimately what he has in mind. Elsewhere he does say it explicitly. Two of these places, where he also uses the precise notion of imitation, are back in the *Secunda secundae*. One, in the section on charity, is a rather striking remark made in the course of arguing that we ought to do more to benefit those who are closer to us. "Grace and virtue imitate the order of nature, which is instituted by divine wisdom. But the order of nature is such that each natural agent first pours forth its action

---

107. *ST* II–II.108.2.

108. *ST* II–II.50.4.

109. *ST* II–II.104.1; cf. *ST* II–II.104.4.

110. *ST* I–II.74.7. He goes on to say that they can also be ruled by the rule of divine law. He makes the rule of reason pertain to what is called the *inferior reason*; that of divine law, to what is called the *superior reason*.

111. See below, 201.

more on the things that are closer to it, as fire heats more that which is closer to it."[112] The other passage concerns the vice of presumption.

> Since the things that are according to nature are ordained by divine reason, which human reason ought to imitate, whatever comes about by human reason that is against the order commonly found in natural things, is vicious and sinful. But this is found commonly in all natural things, that any given action is commensurate with the agent's power, and no natural agent tries to do what exceeds its capacity. And therefore it is vicious and sinful, as being against the natural order, that someone undertake to do things that are beyond his power.[113]

The first sentence of this quotation is almost a synopsis of Thomas's most elaborate account of the imitation of nature, which is the one in the *Politics* commentary. Let me turn to that.

NATURALLY IMITATING THE DIVINE MIND

The passage is the initial portion of the prologue with which Thomas opens the commentary.[114] It begins as follows:

> As the Philosopher teaches in *Physics* II, craft imitates nature. The reason for this is that, just as principles are related to each other, so proportionally are their operations and effects. But the principle of things that come about by craft is the human intellect, which is derived, according to a certain likeness, from the divine intellect, which is the principle of natural things. Whence it is necessary that the operations of craft imitate the operations of nature, and that the things that are by craft imitate those that are in nature. For if a master of some craft were to effect a work of the craft, the apprentice who would take up the craft should consider the master's work so that he might work in a similar way. And so the human intellect, to which intelligible light is derived from the divine intellect, must be informed in the things that it does from the inspection of the things that are done naturally, so that it operate similarly.[115]

---

112. *ST* II-II.31.3.

113. *ST* II-II.130.1.

114. According to Torrell, *Initiation*, the (unfinished) commentary on the *Politics*, was written between 1269 and 1272. Torrell assigns the writing of the *Secunda pars* of the *Summa theologiae* to the years 1271–72.

115. *In Pol. Prologus*, A69, lines 1–19.

Nature and Human Nature in the Promulgation of Natural Law

The reference to intelligible light should remind us of *ST* I–II.91.2. So should the idea that the operations of nature, toward which things naturally tend, are the effect of the divine intellect. But here Thomas inserts the imitation of nature into the picture, and in doing so he makes his way of understanding it quite clear. Imitating, in this case, is by no means the same as copying. The apprentices who examine the work of the master learn more than the specific form given to that work, and more than the process by which it was brought about. If this were all they knew, then at most they would only be able to follow exactly the same steps and to bring about exactly the same form; and in order to do this, or at least in order to produce a good result by it, they would have to be provided with exactly the same material and instruments as those that the master used. The continuation of the passage excludes this reading.

> And hence it is that the Philosopher says that if craft made the things that are of nature, it would operate in a similar way, as nature does; and conversely, if nature made the things of craft, it would operate in a similar way, as craft does. Nature, however, does not effect the things of craft, but only prepares certain principles and in some way offers an exemplar of operating to the craftsmen. Craft, for its part, can inspect the things that are of nature, and can use them in effecting its own work, but it cannot effect them. From this it is clear that human reason only knows the things that are by nature, whereas it both knows and effects the things that are by craft. Whence it is necessary that the human sciences which are about natural things be speculative, and that those which are about things made by man be practical, which is to say, operative, according to the imitation of nature.[116]

The last clause is surely striking. It presents reason's practical works quite universally as existing "according to the imitation of nature." Notions gathered from the experience of natural things get into absolutely everything that reason effects. Let me stress again that Thomas is not talking only about craft (*ars*) in the narrow sense, as the intellectual virtue concerned with production or with the making of external things. He is also talking about moral action or conduct, which is the sphere of the virtue of prudence and of the sciences of ethics and politics. In fact, a little later in the prologue, after making it clear that the imitation of nature plays a role in political science, Thomas also makes it clear that political science is not about

---

116. *In Pol. Prologus*, A69, lines 19–36.

production but about moral action. And moral action is also the concern of moral theology.

It should be obvious that Thomas does not mean to restrict the imitation of nature to the imitation of nature's products. We do often make things that resemble things made naturally. But more important is the fact that we imitate nature's very way of operating. This too is an effect of the divine intellect. Unlike the human craftsman, God can put something of His craft, His very way of operating, into the things that He makes. If human craft imitates the natures of things, it is because the natures themselves *are* conceptions of the divine craft, instilled into the things, by which they are moved toward determinate ends.[117] They are intelligible principles of activity, first conceived by God's intellect, but also grasped by human reason through the experience of the activities that they are the principles of. The example that Thomas goes on to cite in the *Politics* commentary is nature's proceeding, in its operation, from the more simple to the more composite, the goal always being that which, relative to everything else in the process, is most composite and perfect. The intelligibility of this procedure explains why, of the communities of human beings that human reason institutes, political community is the last or the ultimate.

But what mainly interests me is Thomas's understanding of what the imitation of nature really amounts to. Again, it is not the mere production of copies of natural things. Nor is it a strict copying of nature's procedures. The apprentice's job is not to do exactly what the master has done. Rather, what the apprentice learns from the master's works are certain more general rules, rules according to which the masterworks are accomplished, but which also apply, in proportional fashion, to the handling of the matters and the instruments that are at the apprentice's own disposal. Proceeding from the simpler to the more composite is such a rule.

The rules are very general. They are not restricted to the measurement of any one specific type of thing or action. As we saw, in several of the texts on the imitation of nature Thomas looks to an order that is found, not just in some particular kind of natural thing, but commonly in all the kinds. These rules are capable of extending beyond, and in fact tend to direct the mind's vision beyond, the particular forms of their realization to which physical agents are determined and restricted. They enable the intellect both to judge the actions of natural things of various kinds and to direct various kinds of action of its own. This is why the order that reason established in the actions under its control will naturally resemble the order in the actions of natural things. For at least the primary terms under which reason's order is

---

117. *In Phys.* II, lect. 4, 65, ¶6; lect. 14, 96, ¶8.

developed will have first been conceived out of the apprehension of those things and for the purpose of judging them.

In this workshop, we might say, the apprentices are not clever enough to conceive the rules without first observing some examples of their application. But what they are able to gather from that observation is a knowledge enabling them to judge the examples themselves as things well accomplished.[118] And so, when they turn to their own work, it will be true in a way that they do what they do in light of the works that they saw, and their work will in a way resemble these; but the works that they saw, in their own proper forms and procedures, will not be what they actually attend to. Rather, they will attend to the more general rules that they conceived through their encounter with those works. And the resemblance will consist only in the common conformity to these rules.

In short, the apprentice's imitation of the master's work is not slavish. It is a certain share in mastery. Physical things themselves are not quite what constitute reason's standard. The standard is grasped somehow in the things or from the experience of them, but also as something by which they themselves can be explained and judged. It measures the very things in whose presence it is first conceived. The intellect remains superior to all merely physical things by its very capacity for such a conception. For if this conception depends upon sense experience, it is still possible only because what the senses provide is not the only, or even the chief, cause involved. The principal cause is the intellect's own natural light, which is derived immediately from God's.[119] And "nothing subsisting is greater than the rational mind, except God."[120]

What human reason primarily imitates is not nature itself. Rather, as the passage on presumption made clear, nature is only the medium through which the order of divine reason is conveyed. What human reason primarily imitates is divine reason. The primary intelligibles—being, truth, goodness, and so forth—upon which the mind's very first principles are founded, are not proper to any single kind of thing. They pertain to being itself, universally, which is a proper effect of the very highest, divine cause.[121] They are a reflection or a mirror of the very first truth, which is identical with the eternal law, of which human reason is a proper image.[122] Natural law is not

---

118. That is, again, he is able to judge them with what Aquinas calls a "practical" judgment, as "a superior judges of an inferior," as to "whether it ought to be so or not" (*ST* I–II.93.2*ad*3).

   119. See *ST* I.84.6*c*/*ad*3.

   120. *ST* I.16.6*ad*1.

   121. *ST* I–II.66.5*ad*4.

   122. See *ST* I.16.6*ad*1; I.84.5; I–II.93.1*ad*3; I–II.19.4*ad*3.

a participation in the natures of created things. It is a participation in the eternal law. It is mediated by the natures of things, but it also transcends them. It even transcends human nature, inasmuch as it constitutes a glimpse of the perfection toward which human nature is ordered.

> The judgment and efficacy of this cognition, by which we grasp the nature of the [human] soul, belongs to us through the derivation of the light of our intellect from the divine truth, in which the reasons of all things are contained. . . . Whence Augustine says in *De trinitate* IX that "we intuit the inviolable truth, from which we perfectly define, as far as we can, not how each man's mind is, but how it ought to be in light of the eternal reasons."[123]

Clearly, this way of understanding the imitation of nature does not entail positing a rule that we ought to do whatever nature does, just because nature does it. For example, once we get the idea of starting from simple, imperfect things and proceeding to composite, perfect ones, we see at once that it makes sense, in any application. We do not have to go back and check to make sure that natural things do work that way. Thomas is not talking about a deliberate process of interrogating natural things for practical principles. He is talking about a procedure that the human mind follows as it were instinctively or spontaneously, naturally.

Moreover, even if there is indeed a rule that human reason ought to imitate divine reason, it is not the first rule that practical reason grasps. It is something that reason can eventually come to know, but the knowledge of it is not what drives the natural process of imitating nature. The truths that we first know derive from divine truth, but we do not at first know this about them, nor is it because we are seeking divine truth that we come to know them. It is precisely by means of them that we can come to conceive of such a thing as divine truth. Our capacity to relate immediately to God and receive His own truth is a function of our apprehension of universal being and universal good—not the other way around.[124] These are proportioned to Him as effects to their proper cause, and grasping them establishes an initial proportion of our mind to His, as of potency to act.[125] They are presupposed by the faith through which we perceive the sublimity of His authority, and upon which depends His moving us through precepts that we apprehend as divinely pronounced.[126]

---

123. *ST* I.87.1.
124. *ST* II–II.2.3.
125. See *ST* I.12.1*ad*4.
126. See *ST* II–II.104.3*ad*2.

This fits with the idea that natural law is not a law that wins assent through the perception of its authoritative institution, in this case by a divine lawgiver. It is instituted and promulgated in such a way as to win assent per se, by virtue of itself, and naturally. And although natural, physical things somehow mediate its promulgation, the assent to it also does not depend on taking physical nature itself as authoritative. Man's proper excellence does not consist in being duly subjected to nature. It consists in being duly subjected to God. Donagan is right to suspect that Thomas has theological reasons for the role that he assigns to nature in morals. But the role is not what Donagan thinks it is.

This understanding of the imitation of nature also fits with the sense in which it is right to see the knowledge of the precepts of natural law as resting upon an apprehension of natural inclinations. Again, the inclinations are not those of the individual who apprehends them. One's own natural inclinations, at least those that pertain to natural law, are the results of one's understanding of the precepts. But we come to understand the precepts through understanding the actions, and the inclinations that give rise to them, of the natural things around us. The precepts are the practical applications of that understanding. The first precept reflects the understanding of that most common inclination, to the being and the perfection proportioned to a thing's nature—the inclination to the good.

There are also the precepts pertaining to the goods that are proper to human nature, proper to reason itself. These do not directly reflect the inclinations of non-human things. They do however reflect common human inclinations. I suggested earlier that a perception of these inclinations, as they are displayed in the human world to which one belongs, is involved in the understanding of the human goods. Perhaps we can say, then, that reason's imitation of nature includes a certain imitation of *itself*. (That reason does imitate itself is obvious. The apprentice's imitation of the master is an example of it.) The reason of each individual imitates the order in the rational, human things around him, and embedded in that is the order that is common to human things simply.

So there appear to be at least two reasons why Aquinas often appeals to the natural inclinations of physical things in establishing the existence of a moral principle or the suitability of a certain virtue for man. One reason, applicable also to angels, is his general conviction that rational and irrational creatures belong within a universal, divinely established order, and that therefore, to the extent that their natures share common features, so will the due order in the actions and inclinations that are suited to them. The other reason is that the manifest presence of a certain order of action in the common world of human experience is of itself sufficient grounds for attributing the understanding of that order, and of the rule measuring it, to natural reason. Reason's access to it is itself quite natural. Ethics and politics can therefore take it for granted.

For this procedure is not itself a work of ethics or politics. It is metaphysical. Like the other particular sciences, ethics and politics take their own principles for granted. To repeat, the task of determining and defending the principles of all the human sciences belongs to metaphysics.

One might therefore wonder why metaphysical interventions turn out to be so frequent in the moral part of the *Summa*. I think the answer is that the moral part of the *Summa* is not a work of either ethics or politics, or of any human science. It is a work of moral theology.

The point is not just that, for Thomas, theology is a single science which is both speculative and practical, so that we should not be too surprised to find metaphysics and morals side by side. It is also that reaching down to the very principles of the natural moral order serves to integrate it with the supernatural order. The natural moral order, as a whole, is the work of mere natural reason, whereas the supernatural order is conveyed to us by divine revelation. But the principles of the natural order are of divine origin as well. And for Thomas, the natural order itself is in some way a principle, though not a sufficient one, of the supernatural order. Again, even grace imitates the order of nature.

There is also a further and perhaps less obvious point. It is that a truly complete articulation of the natural moral order, the order of reason, requires going all the way down to its first principles, and that such an articulation is highly suited to the inner demands of moral theology, *even more* than to those of moral and political philosophy. This is because the whole order of reason, in all its details, has a bearing on man's relationship with God. And so the moral theologian cannot but regard the disclosure of the metaphysical foundations of that order as a valuable instrument. Lawrence Dewan puts this point better than I could:

> Christians have a responsibility for ethical exploration and pursuit of perfection that surpasses what is required in a non-Christian context. It is interesting to note that St. Thomas Aquinas, explaining a difference between his own ethical discourse and that of Aristotle, sees Aristotle as judging to be evil what is *harmful to other human beings*, whereas he himself calls "evil" what is *repugnant to rightly ordered reason*.[127] Later, speaking about the moral part of the divine law, Thomas relates what is basically the same difference to the fact that the divine (revealed)

---

127. ST I–II.18.9ad2. See Aristotle, *Nicomachean Ethics* IV.3, 1121a26–27.

law orders us toward community with *God*, whereas mere human law orders human beings among themselves; thus, since it is by reason or mind that man is united to God, the divine law goes beyond mere human law, instructing us in all those things whereby the reason of man is well ordered.[128] I take this to imply that we should put *more* emphasis on the desirability of probing the theoretical or contemplative wellsprings of ethical structures.[129]

To the two passages that Dewan cites, we can add another, more famous one:

> Man is not ordered to political community according to all of himself and according to all that he has, and therefore it is not necessary that every act of his be meritorious or demeritorious in relation to the political community. But all that a man is, and that he is capable of and has, is to be ordered to God, and so every good or bad act of a man has the quality (*rationem*) of merit or demerit before God, in proportion to the act's own nature.[130]

I take it that by this last phrase, "in proportion to the act's own nature" (*quantum est ex ipsa ratione actus*), Thomas means in proportion to the goodness or badness that an act has in itself or according to its own object and circumstances.[131] And a human act's goodness or badness is nothing other than its conformity or repugnance to reason.

Every good or bad act of a man has the quality of merit or demerit before God. That certainly suggests that natural law, as naturally understand, establishes genuine obligations. This is what remains to consider: the proper, natural obligatory force of natural law.

---

128. *ST* I–II.100.2.
129. Dewan, *Wisdom, Law, and Virtue*, 363.
130. *ST* I–II.21.4ad3.
131. Cf. *ST* I–II.20.1.

6

The Force of Natural Law

As we saw in chapter 2, Aquinas's analysis of the nature of law in general starts from a formulation expressing what he thinks the term *law* commonly signifies: a certain rule and measure according to which someone is led to act or restrained from acting. Thomas supports this formulation by appeal to the effect from which (according to one etymology) law gets its Latin name, the effect called obligation. *Lex enim dicitur a ligando, quia obligat ad agendum.*[1] Clearly for Thomas the connection between law and obligation is very close.[2] In the article on promulgation as an essential feature of law, he even says that obligatory force is proper to law.[3] We have already seen how natural law satisfies the various components of Thomas's definition of law, but the account of its legal character would not be complete without consideration of its obligatory force. This will serve to resolve the conclusions already reached, concerning natural law's possession of the nature of law, into the notion from which Thomas began the process of defining that nature.

---

1. *ST* I–II.90.1. See above, 42.

2. He is not simply being driven by the etymology that he cites. In fact he also knows another etymology, proposed by Isidore of Seville. It reads, "law (*lex*) is called so from reading (*legendo*), because it is written" (*ST* I–II.90.4*ad*3).

3. *ST* I–II.90.4. The article's second and third objections also hinge on its being proper to law to oblige.

There can be no doubt that Thomas takes natural law to be obligatory. This too comes out in the article on promulgation. In the corpus, he says that law, as a rule and measure, has to be applied to those who are to be ruled by it; only so does it acquire the obligatory force (*virtus obligandi*) that is proper to law.[4] The article's first objection says that law does not need to be promulgated, because natural law has the nature of law to the highest degree, and it is not promulgated. The reply says it is promulgated by God's inserting it into men's minds so as to be naturally known. Taken together, these remarks tie the obligatory force of natural law to what was argued in chapter 2 to be the very meaning of its name: law naturally promulgated. Natural law just is law as it exists in someone to whom a law, the eternal law, is applied.[5] Evidently we can say that it is that through which the eternal law first acquires obligatory force over us. In this chapter, I wish to try to determine how Thomas thinks this is to be understood.

THE NATURE OF OBLIGATION IN GENERAL

The first thing to ascertain, naturally, is what he thinks obligation is. Unfortunately there is no thematic treatment of obligation in the *Summa theologiae*, although it is mentioned in a few places. The most conspicuous ones are those just cited: the first and fourth articles of *ST* I-II.90.[6] In both of them, as we saw, obligation seems to be understood as practically identical with law's work of ruling and measuring human actions in such a way as to induce people to act or to refrain from acting. There is also a pair of remarks in *ST* I-II.91.6. The first is that "every law is obligatory, in such a way that those who do not observe it are called transgressors."[7] The second remark explains this, saying that it "applies to that which is a law in the sense of a rule and a measure; for it is in this sense that those who deviate from a law are constituted transgressors."[8] A transgressor is one who has overstepped a boundary.[9] Being *bounded*, after all, is not unlike being *bound*. It means having limits imposed upon one's movements. A law is not a physical boundary, but an intelligible one. It is the kind of boundary that consists precisely in a certain rule and measure. So the connection between the notions of obligation and transgression also suggests that Thomas identifies

4. *ST* I-II.90.4.
5. *ST* I-II.91.2; *ST* I-II.90.3*ad*1.
6. A few other places where obligation is mentioned in the Treatise on Law are noted above, 42.
7. *ST* I-II.91.6*obj*2.
8. *ST* I-II.91.6*ad*2.
9. *ST* II-II.79.2.

law's obligatoriness with its being a rule and measure that leads people to act or not to act. A later *Summa* text adds a further point. This is that obligation constitutes a certain kind of necessity. "Obligation, which is born of precepts . . . imposes necessity."[10] The necessity that it imposes is not that of force (*coactio*). Rather, "necessity from the obligation of a precept" is "the necessity of an end."[11]

These are certainly helpful indications as to how Thomas understands obligation. However, there is one place in his works where he does take up the topic of obligation in a thematic way. It is an article in the disputed questions *De veritate*. This text predates those of the *Summa* by twelve years or so. I find nothing in it that clashes with them, and it does add considerations that shed some light on them. It also indicates the relevance of a few other *Summa* passages, which I shall introduce in due course. So it is worth looking at in some detail.

In *De veritate* 17.3, Aquinas raises the question "Whether conscience binds."[12] His answer is affirmative. Conscience binds "with the force of divine precept." He arrives at this answer by way of an analysis of binding and its place in voluntary action. A somewhat condensed account of this analysis should suffice for the present purposes.

The term *binding* (*ligatio*), Thomas says, is applied to spiritual or voluntary things by way of a metaphorical derivation from bodily things. To bind something is to restrain it or to prevent it from moving out of the place that it is in. Binding therefore implies some kind of necessity, some impossibility of being otherwise. Moreover, the necessity that it implies is an imposed necessity, one arising from something outside the thing subject to that necessity. By contrast, things that are subject to necessity intrinsically or of themselves, for instance fire as subject to the natural necessity of tending upward, are not said to be bound according to that necessity. Binding refers to a necessity understood to be imposed on one thing by another.[13]

---

10. *ST* II-II.44.1*obj*2. I discuss this objection and the reply to it below, 190.

11. *ST* II-II.58.3*ad*2. I discuss this passage below, 191.

12. This text has received very little attention in contemporary studies of Thomas's notion of obligation. See Farrell, "Roots of Obligation"; Stevens, "Relation of Law and Obligation," 195–205; MacGuigan, "St. Thomas and Legal Obligation"; Hibbs, "Rhetoric of Motives." The text is mentioned in passing in Desjardins, *Dieu et l'obligation morale*, 71n3. It receives a rather curious reading in Brown, *Natural Rectitude*, 126–28, on which see below, 183n17.

13. Elsewhere, Thomas indicates that if the nature of a thing is itself the effect of an external agent, then in relation to that agent, even the natural or intrinsic necessity to which the thing is subject can be regarded as a case of binding. See *ST* I-II.93.4*ad*4; I-II.93.5.

Aquinas then distinguishes between two sorts of necessity that can be imposed from outside. One is the necessity of force, *coactio*. He means sheer physical force. This makes it simply impossible not to do what the external agent's action determines. Necessity of this sort, however, cannot be imposed on the will, but only on bodily things. Thomas also says that if the agent's action does not bring about this sort of necessity, then the imposition would not properly be termed force, but only inducement, *inductio*. (Notice that this is the word he uses for how law gives rise to action.) I suppose he is thinking of the fact that sometimes, as in his own writings—including those on law—the term *coactio* is used for the sort of inducement that consists in a threat of some evil that will result if someone does not do something. If what is done out of fear of the evil that would result from not doing it is, in itself, repugnant to the will and done reluctantly, then it is sometimes said to be done by force. Thus, in another place, Thomas contrasts acting from fear of punishment to acting "with pleasure and from one's own will."[14] But what is done from fear still proceeds from the agent's will—under the circumstances, he prefers to do it—and it is not simply involuntary, as is what is done by force properly so called.[15] Thomas does have another term that I believe he uses only to refer to sheer physical force: *violentia*, violence.[16]

The other sort of necessity that can be imposed from outside is what the *De veritate* calls "conditioned" necessity or necessity "on the supposition of an end." For example, "it is imposed on someone that were he not to do this, he would not obtain his reward." Whereas the simply forced is directly opposed to the voluntary, necessity of an end can be imposed on someone's will, "to wit, such that it be necessary for him to choose this, if he should obtain this good, or if he should avoid this evil."[17] This fits with the *Summa* passage mentioned above, in which he distinguishes between the necessity of force and that of "the obligation of a precept, or necessity of an end."

14. *ST* I-II.92.2ad4.
15. See *ST* I-II.6.5; I-II.6.6.
16. See *ST* I-II.6.4; I-II.6.5; I-II.6.6ad1; I.82.1.
17. *De ver.* 17.3; cf. *ST* I.82.1. Brown, *Natural Rectitude*, 126–28, treats this text of *De veritate* as though it were identifying the necessity that obligation constitutes with the necessity that belongs to what are called necessary truths. But they are not the same sort of necessity. A necessary truth is a proposition that is true and cannot be false. Some necessary truths, such as those of mathematics, have nothing directly to do with obligation. Those that carry obligation are practical truths, such as the primary precepts of natural law. But there are other precepts of law that are only contingently true. Yet this does mean that they are not obligatory; in that case they would not be laws at all. It means that they are contingently obligatory. They oblige *when* they are true. Sometimes the exceptionlessness of the primary precepts of natural law is treated as though it were the same thing as their obligatoriness, but this is a confusion.

Lest there be any doubt whether needing to do something in order to avoid an evil constitutes a case of necessity of an end, Thomas explains that, "in such matters, lacking evil is counted the same as having good, as is clear in *Ethics* V."[18] What also seems clear is that Thomas is thinking of the sort of necessity that Aristotle identifies in *Metaphysics* V: "the conditions without which good cannot be or come to be, or without which we cannot get rid or be freed of evil; for instance, drinking the medicine is necessary in order that we may be cured of disease, and a man's sailing to Aegina in order that he may get his money."[19]

The *De veritate* passage also explains how, in a way comparable to bodily binding, this sort of necessity can be imposed by the action of an outside agent. The action is a command. "The action by which the will is moved is the command of a ruler and governor."

However, Thomas explains, it is not sufficient that a governor make a command, in order that his subjects be bound by it to perform or refrain from a particular action. Again as in bodily things, the action of one thing actually binds another only through contact with it. The contact between the governor's command and his subjects comes about through a reception of knowledge of the command by the subjects. "Whence it is that no one is bound by some precept except by way of knowledge of that precept." One is not obliged to do what is commanded unless one knows the command (or at least could and should have known it). It is in this way, the *De veritate* passage concludes, that conscience binds with the force of divine precept. For conscience is nothing other than the application of the knowledge of a divine precept to the judgment of an act.

We should notice that, in speaking of divine precepts, the *De veritate* passage is not referring only to precepts of positive or revealed divine law. Two articles later, Thomas says that "conscience does not bind except by virtue of a divine precept imposed either according to written law or according to the law of nature."[20] He is taking divine law to include natural law.

Now let me try to work out some implications of the *Summa* and *De veritate* passages on obligation. A first implication is something stated explicitly in the third objection of the *De veritate* article: that no one binds himself. This point squares with Thomas's saying in the *Summa* that, properly speaking, no one imposes a law on his own acts.[21] It also fits with our earlier conclusion, that the imposition of natural law cannot be understood

---

18. The reference seems to be to Aristotle, *Nicomachean Ethics* V.1, 1129b8.
19. Aristotle, *Metaphysics* V.5, 1015a22–26 (Ross).
20. *De ver.* 17.5.
21. *ST* I–II.93.5.

to be the work of man's own reason. Reason is not the agent from which natural law obtains its binding power. It is only the means by which the law, with its binding power, exists in man's soul and thereby rules man's will.

I would call attention to the fact that Thomas does not say that the divine precept's binding the will depends on one's knowing its divine origin. He only says that one must know the precept. In some sense, the precept itself binds. To illustrate the point with a physical analogy, imagine a dog bound to a post by a leash. The agent who has bound the dog to the post is its master. But in a different sense, what binds the dog is the leash. We can call the leash the formal principle of the bond. The master binds the dog by attaching the leash to its neck. The neck need not be in contact with the master, but only with the leash. In the case of obligation, what one is bound to is the performance or the avoidance of a certain kind of action. The formal principle of the bond is the governor's precept, which enjoins or forbids such action. The governor binds the subject by attaching the precept to the subject's mind; that is, by giving the subject knowledge of it. I stress this because Thomas allows for the possibility that the subject know the precept in such a way as to be bound by it, even without being aware of the governor's having imposed it. This would be the case with the precepts of natural law. I shall return to this point later in this chapter.

Another implication is a further restriction on the necessity of an end that obligation constitutes, in addition to its being imposed by a governor. This restriction follows on the fact that the governor's precept binds the subject only insofar as the subject knows it. The bond consists in its being necessary for the subject to perform the action commanded, or to refrain from the action prohibited, in order to attain some end. But since the existence of this necessity depends on the subject's knowledge of the precept, evidently the subject's attaining the end, or failing to attain it, requires more than the subject's operating in a way that merely happens to fit or clash with the precept. It also requires that the fit, or the clash, be voluntary. In short, as the *De veritate* passage makes quite clear, obligation is properly a binding of the will. It pertains only to voluntary things. This fits with the example given in the passage: the necessity of complying with a precept if one is to obtain one's reward. Reward and punishment are matters of merit.[22] Merit belongs only to actions performed by free choice.[23] One merits a reward for acting according to a precept, or a punishment for acting contrary to it, only

---

22. See *ST* I–II.21.3.

23. *ST* I–II.114.1. The division of evil into fault and punishment applies properly only to voluntary things (*ST* I.48.5ad2).

insofar as one does so voluntarily.[24] But antecedent or invincible ignorance is opposed to voluntariness.[25]

Notice that this restriction to voluntary acts does not hold in the cases of necessity of an end cited in the *Metaphysics*. Whether or not one knows that one should take the medicine in order to be cured of the disease, and whether or not one's not taking it is voluntary, one will not be cured if one does not take it; and similarly with the necessity of sailing to Aegina in order to get one's money. Thomas makes a distinction along these lines, between the evil that sometimes follows on the "substance" of an act of wrongdoing (*ex parte substantiae actus*), such as getting sick as a result of overeating, and the evil that follows on the "fault" (*culpa*) of it—that is, upon its being a voluntary wrongdoing.[26]

Does this mean that the only ends that the necessity of obligation concerns are matters of merit—of reward or punishment? I do not think so. I shall take this up in the next section. But I do think the *De veritate* account indicates something pertaining to all necessity of an end, including obligation, when it speaks of a good that the one who is bound "should obtain" (*debeat consequi*) or an evil that he "should avoid" (*debeat evitare*). Elsewhere Thomas makes it clear that *debeo* and related terms such as *debitum* signify necessity of an end. *Debitum* means what ought to exist or be done, what is owed to someone, what is one's own (*suum*). Thomas spells this out, saying that to call a thing due or owed indicates "a certain order" toward that to which the thing is said to be due or owed, an order "of exigency or necessity."[27] Evidently it is not always that the one to whom the thing is owed needs the thing or cannot have his own good without it; in that case nothing created would be due or owed to God. The thought must be rather that the one *from* whom the thing is owed cannot have some good that he needs or avoid something that is bad for him unless he renders the thing to the one to whom it is owed. That which is obligatory, then, is necessary for an end that the one who is under the obligation somehow needs. If it were not something he needed, then the mere fact that he cannot attain it unless he complies with the precept would not put him under any real necessity.

---

24. On how compliance with a precept can be meritorious, see below, 191.

25. *ST* I–II.6.8.

26. *ST* I–II.85.5*ad*3. See also *ST* I–II.87.2. On *culpa* as a function of voluntariness, see *ST* I–II.21.2. Punishment, in the proper sense, is always an effect of *culpa* (*ST* I–II.87.7; II–II.108.4).

27. *ST* I.21.1*ad*3. Such English words as *debt*, *due*, and *duty* derive from *debeo*, *debitum*. Notice, by the way, that *ought* and *owe*, and also *own*, all stem from the same Old English root.

Absolutely speaking, he would not need to comply with it. It would not be obligatory.

Along this line, it should be kept in mind that this Aristotelian and Thomistic notion of necessity on the supposition of an end is not the same as what Kant calls a hypothetical imperative. A hypothetical imperative presents something as necessary for you to do on the supposition that you want something: for instance, "if you want to be cured, you must take this medicine." In Aristotle's and Thomas's necessity of an end, what is supposed is not your wanting something, but simply something's being good for you; or more precisely—at least for Aquinas—its being a due good for you, one that you need to obtain. Perhaps it is something that you *should* want, but it may or may not be something that you actually *do* want. In either case, the necessity still holds.

Working out how this necessity of an end relates to what Kant calls a categorical imperative would be a complicated affair. But one thing that is clear about it, at least as Thomas understands it, is that it is not confined to things that are merely instrumental to a good or to an end. Things can also have this necessity with respect to ends that they are constitutive of or even identical with. Thomas applies such terms as *should* or *ought* (*debet*) and *due* (*debitum*) to what is an end in its own right, one that is desirable or good per se, and not just an intermediate end that is good only by reason of its order to some further end. Indeed he applies such terms *primarily* to ends that are good per se. In the following text, for example, he explains why it is fitting that there be precepts of charity:

> A precept carries with it the quality of something due. Hence something falls under precept insofar as it has the quality of something due. But there are two ways in which something is due: per se and on account of another. What is due per se, in every affair, is that which is the end, because it has the quality of a per se good, whereas what is due on account of something else is that which is ordered toward the end. . . . But the end of the spiritual life is that a man be united with God, which comes about through charity, and everything that belongs to the spiritual life is ordered toward this as its end. Now in every genus, what is per se stands ahead of what is on account of another. And so the greatest commandment is that of charity, as it says in Matthew 22.[28]

---

28. *ST* II-II.44.1. The essence of charity is friendship with God, and so it constitutes a union with Him. See *ST* II-II.23.1; II-II.23.6*ad*3; II-II.24.12*ad*5.

Consider the very first precept of natural law: the good is to be done and sought, and the bad, avoided. Here the gerundive expresses the same sort of necessity as do *ought*, *due*, etc. The precept means that it is necessary to do and pursue the good and to avoid the bad. In what sense is it necessary? Precisely in Aristotle's sense: without it, the good cannot be or come to be and we cannot be free of the bad. If this seems too obvious to need stating, well, that is precisely the point. It is altogether self-evident, both in itself and to us, and it is more so than any other practical principle.

To sum up: obligation is a certain sort of necessity, one that applies only to voluntary agents. It is the necessity of their complying, voluntarily, with a precept enacted and made known by a governing agent, in order to attain some end.

This leaves rather indeterminate what that end might be. I do, however, think that it is possible to determine more precisely what Thomas takes to be the end or ends for the sake of which it is necessary to comply with legal precepts, generally speaking. This will be the task of the next section.

OBLIGATION, PUNISHMENT, AND RECTITUDE

Let me begin with the question whether the end for the sake of which what is obligatory is necessary is always, as in the *De veritate* example, a matter of merit; that is, of a reward to be obtained or a punishment to be avoided. Can there also be other ends, for the sake of which it is necessary to comply *voluntarily* with a superior's precept? And if so, is there any one kind of end that the necessity of obligation chiefly concerns?

As we saw, the *De veritate* passage gives only reward as an example of an end for which something obligatory is necessary. It does not give avoiding punishment as an example. But in other places Thomas clearly does associate obligation, and also law itself, with the threat of punishment. In fact he associates it more with this than with the promise of reward. Later in the *De veritate* itself he says that "we are held to something in two ways. In one way, such that if we do not perform, we incur punishment, which is properly to be held to something.... In the other way, we are said to be held to something, because without this we cannot attain the end of beatitude; and in this way we are held to do something out of charity, without which nothing can be meritorious of eternal life."[29] As for the connection between punishment and law, he makes punishment one of law's effects or attributes, the aim of which is to secure compliance with the law. "That through which

---

29. *De ver.* 23.7ad8. The term that I have rendered *we are held* is *tenemur*. That this is synonymous with *obligamur* (we are obliged) is clear from the third and fifth objections of this article. A similar thought is expressed in *In Sent.* III.36.1.6.

law induces obedience to itself is the fear of punishment; and in view of this, to punish is posited as an effect of law."[30] Here he uses the word *induces*; we should recall once again that Thomas associated obligation with law's work of inducing people to act or to refrain from acting. He also associated obligation with the notion of transgression. There are several texts that connect transgression with deserving punishment. For instance, "the act of sin makes a man liable to punishment, inasmuch as he transgresses the order of divine justice."[31] Similarly, "whoever ... transgresses a precept of law merits punishment."[32] Again, "even if he who honors his father does not have charity, he is not rendered a transgressor of this precept [to honor one's parents], although he be a transgressor of the precept that is about the act of charity, on account of which transgression he merits punishment."[33] And again, "a man carrying out the precepts of the law is said [Lev 18] to live in them, because he did not incur the punishment of death that the law inflicted on transgressors."[34]

But perhaps the text asserting the connection between law and punishment most strongly is this: "A precept of law has coercive force. Hence that directly falls under a precept of law, to which the law coerces. The coercion of law, however, is through the fear of punishment, as it says in Book X of the *Ethics*; for that properly falls under a precept of law, for which legal punishment is inflicted."[35] Here he is using the term *coercion* in the qualified sense of a principle of what is done reluctantly out of fear, not in the sense of sheer force or violence.

Taken together, these texts seem to leave no doubt that, for Thomas, the obligatory force of law consists at least partly in the force of its sanctions; that is, in its making some course of action necessary in order to avoid punishment. However, there are other passages which indicate that the obligatory force of law is not simply identical with this necessity. Avoiding punishment is not the only thing for the sake of which complying with a precept of law, as such, is necessary. What is obligatory in the most proper sense is indeed always something that has punishment attached to the transgression of it, but this is not the only thing that its obligatory force consists in. It seems to me that this is not even the primary thing.

30. *ST* I–II.92.2.
31. *ST* I–II.87.6.
32. *ST* I–II.100.9sc.
33. *ST* I–II.100.10.
34. *ST* I–II.100.12ad2. See also *In Rom.* IV, lect. 2, §358.
35. *ST* I–II.100.9.

The primary thing for the sake of which compliance with the law is necessary and obligatory is not something that one merits or deserves, something that one receives or avoids receiving as a due response to one's action. It has a more immediate connection with one's action. Compliance with the law is necessary, first of all, simply in order that one's conduct be right, or at least not wrong, and therefore good, or at least not bad. I wish to argue that this necessity, necessity for the sake of rectitude, is what the obligation of the law chiefly consists in. There are passages which show clearly that this is Thomas's view. But before considering them, let me offer some preliminary considerations, about the relation between obligation and punishment.

First of all, it is clear that what actually induces or motivates someone to obey the law may not be the threat of punishment. Thomas says that rational creatures "are induced to good and drawn back from evil by precepts and prohibitions, rewards and punishments."[36] Precepts and prohibitions (which are also called precepts, in a broader sense[37]) have their own intrinsic power to motivate action. The person who obeys them may not be acting out of what Thomas calls servile fear. By this sort of fear, one complies reluctantly or unwillingly with a precept, merely in order to avoid the punishment that would result from not complying. If there were no threat of punishment, one would not comply. This is a qualified sort of coercion. But one might obey the law without any such coercion. One might be glad to do what the law enjoins. Thomas says quite generally that one may be under the directive force of the law without being under its coercive force. This is the case with the lawgiver himself, and it is also the case with virtuous and just people, whose wills are in harmony with the law.[38] They gladly do what the law requires. Indeed, in the article immediately preceding the one in which he presents punishment as that by which the law induces obedience to itself, he makes it clear that fear of punishment is not what moves everyone to obey. Some do so "out of the perfect goodness of virtue," and some do so "out of the sole dictate of reason, which is a certain principle of virtue."[39]

The point comes out sharply in the article on the existence of precepts of charity. Thomas raises an objection to the fittingness of such precepts: "Charity ... makes us free.... But obligation, which arises from precepts, is opposed to freedom; for it imposes necessity."[40] The reply is that "the

36. *ST* I.103.5*ad*2.
37. *ST* I–II.92.2*ad*1.
38. *ST* I–II.96.5.
39. *ST* I–II.92.1*ad*2.
40. *ST* II–II.44.1*obj*2.

obligation of a precept is not opposed to freedom except in one whose mind is averse to what is commanded; as is evident in those who observe precepts from fear alone. But a precept of love cannot be fulfilled except from one's own will. And therefore it is not repugnant to freedom."[41] Only the person who *has* charity can fulfill its precepts.[42] But the person is still under the obligation of the precepts. Thomas is granting that precepts give rise to obligation. What the precepts of charity enjoin is not repugnant to the person who has it, and he complies with them gladly, but they do restrict or bound his conduct, inasmuch as transgressing them would make his end impossible.[43] Again, his end is the union with God that charity itself constitutes.

Also pertinent is a passage on the difference between the Old Law and the New Law: "The Old Law is said to restrain the hand and not the mind, because the will of one who abstains from a sin out of fear of punishment does not absolutely recoil from sin, as does the will of one who abstains from sin out of the love of justice. And on this account the New Law, which is the law of love, is said to restrain the mind."[44] The point is that even the New Law is said somehow to "restrain" (*cohibere*). It does impose boundaries not to be transgressed. It is obligatory.

Even more explicit on this point—that there is still obligation, as well as acting in order to fulfill an obligation, where there is no coercion—is a text precisely on the virtue of justice. An objection to the very thesis that justice is a virtue is that "what is done out of necessity is not meritorious. But to render another what is his own, which pertains to justice, is necessary. Therefore it is not meritorious. But by the acts of virtue, we merit. So justice is not a virtue."[45] Thomas replies:

> Necessity is twofold. One kind is that of coercion; and this, since it is repugnant to the will, takes away the quality of merit. But another is necessity from the obligation of a precept, or from the necessity of an end; when, that is, someone cannot attain the

---

41. *ST* II-II.44.1*ad*2.

42. This does not mean that it is given in vain to those who do not have charity. They may, merely out of servile fear—and with divine help—move themselves toward the possibility of complying with it, by doing what they can to dispose themselves for receiving charity. See *ST* I-II.100.10.

43. Thomas even grants that they act with a certain fear; not servile fear, but what he calls filial fear. This is not the fear of what might be inflicted upon them, but simply the fear of offending God, which goes hand in hand with loving Him. Nor does it mean that they comply reluctantly. Thomas holds that filial fear actually grows as charity does, and that it exists even in heaven. See *ST* II-II.19.10; II-II.19.11.

44. *ST* I-II.107.1*ad*2.

45. *ST* II-II.58.3*obj*2.

end of a virtue unless he does this. But such necessity does not exclude the quality of merit, insofar as one does what is necessary in this way voluntarily.[46]

Under *coercion* here, I take it, is included the qualified sort that belongs to what is done out of fear, the sort that makes one do voluntarily, but reluctantly, what is in itself repugnant to one's will. Such reluctance takes away the merit of virtue. But the thought is that the end for the sake of which it is necessary—obligatory—to comply with a precept, may be the very end toward which virtue itself tends. The *Secunda secundae* is full of discussions of precepts pertaining to one virtue or another. It would be odd if doing something because it is necessary for the end of a virtue could not be an exercise of that virtue. Every virtue complies gladly with the precepts regarding it, because the things that they enjoin are necessary for the virtue's own end. Surely virtue tends most of all toward what is necessary for its own end, more than toward what is only helpful and not necessary. Just persons who do something because it is necessary for the end of justice do it from their own will. They are in no sense forced to do it. But they are still obliged to do it.

OBLIGATION AND THE PROPER EFFECT OF LAW

What exactly does Thomas mean by the end of virtue? I think it is what he says in the corpus of this very article. "A human virtue is that which renders a human act good, and makes a man himself good." The proper end of virtue is good action.[47] He also explains that "a human act is rendered good by the fact that it attains the rule of reason, according to which human acts are rectified."[48] This brings us to a crucial point regarding the end for the sake of which law is obligatory or compliance with it is necessary. Thomas sees it is as a common feature of law, just as law—as a binding rule and measure of human acts—to aim at making those who are under it be virtuous and act virtuously. And he sees compliance with it as necessary for the end of virtue—at least the virtue that is proper to those subject to law, as such.

Thus, in the article prior to the one in which he presents punishment as an effect of law, Thomas argues that an effect of law is "to make people

---

46. *ST* II-II.58.3*ad*2. Thomas offers a similar reasoning in a passage on the virtue of obedience (*ST* II-II.104.1*ad*3). Similarly, "a slave can voluntarily exhibit to his master what he ought, and thus he makes a virtue of necessity, voluntarily rendering what is due" (*ST* II-II.81.2*ad*2). See also *ST* I-II.93.6*ad*1.

47. See *ST* I-II.55.4.

48. *ST* II-II.58.3.

good." His answer indicates that he understands this to be the proper effect and end of law, as law:

> Law is nothing other than a dictate of reason in the one who presides, by which the subjects are governed. But it is a virtue of any subject to be well subjected to that by which he is governed, just as we see that the virtue of the irascible and concupiscible powers consists in their being well disposed to obey reason. And in this way the virtue of any subject is that he be well subjected to the ruler, as the Philosopher says in *Politics* I. But each and every law is ordered toward being obeyed by those subject to it. So it is evident that it is proper to law to induce its subjects to their proper virtue. Therefore, since virtue is what makes the one who has it good, it follows that a proper effect of law is to make those to whom it is given good . . .[49]

To be law-abiding is itself a virtue.[50] And, obviously, in order to attain the end of this virtue, it is necessary to obey the law. Relative to this end, compliance with the law is necessary. And it is a due end of those who are subject to law, one that they need, according to their status as parts of the community that the lawgiver oversees.

Not all who obey the law do so out of the virtue of law-abidingness. If everyone had that virtue already, then the law itself would not be making any of them have it. And the law induces some of its subjects to obey by the threat of punishment. Even this is aimed ultimately at their becoming good. They need to become good, even if they do not want to. Obviously law may not always have that effect. But "by becoming accustomed to avoiding what is bad and doing what is good because of fear of punishment, one is sometimes led to do it with pleasure and from one's own will."[51] To be sure, insofar as people comply with the law only out of fear of punishment, they do not yet attain the end of being good; indeed their compliance itself is not unqualifiedly good, since it is reluctant. However, at least to the extent that they comply with the law, just as they avoid punishment, so too they avoid acting in a way that is unqualifiedly bad. And the whole point of the threat of punishment is to lead people toward being good.[52] So the need to avoid acting badly is more fundamental than the need to avoid punishment.

---

49. *ST* I–II.92.1. The reference is to Aristotle, *Politics* I.13, 1259b21–b7.

50. Notice that it is not a mindless disposition. It involves a type of prudence. See *ST* II–II.50.2.

51. *ST* I–II.92.2*ad*4.

52. See also *ST* I–II.90.3*ad*2.

What I am arguing is that, for Aquinas, legal obligation—the necessity that law brings with it—is not only, or even primarily, with respect to obtaining reward and avoiding punishment. It is also, and in the first place, simply with respect to the things upon which these depend: doing what is good and not doing what is bad. And above all, most properly, it is with respect to not doing what is bad. This fits with the fact that punishment is for bad conduct and that what properly falls under a precept of law is what is punishable. It also fits with the fact that it is not obligatory to do everything that is good and deserves a reward, whereas it is obligatory to avoid doing anything bad.

A remark in the *De veritate* article on conscience supports this. Thomas argues that conscience is obligatory even when it is erroneous, and his reason is that a transgressor of conscience necessarily incurs sin.[53] By *sin*, he means action that is morally bad. It is bad because it lacks rectitude. It is wrong. In what follows, instead of *sin*, I shall for the most part use the less theologically loaded word *wrongdoing*. Conscience is obligatory because not transgressing it is necessary for the sake of avoiding wrongdoing.

To avoid misunderstanding, I am not denying that the necessity of law is with respect to the will's *last* end, which is happiness. It is, because acting well or rightly and avoiding acting badly or wrongly are themselves necessary for happiness. Indeed, they are at least partly constitutive of it. I am only saying that the immediate and proper necessity of law is with respect to these. There are things that are necessary for happiness which are not directly in the will's power, and whose necessity does not depend on one's knowledge. These are not properly matters of obligation. Obligation depends on knowledge and concerns things that are in the will's power. The necessity that it most properly constitutes is with respect to the end that one attains just by complying with it; that is, the good of which the will is the very subject—moral good.

A moment ago I quoted Thomas saying that by fear of punishment one becomes "accustomed to avoiding evil and doing good." Law does not just aim at procuring obedience to its own dictates. Generally speaking, the things that it dictates are also good in themselves: avoidances of evil and performances of good. And so law generally tends toward other virtues as well, in addition to law-abidingness. However, Thomas is perfectly aware that not all dictates issued by governors are truly good. I ended the long quotation above, about law making men good, with an ellipsis. The passage continues as follows:

---

53. *De ver.* 17.4.

> A proper effect of law is to make those to whom it is given good, either without qualification or in a certain respect. For if the intention of the lawgiver tends toward true good, which is the common good regulated according to divine justice, it follows that through the law, men become good without qualification. But if the intention of the lawgiver is directed toward what is not unqualifiedly good, but toward what is useful or pleasant to himself, or what is repugnant to divine justice; then the law does not make people good unqualifiedly, but only in a certain respect, namely, in relation to such a regime. In this way good is found even in things that are bad in themselves, as when someone is said to be a good thief because he works in a way that is suited to his end.[54]

This qualification of the thesis that law makes people good does not run contrary to the thesis that law has obligatory force by making what it dictates necessary for avoiding wrongdoing. As we have already seen, in Thomas's view dictates that do not tend toward the common good, or that run contrary to divine justice, are not full-fledged laws, and do not fully oblige.[55] Just as they make people good only in a certain respect, so too they are legal and obligatory only in a certain respect.

On the other hand, Thomas does not seem to think that the true common good of human or civil community requires that all of its members be fully virtuous. Only the community's rulers need to be so. Only they need to be good people, without qualification. The rest only need to be good citizens, which is to say, law-abiding ones.[56] Along the same line, Thomas does not think that even good human law can or should directly prohibit all vices or sins.[57] The obligation of good human law does not extend to the avoidance of every sort of wrongdoing.

At the same time, Thomas does hold that being a good and law-abiding citizen is part of being simply good and virtuous, and avoiding civil wrongs is part of avoiding wrongdoing altogether. Thomas's way of putting this is that all true law, whether divine or human, obliges in conscience. Just human laws oblige in conscience because in fact they derive from the eternal law.[58] This is not to say that human laws are themselves divine laws; human

---

54. *ST* I–II.92.1.

55. On order to common good as a criterion for unqualifiedly binding ought-judgments about human actions, see the chapter "Obligation" in Jensen, *Knowing the Natural Law*, 150–74.

56. See *ST* I–II.92.1*ad*3.

57. *ST* I–II.96.2.

58. See *ST* I–II.96.4.

law "falls short" of the eternal law.[59] Human law must fit with divine law, but it is not itself divine. Natural law, by contrast, although not the whole of the divine law for man, is still part of it. And in fact all acts of virtue, as such, pertain to natural law.[60] So clearly natural law also directs toward good citizenship. Everyone is obliged to obey human law and to seek the virtue or the goodness of a good citizen, because natural law itself requires this. Thomas says that one who obeys human law may do so either out of fear of punishment, or out of the goodness of perfect virtue, *or* "out of the sole dictate of reason, which is a certain principle of virtue."[61] To say that obedience is out of the dictate of reason is to say both that it is rooted in a dictate of natural law and that it is an obligation in conscience.

In fact, to be obligatory in conscience and to be required by reason are one and the same thing. "Since conscience is a certain dictate of reason, it is the same to ask whether a will that disagrees with an erroneous reason is bad, as to ask whether an erroneous conscience obliges."[62] To be obligatory in conscience is to be necessary in order to avoid having a bad will. This is just another way of saying that it is to be necessary in order to avoid wrongdoing. To have a bad will is to will to do wrong and (on the occasion) to do it (voluntarily).

One might ask, how is the mere dictate of reason an *inducement* to act? Thomas's answer is very simple: it engages the natural human inclination of the will to act according to reason. This is the same as the inclination to virtue. We may recall that it was precisely because man is free, rational, that Thomas judged it suitable for providence to rule man by a law properly so called, natural law.[63] It was not because people had to be coerced into doing good. Before sin came into the world, they did not have to be.

But it is in the next two sections that I shall consider the obligatory force of natural law, and there I shall address its relation to conscience and to the natural inclination to virtue more fully. My conclusion here, concerning obligation in general, is threefold. First, it is primarily obligation under law. Second, the obligation of law, taken generally, does include the necessity of complying with the law for the sake of objects of merit—earning a reward and, more fundamentally, avoiding punishment. But third, the obligation of law, taken generally, is chiefly the necessity of complying with the law for the sake of something more basic than objects of merit: attaining goodness

---

59. *ST* I–II.96.2*ad*3.
60. *ST* I–II.94.3.
61. *ST* I–II.92.1*ad*2.
62. *ST* I–II.19.5.
63. *ST* I–II.91.2*ad*3.

or rectitude, and, in the first place, avoiding badness or wrongness. To be sure, this is not an end completely diverse from that of earning a reward and avoiding punishment; Thomas regards merit and demerit as *effects* of the goodness and badness, the rectitude and wrongness, of human acts.[64] Likewise, I believe, obligation with respect to merit and demerit is an effect of obligation with respect to goodness and badness, rectitude and wrongness.

In short, the obligatory force of law is above all its establishing a boundary, a dividing line or criterion, distinguishing good or indifferent kinds of acts from those that are bad and wrong. By *wrong*, I mean the sort of wrongness that is proper to voluntary agents, moral wrongness. This is only partly measured or determined by human law, but it is entirely a function of eternal law and natural law. As we considered at some length earlier, all sin is bad because eternal law and natural law forbid it.[65] What this suggests is that if obligation is chiefly obligation under law, then above all it is obligation under eternal and natural law. And, at least in some sense, obligation under natural law comes first, since even eternal law obliges only insofar as it is made known, and it is first made known in the promulgation of natural law. So let us turn to how the obligation of natural law, as naturally promulgated, is to be understood.

THE BINDING FORCE OF NATURAL LAW AND REMORSE OF CONSCIENCE

If, as I have been arguing in the course of this study, Aquinas understands natural law to be a law in the proper sense of the term, then there really cannot be any doubt that he considers it obligatory. And if it "has the nature of law to the highest degree," then evidently it also obliges to the highest degree. This certainly fits with the thesis that obligation is primarily with respect to the goodness and badness that are proper to voluntary agents, moral goodness and badness. Moral goodness and badness consist in being either according or contrary to the rule and measure of reason and the eternal law. Natural law consists in the first principles of human practical reason. It is that through which the eternal law is first brought to bear on the human will so as to rule and measure it in a necessary way. So compliance with the precepts of natural law is obviously necessary for achieving good action and avoiding wrongdoing. They are the first principles of the very rule by reference to which moral goodness and badness are constituted, the rule of reason. Clearly it is reason understood as informed by the precepts

---

64. *ST* I–II.21.3.
65. See above, 85.

of natural law and as working in conformity with them that Thomas is referring to when he calls natural reason a rule and measure of human action.[66]

We should not forget that, according to the *De veritate*, the notion of obligation also involves a reference to the agent, the superior or the commander, whose command imposes necessity on the will. But this point has already been covered, by the consideration that natural law is understood to be properly a law insofar as it is understood to be from God as the governor of the universe. It is God who promulgates natural law by instilling the light of reason into our minds and thereby making the law something that we naturally come to understand. As discussed earlier, in a sense the precepts of natural law are works of reason itself, but not in the sense that reason itself is their legislator or institutor. It is only in the sense in which all propositions are works of reason.[67] Formulating the precepts belongs to reason, but it is not reason that makes the precepts be true, or be rules and measures of human acts, or be obligatory. Reason does not command its own assent to the precepts. Once it grasps them, it assents to them naturally and necessarily. They have in themselves the power to win its assent. It is to the eternal law that they owe their truth, their power to win assent, and their regulatory force over human action.

Now I argued earlier that the precepts of natural law are to be understood as directing toward all the things that reason naturally apprehends to be human goods, and away from their contraries, and that this means that natural law taken as a whole, under the unity of its first precept, directs toward human happiness or beatitude. One might therefore be inclined to say that it is with respect to beatitude or its opposite, which Thomas calls misery, that natural law properly obliges, and not with respect to moral goodness or badness. Natural law does direct toward moral goodness and away from moral badness—the dictate to act according to reason is one of its precepts—but it also directs toward many other good things and away from many other bad things. And it is certainly true that, for Thomas, complying with the precepts of natural law is altogether necessary for being happy and avoiding misery. Nevertheless, as I argued earlier, if we are to follow the *De veritate* account of obligation, I do not think that this necessity can quite be considered to be obligation in the proper sense. That is because it holds, whether or not one is aware of the precepts. Acting out of ignorance of some precept of natural law could have bad consequences, even if one would not be blamed for them. But on the *De veritate* account,

---

66. See above, 104.
67. See above, 67.

the necessity that pertains to obligation takes effect only through knowledge of the relevant precept.

The goods that pertain to natural law are first grasped by reason as having the "goodness of nature." They are things that human beings need, insofar as they are human, for their fulfillment or perfection. Reason naturally grasps that acting for these goods and avoiding their contraries is necessary for attaining them, which is to say, it naturally judges such action to be due. And this judgment is true, because such action *is* due in this way. It would be so even if reason did not grasp it. It is a natural due. But *by* grasping these goods as due in this way and ordaining action for them, reason brings them and the action for them into the moral order.[68] It makes the proper goodness of the will and its acts, which is moral goodness or the goodness of virtue, depend on willing them and acting for them. It makes them morally due.

To be sure, reason also naturally understands moral goodness to be a human good, a perfection proportioned to human nature. That is why it first dictates the pursuit of it and the avoidance of its opposite, vice or sin. Moral goodness itself—acting according to reason—is dictated by natural law. This dictate makes the very willing and pursuing of moral goodness itself, taken generally, to be part of moral goodness.

There can also be no doubt that the precepts of natural law, just as the rules that they are, have power to induce action in compliance with them. As dictates of reason, they engage the will's natural aptitude for following reason. They naturally do so, being natural themselves, and they are the first dictates to do so. That aptitude of the will is first exercised in the natural human inclinations, which are the inclinations that are according to the precepts of natural law. This is not to say that the will's aptitude to follow reason is what makes it seem good to comply with the precepts. It seems good for us to comply with the precepts because it seems good for us to act according to reason, and this seems good for us in virtue of itself. It presents itself as part of our proportionate due perfection. But the will's aptitude, which is really nothing other than the nature of the will, is involved in explaining why we actually do act in accordance with the precepts.

I mean, why we do, when we do. Obviously sometimes we do not. The power of the precepts to induce compliance with them is not overwhelming. We can and do resist it. Obligation is a sort of necessity, but it is not the sort that consists in being absolutely impossible to be otherwise. No law concerning human action is imposed in such a way that transgression

---

68. See *ST* I–II.19.1*obj3/ad3*.

of it is absolutely impossible. What is impossible is to transgress it without incurring wrongdoing and liability to punishment.

This does however raise a question about the obligatory force of natural law. The question is whether it carries any sanction or punishment of its own for violation of it. Although I have argued against seeing punishment as the primary factor in obligation, I have granted that it is at least a secondary factor. Is there some sort of punishment that pertains to natural law, and one that can function as an inducement to compliance, through the fear of it? This will be the concern of the rest of this section. In the next one I shall discuss how this punishment can be regarded as a genuinely legal effect. With this point, I believe that I shall have brought to completion the account of the legal character of natural law.

Does natural law carry its own sanctions? About this, it is very important to keep in mind that, for Aquinas, natural law does not constitute a complete body of law. It is only a participation in a complete law, the eternal law. And it is not even a complete participation, in the sense of the whole participation that human beings need for life in any community, divine or human. It only provides starting-points, common principles, for the realization of a complete participation. Even merely human community requires the conclusions from these common principles, and the determinations of them, that pertain to human law. And divine community requires not only those but also new, revealed principles. This point bears on the question of punishments attached to natural law, because one of the ways in which natural law is clearly incomplete, in Thomas's view, is with respect to punishment.

> Certain things are derived from the common principles of the law of nature in the manner of a conclusion; for instance this, that one is not to kill, can be derived as a certain conclusion from the fact that one is not to do evil to anyone. But certain things are derived in the manner of a determination; for instance, the law of nature has it that he who sins be punished, but that he be punished with such and such a punishment is a certain determination of the law of nature. And so both [sorts of derivation] are found posited in human law.[69]

Similarly, "natural law has it that malefactors be punished, but that they be punished with this or that punishment is from divine or human institution."[70] Natural law calls for the punishment of things that violate it, but it does not say exactly what the punishment should be. A further

69. *ST* I–II.95.2.
70. *ST* II–II.85.1*ad*1.

intervention, of human or divine law, is required in order for there to be a determinate, actual threat of punishment.

However, it is also clear that this point needs to be qualified in an important way. There is after all a certain kind of punishment that natural law brings with it and that does not require the determination or institution of any other law. Thomas indicates it in a fundamental text on punishment. The text does not speak of natural law explicitly, but the connection is not hard to establish. The passage is long, but it is worth quoting in full. I shall present it in two parts.

In the first part, Thomas offers what is really a quite metaphysical perspective on punishment. He traces it to first principles and sees it in terms of a highly universal phenomenon. In effect, and in the manner that by now is familiar to us—by reference to natural things and natural human inclination—he is showing how it pertains to natural law.

> From natural things it devolves to human things that what rises up against a thing suffers some loss from that thing. For we see in natural things that one contrary acts more vehemently in the presence of the other contrary; this is why, as Book I of the *Meteorology* points out, heated water cools more quickly. Hence among human beings one finds that, by a natural inclination, each one presses back anyone who rises up against him. Now it is clear that the things contained within any given order are in some sense unified in their relation to the principle of that order. Therefore, the result is that whatever rises up against a given order is pressed back by that order and by the principle of the order. But since a sin is a disordered act, it is clear that anyone who sins is acting against some order. And so the result is that he is pressed back by that order. And this repression is punishment.[71]

Here we see that punishment is not solely, or even primarily, something that lawgivers or other governors devise as a useful inducement, by the threat of it, to compliance with their orders. They also actually inflict it, in response to violations actually committed. They do so for the good of the order.[72] And they are right to do so. The tendency to repress disorder is rooted in order itself. Inasmuch as complying with due order is a matter of justice, actually repressing disorder and restoring order, by punishment, is

---

71. *ST* I–II.87.1. A similar natural inclination is cited in *ST* II–II.108.2, on the virtue of *vindicatio*.

72. See *ST* I–II.95.1.

also a work of justice.[73] Specifically, it is a work of commutative justice.[74] It restores equality, "insofar as he who, in sinning, has followed his own will excessively, suffers something against his will."[75] This is important. If the actual infliction of punishment were not just, it is hard to see how even the threat of it would be. And then it would be hard to see how it could pertain to law at all, even as an inducement to compliance.

Turning to the second part of the text on punishment, Thomas distinguishes three orders under which human things fall and ascribes punishment to each of them. I shall argue that one of them is rooted directly in natural law.

> Hence, corresponding to the three orders to which the human will is subject, there is a threefold punishment by which a man can be punished. For, first of all, human nature is subject to the order of one's own reason; second, it is subject to the order of other people, who govern it either spiritually or temporally, whether politically or in a household; and, third, it is subject to the universal order of divine government. Any one of these orders, however, is perverted by sin, while the one who sins acts contrary to reason, contrary to human law, and contrary to God's law. Hence, he incurs a threefold punishment: one from himself, namely, remorse of conscience; another from man; and a third from God.[76]

The punishment that can be ascribed directly to natural law is the first, that which is from one's own reason—the remorse of conscience. But before considering how this is rooted in natural law, let me add two other considerations about punishment in general.

Sometimes Thomas speaks of law itself as performing the work of punishing.[77] This must be metonymy. Properly speaking, law is not an agent. It is a principle by which or according to which an agent acts. Moreover, Thomas is not saying that law is the immediate principle from which punishment arises. It calls for punishment, but the actual infliction of punishment is mediated by something else, something that brings the order of the law to bear on the particular transgressor. "Law punishes on the basis of judgment,"[78]

---

73. *ST* I-II.21.3.

74. *ST* II-II.108.2*ad*1.

75. *ST* II-II.108.4. See the lucid, succinct account of Aquinas on sanction in Gilson, *Thomism*, 305–7.

76. *ST* I-II.87.1.

77. *ST* I-II.92.2; I-II.100.12*ad*2.

78. *ST* I-II.100.9.

and "to punish sins pertains to judgment."[79] It belongs to the judge to declare the person guilty of transgression and deserving of punishment, and to determine what the punishment should consist in. This sort of judgment, Thomas says, involves a certain "compulsion" and has "coercive power."[80]

The other point is that Aquinas attributes a certain punitive quality, a power of harming, to the guilty verdict itself:

> It is one thing to judge about things, and another to judge about people. For in a judgment by which we judge about things, what is at stake is not what is good or bad for the thing itself about which we judge, to which no harm comes, no matter how we judge about it. . . . But in a judgment by which we judge about people, what is chiefly at stake is what is good or bad for the one about whom we judge, who is held honorable by the very fact that he is judged good, and contemptible if he is judged bad.[81]

This text is concerned with the judgment that one person pronounces on the conduct of another, with the resulting esteem or scorn in which the one judged is held by others. But there are also such things as the self-esteem and self-contempt that result from one's judgment of one's own conduct as good or bad. Such judgment is an instance of what Thomas calls conscience:

> For conscience is said to testify, to bind, or to goad, and also to accuse or to rebuke or reprimand. And all of these follow upon the application of some cognition or knowledge of ours to the things we do. This application is accomplished in three ways. First, according as we recognize that we have done or not done something . . . and it is in this sense that conscience is said to testify. Second, according as through our conscience we judge that something should be done or should not be done, and it is in this sense that conscience is said to goad or to bind. Third, according as through our conscience we judge that something that has been done was well done or not well done, and it is in this sense that conscience is said to excuse or to accuse or rebuke.[82]

The term that I have rendered *rebuke* is *remordere*, which literally means to bite back. A *remorsus* is a biting back. To act contrary to a rule of conduct that one holds is, as it were, to offend one's reason, and reason bites back. Or, in the words of the passage on punishment quoted previously,

---

79. *ST* II-II.60.6*obj*2.
80. *ST* II-II.60.6*ad*1/*ad*4.
81. *ST* II-II.60.4*ad*2.
82. *ST* I.79.13.

it presses back. This biting or pressing back is nothing other than reason's judgment that the action is wrong.[83] Such judgment about oneself is naturally displeasing. Of itself it is painful; which is almost to say, punitive. Both *pain* and *punitive* come from *poena*, punishment.

I shall want to look more closely at the punitive character of remorse of conscience, but first let me show why I say that remorse of conscience pertains in a special way to natural law.

In the *De veritate* passage on the obligation of conscience, Thomas says that conscience binds with the force of divine precept. But by now it is clear that Thomas regards the precepts of natural law as divine. And the *De veritate* leaves no doubt that conscience is chiefly an act of applying the knowledge of natural law. Several passages show this.

Thomas holds that, properly speaking, *conscience* names an act—an act of judging—and not a power or a habit. One objection to this position is that Saint Basil identifies conscience with the *naturale iudicatorium*. As we saw earlier, Thomas himself identifies the *naturale iudicatorium* with *synderesis*; that is, with the natural habit of the knowledge of the precepts of natural law. To answer this objection, Thomas explains that conscience can be called the *naturale iudicatorium* "inasmuch as the whole examination or consultation of conscience depends on the *naturale iudicatorium*."[84] This is to say that the judgment of conscience is always formed in light of natural law.

Another objection against understanding conscience as an act is that Damascene calls it "the law of our intellect," and that this is the habit of the "universal principles of right." These are the precepts of natural law.[85] Thomas's answer is that conscience is called the law of our intellect because it is a judgment of reason derived from natural law.[86]

Yet another objection is that Damascene says that conscience is implanted by God, and that what is implanted by God seems to be an infused habit. The reply roots conscience in *synderesis* without qualification. "Even natural habits themselves exist in us by God's implanting them. Therefore, since conscience is an act proceeding from the natural habit of *synderesis*, conscience is said to be implanted by God in the way in which all the

---

83. *De ver.* 17.1.
84. *De ver.* 17.1*ad*5.
85. See *ST* I.113.1*obj*1/*ad*1.
86. *De ver.* 17.1, *ad s.c.* 1. Similarly, in the subsequent reply (*ad s.c.* 2), he distinguishes conscience from natural law itself.

cognition of truth that is in us is said to be from God, by whom the cognition of first principles is instilled in our nature."[87]

But Thomas asserts the connection between conscience and natural law most strongly in his reply to the very first objection against taking conscience as an act. The objection is that Jerome seems to identify conscience and *synderesis*. The reply is long, but the relevant part is this: "The whole force of conscience, as examining or taking counsel, depends on the judgment of *synderesis*, as the whole truth of speculative reason depends on first principles. Therefore he calls conscience *synderesis*, inasmuch as it acts by the force thereof."[88] The *whole* force of conscience depends on *synderesis*, which is to say, on natural law.[89]

Thomas's treatment of conscience in the *Summa theologiae* is much briefer than that of the *De veritate*. But the *Summa*'s fundamental article on it presents the same association of conscience with *synderesis*. "Because a habit is a principle of an act, sometimes the name of conscience is ascribed to the first natural habit, namely *synderesis*, in the way that Jerome, in a Gloss on *Ezekiel* 1, calls *synderesis* conscience, and in the way that Basil calls the *naturale iudicatorium* conscience, and in the way that Damascene says that conscience is the law of our intellect. For it is common for causes and effects to be named by one another."[90] And particularly strong is the reply to an objection that wants to make conscience neither an act nor a habit but a power. The objection says that "conscience must be either an act, a habit, or a power. But it is not an act, because then it would not always remain in a man. Nor is it a habit, because then it would not be one thing but many; for in acting we are directed by many cognitive habits. Therefore it is a power."[91] Thomas answers:

> Even if an act does not always remain in itself, it nonetheless always remains in its cause, which is a power and a habit. And even if the habits by which a conscience is informed are many, all of them nonetheless have their efficacy from one first habit, namely from the habit of first principles that is called *synderesis*. Hence in a special way this habit is sometimes called conscience, as was said above.[92]

---

87. *De ver.* 17.1, *ad s.c.* 6.

88. *De ver.* 17.1*ad*1.

89. Suárez too sees all binding in conscience as somehow the effect of natural law. See *De lege naturali*, 143–44 (*De legibus* II.ix.10, lines 1–18).

90. *ST* I.79.13.

91. *ST* I.79.13*obj*3.

92. *ST* I.79.13*ad*3.

It seems to me, by the way, that the association of conscience with natural law confirms the view for which I have been arguing, that in order to function as precepts of divine law, the precepts of natural law do not have to be considered precisely as divine. For Thomas clearly thinks that not every judgment of conscience involves applying a rule that one considers to be from God. This comes out in his discussion of how even an erroneous conscience obliges, which is to say, how a will that clashes with an erroneous conscience is bad.

> When an erroneous conscience dictates something to be done, it dictates it under some guise of good, either as a work of justice, or as of temperance, and so forth. And therefore the transgressor [of the erroneous conscience] falls into the vice opposed to that virtue under whose type conscience dictates that [work]. Or, if it dictates something under the guise of a command of God, or only of some superior, he incurs the sin of disobedience by transgressing his conscience.[93]

And similarly,

> when reason apprehends something as bad, it always apprehends that under some type of badness; for instance, because it runs against a divine precept, or because it is a scandal, or on account of something of this sort. And then such a bad will [clashing with an erring reason] is traced back to such a type of badness.[94]

On this account, atheists have conscience too. They do so even if they deny it. And this is because they know the common precepts of natural law. Nonetheless natural law is a divine law.

REMORSE AS A PUNISHMENT, AND THE OBLIGATION OF NATURAL LAW BEFORE GOD

If the whole force of conscience depends on *synderesis*, and therefore on the knowledge of natural law, then so does all remorse of conscience. As we saw, Thomas regards the remorse of conscience as a kind of punishment. It is a punishment inflicted upon a wrongdoer by his own reason, for a violation of reason's own order. But its whole force derives from the principles of that order, which constitute natural law. Remorse of conscience is the reaction, against the violation of the order contained in natural law, that

---

93. *De ver.* 17.4*ad*9.
94. *ST* I–II.19.5*ad*3.

springs directly from the order itself. And it springs from the order by way of a judgment, as punishment does. It *is* a judgment, and in human things, judgments themselves can be punishments.

So remorse of conscience seems to be the punishment proper to natural law. Some questions might be raised, however, about whether it is a genuinely *legal* punishment. This is what I wish to consider in this section.

First let me say two or three things about the punitive quality of the remorse of conscience. One is that, if remorse is a punishment, it must be involuntary. "For it is of the nature of punishment to be against the will."[95] Of course it is possible to engage voluntarily in the process that leads to remorse of conscience; that is, it is possible to "examine" one's conscience. But the judgment that constitutes the remorse is not determined by the will. It is not an opinion that one adopts because one is pleased to adopt it. Obviously one would be better pleased to judge that one's conduct was good. Some judgments depend on one's good pleasure, but not all. "The intellect's operation can be against a man's inclination, which is the will; as when some opinion pleases someone, but because of the efficacy of the reasons, he is led to assent to the contrary by the intellect."[96] Unlike the will's own operation, the intellect's operation can be brought about against one's will. "Sometimes the intellect is compelled (*cogitur*) by reasons, as it says in Book 5 of the *Metaphysics*."[97] Actually the *Metaphysics* passage does not speak of compulsion. It only says that unqualified demonstrations are necessary and that they are made so by premises that are simply necessary.[98] Presumably not all demonstrations are positively violent or against the will. But they are not in the power of the will to determine. The intellect's assent to them is not voluntary. And if they are displeasing to the will, then they are indeed forced upon it. They are involuntary.

One might wonder whether this point applies to conscience, inasmuch as conscience is about particular actions—practical things—and according to Thomas, the intellect's practical judgment and assent do depend on the will.[99] The answer is that even though conscience is about practical things, it is a theoretical kind of judgment. It is not the same as what Thomas sometimes calls the judgment of free decision or of choice, which is the practical judgment according to which someone actually chooses and acts. "The

95. *ST* I-II.87.6.

96. *De ver.* 22.5*ad*3.

97. *In Sent.* I.48.1.3*ad*1. Other places where he speaks of the intellect's being compelled include *In Sent.* II.25.1.2*obj*4; III.23.3.3*qc*1*c*&*ad*3; *De ver.* 11.3*ad*11; 22.6*ad*4.

98. Aristotle, *Metaphysics* V.6, 1015b6–9.

99. See *ST* I-II.56.3; II-II.4.2.

judgment of conscience consists in pure cognition, but the judgment of free choice consists in application to affection, and this judgment is the judgment of choice."[100] This passage goes on to provide an example of judging, choosing, and acting against one's conscience, and it describes the judgment of conscience as a case of "speculating according to principles" (*speculando per principia*).[101]

Why is it that remorse of conscience is painful and against the will? It runs contrary to the will's natural inclination toward virtue, which is the same as its inclination toward acting according to reason, and which also constitutes an inclination toward what is consonant with the eternal law.[102] Thomas says that even the damned must retain the natural inclination toward virtue, since "otherwise there would not be in them the remorse of conscience."[103] I suppose the thought is that an inclination toward acting according to reason just is, in part, an inclination toward reason's approval of one's action and away from its disapproval.

One other point regarding the punitive quality of remorse of conscience is that if remorse is to be understood as a legal punishment, then it should also be able to serve as an inducement to act or to refrain from acting, by way of the fear of it. Legal punishments are instituted for the sake of such inducement. Can the prospect of remorse serve as an inducement? I think so. One might propose a certain action to oneself, judge that doing it would be wrong, and reject it, one's reason being that later one would undergo remorse for having done it. It is a delicate point. One might argue that such a person's motive is not really the fear of future remorse, but simply the present judgment that the action is wrong. But passion can sometimes blunt the edge of a present judgment, and that the decisive consideration, based on painful past experience, can sometimes be that of how the judgment would bite back with a vengeance later on, once the passion has subsided. That the will has a natural and permanent inclination to act according to reason obviously does not mean that it is always equally disposed to follow reason. People can be conscious of the variability of this disposition in themselves.

However, is it true that the remorse of conscience can be regarded as a properly legal punishment? The text on the threefold punishment for sin ascribes remorse only to one's own reason, and it distinguishes remorse both

---

100. *De ver.* 17.1ad4.

101. The judgment of conscience is not the conclusion of a demonstration, properly so called. The conclusions of demonstrations are universal propositions. But necessary principles can yield necessary conclusions about particulars. See *ST* I.86.3.

102. *ST* I–II.94.3; I–II.93.6.

103. *ST* I–II.85.2ad3.

from punishments for violations of human law, which are inflicted by other human beings, and from punishments for violations of God's law, which are inflicted by God Himself. If the whole force of conscience is rooted in natural law, why does Thomas speak only of *reason* here, and not precisely of natural law? Is it that remorse somehow falls short of the type of punishment that properly belongs to law? That would seem to be in some tension with the very thesis that natural law *is* properly a law after all. How can it be a law if it lacks one of the attributes or effects of law? And indeed there is reason to wonder whether remorse quite fits the bill as a legal punishment. Sorting this out should shed further light on how natural law functions *naturally* as a law.

The reason why it may seem that remorse of conscience is not properly a legal punishment is that, despite the foregoing considerations, it may seem not to be a punishment at all, properly speaking. Punishment, properly speaking, is a matter of merit, which is with respect to the retribution that is brought about according to justice.[104] And justice, properly speaking, concerns relationships between distinct subjects or agents: either between one person and another, or between one community and another, or between a person and a community.[105] But remorse, although it is involuntary, is brought about by the very one who undergoes it. Can this be an act of justice, something merited?[106] The following passage seems to suggest that it cannot:

> When someone does something that is good or bad for himself, then he is ... owed recompense to the extent that this also has an effect on the community, given that he himself is part of the community—even if he is not owed recompense insofar it is good or bad for the individual person who is the same as the agent, unless perhaps he is owed recompense by himself according to a sort of likeness, insofar as there is such a thing as a man's justice toward himself.[107]

---

104. *ST* I–II.21.3.

105. *ST* II–II.58.5.

106. Koritansky, *Thomas Aquinas and the Philosophy of Punishment*, 134, suggests that remorse is not even an evil: "It is difficult to see what evil, what loss of good, is constituted by remorse." Yet in the immediately preceding sentence he acknowledges that it causes "a certain kind of discomfort." Surely it is a spiritual discomfort, the loss of the peace of a good conscience. Is that not an evil? In any case it is clear that Thomas takes remorse to be an evil, a *malum poenae*. See *ST* I.64.3*obj3/ad3*.

107. *ST* I–II.21.3.

The expression "according to a sort of likeness" makes it clear that Thomas takes this "recompense" to be only metaphorical.[108] I say this because Thomas agrees with Aristotle that the sort of justice which a man can have toward himself—or more precisely, which one part of him can have toward another—is precisely that, metaphorical.[109] It is not justice in the proper sense, even with a qualification. It only bears a certain resemblance to justice. Should we say, then, that in the end, the remorse of conscience only bears a certain likeness to punishment?

To this, the answer rests on a distinction. Even if the remorse of conscience is always inflicted upon oneself, for a transgression of the dictate of one's own reason, that does not mean that it is always inflicted for things that are bad only for oneself. Of course they *are* bad for oneself, just insofar as they offend one's reason. But obviously what makes something that one does offensive to one's reason need not be its being bad for oneself. On the contrary, one may very well hold that, ceteris paribus, doing something that is bad for others is worse than doing something that is bad only for oneself. According to the text on the threefold punishment, remorse of conscience is for violations of the order of reason, and the order of reason, far from concerning only what pertains exclusively to oneself, also and even primarily regards one's relations with others. This is simply to say that practical reason looks chiefly to *common good*. I shall return to this point in the next chapter.

Now, the threefold punishment text says that human nature is subject to the "universal order of divine government." The term *universal*, I think, is significant. I would say that Thomas uses it in view of the fact that the divine government partly overlaps with the order of reason itself. It does so inasmuch as the first principles of that order are the precepts of natural law, which is a divine law.[110] The precepts of natural law do not express the whole order of divine government, but they do express what the natural light of reason can grasp about it. And just as God communicates a portion of the order of His government to creatures, so too He entrusts some of the execution of His government to them.[111] Punishment is part of that execution.[112] Although instituting a law belongs only to the legislator, at least part

---

108. On metaphors as names not said properly, see *ST* I.13.3. On their signifying some likeness to what has the name properly, see *ST* I.13.9.

109. *ST* II–II.58.2. See Aristotle, *Nicomachean Ethics* V.15, 1138b5–13. One thinks of Aristotle's likening of the intellect's rule over appetite to "political" and "regal" rule (Aristotle, *Politics* I.5, 1254b5–6).

110. The other order mentioned in the threefold punishment text, that of human law, also falls under divine rule. See *ST* I–II.95.3.

111. See *ST* I.22.3; I.103.6.

112. *ST* I.103.8ad1.

of its enforcement may be, and usually is, assigned by the legislator to other agents. Again, "law punishes on the basis of judgment."[113] Thomas says that punishment pertains to a minister of the law and that a judge is such a minister.[114] If the whole force of conscience is from natural law, which is God's law, and if reason punishes through remorse of conscience, then evidently God has assigned to reason the role of a minister of His law. Reason can be understood as an instrument of the eternal law's enforcement. We already saw that Thomas considers remorse part of the punishment of the damned themselves. It is the "worm that dieth not."[115]

Someone may object: one who judges, with the sort of judgment that conscience is an instance of, is superior to the one judged. "It belongs to a superior to judge inferiors,"[116] and "a superior judges of an inferior with a certain practical judgment, to wit, as to whether it ought to be so or not so."[117] Is a person superior to himself? Obviously the whole person is not superior to the whole person. Superior and inferior must be distinct. But it is also obvious that a person has distinct capacities and operations and that they are not equal in rank. One's voluntary actions proceed from the particular inclination of one's will. The force of one's judgment of conscience derives from one's understanding the universal precepts of natural law, and this is superior to the inclination of one's will. By it, one can judge the inclination itself. One can also judge those operations of reason that follow the will's inclination and complete the formation of one's voluntary actions: deliberation, choice, and command. One can even judge the will's natural inclinations. (The correct judgment is that they are right.)

This is quite consistent with saying that one cannot impose obligations on oneself. The obligatory judgment of conscience is from reason, but its obligatory force is from God alone.[118] The imposition of obligation is the work of a superior agent, the commander or the lawgiver. When judge and lawgiver are distinct, the judge is not the one to impose obligations on the persons judged. The judge only ascertains and declares what their obligations are. A judge is only a minister, as it were an instrument, of the law.

Human reason is fallible, whether in a court of law or in the forum of conscience. This might pose a problem for regarding conscience as obliging with the force of divine law, if conscience were the one and only judgment

---

113. *ST* I–II.100.9.
114. *ST* I–II.92.2*ad*3; II–II.60.2*ad*2; *In Eth.* V.6, 284, line 84.
115. *In Sent.* IV.50.2.3*qc*2; *ST* I.64.3*obj*3.
116. *ST* I–II.57.6*obj*2.
117. *ST* I–II.93.2*ad*3; cf. *De ver.* 8.1*ad*13.
118. See *De ver.* 17.3*ad*3.

under divine law. But it is not. It can be overruled. As is fitting, the principles by which it can be overruled are the very ones given to it to judge by. "In one who errs in conscience, the falsehood of the witness of conscience is argued on the basis of the very dictate of *synderesis*; and thus in the divine judgment the verdict will not be from the declaration of conscience but rather from the dictate of natural law."[119] Thomas is also aware that the remorse experienced for something understood to be wrong can vary in intensity; for instance, he says that it can be weakened by the influence of bad customs or prevailing opinions.[120] And original sin has weakened the natural inclination to the good of reason, which is what makes remorse painful. But none of this is a problem, if conscience is not the only forum.

Remorse of conscience is not the sole or entire sanction that the transgression of natural law is apt to incur. It is only the immediate and connatural sanction. It is fallible in the way that the movements of natural things, including those of human reason, are fallible. Fortin argues that a natural law, as a law of God, has to carry infallible sanctions, and that if these are not naturally known, then the very notion of natural law is problematic. But clearly he is confusing the theory of natural law with what it is a theory of. He would be right, if the natural knowledge that constitutes natural law had to include the theory of natural law or the knowledge that it is a law given by God. But it does not, and the theory does not say that natural law has to carry all of its sanctions with it. This is obvious, if natural law itself, insofar as it is a principle of human law, calls for punishments by human authorities but leaves their determination up to those authorities. The theory only says that natural law carries those sanctions that are proportioned to its own nature. It is only a participation in the eternal law, and the sanctions that it carries are only a participation in the sanctions instituted by the eternal law. It is to revealed law, not to natural law, that Aquinas attributes the work of ensuring that *no* evil go unprohibited and unpunished.[121]

I am arguing that the remorse of conscience can be seen as a full-fledged legal punishment, the one that is proper to natural law, accompanying its proper, natural promulgation. However, seeing it in this way involves at least one further consideration. Even if reason, not God, is the immediate or proximate source of the infliction of remorse, God is still the primary source, the one who has ordained it and established reason as its minister. It must be the case, then, that transgressions of natural law, as such, deserve punishment from God. Anything that deserves punishment from natural

---

119. *De ver.* 17.2*ad*6.
120. See *In Sent.* II.33.1.2*ad*3.
121. *ST* I–II.91.4.

reason, anything that deserves remorse, must be something that deserves punishment from God. Otherwise His very institution of remorse as a punishment would not be just. To say that every transgression of natural law deserves punishment from God is to say that every transgression of natural law offends Him or constitutes an injustice toward Him. It must do so even if the transgressor is not aware that it does so. Thomas must hold that all actions running contrary to the first principles of practical reason are offensive to God and deserve punishment from Him, independently of whether such actions are understood by their agents themselves as violations of His law.[122] This fits with the general account of punishment that Thomas laid out in I-II.87.1: acting contrary to an order naturally elicits repression from the order and from its principle. The proximate source of the order of natural law is the light of reason. But its first source is God.

And in fact Thomas does say that God justly punishes those who act contrary to "the determinate good that is suited to them according to their nature and status."[123] The same point is implicit in the passage that I quoted near the end of the previous chapter: "Every good or bad act of a man has the nature of merit or demerit before God, in proportion to the act's own nature."[124] There I urged that "in proportion to the act's own nature" means in proportion to the act's own intrinsic goodness or badness. This consists in its conformity or repugnance to the order of reason, and the starting-points of the order of reason are the precepts of natural law.

Moreover, as Thomas explains in the corpus of the same article, God is our ultimate end. This is to say that we and our good belong entirely to Him. And we are parts of the community of the universe, whose good, in the whole and in all of its parts, He oversees.[125] Natural law is founded upon our natural understanding of the human good, and it directs us toward that good and away from its contrary. It is true that the sheer fact of there being such a thing as the human good is more evident to us than is His relation to it. We need to learn that He oversees it and that He is our highest good and the end of all our other goods. As I shall discuss at some length in the next chapter, natural law itself does lead us, quite peremptorily really, in the direction of learning these things. But here the point would be that the

---

122. This is not to say that the awareness of offending God by one's wrongdoings adds no further malice to them or incurs no greater punishment. "That servant who knew his master's will, and did not make ready for him and did not act according to his will, will be beaten with many stripes. Whereas he who did not know it, but did things deserving of stripes, will be beaten with few" (Luke 12:47–48). See below, 235.

123. *ST* I.103.8*ad*1.

124. *ST* I-II.21.4*ad*3.

125. *ST* I-II.21.4. On our belonging entirely to Him, see again *ST* I.60.5.

order of merit and demerit before God is not something merely added on to the order toward our natural good. Nor is it merely a part of that order, one that we eventually discover and engage. Our order toward our natural good, which is the good toward which reason directs us, *is* an order of merit and demerit before God, because it is nothing but a portion of the order of the eternal law.

> Whatever is contrary to the conception of an artifact is also contrary to the nature of the craft by which the artifact is produced. But the eternal law is related to the order of human reason as a craft to an artifact. Hence, the fact that a vice or sin is contrary to the order of human reason is of a piece with the fact that it is contrary to the eternal law. This is why, in *De libero arbitrio* III, Augustine says that all natures have from God the fact that they are natures, and they are vicious to the extent that they depart from that craft by which they were made.[126]

In short, God is the very reason why our good, the good that is according to reason, is good.[127] For Thomas, this is so true that "God is not offended except by our acting contrary to our own good."[128]

This confirms the general thesis for which I have been arguing all along, that natural law, as naturally understood, already functions as a true law, with the proper effects of law, even before it is understood as a law, promulgated by God. One is under His law, and capable of transgressing it, even before or without being aware that it is from Him. His very way of promulgating it makes it function in this manner.

---

126. *ST* I–II.71.2*ad*4.
127. See above, 95.
128. *ScG* III.122, 378a, lines 12–14.

7

The Naturalness of Natural Law

This study of the legal character of Thomistic natural law has already reached its main conclusion, which is a simple confirmation of the literal reading of the text, as set forth at the beginning of chapter 1. For Aquinas, natural law is to be understood as a law in the full sense of the term. Its possession of the various elements of the nature of law is established by way of showing the existence of the eternal law of God, and by seeing that something belonging naturally to man has everything required for being described as another instance of this same law, existing as in an agent ruled and measured by it. It is a naturally promulgated law of God. Its naturalness consists essentially in this, that its precepts are practical principles that the human mind naturally understands and that they correspond to natural inclinations of the human will. In this final chapter I wish to look a little more closely at some features of natural law that pertain in one way or another to its naturalness. In the course of this discussion, starting in the chapter's third section, I shall also offer assessments, mostly brief ones, of the positions surveyed in the opening chapter.

THE DUTIES OF NATURAL LAW ABSOLUTELY CONSIDERED

First, having considered in the previous chapter what the obligation of natural law consists in, and how all obligation in a way depends on it, I want to try to identify, in a general way, the obligations that natural law determines, just insofar as it is natural; which is to say, insofar as it is naturally promulgated and naturally understood. To use Thomas's own expression, this is natural law considered "absolutely."[1] He provides important indications about the scope and general tendency of its obligations. The matter is somewhat complex, but it is worth going into. It should shed some light on the relation between natural law and the moral order as a whole. And, most importantly, it should help to show how natural law naturally functions as a true law and as a law of God. In this section I shall offer an initial sketch of the scope that Thomas seems to assign to natural law considered absolutely. In the next session I shall concentrate on a way in which it especially shows itself to be a law of God. That should help to fill in the sketch a little.

Let me first say something about the terminology that I shall use here. According to what I have been arguing, if the term *obligation* is taken to include reference to a binding agent, a governor who imposes it authoritatively, then natural law does not at first or immediately present itself precisely as obligatory. Nevertheless it does present itself as carrying the necessity, the bond, that obligation constitutes.[2] As we have seen, Thomas has another word that can signify this sort of necessity, the word *debitum*, meaning due or owed.[3] As he uses it, this word does not always make reference to the command of a governor or to an authoritative institution. Thus, in one place where he says that *debitum* conveys necessity, he also distinguishes between "legal" and "moral" *debitum*.[4] He refers this distinction to Aristotle.[5] Legal *debitum*, Thomas says, is what the law constrains someone to render. This is what is owed in justice. Moral *debitum* is what is necessary for the *honestas virtutis* or the *honestas morum*, moral uprightness. In Aristotle's text, it is clear that "the law" means written human law. That Thomas too means written human law is clear, since later he will tell us that *all* of what is necessary for the order of virtue is prescribed by the Old Law.[6] But the

---

1. See below, 221.

2. When Thomas speaks of awareness of an obligation, it is not always the case that he implies awareness of being under a governor's command. Thus he says that "by a certain natural instinct, [a man] perceives himself to be obligated to pay reverence in his own way to God, from whom is the beginning of his being and all good" (*ScG* III.119, 370b, lines 19–22). He could just as well have said that by natural instinct a man perceives himself to have a duty to do this. He is talking about a precept of natural law, and he is not assuming awareness of revealed law or even of God's universal legislation. Cf. *ST* II-II.85.1. For a similar use of *obligatus*, see *ST* II-II.122.1.

3. See above, 186.

4. *ST* II-II.80.1.

5. See Aristotle, *Nicomachean Ethics* VIII.15, 1162b21–23.

6. *ST* I-II.99.5; I-II.100.2.

very fact that he attributes the distinction to Aristotle shows that he does not take the concept of the moral *debitum* to involve a reference to divine law. It signifies what presents itself as *debitum* even without reference to a legal institution. Of course my interest here is not solely in those morally necessary things that are determinately *not* required by written human law. Obviously natural law is not confined to those; it certainly extends to matters of justice, and it does overlap with human law. But we can also take *debitum* in a general sense, to mean simply what is necessarily required by virtue, whether or not human law requires it. I think a good word in English to render it, in this sense, is *duty*. In what follows, I shall often use this word to refer to what has the sort of necessity that characterizes obligation. What I wish to consider is the extent and thrust of the duties to which Thomas thinks natural law binds us.

One might wonder why this requires much discussion. If, as I argued in the previous chapter, our unqualified obligations or duties are precisely the things that we need to observe so as not to incur sin or wrongdoing, then surely natural law extends to all of them. It forbids all wrongdoing, universally. It extends to all moral duties.

However, although there is a sense in which this is true, indeed trivially true, there is also a sense in which it is not even true. It is trivially true insofar as wrongdoing is taken as a single general notion. Natural law prohibits just this: wrongdoing. If something is understood to be wrong, then by that very fact, natural law rules it out. This is simply to say that to do wrong is bad, and that this is self-evident to us. But it is another question, whether every specific kind of wrongdoing is something that natural law itself determines to be wrong. And clearly the answer is no. Many things are made determinately wrong only by positive law. Not all duties are determined by natural law itself. Even if, as I argued earlier, all unqualified obligation is somehow rooted in natural law, the actual determination of many obligations or duties is a matter of positive law. Natural law determines in a general way that whatever is instituted by (legitimate) positive law is an unqualified duty. But how far does natural law itself go to define what our duties are? The question is the scope of the duties that natural law determines directly or per se. This does deserve some discussion.

Now we did see earlier that, on Thomas's view, everything that is repugnant to right reason is to be judged bad.[7] Moreover, in *ST* I–II.94.3, he raises the question whether all acts of virtue are of natural law. He explains that acts of virtue are acts that are according to reason, and his basic answer is yes, they are all of natural law. However, he can hardly mean that all acts

---

7. *ST* I–II.18.9ad2. See above, 179.

of virtue are obligatory or strict duties. In that case there would be no such thing as supererogatory acts.[8] Nor would there be acts that are merely counseled and not commanded.[9] And more importantly, within I-II.94.3, Thomas draws a crucial distinction. Natural law, he says, dictates virtuous acts insofar as they are virtuous. That is, it dictates them in a general way, inasmuch as it dictates acting according to reason. But "if we speak of virtuous acts in themselves, that is, insofar as they are considered in their proper species, not all virtuous acts are of the law of nature. For many things are done virtuously, toward which nature does not at first incline; but men have discovered them through the inquisition of reason, as things useful for living well."[10] So there is room for the question, to what extent are the details of reason's own order or own requirements things that reason naturally understands and does not need to "discover"?

Where we get the most help in this matter is in Thomas's treatise on the precepts of the Old Law: *ST* I-II.98–105. He has a good deal to say about how natural law factors into these precepts. What he says sheds light on how he understands the scope of natural law itself.

First let me introduce a few of the pertinent texts and ideas.

One text, appearing early on in the treatise, is in his answer to the question whether all men on earth were obliged to observe the Old Law:

> The Old Law manifested the precepts of natural law and added certain precepts of its own. As regards the things of natural law that the Old Law contained, everyone was bound to the observation of the Old Law—not because they were of the Old Law, but because they were of the law of nature. But as regards the things that the Old Law added, the only ones obliged to observe the Old Law were the Jewish people.[11]

In line with this distinction, Thomas goes on to adopt the traditional Christian division of the precepts of the Old Law into moral, ceremonial, and judicial precepts.[12] The ceremonial and judicial precepts are positive determinations. They are the ones that apply only to the Jewish people. Their obligatory force depends entirely on their positive institution. But that of the moral precepts does not.

Further on, Thomas explains why the moral precepts are called moral. "Certain precepts of any law whatsoever have obligatory force from the very

---

8. See *ST* II-II.58.3*ad*2.
9. See *ST* II-II.100.2.
10. *ST* I-II.94.3.
11. *ST* I-II.98.5.
12. See *ST* I-II.99.3–5.

dictate of reason, because natural reason dictates that this is due to be done or avoided (*dictat hoc esse debitum fieri vel vitari*). And such precepts are called moral, because human morals bespeak reason."[13] In the same vein, he says later that the moral precepts of the Old Law "have efficacy from the very dictate of natural reason, even if they never be instituted in law."[14] Here, obviously, *law* means only positive law. Natural law *is* a dictate of natural reason.

It is also clear that here he is not using the term *moral* in quite the same sense as in the distinction between moral *debitum* and legal *debitum*. There, the moral *debitum* is something determinately *not* dictated by positive human law; here, at least some of the things that the moral *debitum* covers are or can be so dictated, because they are matters of justice. Thus, "things to be done do not fall under precept except insofar as they have some character of duty. But duty is twofold; one sort is according to the rule of reason, while the other is according to the rule of a determining law; thus the Philosopher, in *Ethics* V, distinguishes a twofold just (*iustum*), namely moral and legal."[15] He is referring to Aristotle's distinction between natural right, or what Thomas elsewhere calls *ius naturale*, and legal right, or what he elsewhere calls *ius positivum* and describes as adding "determinations" to natural right. In this sense, a moral duty is any duty somehow prescribed by natural reason (although, as we will see, it may or may not pertain to natural law absolutely considered).

Thomas does indicate that not all of this moral duty is a matter of justice or even strictly obligatory. Some of it is necessary only in a qualified sense.

> Moral duty, however, is twofold. For reason dictates something to be done either as necessary, without which there cannot be the order of virtue; or as useful, for the sake of better conserving the order of virtue. And in this regard, some moral things are strictly commanded or prohibited in the [Old] Law, such as "Thou shalt not kill," "Thou shalt not steal." And these are properly called precepts. But some things are commanded or prohibited, not as though strictly duties, but for the better.[16]

---

13. *ST* I–II.104.1. Thomas is not denying that the positive enactment of such precepts adds further force of its own to them. See *ST* I–II.95.2; I–II.99.2*ad*2; II–II.22.1*ad*1.

14. *ST* I–II.100.11. Evidently the term *efficaciam* here is equivalent to one that he uses in the previous sentence, *vis* or force.

15. *ST* I–II.99.5.

16. *ST* I–II.99.5. In II–II.80.1, he draws a similar distinction within the moral *debitum* that is not dictated by human law. Some of it is necessary for the very conservation of the *honestas virtutis*, while some of it is only needed for greater *honestas*.

So not every moral dictate in the Old Law is to be taken as a strict duty. Nevertheless everything that is essential to the order of virtue is to be taken in that way. Thomas confirms this point a little later:

> Divine law proposes precepts about all those things through which the reason of man is well ordered. This comes about through the acts of all the virtues. For the intellectual virtues order well the acts of reason in themselves, while the moral virtues order well the acts of reason concerning interior passions and exterior actions. And therefore it is clear that divine law proposes precepts about all the virtues, although in such a way that some, without which the order of virtue, which is the order of reason, cannot be observed, fall under the obligation of precept; while others, which pertain to the well-being of perfect virtue, fall under the admonition of counsel.[17]

This is surely striking. The moral precepts of the Old Law make the entire order of reason or of virtue, in what is essential to it, a matter of strict duty. But the moral precepts of the Old Law contain the natural law, and as such they obliged (and presumably still do oblige) everyone, not just the Jewish people. And they extend, in quite specific ways, to acts of all the virtues. Indeed they extend not only to the moral virtues but also to the intellectual virtues. At first glance, this claim seems hard to square with the passage from 94.3, where he said that natural law dictates virtuous acts only in a general way, not in their proper species, it being only toward virtue considered generally that nature first inclines us. The claim may also seem hard to swallow. Is it really true that everyone is obliged, as a matter of strict duty, to the essentials of the entire moral order?

Sorting out this matter will require some distinctions. The most important ones are with respect to exactly how the moral precepts of the Old Law contain or express natural law. Thomas does take up the question whether all the moral precepts of the Old Law pertain to natural law. He says that they do—but not all in the same way. The passage is long, but it is worth quoting in full:

> The moral precepts, as opposed to the ceremonial and judicial precepts, concern things that of themselves have to do with good morals. Now since human mores are spoken of in relation to reason, which is the proper principle of human acts, mores are called good when they are consonant with reason and bad when they clash with reason. And just as every judgment of speculative reason stems from the natural cognition of first principles,

---

17. ST I–II.100.2.

so too, as was explained above [I–II.94.2], every judgment of practical reason stems from certain naturally known principles. From these one can proceed in diverse ways to judge about diverse matters. For in human acts some things are so clear that immediately, with very little consideration, they can be approved of or disapproved of on the basis of those general first principles. But there are some, the judgment of which requires much consideration of various circumstances, which to consider carefully belongs not to just anyone, but to the wise; just as to consider the particular conclusions of the sciences does not belong to all, but only to philosophers. And there are some things that man needs the help of divine instruction in order to judge, as in the case of things to be believed. So, then, it is clear that since the moral precepts concern things that belong to good mores, and these are the things that are consonant with reason, and every judgment of human reason stems in some way or other from natural reason, it must be the case that all the moral precepts belong to the law of nature, but in different ways. For some precepts are such that every man's natural reason judges immediately on its own to be done or not done, such as "Honor thy father and thy mother," and "Thou shalt not kill," "Thou shalt not steal." Precepts of this sort belong absolutely to the law of nature. But there are other things that are judged to be observed through a more subtle consideration of reason, by the wise. And these are of the law of nature, but in such a way that they require the teaching by which the young are instructed by the wise, such as "Stand up in the presence of a hoary head," and "Honor the elderly person," and so forth. And there are some things that, in order to judge, human reason needs divine instruction, through which we are educated about divine things, such as "Thou shalt not make for thyself a graven image, nor any likeness," "Thou shalt not take the name of thy God in vain."[18]

To sum up: in one sense or another, natural law can be said to include not only the first, common principles that human reason naturally understands—those that Thomas presented in 94.2 as self-evident to us and as corresponding directly to natural human inclinations—but also everything in moral matters that can be judged in light of these principles. Not every such thing, however, belongs "absolutely" to natural law. The things that do are those that anyone's reason, on its own, can readily judge. (As it turns out, these are the things prescribed in the Second Table—the last seven commandments—of the Decalogue; I shall say more about those below.) But

---

18. ST I–II.100.1.

there are other things that only the wise and those whom the wise have instructed are prepared to judge rightly in light of the principles. And there are still other things that can be judged in light of the principles only with the help of divine, supernatural instruction. The things that require either sapiential or divine instruction belong to natural law, not absolutely, but only with qualifications.

It may seem odd to ascribe things requiring supernatural instruction to natural law at all, even in a qualified way. But Thomas is insisting that even things of this sort do somehow fall under the judgment of human reason, and so, ultimately, under its naturally understood first principles. This point is along the lines of what we saw in chapter 3 concerning the precept of faith.[19] The acceptance of any divinely revealed precept supposes faith. For those who have faith, however, no divinely revealed precept of faith itself is needed. Once God's Word is received, all that is needed in order to grasp the duty to believe it, and indeed the duty to comply with whatever precepts it does contain, is the light of faith itself. However, even though the light of faith is needed, the natural light of reason is also involved in this judgment. In fact elsewhere Thomas is explicit about this. "To have faith is not in human nature, but it is in human nature that the mind of man not reject the interior instinct and the exterior preaching of the truth."[20] Were it not so, he says there, unbelief would not be a sin. All sin is somehow contrary to nature, and to reason.

With these distinctions in hand, the claim in 98.5, that all the moral precepts of the Old Law are of natural law, does not seem so hard to square with the denial in 94.3 that all acts of virtue, considered in their proper species, pertain to natural law. Not all of the moral precepts pertain to natural law taken absolutely. Many pertain to it only as informed by the instruction of the wise or by the light of faith (or both). They regard things that, as I-II.94.3 puts it, reason has to "discover."

It is important, however, to see that all the moral precepts do pertain absolutely to *ius naturale*, natural *right*. They have force independently of any merely positive institution. This is another key distinction to keep in mind: between the notion of natural law and the notion of *ius naturale*. These are not the same notion, any more than the notions of law and *ius* generally are the same.[21] Natural law is a body of knowledge. That it is natural means that having it requires only the natural light of human reason. Natural right is not knowledge. It is a thing, one that is naturally right,

---

19. See above, 70.
20. *ST* II-II.10.1*ad*1.
21. See above, 85.

naturaliter iusta.²² That its rectitude is natural means that it is a function of the thing's own intelligibility, as considered either in itself or in light of its natural consequences.²³ But this rectitude may or may not be something that the natural light of reason, by itself, enables us to grasp. In some cases, additional information is needed, beyond what the natural light discloses on its own. It is true, as we saw earlier, that *ius naturale* is "contained" in the *naturale iudicatorium* of human reason.²⁴ But this is only in a secondary way and as to certain common principles that serve for judging of such *ius*. These principles do not, in themselves, fully specify all of *ius naturale*. The eternal law does, but the common principles are only a certain share in in it. Neither *synderesis* nor its natural, untutored results define all of *ius naturale*. They do not even define many of the things that do not require faith and that fall within the "order of reason." A complete articulation of the order of reason is a matter of wisdom, which goes well beyond what reason itself originally or naturally grasps.²⁵

From a philosophical point of view, the precepts that require the instruction of the wise are especially interesting. Some of them directly concern divine things and presuppose supernatural instruction. But many others concern relations among men and pertain to the natural order.²⁶ And some of these have a rather strong basis in human nature. For instance, while the Decalogue forbids false testimony, the universal prohibition of lying requires the instruction of the wise.²⁷ This is so even though truthfulness is "naturally loved" and even though lying is "unnatural."²⁸ We naturally understand that veracity is generally good and that mendacity is generally bad, but it is not so obvious to us that there is never a truly good reason to lie. What Thomas says even suggests that instruction is needed in order to see that, besides false testimony, other lies can also be grievously sinful or violations of strict duty.²⁹

Similarly, in the sphere of chastity, the Decalogue forbids adultery, but the prohibition of fornication (which Thomas regards as grievously sinful) and even the prohibition of the so-called sins against nature pertain to the

---

22. *ST* II-II.57.2*ad*3.
23. See *ST* II-II.57.3.
24. See above, 85.
25. *ST* I-II.57.2.
26. See *ST* I-II.100.11.
27. *ST* I-II.100.11.
28. *ST* I-II.100.5*ad*5; II-II.110.3.
29. See *ST* II-II.110.4.

instruction of the wise.[30] Perhaps it is not really surprising that Thomas thinks these require instruction, since he has been given to understand that "the Gentiles did not deem it [fornication] a sin" and that, at least for some of them, the same is true of the sins against nature.[31] But the point is still striking, because the sins against nature, on his view, are the very worst in the class of sins of lust.[32] For while other sins of lust run contrary to what is determined by right reason, these run contrary to "what is determined by nature about the use of sex."[33] They are contrary to "natural principles." Evidently this not a reference to practical reason's *common* principles, which are the primary precepts of natural law and which require no instruction. It refers to principles proper to the sphere of sex. Their being principles, I take it, means that they are self-evident. But apparently Thomas does not think that they are naturally self-evident *to us*.[34]

What I am trying to delineate is the sphere of the things that belong absolutely to natural law. Now as we saw, Thomas holds that the moral precepts of the Old Law extend determinately to acts of all the virtues, moral and even intellectual. But he also holds that the precepts belonging to natural law absolutely, those requiring no instruction, define duties pertaining to only one specific virtue. The virtue is justice, and in the Old Law, the relevant precepts are those of the Second Table of the Decalogue.[35] Thomas explains: "The character of duty is more hidden in other virtues than in justice. And therefore the precepts about the acts of the other virtues are not as well known to the people as are precepts about acts of justice. Because of this, acts of justice fall specifically under the precepts of the Decalogue, which are the primary elements of the Law."[36]

Why is the character of duty more hidden in virtues other than justice? I believe it is because justice is the only virtue whose acts directly affect things belonging to others. Intellectual virtues regard cognitive acts, which

---

30. *ST* I–II.100.11.

31. *ST* I–II.103.4*ad*3; I–II.94.6.

32. *ST* II–II.154.12.

33. Here *nature* means the nature of the species. See *ST* II–II.154.11; II–II.154.12.

34. Perhaps this is explained, at least in part, by the fact that they do not, of themselves, constitute injustice toward other people. If they are nevertheless so grave, it is because they directly constitute injustices toward God as Author of nature (*ST* II–II.154.12*ad*1/*ad*2).

35. Later on, Thomas also indicates that what is called the *ius gentium* pertains to natural law "absolutely considered." See *ST* II–II.57.3.

36. *ST* I–II.100.3*ad*3.

terminate in the knower.[37] And the other moral virtues—temperance and fortitude and the virtues associated with them—regard interior passions.

Thus, in answering why the Decalogue forbids only sins against God and neighbor, and not sins against oneself, Thomas says:

> The precepts of the Decalogue are those that the people received immediately from God; whence it is said in Deuteronomy 10, "He wrote in the tables, according as He had written before, the ten words, which the Lord spoke to you." Hence the precepts of the Decalogue must be such that they can be understood at once by the people. Now a precept has the character of something owed (*debitum*). And the fact that a man necessarily owes (*ex necessitate debeat*) something to God or neighbor is easily grasped by a man, and especially by someone of faith (*fidelis*). But it is not so readily apparent that something about matters that pertain to the man himself and not to another is necessarily a duty (*ex necessitate sit debitum*) for him. For at first glance it seems that everyone is free about the things that pertain to himself. And so the precepts by which a man's disorders in relation to himself are prohibited come to the people through the instruction of the wise. So they do not belong to the Decalogue.[38]

The expression "necessarily a duty" (*ex necessitate debitum*) is interesting. It sounds like "necessarily necessary." It is an especially clear way of indicating something that ought to be rendered or done, not in just any sense of the word *ought*, but as a strict duty. Thomas is saying that it is relatively easy, requiring no instruction by the wise, to see that we have strict duties toward God and toward other people. To be sure, he adds the qualification, "especially by someone of faith," which is significant; I shall come back to this further on. But in any case, in things that regard only oneself and directly affect no one else, the existence of strict duties is less obvious. As long as one is simply minding one's own business, one seems free to do as one wishes, without risk of incurring anything bad or wrong or sinful.[39] Taking justice in a somewhat extended sense, to include what is due to God, the duties of natural law absolutely considered—those that it naturally defines—all seem to pertain to the sphere of justice.[40] (It is not

---

37. *De ver.* 4.2ad7; *ST* I.16.1; I.59.2; I.78.1.

38. *ST* I–II.100.5ad1.

39. Thomas returns to this idea in his discussion of the precepts of the Decalogue under the heading of the "precepts of justice" (*ST* II–II.122.1).

40. Duties toward God fall outside of justice in the most proper sense, not by being less strictly due, but by falling short of the equality that is achieved in justice properly so called. See *ST* II–II.80.1.

that there are no moral precepts regarding justice that require instruction. There are many of them.[41])

On the other hand, the thought can hardly be that natural law, taken absolutely, determinately affirms that one *is* altogether free in purely private matters. In that case one could never come to learn otherwise. It is simply that, without instruction, the matter is not immediately clear. We should not lose sight of the fact that natural law (absolutely considered) does order toward all acts of virtue at least in a general, confused way. Instruction is needed in order to clarify that order or to specify its requirements. Once these are understood, however, it will be by virtue of natural law that they are understood to be strict duties, duties "in conscience." In that sense they do pertain to natural law.[42]

But there is more to say about the scope of the precepts that concern justice. Even though the moral virtues other than justice are about one's own passions, the passions themselves can lead to actions that do affect others and regard justice.[43] And indeed, the last two precepts of the Decalogue itself forbid *desires* for certain unjust acts. Thomas says that they constitute harming another "in one's heart."[44] Moreover, we should not forget that although certain kinds of justice—commutative and distributive—are special virtues that are fairly neatly distinguished from the moral virtues concerning the passions, there is also a kind of justice that is a general virtue and in a way overlaps with the other moral virtues. Thomas calls it legal justice. It is the justice that rectifies action in relation to the civil common good.[45]

I mention this because Thomas is quite aware that even mere human law prescribes things pertaining to the moral virtues that regard the passions. It does so insofar as these have a bearing on human justice and the common good.

> Human law is ordered to civil community, which is of people with each other. But people are ordered to each other through the exterior acts by which they associate with each other. And this sort of association pertains to the notion of justice, which is properly directive of human community. And therefore human law only lays down precepts about acts of justice; and if it commands acts of other virtues, this is only insofar as they take on

41. See *ST* I–II.100.11.
42. *ST* I–II.100.1.
43. See *ST* I–II.60.2.
44. *ST* I–II.100.5.

45. See *ST* II–II.58.5–7. This is not to be confused with the legally just (*ius positivum*) that is distinct from the naturally just (*ius naturale*). The latter can very well regard the order to the civil common good.

the character of justice, as is clear from what the Philosopher says in *Ethics* V.[46]

The reference is evidently to *Nicomachean Ethics* V.3, where Aristotle discusses the general kind of justice.[47] In his commentary on this passage, Thomas gives examples of acts of moral virtues other than justice, including fortitude and temperance, that human law prescribes.[48]

Now, in the course of that discussion, Aristotle observes that regimes of different kinds have different laws, in accordance with their different ends, and that some laws are better framed than others. Also, in his discussion of natural right, Aristotle remarks that there is one kind of regime that is by nature the best.[49] I take it that this regime would have the naturally best laws. But defining the nature of this regime and the drift of its laws would surely be a matter for the wise. This at least suggests that, for Aristotle, some of natural right requires instruction. Nevertheless, Aristotle's whole discussion of natural right falls under the heading of civil or political justice.[50] It concerns justice among human beings. Obviously Thomas's own conception of *ius naturale* goes beyond that, inasmuch as it includes duties toward God. These duties require divine instruction. That is, *ius naturale* extends even to revealed matters concerning divine things. And it also goes beyond justice among men inasmuch as it extends to duties toward oneself—duties established, not according to the requirements of civil community, but simply according to the requirements of reason. In this regard, Thomas calls attention to the fact that even in one's relation to oneself, although there is no such thing as justice in the proper sense of the term, there is something like it.[51] There is what Aristotle calls metaphorical justice.[52] A natural order, a natural rectitude, exists among a person's parts and powers. What is right is that reason rule.[53] At least for Aquinas, the fact that the justice of it is metaphorical does not entail that it is not a strict duty (even if seeing that it is a strict duty requires instruction). It is metaphorical simply because justice, in the proper sense, is always between separately existing agents.[54]

---

46. *ST* I–II.100.2.
47. Aristotle, *Nicomachean Ethics* V.3, 1129b11–30a13.
48. *In Eth.* V.2, 268, lines 58–70.
49. Aristotle, *Nicomachean Ethics* V.10, 1135a4–5.
50. Aristotle, *Nicomachean Ethics* V.10, 1134b18.
51. *ST* I–II.100.2ad2.
52. Aristotle, *Nicomachean Ethics* V.15, 1138b5–13.
53. *ST* I–II.94.4ad3.
54. *ST* II–II.58.2.

For Thomas, the very "justification of the impious" is metaphorical justice.[55] Perhaps the proper word for that would be *righteousness*. Rectitude about one's own things is an integral part of it. And such rectitude pertains to *ius naturale*, even though it does not pertain to civil justice.

In fact, Thomas's aim, in saying that all of human law is concerned with human justice, is precisely to contrast it with divine law. That passage continues:

> The community directed by divine law is of people with God, whether in the present life or in the future life. And so divine law sets forth precepts having to do with all the things through which people are well ordered toward their common life with God. Now man is joined to God by his reason, or mind, in which the image of God resides. And so divine law sets forth precepts having to do with all the things through which man's reason is well ordered. But this ordering occurs through the acts of all the virtues.[56]

This then is the fundamental reason why divine law prescribes the whole order of virtue, which is the order of reason, and why it does so in a fully determinate way. The end that divine law chiefly has in view is man's union with God, and the complete rectitude of reason is a necessary condition of that union. If there are strict duties in matters that directly bear on what pertains only to oneself, it is ultimately because one's handling of such matters, insofar as it is according or contrary to reason, does affect one's relationship with God. Everything that one is and has, everything that is one's own, is also and first of all His. There are duties in matters that regard only oneself, but they are duties not so much *toward* oneself as toward God. If one does not understand God to be one's end, or does not understand the bearing of such things on one's relationship with Him, will one see them as matters of strict duty? On Thomas's account, even those who were consciously living in community with Him could see this duty only with the help of instruction. It does not pertain to natural law absolutely considered. And, again on Thomas's account, Aristotle did not consider disorders in what regards only oneself as unqualifiedly bad. This means that he did not consider avoiding them to be a strict duty. What Aristotle treats as strict duty is only what is a matter of human justice, special or general.

Does this mean that, after all, the strict duties that pertain to natural law, absolutely considered, simply coincide with what reason naturally understands to pertain to human justice, taken in its proper and not merely

---

55. *ST* I–II.113.1; II–II.58.2*ad*1.
56. *ST* I–II.100.2.

metaphorical sense? That would be a hasty conclusion. There is one other point in Thomas's discussion of the Old Law that we should not overlook. This is the fact that the Old Law contains precepts about acts of the intellectual virtues.

Thomas indicates that these precepts chiefly concern the knowledge and understanding of the divine law itself.[57] Now, Aristotle does suggest something like a duty to know the civil law.[58] That would be a requirement of the common civil good. But the precepts of divine law regarding intellectual virtues go well beyond this, not only because the divine law goes beyond the common civil good, but also because, besides the mere knowledge of the law, those precepts also dictate the frequent *meditation* of it.[59] Notice, moreover, that even though the precepts pertaining to the intellectual virtues are not among those that belong to natural law absolutely, there is indeed a precept of divine law that does not even require the instruction of the wise and that regards the intellect: the very precept of faith, which is self-evident to those who have faith.[60] This is not itself a precept of natural law absolutely considered. But it is certainly connected with things that do belong absolutely to natural law. I am referring to 94.2—hardly a marginal text on natural law—and the first of the goods cited there as objects of the inclination proper to rational nature; namely, the good of "knowing the truth about God." In function of this good, there is the requirement "that a man avoid ignorance." If Thomas does not mention these things within his discussion of the Old Law, it must be because they are already folded into the precept of faith itself.

Is there anything of this sort in Aristotle's ethical teaching—a common duty, of people generally, to know (or even seek) the truth about God? One does think of the famous opening line of the *Metaphysics*, "all men by nature desire to know." I dare say Thomas had it in mind when he wrote 94.2. And indeed, connecting it with the inclination to know the truth about God is not at all far-fetched. Knowing the truth about God, for Thomas, constitutes wisdom. It does so inasmuch as it constitutes knowledge of the highest causes, especially of the highest final cause, the highest good. He certainly regards the science of metaphysics as a kind of wisdom. And in fact wisdom is precisely what Book I of the *Metaphysics* calls the science that is there delineated. Aristotle also has strong exhortations to the theoretical life or

---

57. See *ST* II-II.16.1-2.

58. See Aristotle, *Nicomachean Ethics* III.7, 1113b31-14a1.

59. See *ST* II-II.16.2c/ad4.

60. See above, 70. Properly speaking, faith is a theological virtue, not an intellectual virtue (*ST* I-II.62.2). But its subject is the intellect (*ST* I-II.62.3; II-II.4.2).

the life of the pursuit of wisdom, for instance in Book X of the *Nicomachean Ethics*. But my question is whether he proposes anything like a universal *duty*, a moral requirement, that reflects this natural inclination. Does the desire to know, or the desirability of wisdom, enter at all into Aristotle's conception of natural right? Does he regard those who do not do what they can to attain wisdom as downright bad?

What Aristotle's practical teaching does set forth, and very prominently, is the other of the goods that Thomas mentions as pertaining to rational nature, the good of living in society. Aristotle's natural right pertains to that good. But in 94.2, Thomas puts that good in second place. I think he does so quite deliberately. There is a passage on natural inclinations in Cicero's *De officiis* which, although not cited in 94.2, may very well have influenced it.[61] Many of the inclinations named by Cicero and Thomas coincide. The two authors' ways of distinguishing and ordering them is also quite similar. Moreover, Cicero does posit an inclination proper to man toward knowing the truth. However, it is not specifically truth about God. And Cicero puts the inclination toward social life before it. Regarding the inclination toward truth, he says that we engage in this when we are free from necessary occupations and cares. It sounds very much like *Metaphysics* I.1. What he seems to have in mind is the distinction between the practical and the speculative lives. I think that if this is what Thomas had in mind, he too would have named it second, inasmuch as he thinks the practical life is more common and more "connatural" to us.[62] But my conjecture is that he is seeing this specific truth, truth about God, as standing above the distinction between those two modes of life and as quite fundamental for regulating human life as a whole.[63] He is presenting the need to know the truth about God, the need for wisdom, as the greatest need of man as man; that is, as rational. This is because what the life of reason needs above all is rational direction, and that depends first of all on the truth about the last end. Determining that truth, and ruling human life in light of it, belongs to wisdom.[64] Social life itself should be ordered to it. As we saw, in 94.2 Thomas lays out the way that he thinks practical reason naturally orders these inclinations and their objects.

Natural law, then, certainly does lead us toward life in human society, but also and even first of all beyond it. Political prudence can only be the

---

61. Cicero, *De officiis* I.iv.11–14. See Pinckaers, *Sources of Christian Ethics*, 405–8. More generally on Cicero's influence, see Houser, "Cicero and Aquinas."

62. *ST* II-II.47.15. See II-II.180.8*obj*3.

63. I develop this idea in Brock, "Distinctiveness of the Natural Inclinations," esp. 47–51.

64. *In Meta.*, proem.

minister of wisdom and must be ruled by it.[65] Even if, absolutely considered, natural law only defines duties directly bearing on justice, which is to say, things pertaining directly to the order toward common good, it does not seem to be concerned only with the common good of *human* community. In the next section I shall try to corroborate this conjecture.

THE NATURAL TENDENCY OF NATURAL LAW

The contrast that Thomas draws, in *ST* I–II.100.2, between human law and divine law, clearly fits with the remark that I quoted at the end of chapter 5:

> Man is not ordered to political community according to all of himself and according to all that he has, and therefore it is not necessary that every act of his be meritorious or demeritorious in relation to the political community. But all that a man is, and that he is capable of and has, is to be ordered to God, and so every good or bad act of a man has the quality of merit or demerit before God, in proportion to the act's own nature.

The contrast also fits with the remark that Fr. Dewan called attention to:

> The Philosopher says that he is properly bad who is harmful to other men. And accordingly he says that the prodigal is not bad, because he harms no one but himself. And likewise for all others who are not harmful to their neighbors. But we here are calling bad generally everything that is repugnant to right reason.[66]

Thomas is not saying that Aristotle deems the prodigal, as such, positively good.[67] The point is rather that Aristotle seems to be holding for the possibility of a middle ground between good and bad in a person's conduct. Thomas cannot accept this. The reason why he cannot is highly pertinent to the question of what duties pertain absolutely to natural law and what their overall thrust is. For it is tied to the fact that even though natural law, absolutely speaking, leaves indeterminate much of what pertains to *ius naturale*,

---

65. See *ST* I–II.66.5*ad*1.

66. *ST* I–II.18.9*ad*2. See Aristotle, *Nicomachean Ethics* IV.3, 1121a26–27; above, 179.

67. Perhaps Aristotle would say that he can be a good citizen. Also, Aristotle does seem to regard one who harms only himself and not others as bad in a qualified way, though not absolutely. Thus he says that one who harms both himself and others is the *worst* (Aristotle, *Nicomachean Ethics* V.3, 1130a5–7). That seems to imply that even one who harms only himself is bad, to some lesser degree or in some qualified sense. But it is what somehow harms others that the civil law forbids, and this would be what is unqualifiedly bad.

much even in the political domain, it also extends beyond the political domain, and in a quite fundamental way.

Thomas's reason for there being no middle between good and bad in a person's conduct is this:

> Since reason's work is to order, if an act proceeding from deliberative reason is not ordered to the due end, then by that very fact it is repugnant to reason and has the quality of bad. On the other hand, if it is ordered to the due end, it fits with the order of reason, whence it has the quality of good. But necessarily it either is or is not ordered to the due end. Whence every act of a man proceeding from deliberative reason, considered in its individuality, must be good or bad.[68]

By "the due end," Thomas evidently means the due *ultimate* end.[69] This functions as practical reason's highest criterion. Any act not ordered to it is by that fact bad. And any act that is of itself ordered to an undue last end is bad without qualification, or what Thomas calls a mortal sin. It is a full-fledged transgression, a violation of strict duty.[70]

Now order toward the due last end is not just a necessary condition of acting well and not acting badly. It is also the most essential or primary condition—primary according to reason. In Thomas's judgment, this is why the precepts of the Decalogue are ordered as they are, with the First Table coming first.

> As was said, the precepts of the Decalogue are given about those things that the human mind grasps at once and quickly. But it

---

68. *ST* I–II.18.9. He says "considered in its individuality" because he grants that an act's proper moral species, which is taken from its object, may be neither good nor bad. See *ST* I–II.18.8.

69. If he meant the phrase generically, to cover any end that is somehow due, he would be running afoul of the thesis of the preceding article, that an act may be neither good nor bad with respect to its object; for as he indicates, *inter alia*, in that very article (*ST* I–II.18.8*ad*2), every object of a human act *is* somehow an end. But he insists that even if an act is not morally good with respect to its object (as it would be if its object were due), it may also not be morally bad in that respect.

70. Thomas does recognize a sphere of things that are morally bad only in a qualified way: the sphere of venial sins. And these are things that do not violate divine law. See *ST* I–II.88.1*ad*1. They are not strictly transgressions. Nevertheless they are not fully in accord with the law and do have a qualified badness or repugnance to reason. They involve failures to observe the "mode of reason that the law intends" (*ST* I–II.1*ad*1). Venial sins are not directly ordered toward God, but they also do not entail taking something other than God as one's last end (*ST* I–II.87.5). Some lies are of this sort (*ST* I–II.110.4). Of course not every sin that does not consist in doing harm to another human being is venial.

is clear that something is better grasped by reason to the extent that its contrary is more grievous and more repugnant to reason. It is evident, however, that since the order of reason starts from the end, it is maximally contrary to reason that a man should find himself disordered with respect to his end. But the end of human life and society is God. And so man had to be ordered by the precepts of the Decalogue in the first place toward God, since the contrary of this is the most grievous; just as in an army, which is ordered toward the general as an end, the soldier first of all submits himself to the general, the contrary of this being the most grievous, whereas his being coordinated with the other soldiers comes second.[71]

Several things stand out here. One is that union with God is the end of human life *and* of human society. We are reminded that God is the first, highest common good, embracing all others.[72] Also, as we already saw, it is because the end is God that the essentials of the whole moral order, the order of reason and virtue, are matters of strict duty. None of them is a purely private matter after all. If it were, then perhaps it would not be a matter of strict duty. Some things are private and, in the human order, entirely up to us, because they are incidental to the civil good, but there is nothing that is incidental to the universal good. And the moral order is *primarily* about that. The whole political order is subordinate to it. A nation's duties, too, are not only those of justice toward its own citizens and other nations. The first condition of good human law is that it "agree with religion" and be "proportioned to divine law."[73]

At the same time, we should keep in mind that union with God—friendship with Him, sharing His life—exceeds the power and dignity of human nature. Its being our last end is gratuitous and had to be revealed.[74] And the First Table of the Decalogue does require divine instruction. Nor does Thomas think that divine law should be simply imposed on people, willy-nilly. The acceptance of divine law, whether individual or collective, requires faith, and faith cannot be forced. It is true, as we have seen, that

---

71. *ST* I-II.100.6. See also *ST* II-II.122.2, on why the first precept of Decalogue comes first.

72. The mention of the general and the soldiers is perhaps an allusion to Aristotle, *Metaphysics* XII.10, 1075a11–15. See above, 91.

73. *ST* I-II.95.3.

74. This can be so even though, being of an intellectual nature, man has a natural capacity for receiving the vision of God and cannot be fully satisfied by anything short of it. What is due to a being from its governor is only partly a function of what the being has the capacity for. It also depends on the being's rank or status or dignity. See *ST* I.21.1. Only God is naturally of such dignity as to deserve to be fully satisfied.

Thomas considers the love of God above all things to be dictated by natural law. Clearly he thinks it pertains to natural law "absolutely considered." The precept of it is a common, naturally self-evident principle.[75] The love that natural law enjoins, however, is not that of union or friendship with God, love of charity. It is a natural love, rooted simply in God's being the highest common good and in every creature's belonging entirely to Him. God is naturally the ultimate end of the world, as the general is the end of the army.[76] The soldiers may not enjoy personal friendship with him, but they fight his battles out of love for him. Offering sacrifice to God, in recognition of His dominion, is also a precept of natural law.[77] Still, even though they pertain to natural law, both the precept of the love of God and that of the love of neighbor were, in practice, "obscured on account of sin."[78] That is why they too were dictated in the Old Law. This, I suppose, is why Thomas says that the existence of duties toward God and others is "especially" easily grasped by someone of faith. And as regards sacrifice, he casually remarks that, among the Gentiles, the laws regulating worship really had only the human common good and human morals in view.[79] They did not put duties toward God in the first place, and Thomas does not seem too surprised about that.

In light of these things, we might very well wonder how significant after all is the distinction between the moral precepts that belong to natural law absolutely and those that require divine or sapiential instruction. As it turns out, under the conditions of sin, even many of the precepts that belong to natural law absolutely, and indeed the most important of them, seem to need divine help, not only for actual compliance with them—that certainly requires grace[80]—but also for a more than tenuous, merely notional or theoretical hold on them. If a person is virtually incapable of using the precepts, and this through no fault of the person's own, how strong can the

---

75. This is possible even though His existence is not self-evident to us. See Brock, "Can Atheism be Rational?," esp. 5–14.

76. This may sound odd to us, but it is how Thomas is seeing it; thus he says: "There is a common good that pertains to one individual or another as part of a whole; for example, to a soldier as part of an army, or to a citizen as part of a city; and as to the love that looks to this good, the chief object of love is whatever the good principally resides in, as the good of an army is in the commander, and the good of a city, in the king" (*De virt.* 2.4ad2).

77. *ST* II–II.85.1. This article's *Sed contra* cites no author, but instead appeals to common experience, asserting that "in every age, among all nations of men, there has always been some offering of sacrifices."

78. *ST* I–II.100.5ad1; cf. I–II.99.2ad2; I–II.94.6.

79. *ST* I–II.99.3.

80. *ST* I–II.109.3; I–II.109.4.

obligation that they carry be? It is almost as though they had not even been promulgated to that person. A law does not oblige anyone to whom it is not promulgated. Yet Thomas holds that all people, not just those to whom revelation was vouchsafed, were obliged to observe the moral precepts.

He is not unaware of such considerations, however. He does recognize that the obligation of those to whom revelation has been given is greater. "The sins of unbelievers are more deserving of pardon, on account of their ignorance."[81] Here he is explaining why unconsented disorderly sense-passions in unbelievers is, if anything, even more "venial," more pardonable, than in believers.

Nevertheless, in the very next article—which is also the article immediately preceding the Treatise on Law—we see why he thinks the sins of unbelievers are still truly sins and cannot be wholly excused. Even if one is inculpably ignorant of revelation, once one has become capable of any moral action at all, one comes to be at fault for lacking the light of faith and the help of grace to steer one's conduct. For there is at least one quite elementary inclination of natural law that original sin does not altogether neutralize. It is that very demand, which is a demand of reason, to order oneself to the due last end—whatever it is. And here I think we see in an especially clear way that natural law does carry within itself the mark of a divine law.

Thomas is talking about what happens when a young person who has not been cleansed of original sin by baptism reaches the "age of discretion" and the "use of reason."

> The first task for thought that then occurs to a man is to deliberate about himself. And if he orders himself to his due end, through grace he will obtain the remission of original sin. But if he does not order himself to the due end, as far as he is capable of discretion at that age, he will sin mortally, on account of not doing what is in his power to do.[82]

Although he does not spell it out here, what Thomas thinks is entailed by obtaining the remission of original sin includes many things. It includes everything involved in the "justification of the sinner": the reception of sanctifying grace, the infusion of the virtues of faith, hope, and charity, the

---

81. *ST* I-II.89.5.

82. *ST* I-II.89.6. For a magisterial discussion of this article, see Dewan, *Wisdom, Law, and Virtue*, 221–41. Thomas presents the same teaching, in more or less detail, in *In Sent.* II.42.1.5*ad*7; *De malo* 5.2*ad*8; 7.10*ad*8. Pertinent, I believe, is Augustine, *De libero arbitrio* 3.20.57.

infused moral virtues, the gifts of the Holy Spirit, and also an act of faith, moved by charity.[83]

So now we can see how he can hold that all are obliged to observe the moral precepts of divine law. They are obliged, by a precept that they are indeed aware of, to do something that will in fact lead them to the requisite knowledge and moral dispositions. To be sure, if they fail to acquire these, then it is quite possible that they will not even grasp all of the precepts. Not all of the precepts will inform their consciences. But the final verdict will be according to natural law.

Obviously this position rests in large part on theological truth concerning the availability of God's grace. However, it is crystal clear that Thomas is presenting the demand to order oneself to the due end as a requirement of natural reason. Indeed he seems to be saying that coming face to face with oneself, as a matter to deliberate about, is just what reaching the "use of reason" consists in. To deliberate about something is to consider it as "for an end." Coming to the use of reason means becoming aware of having the direction of one's life in one's own hands. At that moment, one becomes aware of the need to address the question of what one is for and to orient oneself toward it.

I do not think Thomas means that what prompts the deliberation is the very thought of God. Why should we assume that, up to now, the child has formed any notion of God? No doubt the fundamental motive of the deliberation is the child's love for himself and desire for his own happiness.[84] Also involved in prompting it, however, must be the inclination to love himself and to pursue his happiness *rationally*. It is this that calls for inquiry into his due end and the order to it. For this due end is not happiness itself; that is, it is not the child's ultimate *inherent* perfection, the fullness of the good that is *for him*. Rather it is the end that he himself and his own perfection are for.[85] Only in light of his relation to this end can he determine what his due perfection consists in. Thomas is saying that if the child does carry through with this inquiry, as best he can at that age, he will in fact turn to God, unfailingly. Thus, in the same article, Thomas goes on to say that "this

---

83. See *ST* I–II.113; I–II.63.3; I–II.68.5. It is not impossible for someone ignorant of revelation to have the belief required for salvation (though the help of grace is needed). See *ST* II–II.2.7*ad*3.

84. Thus in the places parallel to *ST* I–II.89.6, Thomas puts it in terms of the child's thinking about or seeking his salvation (*In Sent.* II.42.1.5*ad*7; *De malo* 5.2*ad*8; 7.10*ad*8).

85. See *ST* I–II.89.6*ad*3. It is in this sense of *end*, for example, that Thomas says that "the common good is the end of the individual persons existing in community" (*ST* II–II.58.9*ad*3). And it is in this sense that he says that God is the end of all things (*ST* I.6.3; I.44.4; I–II.1.8).

therefore is the time at which one is obliged by the affirmative precept of God by which the Lord says, 'Turn toward me, and I will turn toward you' (Zachariah 1:3)." He can hardly mean that the child knows the passage from Zachariah. Rather he is saying that the obligation of the precept phrased in terms of God and conversion toward Him, and the obligation of the precept phrased in terms of deliberating about oneself, are ultimately one and the same obligation.

And this is why I say that we see here how natural law, though not originally presenting itself as from God, bears the mark of His law. Clearly the requirement to order oneself to the due end is a precept of natural law. What shows this is not only its occurring quite spontaneously to the young person, but also its very indeterminacy. It speaks only of "the due end," whatever that is. But this is the dominant, we might almost say formal, duty accompanying the very use of reason, and fully complying with this duty suffices to bring one face to face with God's truth and God's rule. Natural law, of itself, leads us to understand that good and bad, in the sense of what is according to reason and contrary to reason, are determined primarily in relation to God. It does not start from this understanding, and it certainly does not itself contain all the determinations of our duties toward God. But what it does start from leads to this understanding, which in turn leads toward the discovery of those determinations, if one is willing to follow it.

I would like to connect this discussion with a point on which I insisted in chapter 3: that Thomas's understanding of natural law must be seen in light of his conception of God as the highest *common good*. Now, in the article on what happens upon reaching the use of reason, Thomas does not spell out the path taken by the deliberation that results in turning to God. Perhaps the possible paths are several. But it must be that the original prompting, even if it is only from the desire of one's own good, is not determinately toward one's own *private* good, a good that is for oneself *alone*. In that case one would hardly be in a position to see oneself as existing for something other than oneself. And even if it is only a prompting of one's love of oneself, it cannot be determinately a love of oneself above all else; otherwise charity would destroy it rather than fulfill it. The prompting must somehow be proportioned to a good that is also for others, and even open to a love that is more for another than for oneself. Reason's natural starting-point, what is "first for us," cannot be what is absolutely first in things or first simply, because it is gathered through sensation, and sensible things are far from the first things.[86] But even what is first for us must be at least in

---

86. See *In Phys.* I.1, 5, ¶7; *ST* I–II.57.2; cf. I–II.71.2ad3, quoted above, 113.

potency to what is first simply and must somehow point us in its direction.[87] It must be open to the highest, most universal good.

In other words, the expression *one's own good* does not have to mean only, or even chiefly, one's private good.[88] It does not even have to mean the good that is for oneself. It can also mean the good that one is for, the ultimate good on which the good that one is and has depends, as on its final cause.[89] The rational consideration of oneself must lead quickly, naturally, to seeing that one is part of something larger than oneself, ordered to it, and made to find one's own fulfillment in somehow sharing in its good. Working to bring it into focus will eventually disclose its being for the sake of a mind that is divine. This fits with what we saw in chapter 5: the natural understanding of the practical good falls within a broader understanding of the good as something toward which all things tend. We naturally find ourselves existing within a universal order of striving for the good, and our mind naturally tends to seek the principle of this order and to ascertain the right way of relating to it.

Perhaps a good way to put it is this. The perspective of reason, as reason, is the perspective of universal being, all reality. It is a metaphysical perspective—not in the sense that we are naturally engaged in the science of metaphysics, but in the sense that it extends over the field that metaphysics examines in a scientific way. But having the use of reason means precisely being able to consider oneself, and to conduct oneself, from this perspective. One sees oneself as part of the world, and the world looks as though it at least might be a genuine community. One sees the need to find out whether it truly is one and, if so, what the principle of its unity and its order is, and what one's own role in relation to it is. Only by knowing this principle and subordinating oneself to it can one rightly determine the nature of one's own due perfection; that is, the nature of one's true beatitude, which is one's full *attainment* of the end.[90] What comes first is the truth about God and one's relation to Him.

Something like this explains how, in his treatment of man's last end at the beginning of the *Prima secundae*, even before he addresses the question of what man's true beatitude consists in, Thomas can already say that it comes about "by knowing and loving God."[91] In other words, prior to the question

---

87. Thus in the speculative order, what is first for us is being as found in sensible things; but it is still *being* as found in sensible things, and its exigencies eventually lead the mind to the consideration of the universal cause of being.

88. See *ST* II–II.47.10ad2.

89. See *ST* I.60.5ad2.

90. *ST* I–II.2, *proem*.

91. *ST* I–II.1.8.

of man's *proper* end is the question of the end of all things—the most universal common good. This just is the question of God. Man's proper end, whatever it is, will be attained through his distinctive way (among visible creatures) of relating to God, which is by knowing Him and loving Him. The highest common good naturally comes first in reason's consideration. As Thomas says in discussing the need for faith, the very fact of apprehending "universal being and good" gives us an immediate order toward God as the universal principle of being.[92] This order, again, is what makes us susceptible of the supernatural, divine influence—the influence of His Word—that faith seizes upon. And even apart from faith, that apprehension must also be what makes it quite natural for us to grasp God's supreme lovability, as soon as we are aware of Him. This just is to be aware of a supreme common good that we and all things are for and that we should love above all else.

In any case, it is clear that the primary tendency and function of Thomas's natural law is not to serve as the rational basis of human law. It does have that function, but only secondarily. More fundamentally, it establishes a perspective for practical reason that is even higher, more universal, than that of human law or of the order proper to human association. It is the perspective from which the absolutely highest common good comes into view.[93]

PRIOR IN OUR APPREHENSION BUT NOT PRIOR SIMPLY

At this point I shall begin to assess the positions surveyed in the first chapter. I shall not discuss them in the order in which I presented them there, but according as they pertain to the remaining aspects of the naturalness of natural law that I wish to discuss. Those that are most pertinent to the aspect to be considered in this section are those that I presented in the fourth section of chapter 1, "Natural law as a natural divine law."

This is my own view: Thomas's natural law is a full-fledged law, and it is so inasmuch as it is promulgated to man by the divine lawgiver through the natural light of reason. I have also argued that, for Aquinas, its promulgation is completed in the natural understanding of the truth of its precepts, even before their having been instituted and promulgated by God is itself understood. Compliance with its precepts will indeed lead (at least with the help of grace) toward that understanding, but the force of law that is proper to the precepts does not absolutely suppose or depend upon it. Not

---

92. *ST* II-II.2.3.

93. For a penetrating discussion of Thomas's conception of God as the highest common good and of how it bears on our relation to the political common good, see Dewan, *Wisdom, Law, and Virtue*, 271–78, 577–79.

everyone whom I discussed in that section of chapter 1 sees it this way. First let me consider those who do.

Even though she does not cite Aquinas, I find Elizabeth Anscombe's discussion to be, as far as it goes, quite consistent with my reading of him. She treats natural law as a divine law, and she insists, with regard to it, that "you can be subject to a law that you do not acknowledge and have not thought of as law." This is how I have been arguing that Thomas thinks we are first subject to natural law.

It might seem that Anscombe's further claim, that the notion of moral obligation is unfounded outside the perspective of an ethics based on divine law, runs contrary to Thomas's assertion of a strict *debitum* that is "moral" rather than "legal." This is a strict duty whose basis is the mere natural dictate of reason, and which is understood as a duty even without reference to God as the dictate's origin.[94] But Anscombe's view is not incompatible with this. For Thomas is not making the moral order *as such*—the whole order of reason or of virtue—to be naturally understood as an order of strict obligation or necessity or duty. It only comes to be understood in that way when it is understood to be a condition of due subjection to God. The naturally understood sphere of strict duty—the sphere pertaining to natural law "absolutely considered"—is narrower. It is the sphere of things naturally understood to be matters of justice (particular and general)—the sphere of things regulated by human law. Anscombe certainly seems to recognize the existence of strict duties or obligations in this sphere, and she treats them as intelligible independently of any reference to divine legislation. She has a whole article, published after "Modern Moral Philosophy," that speaks in this vein.[95]

The title of that article also makes implicit reference to conscience—the "internal forum." It seems clear that when Anscombe rejects the appeal to conscience as proof of "moral obligation," what she is rejecting is only the idea that conscience itself could be the very *source* of moral obligation. That is what does not square with the fact that conscience can dictate "the vilest things." But Thomas knows perfectly well that conscience can do that. He says, for example, that those who killed the Apostles were following their conscience.[96] For him, conscience obliges, not in virtue of itself or as the very source of obligation, but only in virtue of divine precept; and it can err

---

94. See above, 219.

95. G. E. M. Anscombe, "On Promising and its Justice, and Whether it Need be Respected *in Foro Interno*," in Anscombe, *Ethics, Religion, and Politics*, 10–21, esp. 14–19.

96. *De ver.* 17.2sc1.

through misapplication or misunderstanding of the precept.[97] Anscombe is not denying that there is such a thing as a rule's being "binding in conscience." In fact, she has a brief unfinished essay, published posthumously, devoted entirely to the question, "is a false conscience binding?"[98] She does not in any way suggest that such binding is intelligible only by reference to divine law. Moreover, what she means by being *binding* is being necessary to comply with so that your conduct will not be wrong. This is just what I have argued that Thomas means by it.[99]

How Geach's view compares with Thomas's is a little more complicated. As with Anscombe, there is evidently agreement as to our being subject to natural law whether or not we have become aware of its being a law. And Geach's example—the natural knowledge of the general objectionableness of lying—seems to fit Thomas's view well enough. Geach's insistence that God's command is a genuine cause of moral obligation also constitutes an important point of agreement. What complicates matters, however, is Geach's way of arguing for this point, which is by appeal to God's irresistible power.

To explain the complication, first let me say something about Thomas in relation to the *Euthyphro*-like question in terms of which Geach frames his discussion. We can ask: does God forbid lying because it is wrong, or is it wrong because God forbids it? On my reading, Thomas's fundamental answer is the latter. Everything that is wrong for creatures to do is wrong primarily because it is forbidden by God's eternal law. At the same time, however, Thomas does not hold that lying is wrong *only* because it is forbidden by the eternal law. The eternal law is only the *first* cause of its wrongness. It is also wrong, secondarily, because it is forbidden by natural reason. Reason forbids it in light of reason's own understanding of what it is and of how it relates to the human good, which is the good proportioned to human nature. The eternal law is the cause of human nature, of reason's natural light, and of the dictates that it naturally forms.[100]

Geach is not saying that our natural knowledge of things like the general objectionableness of lying depends on our own consideration of God's power. He is saying that we see this objectionableness for ourselves. He is not really concerned to explain how our seeing this constitutes a promulgation

---

97. See *In Sent.* II.39.3.3ad3.

98. Anscombe, "Must One Obey One's Conscience?"

99. Really that whole essay is nothing other than a restatement—a very lucid and nuanced one—of *ST* I–II.19.5–6.

100. The situation is somewhat comparable to the way in which creatures are good *both* by participation in the divine good and by their own intrinsic goodness, which they have in virtue of that participation. See *ST* I.6.4.

of God's law. Perhaps he could say simply that God has ordered the world of our experience and the nature of our mind in such a way that lying naturally shows itself to us as, on the whole, something disordered and bad. But Geach's purpose in invoking God's irresistible power is to explain why it is *always* wrong to disobey His dictates. Once we do become aware that we are dealing with a divine dictate, the consideration of His power suffices to show that acting against it can *never* be rational.

Thomas could perhaps agree with that last statement, at least in some cases. However, it is clear that he does not think that the only basis for judging that lying is always against reason is the revelation of God's universal prohibition of it. He thinks that it too is something that we can come to see for ourselves, though perhaps only with the help of sapiential instruction. Moreover, on Thomas's view, there are things that we naturally understand to be generally wrong, and that God does *not* forbid universally; for instance, not returning deposits.[101] The awareness that our naturally understood practical truths are from God does add to their obligatory force, but it does not always rule out the possibility of exceptions to them. If right natural reason allows for exceptions, and revelation does not rule them out, then the eternal law itself does not rule them out.

Moreover, and more importantly, I do not think that Thomas would consider God's irresistible power to be the truly fundamental reason why His command functions as a genuine source of moral obligations. Geach is quite explicit: "I am saying not: It is your supreme moral duty to obey God, but simply: It is insane to set about defying an Almighty God."[102] Thomas is saying precisely that it is our supreme moral duty to obey God. This is not in view of His power. It is in view of His goodness. I do not mean His "moral" goodness, the goodness of His will; I mean the goodness of the "object" of His good will.[103] It is the goodness which is His infinite perfection and lovability, the goodness of the supreme common good, the ultimate end of all things. His will rules us because it is by His will that we are first ordered to that goodness. Geach's approach, however, makes it sound rather as though we have our ends, and God has His, and while these differ, it makes no sense to pursue ours in a way that runs afoul of what He has ordained about us in view of His. Thomas can very well agree that this makes no sense. But what makes even less sense, for him, is to have any ultimate end other than God's own.[104] It is primarily for that end that we exist and are what we are, and this

---

101. See *ST* I–II.94.4.
102. Geach, *God and the Soul*, 127.
103. See *ST* I.5.4*ad*3; I–II.19.9.
104. See *ST* I–II.19.9; I–II.19.10.

is the primary reason why we ought always to comply with His ordination. Geach's reason is merely secondary. It is so in the way that, in general, sanctions are only a secondary basis of the obligation of law.

Could Geach say that he is speaking only to moral philosophers, not to theologians? For Thomas, God's supreme goodness is no less knowable philosophically than is His irresistible power. Their basis is exactly the same.[105] Of the reasons why it is always wrong to disobey God, His power may be the first one that we consider, but it is not the first simply.

Walter Farrell's reading is in agreement with mine on the two most essential points: that natural law is a divinely promulgated law, and that its full promulgation does not require an indication of its divine origin. He is also right, on my reading, to regard the remorse of conscience as the punishment that is proper to natural law. It may be that Farrell takes the obligation of law to be primarily with respect to avoiding punishment, rather than with respect to avoiding wrongdoing, which is how I see it; but this is a comparatively minor issue. However, there is an important point of divergence. This is the role that Farrell assigns to the human will and its natural inclinations in accounting for the obligatoriness of natural law. Agreeing with Suárez that God's will plays an essential role making natural law obligatory, but disagreeing with Suárez's view that natural law is fully promulgated only insofar as it serves as a sign of God's will, Farrell seems to think that what makes reference to God's will unnecessary is that the human will itself is given a share in the work of making natural law obligatory. The human will would be the proximate active source of the force of reason's dictates. In my opinion, this is a misunderstanding not only of the human will's role in natural law, but also of the law's obligatory force itself.

As we have seen, on Thomas's account of obligation, the will of one who is subject to a law is indeed an essential factor in the law's obligatory or binding force. But its function is not to confer such force on the law. It is not an active principle of the binding, but a passive one. It is precisely that which the law binds. Through the subjects' reception of the law, their wills are placed under the necessity of complying with the law. They are not the agents of that necessity, not even secondary ones. The precepts of natural law are not the effect of human reason's own act of commanding. They are truths that reason grasps concerning the due order of human action, and the only act of commanding that gives rise to them is God's. The will does not bind itself. The natural inclinations corresponding to the precepts are not what give the precepts their moving force. They are rather the first,

---

105. See *ST* I.25.2; I.25.3; cf. I.4.1; I.4.2; I.6.1; I.6.2.

natural effect of that force. Just because it is a will, it is naturally apt to be moved according to reason's understanding of what is good and bad for us.

Farrell proceeds on the assumption that the normativity of the law, its being a true rule and measure of human acts, is something distinct from its obligatory force. On my reading of Thomas, these are one and the same thing. The very grasp of the truth of the precepts is what puts the will under the necessity of complying with them and what inclines it to comply. Not even the force of remorse of conscience (which is not properly a precept of the law, but a particular application of a precept) derives from an act or an inclination of the will. Conscience is an act of "speculating according to principles," and the pain that it gives consists precisely in its running contrary to the will's inclination. It is not a voluntary self-punishment. In the proper sense of *punishment*, there is no such thing.

The natural inclinations of the will are not what make our natural duties be duties. They are not what make good conduct be good or bad conduct be bad. They do not make the precepts of natural law true, or intelligible, or obligatory. The light of reason binds us, on pain of transgression or wrongdoing and of reason's own reproach, simply by showing us what is good and what is bad. But it is through the inclinations that the precepts first influence our conduct. They give our wills a foothold on the moral order. It is not that they suffice to guarantee compliance with the precepts; far from it, especially under the conditions of sin. But without them, the thought of duty itself would make no difference to us. We would not care about being good or bad or about reason's judgment. Right action would always be a result of coercion (or perhaps a coincidence); it would not really be right *conduct* at all. The offer of the help that we need in order to fulfill the precepts—the help of grace—would not, in itself, even interest us.[106] This is how appetitive inclination or connaturality pertains to natural law. It is not, as Maritain holds, a principle of the knowledge of natural law. It is a principle of the law's efficacy.

And it really is connaturality, an agreement with human nature. For the truly fundamental inclination, the inclination to the good of reason, is nothing other than the will itself. "The will is related in one way to what is good and in another way to what is bad. For by the nature of its power it is inclined toward the good of reason as its proper object. This is why every sin is said to be contrary to nature."[107] An obligation is a necessity that the will is under. The will may be free to transgress reason's rules, and even unable

---

106. Natural law is an "instilled" law that "indicates" what is to be done, but there is another instilled law that also "helps" to fulfill it—the New Law, which is chiefly the very grace of the Holy Spirit (*ST* I–II.106.1c/*ad*2).

107. *ST* I–II.78.3.

(without help) not to transgress them, but it is nevertheless under them. They cannot but influence it. It cannot be altogether aloof to whether its act is good or bad, according or contrary to reason. This is simply to say that it is will; that is, rational appetite.

We should certainly see the will's natural inclination as pertaining to the promulgation of natural law. "God, who moves all things toward their due ends, instilled in each of them forms through which they are inclined to the ends instituted for them by God, and in this way He disposes all things sweetly, as it says in *Wisdom* 8."[108] The act of instilling in us the light of reason, which is the act by which God promulgates natural law, is one with the act of endowing us with a will. It is simply the creation of the human soul.

I am not denying that the *legislator's* will plays a role in making the law obligatory. It does, inasmuch as it plays a role in making the law normative. The very institution of the law is a free, voluntary act on the part of the legislator. It is by the legislator's will that the law is enacted and applied to the community's members, making it actually rule and measure their actions.

So now let me turn to Suárez. He certainly does not seem to think that the human will is an active principle of the obligatory force of natural law. Nevertheless, on the whole I find his view diverging considerably farther from Thomas's than Farrell's does.

The principal difficulty that I find in Suárez's reading is not his requirement that the promulgation of natural law include the notification of the legislator's will. I do, however, think that this is a difficulty too. Let me say something about it first. Then I shall turn to the principal one, which underlies it.

As I mentioned, Lawrence Dewan professes agreement with Suárez about the need for a notification of the legislator's will. Nevertheless, I am not at all convinced that Suárez's overall position really fits with Dewan's own outlook. I am inclined to see Dewan's agreement, on that particular point, simply as his way of insisting that natural law puts us on a path toward God—God apprehended as the highest good and as the source of the whole moral order—and that, if we follow it from the start, the path is not really very long. It should be clear that I fully agree with that.[109] But

108. *ST* II-II.23.2. The motif of God's disposing all things sweetly recurs often in Aquinas. In the *Summa*, see I.22.2sc; I.103.8; I.109.2; I-II.110.2; II-II.165.1; III.44.4sc; III.46.9; III.55.6sc; III.60.4.

109. I would want to stress that, at least under the condition of sin, this "short path" necessarily involves the help of grace; this is clear from *ST* I-II.89.6. Dewan's appeal to passages in which Thomas speaks of a certain apprehension of God that is easily accessible to nearly everyone is not very telling. Thomas makes it clear that this is a very imperfect and confused apprehension, one that does not even exclude the opinion that God is a body or a powerful human being. See *ScG* III.38, 94a, line 15–94b, line 4. This

as for the notification of the legislator's will, consider what Dewan himself says. "What is *in fact* law is only inferentially grasped by us *as law*. It is first grasped by us in a more immediate way, as the goodness of being."[110] If what we have grasped is in fact law, then it is also a fact that the law has been promulgated to us, and that we are already under it, whether we know this or not. Suárez is saying that it has not been promulgated, and so is not a law that we are under, until either we actually begin to take it as a sign of God's legislative will or we have come to be at fault for not doing so. I want to say that, on the contrary, for Aquinas reason's dictates must be functioning as God's law from the start, even before they are grasped as God's law.

Consider again what Thomas lays down as reason's first requirement upon reaching the use of reason.[111] It is a requirement to deliberate about oneself so as to order oneself to one's due end. This deliberation does not necessarily start from any knowledge of God or of His legislative will. That knowledge may only be attainable through the process of this deliberation itself. Now on Suárez's view, at the moment when the process of deliberation ought to begin, people in this situation cannot yet be said to be subject to God's law. At this moment, they neither know His legislative will nor are at fault for not knowing it. So suppose they do *not* undertake the deliberation and so do not come to the knowledge of God or of His legislative will. To be sure, they would have acted contrary to a dictate of reason. They would have acted badly and even culpably. Nevertheless, on Suárez's view, they cannot be said to have acted contrary to God's law, since it has not yet been promulgated to them. But if they have not violated His law, then neither can they be said to have offended Him or to be liable to punishment from Him. At most they have only offended their own reason and are liable to its punishment. But its punishment cannot be seen as the execution of an order instituted by God's law. Thomas, by contrast, clearly holds that, just insofar as they have violated their own reason, they have also offended Him, as governor of the universe, and are liable to punishment from Him. "Every good or bad act of a man has the quality (*rationem*) of merit or demerit before God, in proportion to the act's own nature."[112]

But as I said, there is also a deeper problem in Suárez's position.[113] Dewan says—and I think Thomas agrees—that the goodness of being is *in*

---

is certainly not an apprehension of God as the author of natural law.

110. Dewan, *Wisdom, Law, and Virtue*, 210.

111. ST I–II.89.6.

112. ST I–II.21.4ad3. See above, 179, 213.

113. I dare say that Fr. Dewan would have considered it a problem too. The crucial point is God's being the highest common good, and Dewan was as alive to this point as anyone could be.

fact law. Suárez is denying that. On Suárez's view, there is in things—created things, including the human creature—an order of right and wrong, of the *honestum* and *inhonestum*, that is not a law, but is prior to all law, even to God's. It is not just prior in our apprehension. Suárez is not saying merely that we grasp it in itself or in its own contents before we refer it to God's legislative will and thereby grasp it to be a full-fledged law. He is saying that it is prior in its own intelligibility to God's legislative will.[114] Reason's dictates, for Suárez, are not the *effect* of God's legislation. His legislation presupposes them. They fall under it only in the sense that He wills to make them obligatory before Him. His legislative will adds obligatory force to them, but their intrinsic rectitude and obligatory force does not depend on it. God's prohibition of the things that are contrary to them is not what first makes such things wrong or bad. Rather He prohibits them because they are already wrong and bad in themselves. The natural dictates of reason can be called a law only in the sense that they eventually function as signs of that will of God, and what makes them signs of His will is not that they are its effects, because they are not. It is merely that the order which they express, being intrinsically right, is one that we can assume Him to have willed to make legally obligatory.

In short, as I argued in chapter 3, Suárez makes God's own law, the eternal law, function in exactly the way a positive law does. In doing so, he also makes natural law itself, *as* law, function in this way.[115] The relation of God's law to the natural dictates of human reason is the same as that of a law instituted by a human legislator. It presupposes them and adds further force to them, and its own force is actualized only through its subjects' knowledge of the legislator's having instituted it. For Thomas, by contrast, even the intrinsic rectitude of the natural dictates of reason is the effect of the law that God voluntarily institutes. Again, "the eternal law is related to the order of human reason as a craft to an artifact."[116] The eternal law determines the very natures of created things. Those natures, and the orders that pertain to them, are prior in our apprehension. This is the natural order of our understanding, which starts from sensible things.[117] But God's law is prior simply. The natures of things are among its effects.

To be sure, Suárez does make creation the effect of God's free will. The natural dictates of reason, just in themselves, do proceed from God, acting

---

114. See above, 98; also Suárez, *De lege naturali*, 95–96 (De legibus II.vi.13).

115. For further discussion along this line, with interesting remarks on the reasons why Suárez takes the position that he does, see Hittinger, *First Grace*, 51–57.

116. *ST* I-II.71.2ad4.

117. See above, 237n86.

as the Father of lights. But Suárez does not see creation as the effect of God's legislative will. Ordaining the mere existence of creatures and giving them the conditions that they naturally need do not pertain to God's legislation. Nor does the order of rectitude that intrinsically follows upon their natures. God's legislation presupposes that ordination and that order. Its object is a further order of obligation, which partly overlaps with the order of natural rectitude. It seems to me that, in saying this, Suárez has simply overlooked the fact that God's ordering things to His own goodness does *not* presuppose His willing to create them. His will to create things is itself part of His freely adopted way of willing His own goodness. To see His goodness as the end of creation just is to see it as a common good, the first and highest one. His ordaining the existence of the world is already His exercising providential care over it, the sort of care that pertains to a legislator. Certain particular creaturely orders that God has instituted presuppose certain others. But there is no creaturely order that His institution as a whole presupposes.

Farrell, like other critics of Suárez, focuses on the fact that Suárez makes law (and command generally) to be essentially an act of will rather than reason. It seems to me, however, that even though Suárez does differ from Thomas on this point, the real contrast is not there, but in how Suárez relates God's law to the natural order. For Thomas, legislation does indeed involve the legislator's will to oblige those who are subject to him. The eternal law definitely does that. But it is the cause of *all* true obligation, including the obligation in conscience that naturally and inseparably accompanies the creature's possession of reason.

To put it in Dewan's terms, the "goodness of being" is not a principle of God's institution of the order of the eternal law. It is an effect of that institution. God's will for His own good is the very source, the agent, of the whole order of being, cause of the nature of being and of its attributes, which include its goodness. There is no end for the sake of which He wills it, other than His own good. His good, alone, is what "universal being and good" are for the sake of. It is in this sense that our natural apprehension of universal being and good gives us an immediate order to Him.[118] And this is why the practical implications of this apprehension constitute a full-fledged law, and one that does not "fall short" of the eternal law as human law does.[119] It is a divine law, one that of itself leads toward God's goodness, and it is not "something diverse" from the eternal law, but simply a participation in

---

118. Again, see *ST* II–II.2.3.
119. *ST* I–II.96.2*ad*3.

it.[120] God as creator and Father of lights and God as lawgiver are one and the same.[121] This is why the light of reason is, intrinsically, a light that binds.

NATURAL IN PRACTICE AND IN THEORY

As we saw, Ernest Fortin's reading of Thomas on natural law has something in common with Suárez's. Fortin thinks that the full promulgation of a law must include a notification of the lawgiver's act of instituting it. He also thinks that it must include a notification of the sanctions that the lawgiver has attached to it. Especially for this reason, however, he differs from Suárez with regard to the naturalness of natural law. The lawgiver of natural law is God, and Fortin finds Thomas far from sure about natural reason's ability to know of the sanctions that God has attached to it. Fortin thinks that Thomas indicates the not-quite-natural status of natural law in a quiet way, by remaining silent on the question of the sanctions that are proper to it and saying only that it calls for sanctions to be established by human law.

We have seen that Thomas does think that natural law brings with it its own kind of sanction. It carries the remorse of conscience. Now, Fortin might deny that this correction completely refutes of his reading, because he does not think (or think Thomas thinks) that natural reason can be certain that remorse of conscience has the inescapability that a divinely instituted sanction ought to have. This would mean that natural reason cannot be certain that the natural principles of conscience are divinely ordained. But the force of this reply depends entirely on the assumption that the principles must be known to be a divine law in order to function as one. Fortin never actually shows that Thomas assumes this, and I think I have shown the contrary.

Fortin's argument, then, starts from a mere misunderstanding, and it does not yield even a plausible interpretation of Thomas's view. What reason can know about the relation between the principles of conscience and God is incidental to the legal character of these principles. They are already functioning as a natural law. Fortin is right to regard Thomas's natural law as a divine law. He is also right to stress that Aristotle's discussion of natural right is entirely within the domain of political right. As discussed earlier, Thomas's natural right extends beyond what falls within political right or

---

120. *ST* I–II.91.2*ad*1.

121. In other words, "Once God is taken as creator, the whole created order and the motions of all the parts of that order to their ends are seen as the result of God's ordering wisdom, i.e., God's providence and his governance. All law of any kind whatsoever becomes a part of that eternal law, including natural law" (Gallagher, "Role of God," 1032).

within the ambit of human law. And even his natural law "absolutely considered" extends beyond that. He grants, or even insists, that human law does not have the task of enforcing all of natural law.[122] However, I do not think that he differs much from Aristotle on the question of the variability of political natural right.[123] Political right generally pertains to the relations among those living together in political association under a rule of law and legal judgment.[124] On the whole, the precepts of natural law that Thomas regards as absolutely universal and invariable in rectitude are the primary, common precepts.[125] These correspond directly to natural human inclinations, which in turn pertain to the very foundations of political association. Can Aristotle possibly think that political natural right is so variable as sometimes to call for things that altogether undermine political life itself?

Another question would be whether Fortin's argument even shows that the *theory* of natural law, as a participation in the eternal law, requires revelation and is not accessible to natural, philosophical reason. Evidently for Thomas it is only through revelation that we are apprised of the full set of sanctions that God has attached to His law. And I suppose Fortin is right that the inescapability of His punishment is not empirically verifiable. But this hardly proves that it is not philosophically knowable. Fortin simply takes it for granted that, for Thomas, the universality and infallibility of divine providence is beyond the reach of natural reason. But this is patently wrong.[126] Thomas does think that no "philosopher"—no pagan thinker—got God's providence and omnipotence quite right.[127] But he does not flatly identify philosophy with what was achieved by the philosophers, even by the Philosopher. He offers what he clearly takes to be conclusive rational arguments for these divine attributes.[128] He also offers such arguments for the existence of divine reward and punishment.[129]

---

122. *ST* I–II.93.3*ad*3; I–II.96.2.

123. See above, 86n65.

124. See Aristotle, *Nicomachean Ethics* V.10, 1134a26–33.

125. *ST* I–II.94.4.

126. Fortin also departs from Thomas in saying that, within the sphere of revelation, what secures God's providence is the First Table of the Decalogue. The recognition of divine providence is prior to the reception of the Decalogue, just as faith is. It is a primary, immediate truth of faith, perhaps even the most fundamental one. See *ST* II–II.1.7.

127. *ST* II–II.1.8*ad*1.

128. He does so in many of his writings. In the *Summa theologiae*, see *ST* I.22; I.25.

129. See, for example, *ScG* III.140. Also interesting is *ScG* III.141, where he explains why it seems to many that sins are not punished by God.

What about Kluxen's view, that the merely philosophical, metaphysical understanding of natural law as a participation in the eternal law is a purely speculative consideration, without practical significance? Kluxen is right to say that, for Thomas, only revealed theology is both a speculative and a practical science. Only revelation provides a knowledge of God that is in itself practical, a knowledge of God himself enunciating rules of human conduct. But it hardly seems to fit Thomas's view to say that only revelation provides a knowledge of God that has practical significance.[130] After all, Thomas does think there are precepts of natural law about God, such as the precept to love Him above all things. And as for the knowledge of God as a provident, omnipotent lawgiver, it is clear that on this point Thomas would agree with Geach: "For those who believe in Almighty God, a man's every act is an act either of obeying or of ignoring or of defying that God; so naturally and logically they have quite different standards from unbelievers—they take a different view as to what people are in fact doing."[131]

NATURAL PRINCIPLES OF THE CONCEPT OF LAW

The remaining positions that I presented in chapter 1 can be dispatched in fairly short order. All of them, in one way or another, present an approach to natural law that leaves its relation to God and the eternal law out of consideration. Now I do not wish to argue that Thomas's teaching excludes any such approach. It is perfectly possible to look at human conduct and the rightness or wrongness of it from a purely human or mundane point of view. Leo Strauss is said to have declared that "natural law is nothing but an attempt to spell out the principles on which honest men act and have acted and will act as long as there are men."[132] It is an elegant formulation. Evidently it was offered in an informal setting and was meant only to clear up a possible misunderstanding about the scope of natural law, without further theoretical pretensions. Thomas could very well agree that what the participation of the eternal law in the rational creature, considered absolutely, consists in, is nothing but those principles, and that in certain contexts, focusing on those might be the best way to get the discussion of it off the ground.

130. Thomas certainly thinks that theoretical truths can have practical consequences or be "occasions" of acting in a certain way. See *ST* I-II.14.6, on how counsel can borrow from every sort of knowledge, theoretical and practical. One example that he gives is the philosophical knowledge of immortality of the soul (*De ver.* 14.4). For some discussion of Thomas on the role that the knowledge of God and of the immortality of the soul can or should (pace Aristotle) play in moral philosophy, see Brock, *Philosophy of Saint Thomas Aquinas*, 158–63.
131. Geach, *God and the Soul*, 128.
132. Quoted in Banfield, "Leo Strauss," 496.

On the other hand, I do not think he would agree with Lottin that it is positively better to treat natural law without reference to the eternal law and as therefore having the nature of law only in a qualified sense. The problem is not that Lottin wants to see the precepts of natural law as constituting an order of "intrinsic morality," a moral order rooted in man's own reason, already carrying its own obligatory force. Obviously Thomas thinks they do just that. And it is true that the eternal law, in itself, is an "extrinsic" rule or measure. But Lottin treats it as extrinsic in the way that positive law is extrinsic; that is, as merely superimposing another order, one that partly overlaps with the order of reason and adds further obligatory force to its dictates. But for Thomas, the eternal law is the source of intrinsic morality, the very cause of the ruling force of the precepts of natural law—cause of human nature and of the nature of reason itself. Not everything that comes to a subject from an extrinsic source is merely added on to what is intrinsic to it. Even the things that are intrinsic to it can have extrinsic causes upon which they essentially depend.[133]

When Thomas defines natural law as the participation of the eternal law in the rational creature, he is not only explaining how it is that the first principles of practical reason fall under his general definition of law, but also providing the fullest account of their own status as rules of reason. "Nothing stands firmly according to practical reason except by ordination to the last end, which is a common good."[134] The absolutely last end and the most universal common good is the divine good, and the proper measure of the order to it is the eternal law. The primary *happiness* is God's. At first, naturally, human reason is ordered to this good only in a confused, indeterminate way, under the general notion of common good. But that very indeterminacy is the mark of its derivation from a higher, determinate principle. Nothing indeterminate is fully self-explanatory. Until it knows its relation to the eternal law, practical reason's own self-understanding and directive power are not complete. The knowledge of the first common principles is a sufficient promulgation of the natural law, but it is not a knowledge that is sufficient to direct human life—not a knowledge *of principles* that is sufficient. The sufficient knowledge of principles is what is called wisdom, which is primarily the knowledge of the truth about God. This is a natural need of human life. That is why natural law dictates the pursuit of it.

If one does wish to consider natural law without reference to the eternal law, to what extent should one regard it as a law? It seems clear that O'Donoghue, in treating it as a full-fledged law enacted by human reason

---

133. On God's acting "intimately" in all things, see *ST* I.105.5.
134. *ST* I–II.90.2*ad*3.

itself, is not quite following Thomas. Among other things, Thomas does not think that natural law exists in an individual human mind as a set of purely private dictates, applicable only to that person. The precepts of natural law are universal, understood to be applicable to everyone. Indeed they are more common, have a more universal applicability, than the ordinations of any human law. What is applicable only to oneself is the judgment of one's conscience, made by application of natural law to one's own case. O'Donoghue thinks that to regard natural law as existing in us in the manner in which law exists in those who are ruled by it makes us merely passive with respect to it, as the irrational animals are passive with respect to God's ordination. For Thomas, however, the very fact that natural law exists in us in the mode of reason suffices to distinguish our subjection to God's ordination from that of the beasts. It means that we are not merely passive in our compliance with it or our obedience to it. It is up to us to apply the law to the regulation of our conduct and to act accordingly. Nevertheless it is true that we are not the agents of our own possession of it. That would mean that we bring it about in ourselves voluntarily. It does not comes about voluntarily, but in a natural way.

Should we then accept Adler's view—with which Finnis and Grisez evidently agree—that without reference to the eternal law, natural law cannot be understood as a law in the full and proper sense, but only in a derivative and analogical way, by its relation to human positive law? Perhaps we should, *if* we are thinking in terms of Thomas's complete definition of law. I wonder, though, whether Thomas himself would insist on thinking in those terms. What if we think simply in terms of his opening formulation, as it were his nominal definition of law: *a rule and measure of human acts, according to which one is effectively led toward or restrained from action*? Or even more simply, what if we think of law as nothing but a truly binding rule of action? Then, even prescinding from the eternal law, natural law does appear to be a full-fledged law, or at least to contain full-fledged laws—those naturally understood rules that pertain to the sphere of justice. Of course the ultimate explanation of its binding force would still be its derivation from the eternal law. And if one were to *deny* the existence of a divine legislator, one might eventually conclude that the binding force of natural law itself is merely specious.[135] But not being aware that it comes from God is hardly the same as positively denying that it does.

---

135. I think it would be comparable to the way in which, for Thomas, the denial of a divine intellect governing things could lead to the conclusion that all appearances are true and nothing is false and that the principle of non-contradiction is specious. See *ST* I.16.1*ad*2.

So there is an important sense in which both Donagan and Stevens, in speaking of natural law as a law even without reference to God, are in agreement with Thomas. However, their ways of understanding its legality do not quite seem to fit with his. Stevens, like Farrell, makes the human will an active principle of natural law's intrinsic obligatory force, rather than its passive principle, that which it bears upon; and, perhaps for this reason, he glosses over the coercive or punitive force—that of the remorse of conscience—which is intrinsic to natural law.

Donagan, for his part, holds that we do not need to invoke a divine governor in order to treat morality as a whole—the entire order of virtue—as a "system of law." If this means a system of strict obligation, Thomas's view seems to be that only what pertains to the virtue of justice can be treated in this way. Also, if by *morality* Donagan means what can be determined in light of the precepts of natural law, I think that Thomas would balk at the term *system*. For him, law and obligation do always refer to life in community and to common good, and he does not think that even the whole set of conclusions that can be drawn from the precepts of natural law suffice to regulate any community, human or divine, to which human beings actually belong. Humankind, the mere multitude of beings that have human nature, is not itself a complete community of the sort regulated by law. It does not have the unity of order that such a community has. Natural law does incline us to belong to such community, but it does not suffice to establish or to regulate one. Natural law is not a self-sufficient law. It only provides fundamental principles for a complete legal system.

But they are truly fundamental. I would like to close by suggesting that, on Thomas's view, natural law provides the principles underlying his complete definition of law itself. One patent feature of this definition is that it is rather abstract. It must be so, in order to apply not only to human law but also to the eternal law (and, through the eternal law, to natural law). And not only must it be abstract. It must also express the possibility of understanding the eternal law as a *higher* than human law; that is, as prior to human law with respect to the very nature of law, or as that from which the very legality of human law derives. But this means that, in some way, the definition itself must already stand above the precepts or ordinations of human authorities and measure their legality. This is to say that it must measure them in a *practical* way, as things that ought or ought not to be so. And even though the eternal law transcends reason, Thomas arrives at the definition of law through purely rational considerations. It seems to me, then, that he must regard his definition as nothing short of a sapiential determination of the naturally understood principles—practical principles—in light of which we can distinguish between what is and what is not a true law.

They are principles contained in natural law, naturally known principles of practical reason.

We can see that this is so just by running through the parts of the definition. A law is an ordination of reason. This means that what presents itself as a rule of human action ought to be rational. Surely Thomas regards that as self-evident to all. And evidently he regards the requirement of ordination to the common good in the same way. "Nothing stands firmly according to practical reason except by ordination to the last end, which is a common good." As for the requirement that the community, or the one who has care over it, be the maker of the law, is this not really an elementary judgment of justice? "For in all other matters, to order toward an end pertains to the one to whom that end properly belongs."[136] It makes no sense for a person or a group to rule over the pursuit or the maintenance of a good that is not their own. And as for the need for law to be promulgated, the thought is simply that people cannot be obliged to comply with rules that they cannot know. This too is a truth that we all understand. Nothing unknowable obliges. It is only the light that binds.

---

136. *ST* I–II.90.3.

Bibliography

THOMAS AQUINAS

With six exceptions, the references for Thomas's works in this book are to the Leonine edition.

Sancti Thomae Aquinatis doctoris angelici Opera omnia iussu Leonis XIII. P. M. edita. Cura et studio fratrum praedicatorum. Rome; Paris: Leonine Commission, 1882.

A list of the Leonine volumes and titles can be found here:
Alarcón, Enrique. *Corpus Thomisticum: Editio Leonina.* Online. http://www.corpusthomisticum.org/repedleo.html.

The exceptions are as follows:
Collationes in decem preceptis. In Torrell, Jean-Pierre, OP. "Les *collationes in decem preceptis* de Saint Thomas d'Aquin." *Revue des Sciences Philosophiques et Théologiques* 69 (1985) 5–40, 227–63.
In librum B. Dionysii De divinis nominibus expositio. Edited by Ceslaus Pera, OP. Turin: Marietti, 1950.
In XII libros Metaphysicorum expositio. Edited by M.-R. Cathala, OP, and Raimundo M. Spiazzi, OP. Turin: Marietti, 1950.
Quaestiones disputatae de virtutibus. Vol. 2 of *Quaestiones disputatae.* Edited by P. A. Odetto, OP. Turin: Marietti, 1965.
Scriptum super Sententiis magistri Petri Lombardi. 4 vols. Edited by Pierre Mandonnet, OP, and Marie-Fabien Moos, OP. Paris: P. Lethielleux, 1929–56. [for Distinctions 23–50, see vol. 7.2 of *Sancti Thomae Aquinatis Doctoris angelici ordinis praedicatorum Opera omnia ad fidem optimarum editionum accurate recognita,* 872–1259. Parma: Petrus Fiaccadorus, 1858.]
Super Epistolas S. Pauli Lectura. Vol. 1. Edited by Raphael Cai, OP. Turin: Marietti, 1953.

OTHER WORKS CITED

Adler, Mortimer. "The Doctrine of Natural Law in Philosophy." In vol. 1 of *University of Notre Dame Natural Law Institute Proceedings*, edited by Alfred L. Scanlan, 65–84. Notre Dame: University of Notre Dame Press, 1949.

———. "A Question about Law." In *Essays in Thomism*, edited by Robert E. Brennan, 207–236. New York: Sheed and Ward, 1942.

Albertus Magnus, OP. *De bono*. Edited by Henricus Kühle, et al. Vol. 28 of *Opera Omnia*. Aschendorff: Monasterii Westfalorum, 1951.

Anscombe, G. E. M. *Ethics, Religion, and Politics*. Minneapolis: University of Minnesota Press, 1981.

———. "Must One Obey One's Conscience?" In *Human Life, Action, and Ethics: Essays by G. E. M. Anscombe*, edited by Mary Geach and Luke Gormally, 237–41. Exeter: Imprint Academic, 2005.

Augustine. *De libero arbitrio*. In vol. 29 of *Corpus Christianorum Series Latina*, edited by W. M. Green and K. D. Daur, 211–321. Turnhout: Brepols, 1970.

Banfield, Edward. "Leo Strauss." In *Remembering the University of Chicago: Teachers, Scientists, and Scholars*, edited by Edward Shils, 490–501. Chicago: University of Chicago Press, 1991.

Bourke, Vernon J. "Is Thomas Aquinas a Natural Law Ethicist?" *The Monist* 58 (1974) 52–66.

Boyer, Charles, SJ. *Cursus philosophiae*. Paris: Desclée de Brouwer, 1936.

Brady, Ignatius. "Law in the *Summa fratris Alexandri*." *Proceedings of the American Catholic Philosophical Association* 24 (1950) 133–47.

Brock, Stephen L. "Can Atheism Be Rational? A Reading of Thomas Aquinas." *Acta Philosophica* 11 (2002) 215–38.

———. "The Distinctiveness of the Natural Inclinations Proper to Man in *Summa theologiae* 1-2.94.2." In *The Truth about God, and Its Relevance for a Good Life in Society. The Proceedings of the XI Plenary Session 17–19 June 2011*, edited by the Review of the Pontifical Academy of St. Thomas Aquinas, 36–53. Doctor Communis 2012, fasc. 1–2. Vatican City: Pontificia Academia Sancti Thomae Aquinatis, 2012.

———. *The Philosophy of Saint Thomas Aquinas: A Sketch*. Eugene, OR: Cascade, 2015.

———. "Practical Truth and Its First Principles in the Theory of Grisez, Boyle, and Finnis." *The National Catholic Bioethics Quarterly* 15 (2015) 303–329.

———. "The Primacy of the Common Good and the Foundations of Natural Law in St. Thomas." In *Ressourcement Thomism*, edited by Reinhard Hütter and Matthew Levering, 234–55. Washington, DC: Catholic University of America Press, 2010.

Brown, Oscar. *Natural Rectitude and Divine Law in Aquinas*. Toronto: Pontifical Institute of Medieval Studies, 1981.

Butera, Giuseppe. "The Moral Status of the First Principle of Practical Reason in Thomas's Natural-Law Theory." *The Thomist* 71 (2007) 609–631.

Cahalan, John C. "Natural Obligation: How Rationally Known Truth Determines Ethical Good and Evil." *The Thomist* 66 (2002) 101–132.

Caldera, Rafael T. *Le jugement par inclination chez saint Thomas d'Aquin*. Paris: J. Vrin, 1980.

Cicero, M. Tullius. *De officiis*. Edited by M. Winterbottom. Oxford: Oxford University Press, 1994.

Copleston, Frederick, SJ. *Aquinas*. London: Penguin, 1955.

Bibliography

Desjardins, Claude, SJ. *Dieu et l'obligation morale*. Montreal: Desclée de Brouwer, 1963.
Dewan, Lawrence, OP. "St. Thomas and the Divine Origin of Law: Some Notes." *Civilizar: Ciencias Sociales y Humanas* 8 (2008) 123–33.
———. "St. Thomas and the Divinity of the Common Good." In *Ressourcement Thomism*, edited by Reinhard Hütter and Matthew Levering, 211–33. Washington, DC: Catholic University of America Press, 2010.
———. *Wisdom, Law, and Virtue: Essays in Thomistic Ethics*. New York: Fordham University Press, 2008.
Donagan, Alan. "The Scholastic Theory of Moral Law in the Modern World." In *Aquinas*, edited by Anthony Kenny, 325–39. Notre Dame: University of Notre Dame Press, 1969.
———. *The Theory of Morality*. Chicago: University of Chicago Press, 1979.
Elders, Leo. "Nature as the Basis of Moral Actions." *Sapientia* 56 (210) 565–88.
Farrell, Patrick, OP. "Sources of St. Thomas's Concept of Natural Law." *The Thomist* 20 (1957) 237–94.
Farrell, Walter, OP. *The Natural Law according to St. Thomas and Suárez*. Ditchling: St. Dominic's, 1930.
———. "The Roots of Obligation." *The Thomist* 1 (1939) 14–30.
Festus, Sextus Pompeius. *Sexti Pompei Festi De verborum significatu quae supersunt, cum Pauli epitome*. Edited by Wallace M. Lindsay. Vol. 4 of *Glossaria Latina*. Leipzig: Teubner, 1933.
Finnis, John. *Aquinas: Moral, Political, and Legal Theory*. New York: Oxford University Press, 1998.
———. *Natural Law and Natural Rights*. Oxford: Clarendon, 1980.
Flannery, Kevin L., SJ. *Acts Amid Precepts: The Aristotelian Logical Structure of Thomas Aquinas's Moral Theory*. Washington, DC: Catholic University of America Press, 2001.
Flippen, Douglas. "Natural Law and Natural Inclinations." *The New Scholasticism* 60 (1986) 284–316.
Fortin, Ernest, AA. "Augustine, Aquinas, and the Problem of Natural Law." *Mediaevalia* 4 (1978) 179–208.
———. "The New Rights Theory and the Natural Law." *Review of Politics* 44 (1983) 590–612.
———. "On the Naturalness and Lawfulness of the Natural Law: A Few Remarks on Ernest Fortin's Doubts: Response." *The Review of Politics* 45 (1983) 446–49.
Gallagher, David M. "Desire for Beatitude and Love of Friendship in Thomas Aquinas." *Mediaeval Studies* 58 (1996) 1–47.
———. "Person and Ethics in Thomas Aquinas." *Acta Philosophica* 4 (1995) 51–71.
———. "The Role of God in the Philosophical Ethics of Thomas Aquinas." In *Miscellanea Mediaevalia: Was ist Philosophie im Mittelalter?*, edited by Jan A. Aertsen and Andreas Speer, 1024–33. Berlin: de Gruyter, 1988.
———. "Thomas Aquinas on Self-Love as the Basis for Love of Others." *Acta Philosophica* 8 (1999) 23–44.
Geach, Peter. *God and the Soul*. London: Routledge and Kegan Paul, 1969.
Gilson, Etienne. *Thomism: The Philosophy of Thomas Aquinas*. Toronto: Pontifical Institute of Mediaeval Studies, 2002.

Golubiewski, Wojciech, OP. "Imitation of Nature as a Source of Practical Principles in St. Thomas Aquinas's *Summa Theologiae* II–IIae." PhD diss., Institute of Philosophy and Sociology, Polish Academy of Sciences, 2016.

Gratian. *Decretum magistri Gratiani* [*Concordantia discordantium canonum*]. Edited by Emil Albert Friedberg and Aemilius Ludwig Richter. Vol. 1 of *Corpus Iuris Canonici*. 1879–81. Reprint, Graz: Akademische Druck- und Verlaganstalt, 1955.

Gredt, Joseph, OSB. *Elementa philosophiae aristotelico-thomisticae*. Barcelona: Herder, 1961.

Grisez, Germain. "The First Principle of Practical Reason: a Commentary on the *Summa theologiae*, I–II Question 94, a.2." *Natural Law Forum* 10 (1965) 168–201.

Grisez, Germain, et al. "Practical Principles, Moral Truth, and Ultimate Ends." *American Journal of Jurisprudence* 32 (1987) 99–151.

Hibbs, Thomas S. "A Rhetoric of Motives: Thomas on Obligation as Rational Persuasion." *The Thomist* 54 (1990) 293–309.

Hittinger, Russell. *The First Grace: Rediscovering the Natural Law in a Post-Christian World*. Wilmington: ISI, 2003.

Houser, Rollen E. "Cicero and Aquinas on the Precepts of the Natural Law." In *Indubitanter ad veritatem: Studies Offered to Leo J. Elders in Honor of the Golden Jubilee of His Ordination to the Priesthood*, edited by Jörgen Vijgen, 244–63. Budel: Damon, 2003.

Hume, David. *A Treatise of Human Nature*. Edited by L. A. Selby-Bigge. Oxford: Oxford University Press, 1888.

Irwin, Terence. *The Development of Ethics: A Historical and Critical Study*. Oxford: Oxford University Press, 2007.

Jaffa, Harry V. *Thomism and Aristotelianism*. Chicago: University of Chicago Press, 1952.

Jenkins, John I., CSC. "Good and the Object of Natural Inclination in St. Thomas Aquinas." *Medieval Philosophy and Theology* 3 (1993) 62–96.

Jensen, Steven. *Knowing the Natural Law. From Precepts and Inclinations to Deriving Oughts*. Washington, DC: Catholic University of America Press, 2015.

Kluxen, Wolfgang. *Philosophische Ethik bei Thomas von Aquin*. Hamburg: Felix Meiner, 1980.

Koritansky, Peter. *Thomas Aquinas and the Philosophy of Punishment*. Washington, DC: Catholic University of America Press, 2011.

Kossel, Clifford G., SJ. "Natural Law and Human Law (Ia IIae qq. 90–97)." In *The Ethics of Aquinas*, edited by Stephen J. Pope, 169–93. Washington, DC: Georgetown University Press, 2002.

Lazure, Jacques. "La loi naturelle en philosophie morale." *Revue de l'Université d'Ottawa, section spéciale* 28 (1958) 5–30.

LeClercq, Jacques, OMI. *La philosophie morale de Saint Thomas devant la pensée contemporaine*. Louvain: Publications Universitaires de Louvain, 1955.

Lio, Ermenegildo, OFM. "Annotazioni al testo riportato da S. Tommaso (S.Th. I–II q. 90 a. 1) '*Lex ... dicitur a ligando*.'" *Divinitas* 1 (1957) 372–95.

Lisska, Anthony. *Aquinas's Theory of Natural Law: An Analytical Reconstruction*. Oxford: Oxford University Press, 1996.

Lottin, Odon, OSB. "La valeur des formules de Saint Thomas d'Aquin concernant la loi naturelle." In vol. 2 of *Mélanges Joseph Maréchal*, 345–77. Paris: Desclée de Brouwer, 1950.

———. *Le droit naturel chez St Thomas d'Aquin et ses prédécesseurs*. Bruges: Firme Charles Beyaert, 1931.
———. *Morale fondamentale*. Paris: Desclée de Brouwer, 1954.
———. *Principes de Morale*. Louvain: Éditions du Mont Cesar, 1946.
———. *Psychologie et Morale aux XIIe et XIIIe siècles*, t. II: *Problèmes de morale, Première partie*. Louvain: Abbaye du Mont Cesar, 1948.
MacGuigan, Mark. "St. Thomas and Legal Obligation." *The New Scholasticism* 35 (1961) 281–300.
Manser, Gallus, OP. *Das Naturrecht in Thomistischer Beleuchtung*. Freiburg: Verlag der Paulusdruckerei, 1944.
Maritain, Jacques. "Du savoir moral." *Revue Thomiste* 82 (1982) 533–49.
———. *Man and the State*. Chicago: University of Chicago Press, 1951.
———. "On Knowledge through Connaturality." *The Review of Metaphysics* 4 (1951) 473–81.
Merkelbach, Benedikt Heinrich, OP. *Summa theologiae moralis, ad mentem D. Thomae et ad normam iuris novi*. Paris: Desclée de Brouwer, 1935.
O'Donoghue, Dermot. "The Thomist Concept of Natural Law." *Irish Theological Quarterly* 22 (1955) 89–109.
Pinckaers, Servais, OP. *The Sources of Christian Ethics*. Translated by Mary Thomas Noble, OP. Washington: Catholic University of America Press, 1995.
Prümmer, Dominicus M., OP. *Manuale theologiae moralis*. Freiburg: Herder 1915.
Ramírez, Santiago, OP. *Edición de las Obras Completas de Santiago Ramírez, OP*. Vol. 4 of *De actibus humanis*. Edited by Victorino Rodríguez, OP. Madrid: Consejo Superior de Investigaciones Cientificas, 1972.
Schultz, Janice. "Necessary Moral Principles." *The New Scholasticism* 62 (1988) 150–78.
Stevens, Gregory. "Moral Obligation in St. Thomas." *The Modern Schoolman* 40 (1962) 17–21.
———. "The Relation of Law and Obligation." *Proceedings of the American Catholic Philosophical Association* 29 (1955) 195–205.
Strauss, Leo. "Natural Law." In vol. 11 of *The International Encyclopedia of the Social Sciences*, edited by David L. Sills and Robert K. Merton, 80–85. New York: Macmillan, 1968.
Suárez, Francisco, SJ. *De lege naturali* (*De legibus* II.1–12). Vol. 3 of *De legibus*. Bilingual critical edition. Edited by L. Pereña and V. Abril. Madrid: Consejo Superior de Investigaciones Cientificas, 1974.
———. *De legis obligatione* (*De legibus* I.9–20). Vol. 2 of *De legibus*. Bilingual critical edition. Edited by L. Pereña, et al. Madrid: Consejo Superior de Investigaciones Cientificas, 1972.
———. *Tractatus quinque ad Primam secundae D. Thomae*. Vol. 4 of *Opera omnia*. Edited by D. M. André. Paris: Vivés 1856.
Summa theologica seu sic ab origine dicta "Summa fratris Alexandri." Studio et cura PP. Collegii S. Bonaventurae. 4 vols. Ad Claras Aquas (Quaracchi): Ex Typographia Collegii S. Bonaventurae, 1924–48.
Torrell, Jean-Pierre, OP. *Initiation à saint Thomas d'Aquin*. 3rd ed. Paris: Cerf, 2008.
Tuninetti, Luca. *"Per se notum": Die logische Beschaffenheit des Selbstverständlichen im Denken des Thomas von Aquin*. Leiden: Brill, 1996.

Turienzo, Saturnino Álvarez, OSA. "La doctrina tomista de la ley eterna en relación con S. Augustin." In vol. 1 of *Thomistica morum principia*, 9–14. Rome: Officium Libri Catholici, 1960.

van Overbeke, Paul-M., OP. "La loi naturelle et le droit naturel selon S. Thomas." *Revue Thomiste* 57 (1957) 53–78, 450–95.

Index of Names

Adler, Mortimer, 10, 30, 253
Alarcón, Enrique, xv
Albertus Magnus, OP, 42n28, 57n94, 72
Anscombe, G. E. M., 14, 28–30, 240–41
Aristotle, 20, 28–29, 41, 42n26, 86, 91, 96n110, 108, 112, 135n93, 136n97, 139–40, 142–43, 146, 169, 178, 184, 187–88, 193n49, 207n98, 210, 216–17, 219, 227–31, 233n72, 249–50, 251n130
Augustine, 34, 49n64, 52, 56, 84, 85n59, 95, 99, 105n142, 176, 214, 235n82

Banfield, Edward, 251n132
Biel, Gabriel, 19n73
Bourke, Vernon J., 11n39
Boyer, Charles, SJ, 2n4
Brady, Ignatius, 40n22
Brock, Stephen L., xiin3, 123n63, 137n103, 230n63, 234n75, 251n130
Brown, Oscar, 11n39, 182n12, 183n17
Butera, Giuseppe, 157n60

Cahalan, John C., 111n13
Caldera, Rafael T., 144n9
Cicero, M. Tullius, 230
Copleston, Frederick, SJ, 13–14, 30

Descartes, René, 151
Desjardins, Claude, SJ, 182n12
Dewan, Lawrence, 23, 90n80, 121, 137n103, 144, 146, 178–79, 231, 235n82, 239n93, 245–46, 248
Donagan, Alan, 3, 14, 30, 59, 63–64, 107–10, 139, 167, 177, 254

Elders, Leo, 111n13

Farrell, Patrick, OP, 12n40
Farrell, Walter, OP, 14n52, 21n80, 22, 24–26, 30, 182n12, 243–45, 248, 254
Festus, Sextus Pompeius, 47n56
Finnis, John, 10, 17, 30, 64–65, 115–19, 121, 123, 129n71, 134, 141–42, 149, 158n63, 164, 166, 253
Flannery, Kevin L., SJ, 27n103, 140n111
Flippen, Douglas, 116n29
Fortin, Ernest, AA, 17–20, 21n80, 24, 26–27, 30, 62, 212, 249–50

Gallagher, David M., 135n96, 249n121
Geach, Peter, 26–30, 78, 241–43, 251
Gilson, Etienne, 114, 202n75
Golubiewski, Wojciech, OP, 167n90, 170n103
Gratian, 51n69

Gredt, Joseph, OSB, 2n4
Gregory of Rimini, 19n73
Grisez, Germain, 9–10, 74n25, 115–16, 118, 123, 125n64, 141–42, 149, 253

Hibbs, Thomas S., 182n12
Hobbes, Thomas, 47
Hittinger, Russell, 247n115
Houser, Rollen E., 230n61
Hugh of St Victor, 19n73
Hume, David, 29, 149–51

Irwin, Terence, 81n55, 90n78

Jaffa, Harry V., 20, 27, 30
Jean de la Rochelle, 34
Jenkins, John I., 147n23
Jensen, Steven J., 195n55

Kant, Immanuel, 108, 187
Kluxen, Wolfgang, 10–11, 30, 251
Koritansky, Peter, 209n106
Kossel, Clifford G., SJ, 120n46

Lazure, Jacques, OMI, 14n52, 15n57
LeClercq, Jacques, 11n39
Lio, Ermenegildo, OFM, 42n28
Lisska, Anthony, 132n87
Lottin, Odon, OSB, 5–8, 11–16, 30, 33–34, 36, 49n63, 62, 66, 88n73, 252

MacGuigan, Mark, 182n12
Manser, Gallus, 14n52
Maritain, Jacques, 116, 119, 123, 137n103, 244
Merkelbach, Benedikt Heinrich, OP, 2n4
Moses, 48

O'Donoghue, Dermot, 12–14, 30, 252–53

Paulus, Julius, 47
Pinckaers, Servais, OP, 230n61
Plato, 146n20
Prümmer, Dominicus, OP, 2n4

Ramírez, Santiago, OP, 75n32, 130n78
Reilly, James P., xiii

Schultz, Janice, 74n25
Stevens, Gregory, 8n27, 15–16, 25n94, 26, 28, 30, 182n12, 254
Strauss, Leo, 19n73, 251
Suárez, Francisco, SJ, 19, 21–23, 25–26, 30–32, 48, 81, 84, 88, 97–98, 205n89, 243, 245–49

Torrell, Jean-Pierre, OP, 172n114
Tuninetti, Luca, 122n54
Turienzo, Saturnino Álvarez, OSA, 11n39

van Overbeke, Paul-M., OP, 111n13

Index of Subjects

angels, 48, 49n65, 51n73, 169
   and natural law, 38n11
   natural inclination or natural love in, 38n11, 130, 135, 139, 167, 177
appetite, 125n65, 137, 151, 153, 210n109
   and natural law, 12, 53–54, 118, 244–45
   sensitive (*see* sense-appetite)
   will as, 128–32, 142–46, 149n36, 157–58, 161, 165, 244–45
   See also desire; good; natural inclination(s); will

bad. *See* evil
beatitude
   and first duty on reaching use of reason, 236–37
   and first precept of natural law, 154–57, 198
   and God, 238–39
   and obligation, 188, 198
   See also happiness; last end
binding
   and boundaries, 181, 191, 197
   and obligation, 4, 14–15, 40n22, 42, 43n28, 182–85, 243–44
   See also obligation

charity
   and connaturality, 121
   and imitation of nature, 170–71
   and obligation, 187–91
   as friendship with God, 187n28, 234–37
   precept of, 69, 70n12, 187–91
coercion
   and conscience, 203
   and law, 10, 15, 17, 19, 24, 189–92
   and natural law, 69, 196, 244, 254
   and obligation, 24, 26, 189–92
   See also fear; force; punishment
command
   and judgment, 211
   and obligation, 184–85, 198, 211
   and petition, 75
   and promulgation, 45–47
   divine, and moral obligation, 14–16, 26–29, 81–100, 241–43, 248
   intellect and will in, 9, 24–25, 43–44, 74–78
   issued to irrational beings, 77
   issued to oneself, 80
   law as, 4, 23, 27, 43–47, 74, 77, 82, 248
   natural law as, 4, 9, 13, 24–25, 77, 100, 243, 252–53
   obedience to, and knowledge of the command, 78–79
   same as precept, 70n13, 74
   versus counsel, 218–20
   See also precept(s)

Index of Subjects

common good
  and obligation, 195, 210
  as distinct from private good, 112, 113n22
  as part of individual's good, 54, 236–38
  as end of law, 13, 44–45, 50, 53, 82–83, 89, 103, 195, 254–55
  God as highest, 56–57, 90–95, 106, 233–39, 252
  in definition of law, 2, 7, 44–45
  law and (*see under* law)
  natural law as ordering to, xiv, 48, 56–57, 103, 231
  of universe, 82–83, 89–94, 236n85, 237–39, 252
  political, 103, 226, 231, 234
  primacy of: according to nature, 113n22, 136, 164; according to reason, 44, 150, 168, 210, 238, 252, 255
  See also under law
concupiscence
  as sense-desire (*see* sense-appetite)
  love of, versus love of friendship, 135
connaturality, judgment or knowledge by, 119–21, 123, 143, 244
conscience
  and God, 204–6, 211
  and *synderesis*, 204–6
  as a kind of judgment, 184, 203–8, 211–12, 244, 253
  fallibility of, 28, 194, 211–12
  obligation in: and divine law or precept, 182–84, 194–95; and human law, 195; and natural law, 196, 204–6, 253; and natural reason, 24–25, 28, 196
  remorse of: and natural inclination to follow reason, 24–25, 196, 208, 212, 244; as punishment (or sanction), 19, 24, 28, 202–4, 206–14, 249; as worm that dieth not, 211
creation, 65, 69, 108, 112, 139
  and eternal law, 52, 56, 82–84, 89–100, 241, 247–49
  and divine legislation, 15, 22–26, 74–84, 89–100, 246–49; Suárez on, 22–23, 81, 84, 97–98, 247–48
  of human soul, 79–80, 133, 245

De anima (Aristotle), 120, 143
  Thomas's *Commentary on* (*In De an.*), 51n74, 123n60, 131n82, 143n6, 144nn7–8
De interpretatione (Aristotle), Thomas's *Commentary on* (*In Peryerm.*), 77n35, 91n84, 94n102, 98n112
De legibus (Suárez), 19n73, 21n80, 22nn81–84, 23n85, 25n97, 48n56, 81nn52–54, 88n73, 98n114, 205n89
De libero arbitrio (Augustine), 49n64, 85n59, 95n107, 105n142, 214, 235n82
De officiis (Cicero), 230
debitum. *See* duty
Decalogue
  as pertaining to justice, 224–26
  as pertaining to natural law, 221–26
  First and/or Second Table of, 17–18, 232–33, 250n126
  vis-à-vis precepts of faith and charity, 69–70
desire
  and good, 95, 106, 124, 128, 141–55
  for existence, different modes of, 137
  for knowledge, natural, 229–30
  sense- (*see* sense-appetite)
  See also appetite; good; natural inclination(s); will
dignity, and the due, 233n74
divine law
  as revealed or supernaturally promulgated law, 2, 49, 86–87, 103n135, 184, 222–23; end of, 228; virtue and, 220–33, 240
  natural law as a, 16–30, 68, 81, 184, 196, 206, 235–41, 248–50
duty (due, *debitum*), 56, 186n27, 217
  and dignity, 233n74

and justice, 56, 216–19, 224–31,
    233, 240, 253–54
and last end, 232–33
and obligation, 216–17
and reason, 71–72, 217, 219, 237,
    240
and the will, 244
concept of, and morality, 29, 240
moral versus legal: as required by
    virtue versus required by law,
    216; as required by natural right
    versus required by positive right,
    218–19
strict: extending to essentials of
    moral order, 220, 233; *prima
    facie* scope of, 221–28, 240;
    scope as determined by natural
    law, 216–31
toward God, 72, 81, 224n34, 225,
    227, 242
See also necessity of an end;
    obligation

Epistle to the Romans, 57, 92
Thomas's *Commentary on* (*In
    Rom.*), 96n110, 189n34
essence
    as nature, 136
    of creature as effect of eternal law,
        91–92
    principles of, as inclinations, 92,
        132
    See also form, nature
eternal law
    and creation, 52, 56, 82–84,
        89–100, 241, 247–49
    and irrational creatures, 12, 77,
        79n48, 171
    and human law, 102–3, 195–96, 248
    and natural law, 2–16, 21–74,
        79–106, 134–35, 167, 175–76,
        181, 197–98, 248–54
    and natural right (*ius naturale*),
        85–90, 96–97, 100, 114, 223
    and natures of things, 82–84,
        89–100, 107, 114, 214, 247
    and philosophy, 10–11, 19, 250–51

and positive law, 69, 73, 83, 84–100,
    247
and providence, 49n63, 52, 91–92,
    105
and reason, 85, 87, 99, 175, 208,
    211, 214, 223, 241–42, 247
and sin, 84–89, 96
and will of God (*see under* God:
    will of)
as containing all law, 99
as first, divine truth, 99n116, 104
as law, 8, 83–84, 89–106, 247–48
existence of, 49n63, 58–59, 85n59,
    101–2, 215
human knowledge of, 9, 19, 79
in *De libero arbitrio*, 49n64,
    105n142
in *Summa fratris alexandri*, 34–40
participation in, all law as, 103
See also creation; eternal reason(s);
    providence
eternal reason(s), 58, 128, 176
ethics. *See* moral philosophy
Ethics, Nicomachean. *See Nicomachean Ethics* (Aristotle)
Euthyphro question, 26, 241
evil (or bad)
    because prohibited, or vice-versa, 6,
        85–89, 96–97, 241
    in first precept of natural law, 105,
        155–57
    moral: as deviation from natural
        and eternal law, 85–89; as repug-
        nance to reason, 178
    prodigal as not, according to Aris-
        totle, 231
    See also good: and evil; moral
        good; sin; transgression; vice;
        wrongdoing

faith
    and Old Law, 69–70, 73–74, 86–87,
        222, 225, 229, 233, 250n126
    and reason, 72n117, 74, 87, 176,
        222–23, 225, 229n60, 233–36,
        239
    precept of, 8, 69–70, 73–74, 87n68,
        222, 229

Index of Subjects

fear
  of punishment, and obligation, 183, 189–94, 196, 200, 208
  servile and filial, 190–91
  See also coercion; force; punishment
first (or common) principles
  as metaphysical matters, xii, 65, 178
  as self-evident propositions, 3, 11, 15, 65, 98, 115–17, 122–24, 126n66, 175
  of practical reason: and human will, 9, 74n25, 119; as effects of God's will, 98–100; as laws, 19, 104–6; as measures of human law, 104–5, 200; as held by *synderesis*, 38; as truths, 79, 98–99, 104–5, 167–68; (primary) precepts of natural law as, 3–16, 23, 36–39, 59–68, 100, 168–69, 252
  of speculative reason, xii, 36, 168, 205, 221
  See also non-contradiction, principle of
fomes peccati, 112, 130n75
  See also lex fomitis; sense-appetite
force (*coactio, violentia*)
  qualified, and sanction or punishment, 183, 189–92
  unqualified (physical), not force of law, 47, 182–83
  See also coercion; fear; punishment
form
  as inclination to being, 92n89, 132, 153n49
  as measure of good, 87, 148–49, 153, 159, 165
  as nature, 92n89, 113, 130–31
  as principle of practical reasoning, 110, 159, 163
  human (soul), as source of powers, 79n48, 86n63
  See also essence, nature
freedom
  and duty, 225–26
  and nature, 108, 176
  and obligation, 190–92
  and reason, 54, 137n103, 138
  and subjection to law, 13, 16, 53–54, 196
  as condition of merit and demerit, 185–86
  divine, vis-à-vis creatures, 22, 82, 89–99, 247–48
friendship, love of, versus love of concupiscence, 135

God
  and conscience, 204–6, 211–12, 249
  as highest common good, 56–57, 90–95, 106, 233–39, 252
  as last end, xiii, 90–96, 100, 179, 187, 191, 212, 232n70, 233, 236–37, 248, 252
  as legislator, 21–29, 52, 69–70, 74–84, 89–100, 134, 198, 245–49
  as mover of human will, 133, 245
  command of, as source of moral obligation, 26–29, 84, 240–42
  duty toward, 72, 81, 224n34, 225, 227, 242
  existence of: Augustinian argument for, 105n142; not self-evident to us, 4, 21, 63, 65, 234n75
  freedom of (*see* freedom: divine)
  goodness (lovability) of, 90–96, 100–101, 106, 248, 252
  happiness of, 252
  image of, 56n90, 58–59, 175, 228
  human knowledge of: and practical reason, 11, 251; and promulgation of natural law, 3–9, 14–30, 62–73, 78, 97–98, 245–50; as wisdom, xii–xiii, 97, 229, 252; natural or spontaneous, versus scientific, 23, 245n109; natural desire for, 229–30
  intellect of: and principle of non-contradiction, 253n135; and human intellect, 81, 172–76; truth in, 103n131
  love in, 90–91, 95
  merit and demerit before, 179, 213–14, 231, 246
  natural love of: as dictated by natural law, 23, 234; in all beings,

90, 135, 139; vitiated by original sin, 139
omnipotence of, as motive for obeying, 26, 241–43
providence of (*see* providence)
will of: and eternal law, 82–84, 89–100, 106, 248; and natural law, 21–26, 82–84, 89–90, 96–100, 106, 247–49; legislative, and creative, 22–26, 74–84, 89–100, 246–49; source of being, 92–94, 98–99; source of necessities in creatures, 98; source of created truths, 98–99; source of goodness, 94–96

good
analogy of, 101
and being, 144–49, 153–55, 162n73, 248
and desire or appetite, 95, 106, 124, 128, 141–55
and evil (or bad): in the first precept of natural law, 57, 105, 124, 155–60; moral (*see under* moral good)
and form, 87, 148–49, 153, 159, 165
and natural inclination, 116, 141, 147
and nature, 117, 142, 148–53, 157–58, 167, 177, 199; according to Hume, 149–50
and is-ought fallacy, 149
and perfection, 80, 95, 146–56, 199
and pleasure, 130n75, 142–44, 147
and potency and act, 149n36, 153
and reason, 117, 120, 124, 157, 163, 197, 237, 241
and truth, 79, 131n81, 144–49, 154, 158
as a metaphysical topic, xii-xiii, 79
as final cause, xii, 100, 109, 124–25, 142, 149, 153, 229, 238
by essence versus by participation, 90, 94
common (*see* common good)
human, and human nature, 57, 80, 109, 116–17, 142, 157–67, 199, 241
intelligibility of, 57, 79, 116, 122n57, 137, 141–50, 154, 160, 162n73; and will, 144–46, 154
moral (*see* moral good)
nature of, 15, 97, 106, 141–50
noble, 143, 147
private, 13, 45, 94, 112–13, 139, 168; only part of individual's good, 237–38
speculative and practical, 153–54, 167–68
universal: God as, 57, 90–93, 233, 238; grasped by intellect, 143–45, 176
will and, 122, 128–29, 133, 137, 142–47, 150, 151n39, 154, 199, 244
See also evil; moral good; virtue

grace
and imitation of nature, 171, 178
and love of God, 139, 234–36, 245n109
and natural inclination of will, 244
and natural law, 234–36, 239, 244, 244n106

happiness
and first duty on reaching use of reason, 236–37
and law, 44–45
and merit, 19
and natural law, 155–56, 157n60, 198
and obligation, 45, 194
of God, 252
See also beatitude; last end
honestas (*see under* moral good)
human law
and eternal law, 103n133, 195–96, 248
and morality, 195–97, 216–17, 219, 226–28, 240
and natural law, 10, 13, 18, 86, 96, 99, 200, 212, 239, 249–50, 253
and revealed law, 179, 196, 210n110, 231, 233n73
and will of legislator, 74

human law *(continued)*
  as law: first in our apprehension, 20, 102–5; secondary by nature, 102–5, 253–54
  as disclosing natural human inclinations, 140
  in *Summa fratris alexandri*, 35
  promulgation of, 4, 48
  punishment by, 18, 202, 209, 249
  See also positive law
human nature
  and eternal law, 252
  and faith, 222
  and God's will, 22, 80–84, 96–99
  and human good, 109–10, 157–67, 176–77, 199, 241
  and immorality or vice, 81, 88, 99, 113–14, 199, 214
  and morality or virtue, 25, 29, 114–18, 135–36, 139, 223–24, 241, 247
  as common to human individuals, 130, 254
  as primarily reason, 130, 159, 164, 177, 199, 202, 241, 244, 252
  as twofold, 113
  dignity of, and union with God, 233
  mutability of, 86
  natural law as a function of, 3, 59, 79n48, 98–99, 107–10
  natural law as based on knowledge of, 24, 107, 110–11, 142, 157–67, 176–77, 199; according to Grisez and Finnis, 115–18, 158n63, 164, 166
  principles of: as inclinations, 132; as scientific matters, 158n63, 160
  See also natural inclination(s); nature

image of God, 56n90, 58–59, 175, 228
imitation of nature, 167–78
  and grace, 171, 178
  and imitation of divine mind, 172–78
  and politics, 136, 164, 173, 178
  and primacy of common good, 136, 164
  and promulgation of natural law, 169–71, 175–77
  in moral matters, 169–74
intellect
  agent, 58, 79n48, 120n46, 122–23
  and faith, 229
  and good (*see* good: and reason; good: intelligibility of)
  and nature, 136, 152, 159–60, 163, 175
  and sense, 143–44, 169
  and soul, 79n48
  and truth, 103–4, 122, 131n81, 146–47, 168–69
  and will, 120, 129–33, 136–38, 143–46, 161, 207; in command, 9, 24–25, 43–44, 74–78
  human: and divine, 81, 172–76; order of understanding in, 160–65, 169–70
  law as work of (*see* law: as work of reason and will)
  light of (*see* reason: light of)
  practical, 164–67; and speculative or theoretical, 159–60, 168–69, 207–8, 251; as moving principle, 120, 133, 146; truth of, 123, 168
  See also reason
is-ought fallacy, 29, 149
ius naturale. See natural right

judgment
  and command, 4
  and concupiscence or passion, 142, 157, 208
  and punishment, 202–7, 211
  as seat of truth, 123
  practical: ought-judgment as some kind of, 105, 168, 175n118, 211, 255; unqualified, versus judgment of conscience, 207–8
justice
  and divine wisdom, 93
  and duty or the due, 56, 216–17, 219, 224–31, 233, 240, 253–54
  and obligation, 191–92

Index of Subjects

essence or nature of, unchangeable, 86
metaphorical, 8, 16, 210, 227–29;
   righteousness as, 228
original, 113
virtue of, as meritorious, 191
See also duty; obligation

knowledge
   of God, and promulgation of
      natural law (*see under* God:
      knowledge of)
   of good, and knowledge of desire or
      inclination, 141–46, 150–55
   of good, and knowledge of nature,
      146–54
   of human natural inclinations, and
      natural law, 111–14, 115–20,
      127–40
   of human nature, and natural law,
      157–67
   of natural things, and natural law,
      150–54, 167–79
   practical: and speculative or
      theoretical, of good, 153–54,
      167–68; as using other kinds of
      knowledge, 159

last end
   as will's primary object, 53, 129,
      133, 154–55, 230
   God as (*see under* God)
   law and, 44, 191, 252, 255
   natural law and, 53, 70, 129, 155,
      166, 230
   order toward, and morality, 232,
      235–39
   See also beatitude; happiness
law
   and promulgation (*see under*
      promulgation)
   and punishment or sanction (*see
      under* punishment)
   and right (*ius*), 88
   and virtue (*see* virtue: and law)
   as analogical, 6–8, 10–11, 15–16,
      100–106, 253

   as command, 4, 23, 27, 43–45, 47,
      74, 77, 82, 248
   as principle of human action, 46–47
   as proposition(s), 51n74, 67, 76,
      122–23, 198
   as work of reason and will, 24–26,
      38, 43, 51, 74, 245; Suárez on,
      25–26, 97, 243, 245–48
   common good and, 13, 44–45, 50,
      53, 82–83, 89, 103, 195, 254–55
   definition of, 1–2, 4, 8–10, 18, 40,
      42–48, 102–4; Hobbes's, 27;
      nominal or working, 42–43, 253;
      rooted in natural law, 253–55
   division of, 40, 42–49
   revealed (*see* divine law)
   written, 72, 86, 184, 216–17
   See also command; divine law; human law; *lex*; legislation; natural
      law; positive law; precept(s)
law-abidingness, as proper virtue of
   citizens, 193–95
legislation
   and judgment, 210–11
   and promulgation, 50–51
   and teaching, 51n71
   as work of reason and will (*see
      under* law)
   divine (*see* God: as legislator)
   self-: natural law as a work of,
      13–14, 67, 198, 252–53; no such
      thing as, 184
   See also law
lex
   and *ius* (right), 88
   etymology of, 4, 14–15, 40n22, 42,
      180n2
   See also law
lex fomitis, 35, 40n23, 42n25, 43n28,
   49, 59, 101n125
   See also *fomes peccati*;
      sense-appetite
love of God. *See* God: natural love of
lust, sins of, and natural law, 131n81,
   223–24
lying, 27, 78, 108–9, 131n81, 223,
   241–42

merit
- and obligation, 186, 188–92, 196–97
- as proper to free or voluntary action, 185
- before God, 179, 213–14, 231, 246
- punishment as matter of, 209
- *See also* punishment

metaphysics
- and moral philosophy, xii, 11
- and moral theology, 178
- and natural theology, 65, 91
- as concerned with first principles, xii, 65, 159, 178, 140n111
- as wisdom, xii–xiii, 229
- perspective of, and that of practical thought, xii–xiii, 117, 134, 238, 251
- *See also* natural theology; wisdom

Metaphysics (Aristotle), 91, 184, 186, 207, 229–30, 233n72

Thomas's *Commentary on* (*In Meta.*), xiii, 91, 93n100, 130n76, 142, 147, 159, 166n87, 230n64

moral good
- and evil, 87, 117, 197–98; and God, 22, 237; middle between, 231–32
- and good of nature, 117, 157, 199
- and reason, 87, 117, 197–99
- and will, 113, 194, 199, 242
- as *honestas*, 22–23, 81n54, 88, 216, 219n16, 247
- *See also* good; rectitude; virtue

moral philosophy (ethics)
- and divine law, 11, 14, 28–29, 32, 66, 240
- and metaphysics, xii–xiii, 178, 251n130
- and moral theology, 14, 173–74, 178
- and natural moral knowledge, 159
- and politics, 173
- modern, 28

moral theology
- and ethics moral philosophy, 14, 173–74, 178
- imitation of nature in Thomas's, 170–74

natural inclination(s)
- and essence, 92, 132
- and knowledge of good, 111–22, 126–33, 162–65, 177
- and lying, 108–9, 223
- and precepts of natural law, 25, 115–30, 131n81, 133, 170
- as participations of eternal law, 53–55, 72–73, 77, 135, 245
- human, 53–55, 129–30, 162–65, 177; identifying, 133–40; order among, 117, 121–22, 133–34, 166–67
- in angels, 38n11, 130, 135, 139, 167, 177
- in irrational beings, 12, 53, 77, 96, 101n125, 109, 128, 134–39, 167–70
- in *ST* I-II.94.2, 111–40
- of sense-appetite, 113, 116, 130n75
- of will (*see under* will)
- rectitude of, 96, 110, 112, 114, 119, 130–32, 135, 139, 211

natural law
- absolutely considered, 18, 215–31, 234, 240, 250
- and God's will, 21–26, 82–84, 89–90, 96–100, 106, 247–49
- and last end, 53, 70, 129, 155, 166, 230
- and notion of good, 69–73 (*see also* good)
- and political order, 20, 136, 202, 227–33, 239, 249–50
- as a divine law (*see under* divine law)
- as a division of law, 42–50
- as dictating virtue, 39, 67–68, 196, 217–18, 222, 226
- as function of human nature (*see under* human nature)
- as based on knowledge of human nature (*see under* human nature)
- as metaphysical topic, xii–xiii, 11, 65, 117, 134, 140n111, 178, 238, 251

Index of Subjects

as not quite natural, 16–20, 212, 249–50
as obligatory (*see* obligation: of natural law)
as ordering to common good, xiv, 48, 56–57, 103, 231
as sanctioned, 17–20, 24, 28, 200–14, 243–44, 250
definition of, 3, 12, 33, 58–60, 63–68, 105, 252
eternal law and (*see under* eternal law)
human law and (*see under* human law)
existence of, proof (ST I–II.91.2), 35–37, 41–42, 49–58, 62, 66–67, 128–29, 134
exceptionlessness of, 27–28, 68, 183n17, 242, 250
first precept (or principle) of, 111, 142, 152; and other precepts of natural law, 125–28, 166–67, 198; as gathered from creatures, 169, 177; as moral principle, 156–57; as obligatory, 188; as ordering to beatitude, 155–57; as referring to bad or evil, 57, 152, 155–57; as truth applicable to all things, 155n55, 167–69; self-evidence of, 9, 15
grace and, 234–36, 239, 244
in philosophy and theology, xi, 3–4, 9–11, 14, 59, 64–66, 139, 251
in *Summa fratris Alexandri*, 34–40
knowledge of, natural versus theoretical, 64–65
other expressions for, 38–39
precepts of: as necessary truths, 15, 75n25, 98–99, 183n17; as propositions, 64, 98; as universally applicable, 80, 253; order among, 117, 124, 166–67; primary, as first or common principles of practical reason, 3–16, 23, 36–39, 59–68, 100, 168–69, 252; primary, as self-evident (*per se nota*), 3, 115, 122; secondary, 27n103, 64n3, 68, 131n81

promulgation of, 1–31, 36, 49–52, 62–63, 70–72, 215–16, 243–49, 252; natural inclinations in, 107–40; nature in, 141–79; Suárez on, 21–23, 25–26, 243, 245–49
unity of, 166–67, 198
See also conscience; eternal law; natural right; positive law; *synderesis*
natural right (*ius naturale*)
and natural inclination, 118, 170
and order in natural things, 170–71
and political right, 20, 227–30, 249–50
and positive right (*ius positivum*), 85–90, 219, 226n45
and written law, 72, 86, 184, 216–17
as contained in eternal law and natural law, 39, 85–90, 96–97, 100, 114, 222–23
as in part revealed, 86–87, 223, 227
distinction from natural law, 10, 20, 88, 222–23
in Aristotle, 20, 219, 227–30
variability of, 20, 86, 250
natural theology, 3, 27, 65
See also metaphysics; wisdom
naturale iudicatorium. See *synderesis*
nature
and good, 117, 142, 148–53, 157–58, 167, 177, 199; according to Hume, 149–50
as essence, 132, 136
as inclination, 132
by, versus suited or according to, 109–14, 118, 136
ends of, and human ends, 108–10
human (*see* human nature)
imitation of (*see* imitation of nature)
knowledge of, scientific and non-scientific, 151–52, 159–66
of creatures, as effects of eternal law, 82–84, 89–100, 107, 114, 214, 247
sins against, and natural law, 131n81, 223–24

nature *(continued)*
  See also essence; form; human nature; natural inclination(s)
necessity of an end
  and obligation, 182–99, 216–17, 219, 241
  versus absolute necessity, 199
  versus force or violence, 183
  versus hypothetical imperative, 187
  versus necessary truth, 183n17
  See also duty; obligation
New Law, 48–49, 191, 244n106
Nicomachean Ethics (Aristotle), 20n76, 20n78, 86n65, 96n110, 135, 142, 146, 178n127, 184, 189, 210n109, 216n5, 219, 227, 229n58, 230, 231nn66–67, 250n124
  Thomas's *Commentary on (In Eth.)*, 45n41, 79n47, 86n65, 130n76, 142n1, 146n20, 147n22, 148n26, 151n38, 211n114, 227
non-contradiction, principle of
  and desire of beatitude, 154
  and first precept of natural law, 124, 134, 155
  as effect of divine providence, 98n113, 253n135
  See also first (or common) principles
normativity, and obligation, 23–24, 31–32, 46, 74, 105, 181–82, 244–45
  See also obligation; rectitude

obedience
  and fear, 189–92, 193
  and imitation of nature, 171
  and law or command, 46, 78, 79n44, 189–96
  and precept of faith, 69–70, 73
  and precepts of natural law, 70–73, 83, 105, 206, 253
  to God, 70–73, 79n44, 83, 171, 206, 242–43, 251
obligation
  and binding (*see* binding: and obligation)
  and common good, 195, 210
  and conscience, 24–25, 28, 182–84, 194–96, 204–6, 211–12, 240, 253
  and duty, 216–17
  and justice, 191–92
  and knowledge of precepts, 46–47, 77–78, 184–86, 198–99, 234–35; as imposed by a superior agent, 13–16, 21–30, 69–73, 77–84, 89–90, 97, 185, 206, 216n2, 240
  and normativity, 23–24, 31–32, 46, 74, 105, 181, 244–45
  and punishment, 186, 188–94, 200, 206–14, 243
  and rectitude, 98, 190, 194–97, 247–48
  and virtue, 190–97, 208, 217–18
  and voluntariness, 182–88, 197
  and will: of the obliging agent, 21–22, 75–84, 89–99, 213n122, 243, 245, 247–48; of the one obliged, 25, 80, 182–86, 196, 199, 202, 207–8, 211, 243–44
  and wrongdoing, 193–97, 200, 213n122, 217, 243–44
  as a kind of necessity of an end, 182–92, 194–99, 216–17, 219, 241; imposed by a superior agent, 15–16, 181–84, 188, 198, 216
  law as principle of, 4–5, 14–15, 25, 42–43, 45, 103, 180–81, 192–97
  moral, 14–16, 72, 84; God's command as source of, 26–29, 84, 240–42
  of natural law, 13–16, 21–30, 69–74, 80–84, 89–90, 181–82, 196–214, 217–20, 243–48, 252–54
  See also conscience; duty; necessity of an end; punishment
Old Law, 48–49, 51n73, 69, 191, 216, 232–33
  precepts of natural law in, 64n3, 218–29, 234
original sin, 112–13, 139, 212, 235

participation, as partial likeness, 99n116
Physics (Aristotle), 136, 169, 172
   Thomas's *Commentary on* (*In Phys.*), 169n99, 174n117, 237n86
Politics (Aristotle), 193, 210n109
   Thomas's *Commentary on* (*In Pol.*), 169–70, 172–74
positive law
   and the definition of law, 6–10, 62, 253
   distinction from positive right (*ius*), 85
   eternal law and (*see under* eternal law)
   mode of promulgation of, 62–63
   See also divine law; human law; law: written; natural law; natural right
Posterior Analytics (Aristotle), 42n26
   Thomas's *Commentary on* (*In Post. an.*), 42n26, 160n68, 169n102
powers of soul, as concreated and flowing from soul, 79n48, 86n63, 107, 245
   See also appetite; intellect; reason; sense-appetite; will
practical reason. *See* intellect: practical; knowledge: practical; reason: practical
precept(s)
   moral, 72, 218–26, 234–36
   of faith, 8, 69–70, 73, 87n68, 222, 229
   of natural law (*see under* natural law)
   of Old Law, division of, 218, 220
   same as command, 70n13, 74
   See also command; law
prodigality, 231
promulgation
   as basis of division of law, 45–50
   in definition of law, 45–46
   of natural law (*see under* natural law)
   of precept of faith, 8, 69–70
providence (divine)
   and creation, 91–94, 98n113, 139, 248, 249n121
   and eternal law, 49n63, 52, 91–92, 105
   and natural law, 24–25, 37, 52–55, 105, 117, 134, 196
   and irrational things, 52–55, 109, 165, 171
   as eternal, 49n63
   as distinct from governance, 50n68
   knowledge of, 3, 17–20, 105, 250
   man as sharing in, 55–56, 129
   See also creation; eternal law
Psalm 4, 57–58
punishment (or sanction)
   and obligation, 24, 31–32, 188–97, 243–44
   as effect of law, 18, 100n124, 188–89
   as proper to voluntary things, 185n23, 186n26
   as work of justice, 201–2, 209
   by God, 17–20, 83, 202, 210–14, 246, 250
   judgment and, 202–4, 207, 211
   natural law and, 17–20, 24, 28, 200–214, 243–44, 250
   remorse of conscience as, 19, 24, 28, 202–4, 206–14, 243, 249, 254
   See also coercion, fear; force; merit; obligation

reason
   and will (*see* intellect: and will)
   as instrument or minister of divine law, 66, 211–12
   as man's differentia, 113, 160–61; and unifying principle, 165
   human or moral good as according to, 113n23, 130, 157, 163–65, 198–99, 214, 232, 237
   law as work of (*see under* law)
   light of (or of intellect): agent intellect as, 58, 79n48, 122–23; and divine light, 57–58, 79, 172, 175–76; and faith, 222–23; and promulgation of natural law, xi, 22–26, 36, 66, 72–74, 79–80, 128–29, 244–45, 249
   natural order of understanding in, 160–65, 169–70

reason *(continued)*
  practical: and imitation of nature, 169–78; and speculative or theoretical, 159–60, 168–69, 207–8, 251; truth of, 123, 168; first principle of (*see* natural law: first precept [or principle] of)
  use of (*see* use of reason)
  See also intellect
rectitude, 42–43, 87
  and obligation or duty, 98, 190, 194–97, 216, 247–48
  See also moral good, virtue, wrongdoing
Republic (Plato), 146n20
Rhetoric (Aristotle), 20n77
righteousness, as metaphorical justice, 228

sanction. *See* punishment
sense-appetite (or sensitive or sentient appetite)
  and natural inclination, 136–38
  and reason, 112–13, 138, 142–46, 165, 193
  and will, 118–20, 132
  as selfish, 112–13
  concupiscible and irascible, 170–71, 193
  See also fomes peccati; *lex fomitis*
sin
  and eternal law, 84–89
  and natural law, 87–89
  as contrary to natural right, 85–89
  as contrary to nature, 113, 222, 243
  as contrary to reason, 19, 202, 222
  as offense against God, 19, 26, 88, 213–14, 246; Suárez on, 25–26, 88
  definition of, 84–85
  mortal versus venial, 232n70, 235
  See also evil; transgression; vice; wrongdoing
soul, human, creation of: 79–80, 133, 245
Summa fratris Alexandri, 34–40, 47n55

Summa theologiae
  other expressions for natural law in, 38–39
  quaestio on natural law in (I–II.94), 38, 63–68, 119, 166; most famous article of (94.2), 56–57, 114–37, 142, 151, 154–62, 166–68, 229–30
synderesis, 37–38, 67, 121–22, 132
  and conscience, 204–6, 212
  and natural right, 87–88, 223

temporal law, 40, 49n64, 85n59
theology (revealed)
  and metaphysics, xiii, 90, 178, 243
  as both theoretical and practical, 11, 251
  imitation of nature in, 167, 170–72, 174–78
  natural law in, xi, 3–4, 9–11, 14, 59, 64–66, 139, 251
  scholastic, eternal law in, 6, 34
  sin in, 19, 194
transgression
  and obligation, 181, 189–91, 199–200, 232
  and punishment, 189
  as overstepping a boundary, 112, 181
  of conscience, 194, 202–3, 206, 210, 244–45
  of natural law, 81; as offensive to God, 19, 22, 26, 88, 96, 214; with respect to its first precept, 157, 167–68; punishments for, 212–14
  See also wrongdoing
truth, nature of
  in divine and human intellects, 103n131
  speculative and practical, 123, 168

use of reason, 110, 162
  first duty on reaching, 235–39, 246

vice
  and conscience, 28, 206, 240
  and human law, 195
  and imitation of nature, 170, 172

as contrary to nature, 99, 113–14, 199, 214
as intrinsic principle of action, 46
See also evil; sin; virtue; wrongdoing
vindicatio, 170, 201n71
virtue
  and law, 192–96; divine (*see* divine law: and virtue); human (*see* human law: and morality)
  as according to nature, 114, 136
  as dictated by natural law, 39, 67–68, 196, 217–18, 222, 226
  as perfecting natural inclination, 118, 201n71
  conscience and, 206
  duty and, 219–20, 224–27, 240
  end of, and obligation, 192–94
  imitation of nature and, 170–71, 177–78
  intellectual, 174; moral duty to cultivate, 220, 224, 229–31
  moral, 29, 120–21, 220, 225–27, 236
  natural inclination toward, 129, 136, 139, 196; and eternal law, 72–73, 135; and remorse of conscience, 208
  obedience and, 71, 190–92
  of citizens, 136, 164, 195–96, 231n67
  See also good; moral good; rectitude; vice
voluntariness, and obligation, 182–88, 197

will
  and intellect (or reason), 120, 129–33, 136–38, 143–46, 161, 207; in command, 9, 24–25, 43–44, 74–78
  and obligation (*see under* obligation)
  and understanding of good, 144–46, 154
  human, moved by God, 133
  legislator's (*see* law: as work of reason and will)
  natural inclinations of, 53, 79–80, 119–20, 127–40, 157–59, 245; toward virtue or the good of reason, 79, 131, 163, 165, 208, 212
  of God (*see under* God)
  See also appetite; desire; good; intellect; natural inclination(s)
wisdom
  as knowledge of God, 229–30
  as knowledge of highest causes or principles, xii, 97, 225, 252; especially of the last end, xii–xiii, 230–31
  divine, 8, 93–94, 106, 171, 249n121
  gift of, 121
  metaphysics as, xii–xiii, 229–30
  See also metaphysics; natural theology
wrongdoing
  and obligation, 186, 193–97, 200, 213n122, 217, 243–44
  inescapability of punishment for, and natural law, 19, 206, 213, 249–50
  See also evil; rectitude; sin; transgression; vice

www.ingramcontent.com/pod-product-compliance
Lightning Source LLC
Chambersburg PA
CBHW071239230426
43668CB00011B/1509